Globalisation and the New Terror

D0150206

Globalisation and the New Terror

The Asia Pacific Dimension

Edited by

David Martin Jones

University of Tasmania, Australia

Edward Elgar
Cheltenham, UK • Northampton, MA, USA

Published by
Edward Elgar Publishing Limited
Glensanda House
Montpellier Parade
Cheltenham
Glos GL50 1UA
UK

Edward Elgar Publishing, Inc.
136 West Street
Suite 202
Northampton
Massachusetts 01060
USA

A catalogue record for this book
is available from the British Library

Library of Congress Cataloguing in Publication Data

Globalisation and the new terror: the Asia Pacific dimension/edited
    by David Martin Jones.
        p. cm.
    Edited papers presented at an international conference held in Hobart,
    2002.
    Includes bibliographical references and index.
    1. Terrorism—Congresses. 2. Terrorism—Asia—Congresses.
    3. Terrorism—Pacific Area—Congresses. 4. Globalisation—Congresses.
    5. World Politics—1995–2005—Congresses. I. Jones, David Martin.
    HV6431.G566   2004
    303.6'25'095—dc22

                                                                2003064252

ISBN 1 84376 442 3

Printed and bound in Great Britain by MPG Books Ltd, Bodmin, Cornwall

Contents

Contributors

Richard Butler is currently Diplomat in Residence at the Council on Foreign Relations. He was Australia's Permanent Representative to the United Nations from 1992–1997. Mr Butler was Executive Chairman of the United Nations Special Commission (UNSCOM), concerned with the disposal of Iraq's weapons of mass destruction from 1997–1999. In 1989 Mr Butler served as Australia's ambassador to Thailand and, simultaneously from 1991, served as Ambassador and Permanent Representative to the National Council of Cambodia. He was President of the Economic and Social Council in 1994 and Chairman of the Preparatory Committee for the Fiftieth Anniversary of the United Nations in 1995. He was Vice-Chairman of the 1995 World Summit for Social Development held in Copenhagen. In 1995 Mr Butler was appointed Convenor of the Canberra Commission on the Elimination of Nuclear Weapons. His books relating to global security include *The Greatest Threat: Iraq, Weapons of Mass Destruction* and *The Crisis of Global Security and Fatal Choice: Nuclear Weapons and the Illusion of Missile Defense.*

Dr Gavin Cameron is a lecturer in politics and military history at the University of Salford, UK. His research focuses on terrorism with non-conventional weapons, and on strategies to counter this threat. His book, *Nuclear Terrorism: A Threat Assessment for the 21st Century* was published in 1999. He received his doctorate in international relations from the University of St Andrews (UK), and has been a research fellow at the Center for Nonproliferation Studies in Monterey, California and at the Belfer Center for Science and International Affairs at Harvard University.

Dr Peter Chalk is a Policy Analyst at the RAND Corporation, Washington, DC. His projects include examining unconventional security threats in Southeast Asia, and evolving trends in national and international terrorism. Prior to joining RAND, Dr Chalk was an Assistant Professor of Politics at the University of Queensland, Brisbane, and a Postdoctoral Fellow in the Strategic and Defence Studies Centre of the Australian National University, Canberra. In addition to numerous journal articles and other scholarly publications, Dr Chalk is a contributor to *Drugs and Democracy: In Search of New Directions* (2000) that examines Australia's unsuccessful attempts to control the illicit drug trade, and discusses how – within the confines of our liberal democratic values and culture – we could improve our strategies.

Professor James Cotton currently teaches at the Australian Defence Force Academy. He studied at Flinders and Durham Universities, the London School of Economics and the Beijing Language Institute and was a graduate fellow at Princeton University. He taught at the Universities of Western Australia, Newcastle-upon-Tyne, National University of Singapore, Australian National University and the University of Tasmania. In 1997 he was a Visiting Professor, Universiti Malaysia, Sarawak, and a Visiting Fellow at the University of Hong Kong. In 2001 he was Visiting Centennial Professor, Department of International Relations and Asian Research Centre, London School of Economics. He is the author of over 150 publications on Asian politics and political thought.

Dr Rohan Gunaratna is Research Fellow, Centre for the Study of Terrorism and Political Violence, University of St Andrews, UK and Honorary Research Fellow, International Policy Institute for Counter Terrorism, Israel. Currently, he heads the International and Domestic Terrorism Database and Terrorist Group Profiles Projects at St Andrews. Previously he was Principal Investigator UN Terrorism Prevention Branch; Principal Investigator, Terrorist Information Operations Project, DERA, UK; and Co-Director, UN University Project on Managing Contemporary Insurgencies. He has authored six books including *Inside Al-Qaeda: Global Network of Terror*.

Professor François Haut is currently head of the Department of Research on Contemporary Crime at the University of Paris II. Professor Haut's particular specialism is in the study of emerging criminal threats. He has published many articles and studies including most recently *The 8th Street Gang*. He is also the author with Xavier Raufer of *Le Chaos Balkanique*, and with Stéphane Quéré of *Les Bandes Criminelles*.

Dr David Martin Jones is Senior Lecturer in Government at the University of Tasmania. He acquired a PhD from the London School of Economics in 1984, which rendered him virtually unemployable until the Politics Department at the National University of Singapore offered him a lectureship. He left the city-state in the latter part of 1995 materially enhanced but psychologically diminished for deep Green exile in the Southern Ocean where, despite occasional forays to the North Island and beyond, he has been immured ever since.

John MacFarlane is the Executive Director of the Australian Member Committee of the Council for Security Cooperation in the Asia-Pacific (AUS-CSCAP), located at the Strategic and Defence Studies Centre at the Australian National University in Canberra. Mr McFarlane retired from the Australian Federal Police (AFP) in December 1999 where he served as a Special Adviser in the Office of the Commissioner and Director of Intelligence. Before joining the AFP, he served with the Australian Security Intelligence Organisation. He has written extensively on matters relating to transnational crime, military support for law enforcement and related issues.

Dr Angus Muir has a PhD from St Andrews (UK). He is currently attached to the Office of National Assessments, Canberra.

Dr Kevin A. O'Brien is a Senior Policy Analyst with RAND Europe, based in Cambridge (UK). Previously, he served as the Deputy Director of the International Centre for Security Analysis and a Visiting Fellow – teaching and researching in intelligence studies – in the Department of War Studies, King's College, London. He has published widely on intelligence and security issues, as well as on the continuing transformation of national security structures and operations in the post-Soviet era, especially with regard to information operations and asymmetric warfare strategies – including terrorism.

Dennis Richardson has been the Director-General of the Australian Security Intelligence Organisation (ASIO) since October 1996. Prior to this appointment, Mr Richardson held the position of Deputy Secretary to the Department of Immigration and Multicultural Affairs. In addition to two periods in the immigration portfolio, he has worked extensively within the Department of Foreign Affairs and Trade, both in Australia and overseas, and in the Department of the Prime Minister and Cabinet, where he had responsibilities in the areas of foreign policy, defence and intelligence. In 1992 he conducted a wide-ranging review of the Intelligence Community in the post-Cold War era. Many of his recommendations made in the course of that review have helped to guide and direct the current strategic directions of ASIO today.

Paul Schulte joined the Ministry of Defence (MOD) in 1973 and is currently the Director, Proliferation and Arms Control in the MOD and UK Commissioner on the UN Special Commission for Iraq (UNMOVIC – previously UNSCOM). He was a member of the UN Security Council's Special Panel on Iraqi Disarmament in February and March 1999. He has been involved in non-nuclear arms control (where he invented the important verification method of 'Managed Access') and arms control policy analysis, Middle East defence commitments, land systems procurement, armed forces medical planning, and handling Gulf War Syndrome allegations. He has published papers on terrorist psychodynamics and the future of European political violence.

Dr Mike Smith is Lecturer in the Department of War Studies, King's College, University of London having previously worked as Senior Lecturer in the Department of History and International Affairs, Royal Naval College, Greenwich and later at the Joint Services Command and Staff College. From 1992–1995 he was lecturer in the Department of History, National University of Singapore. In 1986 he was Robert Schumann Scholar at the Directorate of Research at the European Parliament, Luxembourg. Last and not least, from 1997–2001 he was consultant at the Institute of Defence and Strategic Studies at the Nanyang Technological University, Singapore.

Dr Andrew Tan is Assistant Professor at the Institute of Defence and Strategic Studies (IDSS), Singapore. He obtained his PhD from Sydney University and his Master's (International Relations) from Cambridge University. He has had extensive experience in the private and public sectors, including the Singapore Foreign Service. He worked and taught in Australia for five years before joining the IDSS. His research interests are conflict in Southeast Asia, non-traditional security issues and force modernisation. He has published a number of books and articles in these areas. He is currently coordinating a programme on terrorism at his institute.

Dr Grant Wardlaw was appointed Executive Director of the Australian Bureau of Criminal Intelligence (ABCI), Australia's national criminal intelligence service, in February 2001. He has held senior executive positions in intelligence, research and policy organisations, including the inaugural Director of the Commonwealth Government's Office of Strategic Crime Assessments (OSCA). Dr Wardlaw has published widely in the fields of terrorism and law enforcement intelligence and is the author of *Political Terrorism: Theory, Tactics and Countermeasures*. In 1988 and 1991 Dr Wardlaw worked in Washington, DC, as a Distinguished Visiting Professor at the Defense Intelligence College, Defense Intelligence Agency.

Mark Weeding is a postgraduate student at the School of Government, University of Tasmania. He is currently working on his doctoral dissertation, examining legislative responses to the September 11 2001 terrorist attacks as they affect intelligence services.

Dr Clive Williams is one of Australia's leading experts on international terrorism. He is based at the Australian National University.

Dr Michele Zanini is currently a consultant at McKinsey & Company. He has written extensively about information-age terrorism during his tenure at the RAND Corporation from 1996 to 2001. Dr Zanini co-authored the book *Countering the New Terrorism*, and contributed to *Networks and Netwar*. He received his Master's in public policy from Harvard University in 1996 and a PhD in Policy Analysis from the RAND Graduate School in 2001. Dr Zanini has worked on a number of RAND research projects focusing on NATO strategy in the Balkans and Mediterranean, terrorism, ethnic conflict, and European defence planning.

Acronyms

APG	Asia-Pacific Group on Money Laundering
ARF	ASEAN Regional Forum
ASEAN	Association of Southeast Asian Nations
ASIO	Australian Security Intelligence Organisation
AUSTRAC	Australian Federal Police's Transaction Reports and Analysis Centre
ATCSA	Anti-Terrorism, Crime and Security Act 2001
BIAF	Bangsa-Moro Islamic Armed Forces
BIS	Bank for International Settlements
BNPP	Barisan Nasional Pembebasan Patani
BRN	Barisan Revolusi Nasional
C^2W	Command and Control Warfare
C^4	Command, Control, Communications and Computers
CAFGU	Citizen Armed Forces – Geographical Units
CBRN	Chemical, Biological, Radiological and Nuclear Weapons
CIA	Central Intelligence Agency
CIP	Critical Infrastructure Protection
CNA	Computer Network Attack
CND	Computer Network Defence
CNE	Computer Network Exploitation
CNI	Critical National Infrastructures
CNO	Computer Network Operations
COMINT	Communications Intelligence
CPM	Communist Party of Malaya
CSA	The Covenant, the Sword, and the Arm of the Lord
CSCAP	Council for Security Cooperation in the Asia Pacific
CSIS	Center for Strategic and International Studies
DAN	Direct Action Network
DDoS	Distributed Denial of Service
DIN	Dahm Y'Israel Nokeam
DOS	Denial of Service
EIJ	Egyptian Islamic Jihad
ESN	Electronic Serial Number
ETA	Basque Fatherland and Liberty Group

FARC	Revolutionary Armed Forces of Colombia
FATF	G-7 Financial Action Task Force
FBI	Federal Bureau of Investigation
FDA	US Food and Drug Administration
FIS	Islamic Salvation Front
FISA	Foreign Intelligence Surveillance Act
FIUs	Financial Intelligence Units
GAM	Free Aceh Movement
GAMPAR	Association of Malays of Greater Pattani
GAP	Grey Area Phenomena
GIA	Algerian Armed Islamic Group
GSPC	Salafist Group for Call and Combat
HEU	Highly Enriched Uranium
HUMINT	Human Intelligence
IAAC	Information Assurance Advisory Council
IAEA	The International Atomic Energy Agency
ICFM	Islamic Conference of Foreign Ministers
ICT	Information and Communications Technology
IMF	International Monetary Fund
IMINT	Imagery Intelligence
IMU	Islamic Movement of Uzbekistan
IO	Information Operations
IRA	Irish Republican Army
IS	Information Superiority
ISA	Internal Security Acts
ISD	Internal Security Department
ISI	Pakistan's Inter-Services Intelligence
IT	Information Technology
IW	Information Warfare
JI	Jemaah Islamiah
JRA	Japanese Red Army
JTF-CNO	Joint Task Force-Computer Network Operations
KLA	Kosovo Liberation Army
KMM	Kumpulan Mujahidin Malaysia
LTTE	Liberation Tigers of Tamil Eelam
MILF	Moro Islamic Liberation Front
MIM	Mindanao Independence Movement
MIN	Mobile Identification Number
MNLF	Moro National Liberation Front
MTA	Mong Tai Army
NATO	North Atlantic Treaty Organisation
NCB	Narcotics Control Board

NCCTs	Non-Cooperative Countries and Territories
NCII	National Critical Information Infrastructures
NII	National Information Infrastructure
NSA	National Security Agency
OCIPEP	Office for Critical Infrastructure Protection and Emergency Preparedness
ODCCP	Office of Drug Control and Crime Prevention
OECD	Organisation for Economic Cooperation and Development
OIC	Organisation of Islamic Conferences
PAN	National Mandate Party
PAS	Parti Islam se-Malaysia
PFLP	Popular Front for the Liberation of Palestine
PKK	Kurdistan Workers Party
PLA	Chinese People's Liberation Army
PLO	Palestine Liberation Organisation
PPM	Pattani People's Movement
PULO	Pattani United Liberation Organisation
RAF	Red Army Faction
RUF	Revolutionary United Front
SEC	Securities and Exchange Commission
SIGINT	Signals Intelligence
SIPRNET	Secret Internet Protocol Router Network
SPDC	State Peace and Development Council
TNCWG	Transnational Crime Working Group
TNI	Indonesian Armed Forces
TOC	Transnational Organised Crime
TSWG	Technical Support Working Group
UIFO	Union of Islamic Forces and Organisations
UMNO	United Malays National Organisation
UNDCP	United Nations International Drug Control Program
UNSCOM	United Nations Special Commission
USSPACECOM	US Space Command
UTN	Umma Tameer-I-Nau
UTO	United Tajik Organisation
UWSA	United Wa State Army
WMD	Weapons of Mass Destruction
WTO	World Trade Organisation
WVS	World Values Survey

Acknowledgements

This edited book arose from an international conference on Globalising Terror: Political Violence in the New Millennium, held in Hobart in May 2002. The range and variety of speakers, who subsequently turned their papers into chapters for this edition, would not have been possible without the financial support and encouragement of the Commonwealth Attorney General's Office, Canberra and the Standing Advisory Committee on Commonwealth/State Cooperation for Protection Against Violence who hosted the conference.

In particular special mention must go to: Lindsay Hansch, Assistant Secretary Security Programs, Protective Security Coordination Centre, Commonwealth Attorney General's Department; Jack Johnson, Deputy Commissioner, Tasmania Police; and Phil Foulston, Assistant Director, Department of Premier and Cabinet, Tasmania. Their foresight, generosity, good humour and excellent coordination and planning made the organisation of the conference and the production of this edited book a relatively painless process.

David Martin Jones, Hobart, 2003

1.   Contemporary Political Violence –
New Terror in the Global Village

David Martin Jones and Mike Smith

THE ASYMMETRIC THREAT

George Shultz, Ronald Reagan's Secretary of State in the 1980s, observed that terror constituted 'the matrix of different kinds of challenges varying in scope and scale. If they have a single feature in common it is their ambiguity – they can throw us off balance.' As recent events in Washington, New York and Bali provide graphic testament, the carefully coordinated terrorist act can be extremely effective in throwing western governments off balance.

The threat posed to the US, and the West more generally, by such acts is asymmetrical. The US military considers asymmetric warfare a condition where: 'adversaries are likely to attempt to circumvent or undermine strengths while exploiting its weaknesses, using methods that differ significantly from the usual mode of operations'. It consists of 'unanticipated or non-traditional approaches to circumvent or undermine an adversary's strengths while exploiting his vulnerabilities through unexpected technologies or innovative means'.

As the US *Quadrennial Defense Review* noted, it can take many forms, including 'the use of chemical, biological and possibly nuclear weapons; attacks against the information systems ... as well as insurgency, terrorism and environmental destruction'. It presciently forecast that a future adversary might 'employ asymmetric methods to delay or deny US access to critical facilities; disrupt our command, control, communications and intelligence networks; or inflict higher than expected casualties in an attempt to weaken our national resolve'.[1]

As Thomas Friedman has shown, the defining character of globalisation is its speed of communications, travel, commerce and innovation.[2] In this context, globally connected networks facilitate the recourse to asymmetric attacks. Indeed, the application of asymmetrical methods is fast becoming a defining feature of post-Cold War conflict.[3] Significantly, this new warfare is conducted at the expense of the civilian population rather than by conventional arms. At the turn of the century, the ratio of military to civilian casualties in wars was eight to one. Today this has been almost exactly reversed. In the wars of the 1990s, the ratio of military to civilian casualties is approximately one to eight.

Consequently, alongside the growth in number of attacks on civilians is their increasing lethality. According to Rand, 50,000 people died in terror attacks between 1990 and 1996. This doubled the number of casualties that occurred in the previous fourteen years. Moreover, terrorist groups no longer distinguish between limited and restricted uses of violence. Instead terrorist acts, following the example of the Real Irish Republican Army, Islamic Jihad and Hizbollah, have become more extreme with indiscriminate killing becoming the rule rather than the exception.

All this strikingly contrasts with the terrorist violence of the 1970s and 1980s where hostage taking, hijackings and even urban bombings were deemed effective to the extent that they generated international coverage, rather than massive loss of life. The adage that guided terrorist actions during this era, as Brian Jenkins observed, was that 'one wanted a lot of people watching rather than a lot of people dead'.

This strategy changed with regard to lethality as a religious or ethnic consciousness, rather than an abstract ideological motive, came to inform the recourse to terror. As Mark Juergensmeyer shows, 'in 1980 the US State Department roster of international terrorist groups listed scarcely a single religious organisation'.[4] By 1998, however, US Secretary of State Madeline Albright considered more than half the world's most dangerous terrorist organisations of a religious provenance, a figure largely supported by the Rand-St Andrew's Chronology.

A further by-product of assaults on civilian populations in states enduring civil conflict is a heightening of refugee and economic migrancy flows towards those states that are either adjacent to conflict zones or seen as desirable destinations (almost exclusively in the developed West). Transnational criminal networks dedicated to people, narcotics and arms smuggling facilitate such flows (as both Peter Chalk and John MacFarlane discuss in Part III). Why we might wonder has the asymmetrical threat become the defining feature of post-Cold War security and does this mean that we have entered a distinctively new era of what Mary Kaldor terms 'new wars'?[5] Furthermore, does Islamist terrorism, particularly in the aftermath of the attacks against New York and Washington, DC on September 11 2001, which has given rise to the 'war against terrorism', constitute a distinctive manifestation of the new war/new terror phenomenon?

Post-Cold War Wars: Armed Conflict in the Era of Globalisation

The growth of the asymmetric threat reflects two phenomena that have intensified and mutated with the termination of the Cold War: the proliferation of low intensity conflict in the former communist or developing world and the anxious pursuit of identity politics in response to the perceived threat posed by an increasingly globalised marketplace. There are a number of reasons for the proliferation of low intensity conflicts in the post-Cold War era and the attraction of asymmetric warfare for belligerents. Firstly, the end of the Cold War gave rise to one global hegemon, the United States.[6] Outside an American sphere of influence, yet at the same time often in conflict with it, international relations between states and sub-state actors was increasingly characterised by civilisation issues of an ethnic or religious nature. Benjamin Barber characterised the deracinating confrontation between a US-led 'global commerce' and 'the parochialism of ethnic identity' as *Jihad vs McWorld*.[7]

The proliferation of low intensity conflicts that reflected this dialectic were localised, yet increasingly depended on a variety of transnational connections to sustain them. Consequently, conventional distinctions between internal and external, between aggression (from abroad) and repression (attacks from inside the country) are difficult to sustain. Some commentators even contend that the globalisation of the 1990s is a qualitatively new phenomenon. Its consequences are unstable and contradictory, and involve integration and fragmentation, homogenisation and diversification.[8]

Secondly, the goals of these wars concerned identity construed either in religious or ethnic terms rather than the ideological goals that drove the Cold War. This concern with identity also required that the struggle be fought simultaneously at both a local and global level. For the desired identity relies for support and international pressure upon a significant diaspora community and requires the media and the new communication technologies of the Internet and the mobile phone.

Yet, it is important to recognise that globalisation merely intensified and facilitated patterns of resistance to state sovereignty that have been a feature of world history since at least the American and French revolutions of the late eighteenth century, and arguably long before that. In their enthusiasm to emphasise the newness of new war and new terror, a number of commentators have overlooked the fact that during the nineteenth century European revolutionaries of various persuasions, anarchists, Marxists and nationalists, justified emancipation by recourse to violence and the blood sacrifice. Indeed, by the late 1960s extremist political violence had become a notable feature of the international system. The doctrine of the armed struggle flourished from Ireland through Italy and Germany to the Middle East, East Asia and South America. Its protagonist/heroes ranged from French intellectuals like Régis Debray, to incompetent revolutionaries like Ernesto Che Guevara and genocidal maniacs like Pol Pot. New left ideologies of violence drew inspiration from both the tactics of the Palestinian resistance (primarily hostage taking, aircraft hijacking and assassination), which drew world attention to the Palestinian struggle after the defeat of the Arab powers by Israel following the Six Day War in 1967, and from Viet-Cong and North Vietnamese tactics in overcoming the US imperium in Southeast Asia. In other words, what we have witnessed since the end of the Cold War is not so much a 'new' recourse to terror as the intensification of sub-communal rather than ideological conflict and a subsequent dramatic rise in the range and extent of militant identity-driven assaults on the US and her allies.

However, the groups that have modified strategies pioneered by Marxist or Maoist revolutionaries during the Cold War aimed not to capture hearts and minds – the avowed intention of Mao Tse-tung's Protracted People's War in China, or Guevara's *focoquismo* strategy in Cuba. Instead, they explicitly targeted the civilian population either through expulsion, forcible resettlement, or by a range of intimidatory tactics. These have ranged from systematic rape, through to mass killing, like the Trade Center attack of September 11 2001, genocide as in Rwanda or the massacre of Muslims in Srebrenica in Bosnia in 1995. In other words, the end of the Cold War that facilitated both the proliferation of capitalism and a new multilateralism also facilitated the recourse to asymmetric warfare by terrorist networks who deployed this strategy both locally and globally to advance identity rather than ideologically driven goals. To explore this strategic mutation let us first revisit the Cold War notion of the terrorist network and see if it can shed further light on our understanding of the post-Cold War asymmetric threat and its de-territorialised and transnational character.

The Terror Network Revisited

The initial concept of the terror network held that the Soviet Union sponsored many, if not all, of the terrorist movements in Western Europe and beyond. The theory saw the hidden hand of the KGB together with its East European, Middle Eastern and Arab proxies promoting international terror. Thus the Red Army Faction (RAF) in West Germany, the Irish Republican Army (IRA) in Northern Ireland, the Red Brigades in Italy, and the Basque Fatherland and Liberty group (ETA) in Spain's Basqueland, together with the Japanese Red Army (JRA), the Popular Front for the Liberation of Palestine (PFLP) and Abu Nidal represented the national faces of a putative but indistinct international organisation that coordinated operations ranging from the assault on the Munich Olympic Village 1972, and the JRA attack on Lod Airport 1973 to the attempt on the Pope's life in 1980 by Mehmet Ali Agca.[9]

Critics at the time and since have alleged that such a coordinated terror campaign existed only in the febrile brains of right-wing conspiracy theorists, sensationalist journalists and insecure governments eager to use such revelations to erode civil liberties and impose a panopticon of total surveillance.[10] Retrospectively, however, the idea of the 'terror network' is neither as hysterical as its detractors nor as clear-cut as its protagonists claimed. The prosaic reality was that national terrorist organisations, often committed to a shared international and Marxist agenda, established connections and affiliations during the Cold War. Informal ties evolved, based on shared perceptions of resistance against oppressors, and personal contacts between operatives who trained together in guerrilla camps from Libya to the Lebanon.[11] Sometimes disparate groups forged alliances. Thus, the JRA and the German Red Army Faction undertook operations both on behalf of, and sometimes in unison with, extremist Palestinian elements. The combined hijacking of a Lufthansa 737 by members of the RAF and the PFLP in 1977, illustrates the extent of Cold War cross-terrorist cooperation.

Nevertheless, this initial version of the terror network thesis failed to establish convincingly that the Soviet Union coordinated it.[12] Indeed, the absence of any compelling proof of Soviet involvement in the sponsorship of anti-western terrorism,[13] combined with more general accusations that terror analysts pursued government-framed agendas that produced superficial research outputs, tarnished the image of terrorist studies for the better part of two decades.[14]

The Evolution of an Islamist[15] Terror Network

However, after the events of September 11, the notion of the terror network, albeit in an Islamist rather than a Marxist manifestation, has much greater plausibility. The new Islamist network, moreover, does not take the hierarchical form assumed in the 1970s by groups like Sabri al-Banna's Abu Nidal, rather the network that groups like al-Qaeda prefer takes a more diffuse and less penetrable transnational shape (as Rohan Gunaratna explains in Part I and Michele Zanini explores in Part II).[16]

In this context of an increasingly interconnected post-Cold War world, neoliberal-institutional theory as it developed after 1990 offered a plausible explanation of the genesis of such a terror network, whilst simultaneously sustaining a mindset that refused to countenance it. The institutionalist approach holds that political entities within the international system seek out sympathisers, both state and non-state, affiliate with like-minded actors, and reach *de facto* alliances based on mutual self-interest to facilitate their goals.

Yet this understanding further assumes that such relationships occur between essentially benign, rational and synergetic political and economic actors.[17] From this perspective, multilateral institutions could only improve the prospects for international cooperation.[18] Consequently, this approach ignored the downside of transnational criminal interactions that were equally facilitated by the end of the Cold War.[19]

However, although the end of the Cold War evidently sped the pace of terror networking and facilitated its increasingly protoplasmic character, globalisation ultimately only intensified an evolving process. For, as we have seen with Cold War terror, violently motivated actors traditionally relied upon transnational connections, exiles, diaspora communities, sympathetic states and links with international crime to provide money, weapons and propaganda for their cause. Moreover, in terms of the political antecedents and strategic *modus operandi*, it is also misleading to speak of a 'new' warfare phenomenon. The fact that terrorists wielding nothing more technologically advanced than box cutters could hijack planes and fly them into skyscrapers suggests that little has altered in what those who practice terror do to sustain and equip themselves (as Angus Muir discusses in Part II). Nowhere is this fact more apparent than in the case of militant Islamist terrorism.

To trace the antecedents of an Islamist terror network, therefore, is not without difficulty.[20] Nevertheless, in its more virulent anti-United States and transnational manifestation, the obvious starting point is not the end of the Cold War or the evolution of the al-Qaeda network but the Iranian Revolution. The overthrow of the secularising and modernising Pahlavi dynasty in 1979 brought an aggressive Islamist ideology, albeit of a Shiite doctrinal provenance, into political power for the first time in the twentieth century. By its success, the austere Iranian Islamic juridical republic based on the Ayatollah Khomeini's 'little Green Book' of political and hygienic theology profoundly influenced the subsequent contours of Islamist extremism. It was the Iranian Revolution that gave rise to the expression 'the Great Satan' and perpetrated the first act of anti-American hostility – the seizing of the American Embassy in Tehran.

The Iranian revolution, moreover, helped crystallise growing resentment across the Islamic world at both the failure of modernisation, and the ineffectiveness of secular, nationalist, post-colonial rule across the Middle East as witnessed by developments in Arab-Israeli relations. Thus, in Pakistan, military regimes like that of General Zia ul-Haq, who in 1977 seized power in a military coup from the secular Prime Minister, Ali Bhutto, inaugurated an Islamisation programme in order to draw legitimacy from spiritual sources.[21] Similarly, by the late 1970s longer standing Arabist regimes like Colonel Mu'ammar Ghaddafi's Libyan People's Republic began to abandon their admiration for the pan-Arab nationalism of Colonel Gamal Nasser in favour of stricter Islamic observance for similar reasons.

Meanwhile, the Egyptian *modus vivendi* with Israel reached at Camp David in 1979 raised both the ire of Palestinians and fuelled a burgeoning fundamentalism within Egypt, where those who felt betrayed by the nationalist elite sought solace in the fundamentalist ideas first promulgated by the Muslim Brotherhood.

The Brotherhood believed that the weakness of the Islamic world resided in the failure of post-colonial nationalist regimes to embrace the tenets of Islam and the rules that ought to preside over a healthy Islamic society. In this view, initially articulated by Hassan al-Banna in the 1940s, 'Islam was to be the banner and the Koran the constitution of Muslim society'. Certain political conclusions followed, 'the Prophet had not only been a prophet, but also a ruler and a war leader. Thus, it was only by the state itself becoming Islamic through and through that Islamic society would find salvation.'[22] Subsequent followers of this increasingly ideologised understanding of Islam, like Sayyid Qutb, maintained in the 1950s that existing 'Islamic states so-called actually inhabited an age of Ignorance, the very condition of idolatry from which the Prophet was sent to deliver the world' (Clive Williams examines this salafist ideology further in Part I). Thus rulers of Islamic countries in the 1960s like Nasser in Egypt with his promotion of pan-Arabism, or the Baa'thists in Syria and Iraq, merely aped the idolatry practised in both the western and communist world, 'the essence of which is to deny the sovereignty of God and to confer sovereignty on merely human institutions'.[23] From this, it was a short, but fateful, step to consider, as al-Salam Faraj did, that the 'neglected duty' of Muslims was jihad against the Muslim ruler who collaborated with unbelievers to the detriment of Islam.[24]

This growing use of Islam for ideological purposes initially presented a challenge, not to the West, but to those more secular Arab states whose autocratic rulers had characteristically come to power by military coup in the 1950s and 1960s and who subsequently legitimated their authoritarianism by the need to unify the people in defence of national and pan-Arab values. Ironically, the growing attraction of Islamism in the Arab world (non-Arabic Iran notwithstanding) did not appear, at first, to threaten western political interests. Indeed, the Islamic revival in Saudi Arabia and some of the other Gulf States appeared actually to strengthen the rule of essentially pro-western monarchies against internal opposition forces.[25]

Beyond the Middle East, notably in Afghanistan, Islam was seen as a bulwark against the forces of Godless communism in general and Soviet adventurism in particular. Indirect American support of the Mujahidin forces, administered through Pakistan's Inter-Service Intelligence, especially the supply of hand-held Stinger and Red-Eye surface-to-air missile launchers, helped turn the tide of the war against the Soviet occupation.[26] It was only in the wake of the Soviet withdrawal and the descent into faction fighting that eventually brought the Taliban regime to power in Kabul in 1996 that its erstwhile American backers felt the blowback from aiding the Afghanistan jihad.[27]

In the first instance, and before the end of the Cold War, it was primarily the non-Arab, and non-mainstream Muslim, Iranian revolution that intimated the possibility of a terror network, with Iran and Libya seen as key protagonists within a growing web of international terrorism. Moreover, both Iran, with its distinctive, millennially flavoured *Imami* (twelver) Shiite brand of Islam, and Ghaddafi's Libya with its Third Theory, an idiosyncratic blend of Islam and pan-Arab nationalism, seemed distinctly anomalous in their cultivation of links to West European and Palestinian terror groups. Thus, Ghaddafi's regime had a long-standing relationship with the IRA dating from the early 1970s. Meanwhile, Iranian backing for militant groups like Hizbollah in the Lebanon helped pioneer modern suicide bombing against American targets. On 23 October 1983, the Iranian backed 'Husaini Suicide Forces Movement' mounted simultaneous attacks against the US Marine Headquarters and French Forces in Beirut, which killed 241 Marines and Navy personnel along with 58 French paratroopers.

In retrospect, this period may be construed as the first premonitory snuffling of the Islamist terror network: emanating from the Iranian revolution and culminating in the destruction of Pan Am 103 over the Scottish town of Lockerbie on 21 December 1988, with the loss of 270 lives. The investigation into the bombing of Pan Am 103, for example, revealed a trail of transnational associations stretching from Libya and Syria, to Germany and Malta. Interestingly these events, largely overlooked in the current pursuit of 'new' terror, gave currency to terms like 'state-sponsored terrorism', 'arc of crisis' and 'rogue-state'. In other word, the Lockerbie incident evinced in 1988 all the features of a transnational terrorist infrastructure that analysts now detect at work in the al-Qaeda movement.

The asymmetric threat, therefore, is not a new phenomenon, neither is Islamic militancy, or anti-American suicide bombing. To be precise, the attacks on the United States in September 2001 do not represent a new form of terrorism. To assert this neglects both the origins of Islamist terror and the United States initial response to it. Although not officially labelled a 'war against terror', American actions after 1983 bore many of the hallmarks that have characterised the current Bush Administration's multifaceted reaction to the assault on the World Trade Center and the Pentagon. They comprised a mixture of active military responses, intelligence measures, international coalition building, accompanied by long-term economic and diplomatic sanctions to isolate sponsor states.

Following the La Belle disco bombing in April 1986, American intelligence identified evidence of Libyan involvement in the attack.

American fighter aircraft subsequently struck at military and political centres in Tripoli and Benghazi. The application of a combination of military and diplomatic pressure yielded results. Although the Libyan regime continued to support terrorist acts, notably the Pan Am 103 bombing, Ghaddafi began slowly to desist from attacks on Americans, turning his attention instead to the US's British allies, by supplying weapons to the IRA. It was, moreover, the determined pursuit of the perpetrators of the Lockerbie atrocity, resulting in the UN-sanctioned banning of air flights from Libya and, in April 1992, formal economic sanctions that finally secured Libyan compliance. This sector of the war against global, state-sponsored terrorism ended when Libya handed over two suspects to the Scottish Court in the Netherlands. In May 2001, Ghaddafi formally announced Libya's rejection of terrorism.[28]

The Transformation of Islamist Terror in the 1990s

In the course of the 1980s the US and its allies dealt firmly with Libyan state-sponsored terror. However, the West was notably less effective in dealing with less state-dependent forms of terror like that subsequently developed by al-Qaeda. Let us next examine the character of the de-territorialised terror promoted by Osama bin Laden and his affiliates, before considering the reasons for the West's conspicuous failure to recognise, let alone coherently address, the threat it poses.

Examined against the background of pre-existing Islamic militant threats to western interests, the recent activity of Osama bin Laden, the wealthy Saudi exile, is the latest incarnation of an evolving Islamism directed at the United States. This was responsible, *inter alia*, for: the blowing up of a Jewish community centre in Buenos Aires in 1992; the bombing of the World Trade Center in New York in 1993; the suicide bombing against the Khobar Towers, Dhahran in June 1996; the Luxor tourist massacre of November 1997; the American embassy bombings in Nairobi and Dar-es-Salaam of 1998; and the attack on the USS Cole in the Yemen in 2000. Central to this escalation of terror aimed at the civilian population has been the strategy of the suicide bomber, or in Islamist parlance the practice of self-chosen martyrdom (ishtishhad), pioneered by both Hizbollah in the Lebanon and Hamas (the Party of Zeal) in the Gaza Strip, prior to 1990 and recently extended to New York by the attack on the World Trade Center.

The factors promoting the current mutation of Islamist terrorism are threefold. Firstly, and of decreasing importance, sponsorship by 'rogue' states like Sudan, Syria, Iran, Iraq and Libya; secondly, the legacy of the Afghan war viewed in the Islamic world as a triumph over the forces of Satan; and thirdly, the fallout from the stalled Israeli-Palestinian peace process.

Significantly, what does seem to be distinctive in the mutation of the Islamic terror network, is that since coming to power in Tehran, Khartoum and Kabul, Islamist regimes have conducted foreign policy in terms of the *al-jihad al saghir*. This understanding maintains the necessity of conducting internal and external political relations through struggle in order to transform the quotidian sphere of war (dar al harb) into a realm of harmony (dar al Islam).

Such uncompromising thinking informed groups like Osama bin Laden's al-Qaeda, which functions as a de-territorialised franchising agency for jihadist activity on a global basis – a Kentucky Fried Chicken of Global Terror. In other words, it operates through increasingly available globalised religious, internationalist and 'nomadic' networks as well as the more conventional Cold War mechanism of sponsor states.[29] Thus al-Qaeda drew upon resources from rogue states like Afghanistan and Sudan and also from its formal and informal ties with the Algerian Islamic Group (GIA), al Jihad in Egypt and groups like Laskar Jihad, Jemaah Islamiah (JI) and Abu Sayyaf in Southeast Asia.

In this respect such de-territorialised terror posed a mounting challenge to the state system, after 1990, in that it aimed to wage jihad in order to reconstitute the Muslim community beyond national frontiers.[30] Paradoxically, the strategy depends upon the globalisation that the Islamist professes to despise in order to achieve the vision of a dar al islam stretching from the Mediterranean to Indonesia. By their use of English, the internet, satellite phones, satellite TV stations like al-Jazeera and other technology, these sub-state actors are an authentic product of the modern, globalised world and yet in fundamental conflict with it (Kevin O'Brien and Michele Zanini discuss the paradoxical character of information age terrorism further in Part II). Thus, both the 1993 and 2001 participants in the assault on the World Trade Center attended western universities, wore western clothes and liked to party.[31] Meanwhile, in Southeast Asia, Al Ma'unah (Brotherhood of Inner Power), a sect in Northern Malaysia, which was potentially open for an Osama franchise, before it was busted by Malaysian Internal security in June 2000, consisted of silat practising warriors who believed their leader, Mohamad Razali, could freeze opponents by the blink of an eye (as Andrew Tan explores in Part III). At the same time, they also used the World Wide Web to advertise their belief that 'Jihad is our way'.[32] Other groupings like Abu Sayyaf, an al-Qaeda franchise in Mindanao, attained international notoriety by kidnapping tourists,[33] raising funds for its struggle through hostage taking and operating in a hazy underworld of transnational crime and politically motivated violence.[34]

Elsewhere, in Indonesia, Laskar Jihad, an organisation responsible for sending Islamic fighters to cleanse the Moluku Islands of Christian infidels in the 'holy war in Ambon',[35] takes its inspiration from the Afghan war and the Taliban's success (albeit short lived) in creating an Islamist state. Ostensibly, Laskar Jihad, like the Taliban and Osama bin Laden, adhere to the Salafi school of Islam, a movement that draws inspiration from the uncompromising Wahhabism of Mohamed Abdul Wahhab (1703–87) and Ibn Saud, founder of the house of Saud and unifier of the desert tribes.[36] Its negative view of women's rights, democracy, and relations with the West reflect more recent Middle Eastern influences. Interestingly, from the globalising perspective of Islamist terror the fatwa-declaring jihad in Ambon was issued in Yemen.

The pattern of Islamist organisation in groups like Laskar Jihad, al-Qaeda or the Shiite Hizbollah in Lebanon (as Gunaratna shows in chapter 3) challenges both the international order and the unreformed state in which they operate. They function both locally and globally. They consequently combine social, educational and humanitarian work with paramilitary activities. In Sudan, bin Laden's operation established a broad education, health and welfare network. Al-Qaeda possessed a board of directors, the Shura, a panel of a dozen trusted lieutenants who discussed and coordinated the organisation's wide-ranging activities. Prior to the movement of the base to Afghanistan in 1998, there were four executive committees subordinate to the council. These were responsible for: military operations; finance and business; Islamic studies and media relations. The media department ran its own newspaper *Abu Massad Reuters*, named in honour of the British wire service, whilst the financial committee paid salaries and organised healthcare. Analogously, Hizbollah has its own satellite TV station, al-Monar, that operates across the Middle East and prefaces programmes with the injunction 'O Arab Rise Up'. Somewhat differently Laskar Jihad entered Ambon by providing schools and health centres, as well as providing services such as garbage removal.

Such activities, however, merely support the core business, which is jihad. On the paramilitary side of the business, recruits to Laskar Jihad or the various Middle Eastern jihadist franchises, undergo training in one of these organisation's training camps, dotted around the globe from Algiers through Southern Lebanon to Bogor in Indonesia. Training consists of akidah (faith), physical exercises, and the use of traditional arms. In Laskar Jihad's case several sources provide training. These include both indigenous Indonesian Armed Forces (TNI) personnel, fighters who have returned from Ambon, Indonesians who gained experience in Afghanistan, and members of Afghanistan's Taliban itself. The globalised link with Afghanistan featured prominently in the activity of all these groups.

The Failure of Western Threat Perception in the Post-Cold War

The networks developed by al-Qaeda and its affiliates effectively manipulated the technology and opportunities afforded by globalisation for their own particularist ends. Given that, as we have shown, the strategies employed to remove Libya from its sponsorship of an international terror network that extended from Dublin to Mindanao proved successful, why did the Osama mutation of the network prove so effective? Did the earlier success in curbing the ambition of one particularly egregious rogue state, combined with the relative ease with which US-led forces ejected Saddam Hussein's expansionist pretensions from the Gulf by conventional means in 1991, prove conducive to an international atmosphere of complacency towards the mutating Islamist threat? And if so, what was the basis of this complacency?

Evidently, the devastating attacks on New York and Washington that launched the war on terrorism in 2001 are new neither in terms of scope nor intended impact.[37] Ultimately, all that differed was the scale and effectiveness of the planning, the lethality of the attack, the fact that it took place on US soil, and the fear it generated. Retrospectively, what now seems hard to credit is the degree of governmental indifference to the level of threat. This is particularly astonishing given the fact that for most of the 1990s the incidences and severity of attacks directed at US targets escalated steadily. By the time of the New York and Washington outrages, hundreds of American lives had already been lost to Islamist suicide operations.

Some analysts attribute this complacency to a failure of intelligence. Yet, the CIA evidently recognised the nature of the threat and advertised its concern.[38] Moreover, intelligence agencies only reflect national priorities. In the context of their threat perception, governments in both the US and the UK deprioritised the transnational threat posed by Islamist terror after 1991. This in turn affected the resources directed towards its management.[39] As Bruce Hoffman has observed, up until the attacks against the US, 60 percent of the intelligence gathering effort was devoted to acquiring information on the armed forces of states perceived as potential threats.[40] Likewise, the Presidential directive of 1995 banning the recruitment of agents with criminal associations, and encouraging agents to undertake sensitivity training towards minorities, militated against the penetration of Islamist terror cells.[41]

Why this curious neglect of the manner in which Islamist terror groups in Egypt, Algeria, Saudi Arabia, Lebanon, Pakistan and Afghanistan were both evolving and extending their local and global interconnections? The answer appears to involve a number of ideological and political factors at play in both the West and the non-West. Firstly, it would seem scholars and analysts assumed that Islamism in its Iranian mutation was an isolated and anomalous phenomenon. In the aftermath of the Shia-inspired Iranian revolution it became a growing scholarly orthodoxy that mainstream Islam of a Sunni provenance, and its variations like the Wahhabism practised in Saudi Arabia and by the Taliban in the madrassas of Northern Pakistan, would prove more accommodating both to modernisation and the West. By the 1990s, western scholars of Islam increasingly discountenanced a 'monolithic' Islamic threat. Thus John Esposito poured scorn on the notion of 'Muslim rage' and considered western fears of Islam highly exaggerated. Meanwhile, Robert Hefner found in Islamic revivalism not ideological intolerance but the possibilities of democratisation and civil society.[42]

Such an accommodationist interpretation of Islam neatly coincided with the view that history had somehow ended and what remained, as Francis Fukuyama explained, was merely a gradual global dawning that 'liberal democracy' constituted 'the end point of mankind's ideological evolution'.[43] This understanding also suited a post-ideological Presidency in America dedicated to a third way in governance that considered that 'the calculation of pure power politics simply does not compute'.[44] In the wake of the Gulf War, the Clinton presidency in the US and the Blair government in the UK shared an incoherent pursuit of ethics and human rights in foreign policy that promoted a vacuous multilateralism abroad allied to a multicultural sensitivity at home.

However, the assumed compatibility of all values in the postmodern state at the end of history confronted an uncomfortable but largely unrecognised fact. As Ernest Gellner observed, 'the tolerant endorsement of human diversity becomes very tangled if one realises that very many past and alien visions have been internally inclusive, intolerant and ethnocentric; so that if we, in our tolerant way, endorse *them*, we thereby also endorse or encourage intolerance at second hand. This might be called the dilemma of the liberal intellectual.'[45] It might also be called the current dilemma of the western liberal democratic state.

For after September 11 the extent to which government-promoted diversity had led to the open toleration of religiously motivated militancy both within the UK and the US exposed some uncomfortable facts. For example, the US State Department hampered the investigation into the Khobar Towers massacre when it refused an FBI request to threaten a suspect, Hani al-Sayegh, with repatriation to his native Saudi Arabia, on the grounds that such action would transgress international legal conventions.[46] One of the more piquant illustrations of the contradictions in western policy after September 11 came when British Foreign Secretary, Jack Straw, briefly in Cairo to solicit support for the 'war against terrorism', was berated by President Hosni Mubarak for Britain's refusal to extradite convicted Islamist terrorists to Egypt.[47] Western nations in their desire to promote global human rights and accede to universal standards of justice allowed international conventions on asylum to be manipulated for terrorist ends. Ironically, having put the rest of the world on notice about punishing countries that harboured terrorists, western governments awoke after September 11 to discover that they, in fact, harboured many of the extremists who planned and executed terror outrages.[48]

The War 'Against the Abstract Noun':[49] The Challenge in Global and Local Perspective

Ultimately, it would seem that the intensification of asymmetric threats of an Islamist or ethnicist hue in the post-Cold War era represents a complex amalgam of factors that can trace their recent historical origins to the period before the end of the Cold War, but which now exploit the economic and media opportunities provided by globalisation in order to deploy a range of anti-state tactics that have evolved since Robespierre pioneered the view that virtue without terror was impotent in 1793.

In particular, the end of the Cold War removed the superpower patronage system that held many weaker states together. As a result, many of the post-Cold War states such as Afghanistan, Sudan, Somalia, the Philippines and Indonesia became notably unstable and thus a source of sanctuary where al-Qaeda training grounds could flourish unmolested (as Cotton explores in Part III). This has given rise to a sharp cleavage in the international system. At one level, the forces of globalisation have ushered in complex transnational processes that have, to a degree, eroded national boundaries. In this pluralist world, cosmopolitans inhabit and work in relatively stable systems and adapt to the secular values of a globally connected marketplace, often communicating in English as a *lingua franca*.

However, beyond this cosmopolitanised world, which likes to conduct its international relations through multilateral institutions and rule-governed arrangements that promote both free trade and human rights, there resides another domain where people exist in different 'ages', with another sense of time and reality. Here, people inhabit a world of traditional rivalries where national, or religious, myths flourish and where force rather than persuasion remains the essential arbiter of life. It is in this twilight zone of state disintegration, economic chaos and genocide that the terror strategy has mutated and which the cosmopolitanised world in terms of both its threat perception and Olympian ideology of globalised rights appears singularly ill equipped to address.

Paradoxically, the very openness of western democracies to processes of globalisation and borderlessness has rendered them peculiarly vulnerable to asymmetric threats generally and those perpetrated by al-Qaeda type terror in particular (as Paul Schulte discusses in Part I and François Haut and Gavin

Cameron explore in Part II). If the West is at war, it is evidently not at war by conventional means, nor do conventional forces offer necessarily the most effective response. This problem is ultimately twofold – political and military – and requires a political reassessment of the relationship of external and internal threats to the stability of complex modern industrial societies.

On a theoretical level it requires a radical reappraisal of the categories 'war' and 'terror'. For much of the twentieth century, culminating with the atomic denouement to World War II, the dominant understanding of war has been to conceive it in either eschatological or cataclysmic terms rather than strategic ones controlled and regulated by political tutelage towards specific goals. The Cold War years, despite avoiding an all-engulfing military confrontation between the superpowers, fitted this eschatological framework. More recently, the current war on abstract terror reflects a characteristic American propensity to view war as an ideological showdown between the forces of good and evil. For ultimately, a 'war against terror' has no more meaning than a 'war against war' or a 'war against poverty'. It defines no specific threat, does not delineate a precise enemy, and thus, defines no realisable political ends.

Islamism offers a mirror image of this view. It too seeks the final apocalypse that will render the forces of the great secular Satan otiose. Ironically, whilst western theorists envisaged an end of history narrowly conceived in rights-based, secular and tolerant liberal democratic terms, their Islamist equivalents conceived themselves in an apocalyptic conflict to establish a political Islam that actively confronted the West. Moreover, while western analysts considered the Russian reversal in Afghanistan a result of imperial overstretch, Islamism conceived it vindicating the will of Allah. The demise of the Soviet Union left only the Great Satan of the US, whose imminent demise was prefigured in the collapse of the twin towers.

The failure to recognise the Islamist take on a clash of civilisations illustrates a curious western hubris masquerading as sensitivity to diversity. Moreover, the central strategic problem for any coalition against terrorism is that if the enemy views its struggle in eschatological terms, then it assumes that its ideology will eventually triumph, no matter the short-term setbacks or the losses inflicted upon itself. If the enemy one is taking on represents an entrenched religiously motivated movement, then one has a serious problem, especially if it is as large and amorphous as Islam – which has been around a lot longer than the United States, 'democracy' or 'the West' and which sees itself as outlasting them all.

In eschatological terms, the technological superiority provided by the revolution in military affairs ultimately gave allied forces a significant edge over an enemy like the Taliban, but how does the West subsequently respond to the increase in people flows and the rights of refuge and asylum that populations subject to and not always immune from the blandishments of Islamism will provoke? The answer again is worryingly unclear, for the third way approach to war, propounded in October 2001 by British Prime Minister, Tony Blair, which seeks resolution through an evolving global communitarian ideal permitting a proliferation of cultures, debt forgiveness and endless humanitarian aid appears worryingly incomplete. Such an ideology, despite growing evidence to the contrary, refuses to recognise that non-western minorities do not accept the practices of secular western institutions and evince minimal tolerance for the values of a plural democracy. Ironically, to launch an ideological war on the basis of an Anglo-American commitment to distributive justice and multilateral institution building undermines the strategy of internal and external intelligence gathering and policing that constitutes the only effective long-term response not to abstract terror but to those groups from religious fundamentalists through ethno-nationalists to radical anti-capitalists who consider their cause legitimates an apocalyptic recourse to violence (as Dennis Richardson suggests in Part IV).

The prognosis, then, is grim and requires a political mindset more Machiavellian than Kantian (as Paul Schulte discusses in Part I). In the domestic sphere there is a need for intelligence and domestic security arrangements that are configured to meet the realities of post-Cold War threats along with tougher law enforcement, tighter border controls, increased security measures and general vigilance, along with additional measures for bureaucratic surveillance.[50] Externally, it means being prepared to disrupt terror networks and to subvert fundamentalist regimes as soon as they appear in order to render them unsustainable. Generally, the struggle entails employing force where necessary, coercive diplomacy, playing off states or non-state groups against each other, forging temporary alliances with states that are not intrinsically friendly, and even sometimes a willingness to negotiate with certain sections of 'terrorist' movements.

The most important realisation is that there can be no conclusive victory. As Andrew Brown, notes: 'you cannot beat terrorism without killing terrorists. But just killing them won't do the job ... In the end, you reach the goal of "no more terrorists" not when they are all dead, but when some are dead, some have stopped terrorism and no new young men are coming along to take their places'.[51] For the defeat of terrorism in all its manifestations is a messy and complex enterprise, one that requires a new appreciation of Martin Wight's dictum that there are only three permanent institutions in the international system: diplomacy, alliances, and war.

THE STRUCTURE OF THE BOOK

Part I: Theorising New Terror

To explore the character of this evolving terrorism and the messy response to it, Part I examines the motivations that inform new terror and the uncertainty it engenders not only in states of concern but also since September 11 in the increasingly interconnected, open, and cosmopolite states of Europe, Asia and the Americas that once envisaged a borderless world, but are now troubled by what lies both within and beyond the borderline.

Thus in chapter 2 Paul Schulte offers an 'uncertain diagnosis' of a potential unending war for the future. For Schulte, September 11 crystallised and confirmed culturally emergent anxieties about the character of this war. Nevertheless, Schulte argues, the scale, significance and operational effectiveness of terrorism as a global phenomenon remains far from certain. It is plausible that the techno-strategic balance between offence and defence has changed, especially with the possibility of bioterrorism. Apprehensions about this could have profound psychological and cultural consequences. Yet the realistic chance of occurrence or actuarial probability of falling casualty to the New Terrorism will almost certainly be grossly exaggerated – as with the Old Terrorism.

It is still not clear, Schulte maintains, to what extent New Terrorists will link with each other, with criminals, or with existing practitioners of political violence. International actors will differ – for cultural, historical and capability reasons – in their relative reliance on each response. Some responses should be pursued anyway, most are combinable and synergistic; others may conflict. Ultimately, Schulte avers, we need to keep a sense of proportion and of realistic risk, or else terrorists will already have begun to intimidate us. 'Megalomaniacal Hyper-Terrorism' is only one possible perturbation among many facing densely networked societies – we should plan with overall 'national resilience' and generic risk management in mind.

Subsequently, in chapter 3, Grant Wardlaw looks at how anti-globalisation protest has exacerbated the perturbation of modern western democracies. For Wardlaw globalisation has become the driving force behind many aspects of contemporary society. In its many manifestations it is held responsible for both progress and increases in living standards globally and increasing poverty, a widening of the divide between rich and poor and the subjugation of individual and local values to those of an unaccountable global elite.

This clash of worldviews has spawned a wave of international protests – often with a violent edge – whose organisation and impact paradoxically rely on the technologies that symbolise the globalised world they oppose. The Internet, the mobile phone, encryption and other sophisticated technologies have enabled anti-globalisation protesters to plan, communicate, coordinate, energise, promote and protect their activities in a way that has not been possible in the past. The devices pioneered by anti-globalisation protesters are, of course, also those increasingly favoured by protoplasmic new terror groups.

In the context of globalisation, therefore, Rohan Gunaratna examines in chapter 4 the al-Qaeda threat and the international response. In particular, Gunaratna explores the character of the networked and de-territorialised threat posed by al-Qaeda, which he views as the defining conflict of the twenty first century. Gunaratna traces how al-Qaeda functions both operationally and ideologically at local, national, regional and global levels. To challenge al-Qaeda and its associate groups successfully, Gunaratna contends, the international community must seek to develop a multi-agency, multi-dimensional and multi-lateral responses.

Subsequently in chapter 5, Clive Williams examines in greater detail the ideology of Islamic extremism and particularly its Wahhabist variation. Williams explores the religious thinking that informs the ideology, personnel and strategies of radical groups in Saudi Arabia, Pakistan, and Southeast Asia as well as that of the al-Qaeda network and their former hosts, the Taliban and seeks to explain its appeal in societies and amongst diasporic communities experiencing uncertain globalisation.

Part II: Terror Tactics and Asymmetric Strategies – New and Old

Part II of the book shifts from theories and practitioners to actual practices. In particular, it examines the weaponry, terror tactics and asymmetric strategies both new and old deployed by contemporary terror networks. In chapter 6 Angus Muir analyses how the terrorist weapon of choice, the bomb, has evolved and might develop in the future. Muir examines, from an historical perspective, the way terrorist targeting and tactics have developed over recent years. In particular, Muir examines the post-war evolution of bombing tactics from using cars as bombs to aeroplanes to more recent and disturbing innovations in the area of suicide bombing.

In chapters 7 and 8, Gavin Cameron and François Haut examine the character of the Chemical, Biological, Radiological and Nuclear (CBRN) threat and the extent to which such a threat is exaggerated. For Cameron, the acts of terrorism on September 11 2001 appear to herald a new era of high-casualty and high-consequence terrorism, unmatched even by previous incidents such as Aum Shinrikyo's release of sarin gas in the Tokyo subway in March 1995. Although relying on a familiar tactic, airline hijacking, the attacks on the World Trade Center and Pentagon were unlike their predecessors in the 1970s: the terrorists were not intent on escaping after the attack. However, until relatively recently, Aum Shinrikyo's attack was regarded as being a watershed, itself supposed to be the start of a wave of high-consequence terrorist attacks with CBRN weapons. Such pessimism was not borne out by events in the subsequent years. It is therefore important to consider whether the events of September 11 are really indicative of a greater likelihood of terrorists resorting to CBRN weapons.

In considering the implications of September 11 for subsequent terrorist uses of CBRN weapons, both Cameron and Haut further differentiate between the various types of these weapons, analysing the threats posed by each. They assess the relative difficulties of effective acquisition, weaponisation, and delivery of CBRN weapons, and the potential impact of such weapons use, suggesting that this impact would have psychological, social and political ramifications, as well as the obvious potential for casualties. However, both authors also examine, from a historical perspective, the record of previous examples of CBRN use by sub-state actors. Cameron argues that many previous threats have used low-level agents or have used high-level agents ineffectively and suggests that there is a disconnection between those sub-state actors who have used CBRN weapons and those whom one would most fear using such weapons.

By contrast, for Haut, CBRN terror constitutes the most asymmetrical tactic available to terrorist groups and considers its capacity to generate a 'Damocles effect' with the citizens of the modern cosmopolis living in a permanent situation of paralysis created by this form of psychological warfare. They would have to live with the fear that, at any time, as in the legend, the horse's hair preventing the sword from falling might be broken.

Moving away from CBRN terror, in chapters 9 and 10 Kevin O'Brien and Michele Zanini assess the nature of information age terrorism. In chapter 9, O'Brien explores the future potential use of the Internet by terrorists. He asks: is it a weapon that suits the terrorist psyche, or is it more valuable as a tool to organise and manage a campaign?

This chapter therefore examines the notion of Netwars and the manner in which terrorists could use cyberspace as a means for organisation, control and information warfare. More precisely, it raises the cyber threat paradox that if terrorists undermine net-based communication, they will also undermine their own access to an increasingly valuable organisational tool. O'Brien also examines the links between 'real world' terrorism and cyber terrorism particularly with regard to critical infrastructure protection.

Meanwhile in chapter 10, Michele Zanini observes that while the information revolution has fuelled the longest economic expansion in US history, it has arrived with a dark side in the form of cyberterrorism. The idea of terrorists surreptitiously hacking into a computer system to introduce a virus, steal sensitive information, deface or swamp a website, or turn off a crucial public service, seriously concerns computer security personnel around the world. The exponential increase in reported incidents over the last ten years, along with recent high profile attacks – such as the denial-of-service (DOS) attacks against major e-commerce sites Yahoo! and eBay in 1999 or the ongoing 'cyber-jihad' against Israeli and American web sites being waged by Pakistani-based hackers in support of the Palestinian al-Aqsa Intifada – continue to raise the spectre of cyberterrorism.

Despite such publicity, however, Zanini further argues that the information age affects not only the types of targets and weapons terrorists might choose, but also the ways in which such groups operate and structure their organisations. Several of the most dangerous terrorist outfits use information technology (IT) to organise and coordinate dispersed activities. Like the large numbers of private corporations that have embraced information technologies in order to operate more efficiently and with greater flexibility, terrorists are harnessing the power of IT to enable new operational doctrines and forms of organisation. In this context, terrorist groups are 'disaggregating' from hierarchical bureaucracies and moving to flatter, more decentralised groups united by a common goal.

The rise of networked terrorists groups is part of a broader shift to what Arquilla and Ronfeldt have called 'netwar'.[52] Netwar refers to an emerging mode of conflict and crime at societal levels, involving measures short of traditional war in which the protagonists are likely to consist of dispersed, small groups who communicate, coordinate, and conduct their campaigns in an internetted manner, without a precise central command. Netwar differs from modes of conflict in which the actors prefer formal, stand-alone, hierarchical organisations, doctrines and strategies, as in past efforts, for example, to build centralised revolutionary movements along Marxist lines. This chapter assesses the degree to which – and how – networked terrorist groups are using IT, particularly in the Middle East. The analysis reviews past trends, and offers a series of educated guesses about how such trends will evolve in the future.

Part III: Implications for the Asia Pacific

While the first two parts of this book examine the motivation of and the asymmetric strategies deployed by increasingly networked and disaggregated terror groups, Part III considers the strategies and financing of terror groups with particular reference to the Asia Pacific and explores the links between organised crime, and the increasingly globalised pursuit of terror. This section also addresses the infrastructure of terror, how it is financed, its links to grey area activity like drug and people smuggling that is linked to the illegal global economy and the problem it represents for policing and international law regimes.

In chapter 11 James Cotton notes that Southeast Asia has become the 'second front' in the global campaign against terrorism. Cotton contends that the region embracing southern Asia, Southeast Asia and the Southwest Pacific has seen considerable instability since the end of the Cold War. A number of the conflicts that have emerged have spawned domestic terrorism, some of which has spilled into neighbouring countries. This chapter surveys regional trends in the post-Cold War period followed by a discussion of cases in the region where government incapacity has allowed significant terrorist threats to emerge or where governments (notably North Korea) have used terrorism as a strategy of state policy. The poor performance of regional organisations in addressing such security issues will be assessed in the context of multilateral and bilateral security diplomacy. Having reviewed the regional context, this chapter considers the response of the major countries in the region to the terrorist threat, before locating that response within the narrative of domestic and regional political developments. It then argues that while whatever network al-Qaeda had established in Southeast Asia will be disrupted by concerted United States action, in the process the pronounced illiberal tendencies in a number of political systems will become more deeply entrenched.

Following this regional overview, Andrew Tan in chapter 12 addresses more specifically the phenomenon of armed Muslim rebellion in Southeast Asia. Tan considers the persistence of armed separatist movements in Southeast Asia, demonstrated by the continuing separatist/irredentist rebellions in Aceh, Mindanao and Pattani that date from the era of decolonisation. He further examines the security implications of this persistence particularly in relation to the globalising pressures in the wake of the Asian financial crisis that has volatised separatist movements in Southeast Asia and their evolving relationship to terror networks beyond the region.

In chapter 13 John MacFarlane assesses the nature of organised crime and terrorism in the Asia Pacific region. MacFarlane shows that organised and entrepreneurial crime groups are well established throughout the Asia Pacific region and have been very active in the whole spectrum of criminal activity from drug trafficking, human and arms smuggling, sea piracy and kidnapping, to credit card fraud, investment scams, money laundering and intellectual property crime. These groups range from the highly structured Japanese yakuza and Chinese triads to small entrepreneurial groups specialising in providing a particular criminal service and street gangs engaging in opportunistic crime. There are also states like Myanmar, where senior officials periodically engage in criminal activities with the apparent blessing of the state itself.

With little or no state sponsorship, terrorist groups operating in the region have little option but to engage in criminal activities in order to generate the necessary funds to support their political objectives. Such activities embrace a wide variety of illegal activity from drug trafficking to kidnapping and bank robbery. Some groups, like Abu Sayyaf, straddle an uncertain line between crime and terror. This chapter also considers a range of international and regional initiatives devised to curtail the effectiveness of transnational criminal and terrorist groups.

Subsequently in chapter 14 Peter Chalk discusses one prevalent manifestation of transnational organised crime in contemporary Southeast Asia: the heroin trade. He first examines opiate production in Burma, outlining major trafficking routes and markets for the trade, regionally and internationally. The chapter then analyses the issue of narco-terrorism and the prospect of this type of nexus emerging in Southeast Asia.

Part IV: Towards a Conclusion

Part IV examines western democratic legal responses to terrorism and the relationship between terrorism and international regimes. Mark Weeding in chapter 15 considers the character of western liberal legislative responses to mass casualty terror attacks after September 11. Dennis Richardson in chapter 16 explains the current multivalent approach adopted by the Australian government. Finally, Richard Butler concludes with an overview of the structural characteristics of globalisation that informs contemporary terrorism. Butler contends that the current state of our globalised world indicates that major action is required on three fronts to address the asymmetric threat posed by new terror emanating from low intensity conflicts in states of concern or that have broken down. Butler argues that this action is required not because of terrorism, but because these are the areas in which profound failure is occurring. These are: the realignment of global economic relations; the field of communications that retails, on a global basis, information that is false and incites violence; and the expansion in the proliferation of the means of mass destruction since the end of the Cold War. These three related phenomena that shape the post-Cold War order require, Butler concludes, a new international paradigm to address them.

NOTES

1.   O'Brien, Kevin A. and Nusbaum, Joseph (2000), 'Intelligence gathering on asymmetric threats – Part One', *Jane's Intelligence Review*, 12, 10 October, p 52.
2.   Friedman, Thomas (1999), *The Lexus and the Olive Tree*, London: HarperCollins.

3. Bowen, Wyn (2003), 'The Dimensions of Asymmetric War', in Dorman, Andrew, Smith, Mike and Uttley, Matthew (eds), *The Changing Face of Military Power*, London: Palgrave.
4. Juergensmeyer, Mark (2000), *Terror in the Mind of God: The Global Rise of Religious Violence*, Berkeley: University of California Press, p 6.
5. Kaldor, Mary (1999), *New and Old Wars: Organized Violence in a Global Era*, Stanford: Stanford University Press.
6. Smith, Steve (2001), 'The United States will emerge from this as a more dominant world power', *The Times*, 19 September.
7. Barber, Benjamin (1996), *Jihad vs McWorld*, New York: Ballantine, chapter 15.
8. Kaldor (1999), *New and Old Wars*, p. 7. See also other important works of this genre: Huntingdon, Samuel (1996), *The Clash of Civilizations and the Remaking of World Order*, New York: Touchstone; Holsti, Kalevi (1996), *The State, War, and the State of War*, Cambridge: Cambridge University Press; Kissinger, Henry (1994), *Diplomacy*, New York: Touchstone; Van Creveld, Martin (1991), *The Transformation of War*, New York: Free Press; Van Creveld, Martin (1999), *The Rise and Decline of the State*, Cambridge: Cambridge University Press; Friedman (1999), *The Lexus and the Olive Tree*.
9. Sterling, Clair (1981), *The Terror Network*, New York: Holt, Rinehart & Winston.
10. Herman, Edward and O'Sullivan, Gerry (1990), *The Terrorism Industry*, New York: Pantheon.
11. For example, the IRA in Northern Ireland and the Basque militants of ETA-Militar and its political offshoot *Herri Batasuuna*, have maintained close affiliations based on a perception of a shared legitimate struggle against an oppressor state. It is a relationship that in the past has extended to sharing information on tactics and facilitating weapons shipments. See *An Phoblacht/Republicans* (1990), 'Many Parallels Between Ireland and the Euskadi', 10 May.
12. Guelke, Adrian (1995), *The Age of Terrorism and the International Political System*, London: IB Tauris, p 35.
13. Chomsky, Noam (1991), 'International Terrorism: Image and Reality', in George, Alexander (ed.), *Western State Terrorism*, New York: Routledge, p 34.
14. See Herman, Edward and O'Sullivan, Gerry (1991), '"Terrorism" as Ideology and Cultural Industry', in George, *Western State Terrorism*, pp 39–75.
15. By Islamism we understand the use of Islam for political and ideological purposes of a radical utopian character. See in this context Pipes, Daniel (2000), 'Islam and Islamism Faith and Ideology', *The National Interest*, Spring, p 90.
16. See in this context, Bergen, Peter (2001), *Holy War Inc. Inside the Secret World of Osama bin Laden*, London: Weidenfeld & Nicolson, p 127.
17. See Keohane, Robert (1984), *After Hegemony*, Princeton: Princeton University Press; Baldwin, David (ed.) (1993), *Neorealism and Neoliberalism: The Contemporary Debate*, New York: Columbia University Press.
18. For the antidote see Mearsheimer, John (1994/95), 'The False Promise of International Institutions', *International Security*, 19/3.
19. Paz, Reuven (1998), 'Is There an Islamic Terrorism?' Online. 7 September. Available: http://esoterictexts06.tripod.com/EsotericTexts06/Islam.Terrorism.Essay.htm. 13 April 2003. See also Dunlap, Charles (1998), 'Preliminary Observations: Asymmetrical War and the Western Mindset', in Matthews, Lloyd (ed.), *Challenging the United States Symmetrically and Asymmetrically: Can America Be Defeated?*, Carlisle, PA: United States Strategic Studies Institute, p 2; Arquilla, John and Ronfeldt, David (1993), 'Cyberwar Is Coming!' *Comparative Strategy*, 12/2, Summer, pp 141–65; Schwartzstein, Stuart (ed.) (1996), *The Information Revolution and National Security: Dimensions and Directions*, Washington, DC: Center for International and Strategic Studies.
20. In its broad anti-western manifestation and its desire for Islamic purity it can be traced to the emergence of Hanif al-Banna's Muslim Brotherhood in 1928, the forerunner of Islamic Jihad. In this context see Kedourie, Elie (1980), *Islam in the Modern World and Other*

Studies, London: Mansell, p 56; Hiro, Dilip (1989), *Islamic Fundamentalism*, London: Paladin, chapter 4.

21. Nordland, Rod (2001), 'A Dictator's Dilemma', *Newsweek*, 1 October, p 28.
22. Kedourie, Elie (1994), *Democracy and Arab Political Culture*, London: Frank Cass, p 94.
23. *Ibid.*, p 97.
24. *Ibid.*, p 99–100. See also Juergensmeyer, (2000), *Terror in the Mind of God*, p 81.
25. Zakaria, Fareed (2001), 'The Allies Who Made Our Foes', *Newsweek*, 1 October, p 17.
26. For an account of the CIA's links with Pakistan's Inter-Services Intelligence (ISI), but not with either Osama bin Laden or the Taliban, see Bergen (2001), *Holy War Inc.*, chapter 3.
27. In this context see Rashid, Ahmed (2000), *Taliban: Militant Islam, Oil and Fundamentalism in Central Asia*, New Haven: Yale University Press; Bergen (2001), *Holy War Inc.*
28. Agence France Presse (2001), 'Gaddafi: Libya Ordered 1986 Berlin Bombing', 15 May. See also Hooper, John (2001) 'Gadafy Told Berlin Diplomat of Libyans' Lockerbie Role', *The Guardian*, 16 May. The second suspect, Al-Amin Khalifah Fhima, a Libyan airline official, was cleared of any involvement.
29. Simon, Steven and Benjamin, Daniel (2000), 'America and the New Terrorism', *Survival*, 42/1, Spring, p 59.
30. Roy, Oliver (2000), 'Islam, Iran and the New Terrorism', *Survival*, 42/2, Summer, pp 89–106.
31. See in this context Pipes (2000), 'Islam and Islamism Faith and Ideology', p 90.
32. *Straits Times*, 8 July 2000.
33. *Asian Wall Street Journal* (2001), 'Philippine Police Say Rebels Have Links to Bin Laden', 24 September.
34. See Gunaratna, Rohan (2001), 'The Evolution and Tactics of the Abu Sayyaf Group', *Jane's Intelligence Review*, July, pp 29–32.
35. *The Australian* (2000), 24 May.
36. See Hiro (1989), *Islamic Fundamentalism*, chapter 5; Lapidus, Ira (1988), *A History of Islamic Societies*, Cambridge: Cambridge University Press, pp 673–4.
37. *Newsweek* (2001), 'The Road to September 11', 1 October, p 46. In 1993, the original World Trade Center bomber, Ramzi Yousef, planned to knock down one tower into the other and at other times talked of crashing a plane into the CIA building in Virginia or a nuclear facility.
38. Woodward, Bob and Ricks, Thomas (2001), *Washington Post*, 3 October.
39. For instance a specialist British unit set up by the counter-intelligence service, MI5, to deal with Islamic-based terrorism was disbanded in 1994.
40. Hoffman, Bruce (2001), 'A Counterterrorism Policy for Yesterday's Threat', *Los Angeles Times*, 16 September.
41. Sullivan, Andrew (2001), 'The Damage Clinton Did', *Sunday Times*, 30 September. See also Roberts, Andrew (2001), 'Bring Back 007', *The Spectator*, 6 October.
42. See Esposito, John (1992), *The Islamic Threat Myth or Reality?* Oxford: Oxford University Press, chapter 6; Hefner, Robert (2000), *Civil Islam Muslims and Democratization in Indonesia*, Princeton: Princeton University Press, chapters 1 and 8. For the development of this argument of tolerant, modernising Islam more generally see Lapidus, Ira (1983), *Contemporary Islamic Movements in Historical Perspective*, Policy Papers in International Affairs, No. 18, Berkeley: University of California Press.
43. Fukuyama, Francis (1992), *The End of History and the Last Man*, London: Penguin, p ix.
44. Cited in Harries, Owen (2001), 'An End to Nonsense', *The National Interest*, p 65.
45. Gellner, Ernest (1985), *Relativism in the Social Sciences*, Cambridge: Cambridge University Press, pp 83–4.
46. *Newsweek* (2001), 'The Road to September 11', p 47.
47. Johnston, Philip (2001), '"Terror Groups" Hiding in the Heart of Britain', *Daily Telegraph*, 28 September.
48. See, for example, Marin, Minette (2001), 'It is Decadent to Tolerate the Intolerable', *Daily Telegraph*, 22 September.

49. Utley, Tom (2001), 'The Moment I Saw Bush Had Grasped the Point of this War', *Daily Telegraph*, 28 September.
50. Hoffman (2001), 'A Counterterrorism Policy for Yesterday's Threat'.
51. Brown, Andrew (2001), 'Lessons on How to Fight Terror'. Online. *Salon*, 19 September. Available: http://www.salon.com/news/feature/2001/09/19/fighting_terror/print.html. 3 May 2003.
52. See Arquilla, John and Ronfeldt, David (2001), *Networks and Netwars: The Future of Terror, Crime, and Militancy*, Santa Monica: RAND.

PART I

Theorising New Terror

2. Uncertain Diagnosis: Megalomaniacal Hyper-Terrorism and an Unending War for the Future?

Paul Schulte

September 11 crystallised and confirmed culturally emergent anxieties about the 'War of the Future'. Nevertheless, the scale, significance and operational effectiveness of terrorism as a global phenomenon remain far from certain.

It is plausible that the techno-strategic balance between offence and defence has changed, especially with regard to the possibility of bioterrorism. Apprehensions about this could have profound psychological and cultural consequences. Indeed, humans may be hard-wired to exaggerate this kind of risk. Yet the realistic chance of occurrence or actuarial probability of falling casualty to the New Terrorism will almost certainly be grossly exaggerated – as it was with the Old Terrorism.

It is still not clear to what extent New Terrorists will link with each other, with criminals, or with existing, 'ordinary decent' practitioners of political violence.

PRESCRIPTION

Seven Responses and a Sense of Proportion

Given the nature of this new threat, combinations of the following responses will be increasingly necessary:

1. *Dissuasion* (resolving, moderating or at least 'detoxifying' the underlying causes of terror).
2. *Disarmament* (reducing the amount of weapons of mass destruction [WMD] material and expertise available in the world and the extent of international tension).
3. *Denial* (of resources and space to organise).

4. *Disruption* (of terrorist networks by police or military action).
5. *Detection* (by human or technical means).
6. *Deterrence* (by denial of effective action and/or the threat of retribution).
7. *Defence* (and protection of both homelands and citizens and assets abroad).

International actors will differ in their relative reliance on each response. Such responses will be dependent on specific cultural or historical backgrounds and differing resource capabilities. Some responses should be pursued anyway, most are combinable and synergistic, and others may conflict with each other.

Yet we need to keep a sense of proportion and of realistic risk, or else terrorists will already have begun to intimidate us. The notion of 'Megalomaniacal Hyper-terrorism' is only one possible perturbation among many facing densely networked societies – we should plan with overall 'national resilience' and generic risk management in mind.

UNCERTAIN DIAGNOSIS

We have entered a time when global political violence may be changing its features, increasing its significance and requiring new, more serious and integrated responses from us. Yet caution, as always, is required.

One must begin with a developmental diagnosis. To generalise, plainly, there seemed to be a consensus by the end of the 1980s about what terrorism was, as far as Western governments were concerned. Terrorists, whether separatists like the Irish Republican Army (IRA) or Basque Fatherland and Liberty (ETA), or revolutionary leftists like Baader-Meinhoff and the Red Brigades, or so-called national liberationists like the Palestinian groups were callous, tenacious and murderous. However, in the summarised theories of motivation that have entered popular discourse, they mounted operations which left a lot of people watching, rather than a lot of people dead, because they wanted the oxygen of publicity. To be beneficial, that publicity largely had to be favourable, because they wanted to use assassinations, bombings and hostage taking as tools to achieve concessions and (often very vague and improbable) political settlements. The Middle East was different, as the scale of violence, especially from any intervention there, was unpredictably greater. But Middle East governments, too, tended to use state-sponsored terror by various groups as a rationally calibrated but clandestine extension of politics by other means.

From about the mid-1990s it was becoming clear that we might have to expand our sense of the threat. Although the collapse of Marxism for the most part removed extremist leftist motivations, movements like the Islamic Salvation Front (FIS) and Armed Islamic Group (GIA) in Algeria, and Egyptian Islamic Jihad, reinforced by brutalised and religiously intoxicated returnees from the Afghan War against the Soviets (the Spanish Civil War of the Islamic world) were showing willingness for extraordinary savagery and utter indifference to public opinion. In the United States, Christian fundamentalists, overlapping with right-wing militias, were discovered to be working on chemical and biological weapons as an aid to a sacred apocalyptic race war.

In 1994 Baruch Goldestein shot dead thirty Muslims at prayer in Hebron and Palestinian suicide bombings were becoming increasingly frequent. In 1995 Timothy McVeigh blew up several hundred people in Oklahoma and Aum Shirikyo fatally gassed twelve and affected over 5,000 others on the Tokyo underground. In all of this, there were no press releases or calls for negotiations. There was a strong emphasis on holy motives and a sense that modern, earthly, secular-based societies, nation-states or compromise settlements were intolerable to the 'true believers'. Something ugly and extreme was happening in the global village, Walter Laqueur coined the term 'New Terrorism' to describe it.[1]

WHAT DOES NEW TERROR MEAN?

Fears associated with the New Terrorism now incorporate:

1. *Non-negotiability.*
2. *Internationalism*, of actors, resources and grievances and its habitat, in expanding global diasporas and email and airline-linked ethnicities or affinity groups.
3. *Network centricity*, rather than any kind of traditional hierarchical structure.
4. Its ability to eclipse the power of *failing states*. Bin Laden as an individual could settle in and influence Sudan, and later effectively merge his operations with the government of Afghanistan.
5. A generally *religious basis* and the resultant indifference to the mortal lives of operatives and victims.
6. Its apparently predictable *interest in the most modern and lethal weaponry* especially WMD and probably of mass effect, such as cyberterrorism.
7. Above all, its likely *willingness to carry out mass casualty attacks* which would leave a lot of people dead, with audience ratings that would also be enormous, but even so might not be the main purpose of the action.

By 1998, after the Embassy Bombings in East Africa, with their huge bystander casualties, Madeline Albright began referring to the 'War of the Future', setting the New Terrorism in terms of a long-running total campaign, a kind of low intensity World War III. A whole genre of Hollywood movies (*Executive Decision, Navy Seals, Die Hard, GI Jane, The Siege*) began to implant its image into our collective consciousness. We began to imagine (perhaps to dream of) a long, conceivably interminable, ugly, globally widespread, intensely asymmetrical conflict with racial and religious overtones. This conflict would largely exist between an affluent, secular and hi-tech, but post-heroic and ageing West, and an angry, poor, young belligerent South and East. Complicating matters is the fact that many of the latter's potential recruits or sympathisers might now live physically within Western political communities, but not, we might have to fear, inside our public space.

The events of September 11 crystallised, amplified and apparently certified these fears, adding in the mass murderous suicide of brilliantly coordinated operatives. It led to the declaration of the 'War against Terror' that is now taking place.

Yet how much of this is new? That's largely a question for academic terrorism buffs. Elements of the New Terrorism have been around for some time. Russian terrorism of the late nineteenth century was effectively suicidal for the hundreds of those involved. Indiscriminate bomb-throwing French anarchists of the 1890s were insisting 'there are no innocent victims' before they went to the guillotine. Joseph Conrad's characters in *The Secret Agent* (1907),[2] still the greatest novel on the shabby deceptive dynamics of terrorism, speak of the need for an 'act of destructive ferocity' so absurd 'as to be incomprehensible, inexplicable, almost unthinkable'. They argue, rationally, that apparent 'madness alone is truly terrifying, as you cannot placate it either by threats, persuasion or bribes' and proceed to arrange an attack on a prominent metropolitan architectural landmark.

As long ago as 1920 a car bomb on Wall Street killed thirty-five random people and injured hundreds. Aircraft hijackings began in the 1930s. The first reported mid-air bombing in the US took place in 1933. Communist intelligence services were coordinating international revolutionary violence between the 1920s and 1980s. International Muslim activism, based on struggle and martyrdom (encouraged and aided by Western agencies), was decisive in Afghanistan by the end of the 1980s. Suicide bombings have been an evidently highly effective Tamil Tiger speciality for twenty years. The IRA made a semi-religious cult of suicidal hunger strikes in the 1980s. Sayyid Qutb, perhaps the key theologian of relentless jihad against the secular West and its alleged puppets, was executed by another Muslim, General Abdul Nasser, in 1966.

What seems new is that all these strands are now converging. Underneath this, perhaps something less visible, more profound, and genuinely original has been changing. It is what I would call the *techno-strategic balance.*

Over two centuries ago, the English historian Edward Gibbon, at the end of his *Decline and Fall of the Roman Empire* (1776–1788) wondered whether this was going to happen again. He thought not. He judged that 'since Mathematics, Chymistry and Mechanics' had been applied to the service of war 'we cannot be displeased that the subversion of a city should now be a work of cost and difficulty' and that 'the gradual advances in the sciences of war would always be accompanied with a proportionate improvement in the arts of peace and civil policy'.[3] So, overall, he reasoned that the barbarians were unlikely to succeed in coming back. I think he was wrong about our ability to learn to cope with human destructiveness, but he was certainly correct about late eighteenth century techno-strategic balances.

There can be little doubt that they did favour the defence and the power of well-organised states. However, great deals of 'Mathematics, Chymistry and Mechanics' have been applied in many directions since then. All saboteurs in Gibbon's day could use was a cart of gunpowder. Yet today's increasingly potent, concentrated, compact or portable technologies are orders of magnitude more devastating when misused. Consider the potential lethality of oil refineries, nuclear reprocessing plants or chem-bio laboratories, container ships and, as we have seen so starkly, airliners. All of these advances change the nature of the problem. Perhaps the barbarians *can* come back, at least from time to time, in ways that will be culturally, psychologically and politically preoccupying. Perhaps post-modernity will mean no longer having only to worry about the organised violence of the modern state, but having to envisage culturally and come to terms with the re-privatisation of large-scale violence.

September 11 was the irrefutable confirmation that, in his other sense, Gibbon was wrong. We cannot any longer easily expect advances in human relations, civil or international order to advance in parallel with technical progress. We can no longer reject the worse-case possibilities of highly organised scientifically empowered human malice.

At least some of us, professionally, will now have to view the humanly constructed world very differently. Two points become very clear in this respect. Firstly, enticing interlinked cosmopolitan societies with their intricate feeder networks become sprawling vulnerabilities. Secondly, lucrative trade nodes and thriving cultural crossroads appear to make shockingly poor fortresses.

We will have to decide what kinds of nations and society we want. We may all, or mostly all, want to remain Athens. Sayyid Qutb believed that the corrosive freedom and rationality deriving from Athens was the essential elemental enemy of an Islam based on the opposing principle of virtue. Christian fundamentalists and fascists would tend to feel the same. Depressingly though, we may have to consider how far one must move in the Spartan direction. How far can we maintain our essential values if we now have to build modern versions of the Long Walls that protected the city and the civilisation of Athens.

RESPONSES

If this is our diagnosis, how should we respond? The West and its allies across the globe (including the many non-murderous or fanatical millions in the Muslim world) have huge resources and a number of possible reactions. By applying them systematically it is not impossible, though it is far too early to be certain, that we can in time thwart, reduce and marginalise al-Qaeda to the status of a short-lived death cult. In this way they could seem to be attempting a doomed revolt against Modernity in the same way as the Ghost Dancers, the Boxer Rebellion or the Mahdist Rebellion.

I shall suggest seven principal ways in which efforts could be made: dissuasion, disarmament, denial, disruption, detection, deterrence and defence. Some of them are new, some we should be doing anyway, many of them reinforce each other, and others may on occasion conflict. They all need attending to. Different international actors, even allies, will differ in their reliance on the various responses. Such differences will result from alternative priorities, world-views, historical experiences and national capabilities. Realistically, we should not expect exact coincidence, but enough agreement for constructive cooperation to use the leverages that resources of modern states and societies provide.

First, in roughly reverse order of concreteness is *dissuasion*. In this context I propose essentially non-military attempts at resolving, moderating or at least detoxifying conflicts by appeals to 'hearts and minds'. These would include those political or economic measures that would reduce the risk that anyone would script themselves as victimised activists into a cosmic war justifying mass murder, or at least minimise their support if they do. Worldwide efforts to respond to injustice and address root causes will be prudent and even morally necessary, but also slow and difficult.

Discrimination between causes and factions will be important, but so too will be non-discrimination on irrelevant racial or religious grounds. Concomitant with this will be far-sighted diplomacy. We must approach dialogue with great seriousness, but should not forget that dialogue favours our relativism and our huge cultural intellectual and economic weight in the world. In terms of *Star Trek*, our contemporary 'global', but in fact very western Greek myth, we are the Borg, and our favoured means of disposing of enemies is to assimilate them. We should not, therefore, expect our opponents to play our favourite persuasive language games, any more than we should expect them to fight us in our preferred open, hi-tech ways. Nonetheless we should be interested in mixtures of altruism and propaganda and in the possible confluence of Islamic theology and information operation.

Overall, we can neither give up hearts and minds efforts nor rely too much on them for early effect. It may never be possible to dissuade some present and future fanatics. Although apparently soft, 'fuzzy' hearts and minds measures such as aid, assistance and constructive diplomacy can also help legitimate and leverage some of the harder responses that will be discussed later.

Secondly there is *disarmament*. Maintaining and developing a global legal and moral taboo on possession or use of WMD remains crucial. Terrorists don't sign disarmament treaties. Yet the fewer such weapons and materials possessed by states the less chance that they will spread to terrorists. Moderated tensions at state level also imply less support for bio-terrorism in general. Serious questions, however, over the verifiability and effectiveness of disarmament will remain unless recalcitrant states such as Iraq can be forced to give up their prohibited weapons.

The third proposed response is that of *denial*. Obviously, we need to deny terrorists and state sponsors their materials for creating chemical, biological, radiological or nuclear (CBRN) weapons. The best-established way of doing this is through export control arrangements like the Australia Group, which in turn gain their foundation and justification from disarmament treaties. We need to keep strengthening, extending and adjusting controls as the technologies keep developing.

In another sense, we need to actively deny space for bases and infrastructure facilities for bio-terrorists, like the al-Qaeda laboratories discovered in Kabul. We cannot any longer safely ignore endless civil conflicts or allow failing states to decompose into black holes on the map. There can be no predicting what pathological developments may emerge from them. For that reason, we need better 'global security hygiene' to sanitise the sites from which New Terrorism can be expected to spread. This overlaps benignly with dissuasion and the notion of claiming 'hearts and minds.'

Fourth is *disruption*. Similarly, we need to be prepared to act vigorously against preparations for mass casualty terror. Strong pre-emptive international police or, if necessary, military action, will be essential in eliminating terrorist networks anywhere in the world as we become aware of them, because distances from our homelands now gives little security. Disruption will mostly have to be achieved through local governments, which will put a premium on diplomacy and coalition building, and we should remember that a clumsy over-emphasis on disruption might damage hearts and minds efforts. Less controversially, we also need to uncover and disrupt illicit flows of money and materials for terrorist groups. Computer experts, accountants and customs officers may be as important as special forces in this regard. Once again authentic international cooperation will be important, and not necessarily easy to achieve.

Fifth is *deterrence*. We should also be interested in deterring terrorism through justified fear of its consequences. Everyone accepts that suicidal terrorist operatives may be beyond deterring when launched on their mission. However their leaderships, or the leaders of sponsoring states, will observe that some nations and individual targets are less rewarding in their vulnerabilities (deterrence by denial) or more dangerous in their reactions (deterrence by retaliation) than others.

The second kind of deterrence, at least, depends upon credible coercive military capabilities. There are grounds for optimism about its effectiveness. The military success of the US-led coalition with near global diplomatic support, in terminating the Taliban regime in a particularly remote, rugged and inaccessible country has been the best possible precedent. It will help to deter other regimes from being tempted into the dangerous game of sponsoring terrorists. Increasing US global military predominance from huge new investments will further raise the strategic credibility of the deterrent response by military means.

Legal deterrence too will also have to be pursued, although the predictable difficulties over acquiring proof for extradition of suspects from unwilling states seem immense.

The sixth concept is *detection*. I think this is important enough to be in a category in itself but the concepts of denial, disruption, deterrence and defence will also gain a good deal from investment in excellent police and intelligence and detection capabilities which can locate and stop individuals and penetrate networks before they strike, or apprehend and convict them afterwards.

The primary importance of human intelligence is obvious. Yet technological improvements may be an important underlying factor. International information sharing and improved data analysis capabilities should help the early recognition of patterns of movement, of association and of behaviour by more and more sensors (including human agents) across the world. Consider the potential of face recognition systems able to match images collected from Peshawar with crowds emerging from the New York subway. Such international capabilities will need to be constantly monitored and addressed. However, there will be weak links in the foreseeable international efforts, through lack of national investment, good faith or concerns over confidentiality.

Seventhly, if all else fails, there is *defence.* Since September 11, most western countries have publicised improved efforts in national defences against a mass casualty terrorist attack. Police, military, medical, scientific, legal and administrative precautions and preparations are necessary but expensive and hard to practise.

There is one final perspective to emphasise: we must preserve or develop a sense of proportion. The risk of outbreaks of New Terrorism is no doubt genuine. Megalomaniacal hyper-terrorism like the destruction of the World Trade Center is a demonstrated possibility. Yet it will not necessarily be likely or frequent or technically successful. Even entirely ruthless terrorist leaderships may have strong practical or prudential reasons not to attempt this particular tactic and, as already noted, we can and should strengthen these reasons. If we become generally culturally obsessed with worst-case possibilities, terrorists achieve an automatic success of a kind. They prove that their variously motivated cosmic wars are the main reality of the planet. While we should not be complacent, we should not let our imaginations or policy decisions become overshadowed by this threat, among the many complexities we currently face.

For citizens of western societies the realistic chance of occurrence or actuarial probability of falling casualty to the New Terrorism will be minute, though it will, even so, almost certainly be grossly exaggerated, as it was with the Old Terrorism.

RESILIENCE

One must acknowledge the concept of national resilience, which we are starting to implement in the United Kingdom. We realised that we had to think very deeply, even before September 11. Because Britain is more tightly coupled and networked in a small space, we realised painfully that events with small beginnings would now have wide effects. We have seen enough evidence of this recently: self-organised tanker driver strikes coordinated by mobile phones; an outbreak of foot and mouth; floods; and an article on the measles, mumps and rubella vaccine which threatened to generate a powerful distrust of government policy. Consequently, we have set up a new Civil Contingency Secretariat that will:

- Scrutinise the horizon for small trends and events.
- Identify and manage national capacities.

- Plan and exercise for risk management.
- Set up sector resilience groups.
- Undertake scenario planning.
- Carry out public perception research and work out optimum strategies of public information and reassurance.

We are beginning to think about resilience as the ability, at every level, to anticipate, pre-empt and resolve disruptive challenges into healthy outcomes.

The eventual idea is to make resilience everyone's responsibility: corporations, local governments, health providers, auditors, investors, insurers and customers. This is a work in progress and for the moment it remains too early to offer firm lessons. In any event, each separate nation is resilient in its own unique way.

One must conclude on a broader scale. For the rest of human history the majority of us will be living in dense, complex, technically proficient, globally interconnected societies. Human beings will continue encountering fundamental value disputes around issues we perhaps cannot yet imagine.[4]

Terrorism, even mass casualty terrorism, is just one more kind of network perturbation. We should draw upon the ingenuity and experimentation, which arose in the West, but is available to all mankind and is being selectively taken up across the world. Therefore we should plan systematically for trouble. We should try holistically to dissuade, disarm, disrupt and deter threats before they reach us, to deny our self-declared enemies resources, to defend against them, but suppose that bad unexpected things *will* go on happening.

In a strong sense we are the heirs of both Qutb's detested Athens and Gibbon's eventually techno-strategically overmatched Rome. At their best each was a resourceful, well-organised, intellectually unhindered society, tenacious, occasionally ferocious, but open and hospitable to immigrants of any origin.

There can be no doubt that we owe it to ourselves neither to let the new barbarians return (or emerge in our midst), nor to become obsessed by what they might do and eventually barbarise ourselves, which would be to give them victory of a kind.

NOTES

1. Laqueur, Walter (1999), *The New Terrorism: Fanaticism and the Arms of Mass Destruction*, New York: Oxford University Press.
2. Conrad, Joseph (1907, 1990), *The Secret Agent*, London: Penguin Books.
3. Gibbon, Edward (1776, 1977), *The Decline and Fall of the Roman Empire*, Harmondsworth: Penguin.

4. I would hazard a personal guess that reproductive technologies, inequality, race and religion will be the most likely blend in this country.

3. Anti-Globalisation.com: The Paradox and the Threat of Contemporary Violent Protest

Grant Wardlaw

Globalisation has become the driving force behind many aspects of contemporary society. In its many manifestations it is held responsible for both progress and increases in living standards globally and increasing poverty, a widening of the divide between rich and poor and the subjugation of individual and local values to those of an unaccountable global elite.

This clash of worldviews has spawned a wave of international protests – often with a violent edge – whose organisation and impact paradoxically rely on the very technologies that symbolise the globalised world they oppose. The Internet, the mobile phone, encryption and other sophisticated technologies have enabled anti-globalisation protesters to plan, communicate, coordinate, energise, promote and protect their activities in a way that has not been possible in the past.

I would like to outline the nature of anti-globalisation protest and examine the extent of and reasons for the violence that has accompanied recent protests internationally. I will note the paradoxes inherent in these protests, especially the coalition of strange bedfellows that make up the anti-globalisation movement and the use of the tools of globalisation to oppose their influence. The problems posed for law enforcement by these threats to public order are assessed and some comments made about the likely future development of anti-globalisation.com.

GLOBALISATION AND POST-MODERN VALUES

In discussing the phenomenon of anti-globalisation.com, many people leap straight into accounts of the violence at particular events and describe the inevitability of it getting worse. However, I would like to start by turning briefly to social science to help put the nature of the protest into context.

Part of trying to understand the extent and types of protest we may face in the future involves understanding whether or not the demonstrations in cities such as Seattle, Prague, Melbourne and Genoa reflect some fundamental shift in social attitudes and values. Or was this a passing phenomenon with little long-term significance?

In fact, a range of studies indicates that there are quite deep-rooted changes in social values occurring in advanced industrial societies that are the result of many of the forces that drive globalisation. Evidence from surveys such as the World Values Survey (WVS), which surveyed the values and beliefs of publics in more than 60 societies in 1981, 1990 and 1995, has found strong links between the beliefs of individuals and the characteristics of their societies. Professor Ronald Inglehart of the Institute for Social Research at the University of Michigan has extensively analysed the survey results.[1]

For our purposes, his most important finding is that: 'Economic development eventually reaches a point of diminishing returns ... in terms of human happiness. This leads to a gradual but fundamental shift in the basic values and goals of the people of advanced industrial societies'. Moving beyond a certain threshold of economic development seems to eliminate the subjective payoff for people, with a 'gradual intergenerational shift in basic values in the societies that have passed this threshold'.[2] As they move beyond this threshold, people increasingly emphasise quality of life issues such as environmental protection and lifestyle choices.

Perhaps this finding helps explain the often sarcastic comment of many observers of recent demonstrations that the protesters are overwhelmingly the citizens of rich countries who are indulging themselves in their ample spare time by concerning themselves with the plight of the poorer nations. A number of commentators have noted the fact that significant blocks of protesters have flown into town for the protest, stayed in good hotels and payed for their experience with credit cards. While this critique misses a number of points, most fundamentally it fails to recognise that the composition of the demonstrators reflects a widespread value shift that affects substantial portions of the populations of richer nations and which has significant implications for the ongoing nature of protest. While there are continuities with the protests of the past, we are seeing a significantly different – and considerably wider, more representative of society-at-large, and better-connected (in all senses) – group of protesters than we have in the past.

An important finding from the WVS is that, while economic growth is still valued by the citizens of advanced industrial societies, an increasing proportion of the public is willing to give environmental and social concerns priority over economic growth when they conflict. The survey found that in such countries the needs for belonging, self-expression and a participant role in society are becoming more prominent and widespread. These postmodern values 'emphasise self-expression instead of deference to authority and are tolerant of other groups and ... regard exotic things and cultural diversity as stimulating and interesting, not threatening'.[3]

As a result of these value shifts there is a sharply reduced acceptance of bureaucratic organisations. A dramatic decline in trust in government across the globe both reflects and intensifies the desire for many people to turn to alternative institutions or to take community action. Thus although voter turnout is at record lows in many countries, this does not reflect political apathy. Although established political parties are losing their ability to bring out the voters, elite-challenging political actions are steadily rising.

The value shifts appear also to be enduring, especially following prolonged periods of prosperity. The indications are that such values will incline a growing number and range of people to participate in or support protests about the perceived negative impacts of globalisation. Of course, the vast majority of this protest will be non-violent, but it will provide the context within which violence could occur or be planned by some elements of protest movements.

A number of other social trends will also ensure that the protest movements are here to stay. Most important is the changing nature of notions of community and people's understandings of self. This is a complex and controversial area of social science. For our purposes, the most relevant thing is that the traditional way of knowing 'who we are' – the community or communities within which we live – has fundamentally changed in the past century. Social, economic and technological forces have led to increasingly mobile populations, a wider but often more superficial range of personal relationships, an erosion of strong bonds, a loss of traditional faiths, and competing and often inconsistent sources of information leading to increasing confusion and distrust.[4]

These changes in themselves contribute to an increase in levels of dissatisfaction with social and economic conditions and a search for the causes of people's disquiet – a search that often ends seeing the catch-all word 'globalisation' as the main culprit. Most important is the finding of a number of studies that, after a period of celebration of the individual (a period by no means over), the group is once again moving to centre stage as an important anchor for people's views of their identity. Significantly, many of these groups will not be the previous anchors of the traditional extended family, established religion and so forth. Many of the groups will revolve around interests and, particularly important for analysing the nature of protest, around identifying themselves with otherwise marginalised groups (such as those centred on ethnic or sexual identity or single-issue politics, for example).

The effect of all of this is that the coalitions of interests, the desire to belong to the evolving networks of dissent and the focus on the sorts of issues that disturb the many elements of the anti-globalisation movement are likely to be with us for some time. They will drive the nature of much international protest in the foreseeable future.

THE ANTI-GLOBALISATION DEMONSTRATIONS IN SEATTLE, NOVEMBER 1999

Let us turn now to the protest in Seattle that seems to mark a reversal in contemporary dissent. The demonstrations and associated violence that accompanied the Seattle World Trade Organisation (WTO) Ministerial Conference in November 1999 are seen by many as the beginning of a new area of protest characterised by: the target – the symbols of globalisation; style – decentralised organisation, but considerable preparation; composition – a moving coalition of groups united in their opposition to what they see as the evils of globalisation, but otherwise having little in common; use of the tools of globalisation to protest the fact of or ill-effects of globalisation; and being part of an ongoing series of similar events.

Because of the central role that Seattle has played in the views expressed by commentators about anti-globalisation protest it is worth spending a bit of time examining just how important it was as an indicator of what to expect in the future. We should start by noting that Seattle was not the first protest to exhibit the characteristics just described. There are many similarities with past protests, especially those involving the anti-Vietnam War, civil rights and peace movements. In addition, there had been a number of large anti-globalisation demonstrations in the period immediately preceding Seattle that shared many of the characteristics. In June 1999, protests known as J18 were organised in a number of European and North American cities to coincide with the G-8 Summit in Cologne. The protest in London was the most notable, in which the demonstration involving a crowd of only 2,000 – not large by London standards – got out of hand resulting in rioting, 42 injured people and one million pounds worth of damage. Financial districts were the targets of many of the J18 demonstrations, a trend that has continued since then.

Even earlier, when G-7 leaders gathered in Birmingham in 1998, they emerged from their meeting to be confronted by 60,000 people demanding debt relief in the world's poorest countries. They were inspired by a line in Leviticus calling for all debts to be forgiven every 50 years, in a Jubilee year. As the *Financial Times* put it: 'Global economic activism was not hatched on the barricades in the Pacific Northwest, but first mobilised from the pews of England's churches'.[5]

What was significant about Seattle was not the target and style of the protest but rather: the extent of the violence; the nature of the organisation of the demonstrations; and the fact that it was followed by a succession of large-scale protests at meetings of other symbols of globalisation (the World Bank, International Monetary Fund, World Economic Forum, various Ministerial groups). Many of these protests involved violence and significant property damage.[6]

De Armond argues that it is networked forms of social organisation that distinguish the new protest movement. Drawing on Arquilla and Ronfeldt's concept of 'netwar', he shows how the style of conflict typified by Seattle depends on information and communications technology, non-hierarchical organisation and some novel tactics. Nevertheless, the actual dimensions and outcomes of Seattle were as much dependent on the behaviour of the police and the protesters' underestimate of the consequences of some of their actions as they were on the successful execution of a battle plan.

Central to the events in Seattle were the actions of the Direct Action Network (DAN), a networked group of groups (such as the Rainforest Action Network, Art and Revolution and the Ruckus Society – the latter being a civil disobedience group that trains activists for tree sit-ins, banner-hangs and barricades). Through DAN, these groups coordinated non-violent protest training, communications and collective strategy and tactics through a decentralised process of consultation/consensus decision-making.[7]

The advantage of the network form of organisation is that its decentralised command and control structures (if they can properly be described as such at all) are resistant to decapitation attacks targeting leaders, as there are no identifiable leaders in the sense that past demonstrations have had them. They are also sufficiently amorphous to form an umbrella for organisations with very different agendas, memberships and preferred styles of action whilst still concentrating action on a single symbolic target – in this case globalisation.

In Seattle, DAN's overall strategic objective was to shut down the WTO meeting. It aimed to do this by mobilising a few dozen 'affinity groups' – small units that the activists organised individually. The Ruckus Society ran central training for approximately 250 protesters who were willing to risk arrest and violent confrontation with the police (although their tactics emphasised non-violent confrontation). This first wave of protesters were to seize and hold a number of strategic intersections and to immobilise the police. Thus the method was one of what de Armond describes as: 'a variety of independent but strategically congruent actions'.[8]

A second wave comprising other affinity groups and supporters, who were still militant, but less willing to risk arrest, was designed to converge on the anchor groups from the first wave, thereby reaching a critical mass at a number of blockade sites. A third wave involved a larger number of protesters from a wide range of interest groups who wanted to express their opposition to the WTO's policies, but who had no intention of being involved in any direct confrontation with authority.

In Seattle, the picture was complicated by the presence of a large number of supporters belonging to organised labour groups that essentially had little to do with DAN, but a significant number of whom were caught up in the action as it unfolded and unintentionally reinforced the third wave of protest that ultimately overwhelmed the police. Finally, there was a small group, probably 100–200 strong, of members of radical anarchist factions known collectively as the Black Blocs. These people took a much more confrontational approach to violence and came prepared to destroy property and were quite prepared to use personal violence. They came not only to smash the symbols of globalisation but, more importantly, to radicalise the protest. There was considerable friction between the Black Blocs and the DAN, with a number of scuffles involving the latter trying to prevent the Black Blocs from continuing with violent action.

On the other side of the equation, the police found themselves factionalised and ill-prepared for the strategy deployed against them. A prominent feature of the police response was the political rivalry inherent in working in an environment of overlapping federal, state, city and local jurisdiction. There were significant differences in policing philosophies that characterised the various police agencies involved. These problems contributed to a failure to agree on a concerted response and delay in deploying resources at the optimum time. Some of the planning was clearly off the mark – for example, in relation to the placing of and distance between control zones.

In addition, there were some major failures in intelligence. Sufficient information about the protesters was available either from the public nature of their deliberations, the use of undercover operatives in the various movements and the close observation and tracking of the groups once the action began. However, the picture put together on the basis of this information was woefully inaccurate, reflecting a good deal of wishful thinking, a tendency to exclude contrary information that did not confirm the views already arrived at and a lack of appreciation of the strategy of the demonstrators – especially DAN.

Finally, there were some clear instances of loss of control of their own forces by police commanders, including open resistance to the official response strategy and police attacks on uninvolved citizens, including at least one instance of assault on an elected official trying to attend an official WTO function.

The police strategy centred on the ability of a large union rally to co-opt the other protesters, contain them within the larger group and keep them out of the downtown area. This was never realistic, with the DAN and, more particularly, the Black Bloc having no intention of agreeing to the union's terms. DAN was effectively organised to use its affinity groups to seize the dozen strategic intersections and hold them until reinforcements arrived. They estimated correctly the size of participation in this first wave.

The second wave soon arrived to protect the affinity groups and to interfere with police operations by sheer numbers and passive resistance. Many more people joined this wave than DAN had estimated.

The third wave, consisting of thousands of people representing environmental and human rights groups, who had been expected by the police to attend the union rally rather than join the protest, greatly exceeded DAN's estimates. The numbers were inflated even further when a significant group of marchers from the union rally joined the street protests. As a consequence the police failed in their attempt to have the union rally contain the protest, lost the ability to effect arrests, remove prisoners efficiently and lost control of the streets. The Black Bloc systematically vandalised symbolic properties (Starbucks, banks and so on), and much more damage and looting was caused by local youths who opportunistically capitalised on the situation. Police discipline broke down in some parts of the city, with police chasing, teargassing and batonning demonstrators who were already leaving the scene. Police charges and use of tear gas also caused crowds to surge from one place to another without allowing police to gain control.

Meanwhile, the original affinity groups remained in place, handcuffed to each other and to objects, controlling the intersections and keeping the demonstration focused on the Convention Centre where the WTO was meeting. Eventually the Seattle mayor declared a civil emergency allowing the State Police and other law enforcement agencies to be deployed in reinforcement. Nevertheless, by then the WTO had already cancelled its activities. Over the next two days, mass sit-down protests and arrests continued and there were a number of ugly confrontations between police and demonstrators. Unfortunately, a good deal of this owed much to police tactics and lapses in discipline, some egregious examples of which were filmed by television crews and given nationwide exposure. In the aftermath, the Chief of Police and three of his seven Assistant Chiefs resigned.

What made the Seattle demonstrations stand out as unusual? De Armond believes that two factors are noteworthy. First, the actions of the DAN affinity groups exemplified the notion of 'swarming' that has been introduced into analysis of modern strategy and tactics by Arquilla and Ronfeldt.[9] Swarming strategies involve having a multitude of small units that are usually held dispersed suddenly converge on a target from all directions, conduct an attack, and then redisperse to prepare for another attack. A similar approach is being taken among some of the hacktivists who like to style themselves as electronic civil disobedience groups and that are often likely to operate in parallel with on-the-ground anti-globalisation protesters. These groups advocate the use of online tools to flood a target's computer systems, e-mail in-boxes and websites thereby rendering them inoperable. In a probably unwanted tribute to Arquilla and Ronfeldt one group of hacktivists wants to develop a device called SWARM to create new forms of digital activism.[10] According to de Armond:

> Throughout the protests, the Direct Action Network protesters were able to swarm their opponents; seizing key intersections … DAN communications channels blanketed the Seattle area and had global reach via the Internet. Indeed, DAN's cohesion was partly owed to an improvised communications network of cell phones, radios, police scanners, and portable computers. Protesters in the street with wireless handheld computers were able to link into continuously updated web pages giving reports from the streets. Police scanners were used to monitor police transmissions and provided some warning of changed police tactics. Cell phones were widely used. In addition to the organizers' all-points network, protest communications were leavened with individual protesters using cell phones, direct transmissions from roving independent media feeding directly into the Internet, personal computers with wireless modems broadcasting live video, and a variety of other networked communications.[11]

Taken overall, the Seattle demonstrations were indeed a watershed. But we must be careful to learn the right lessons from them. Firstly, the contribution of the violent anarchist fringe to the destruction of property and general level of violence should not be overestimated. A hardcore of violent protesters or professional agitators is often blamed for more violence than they actually cause. True they have a part to play, but overstating their influence allows us to overlook the accidents of fate, chance circumstances, unplanned violence of relatively uninvolved groups and poor police tactics that may often play a bigger role. We will not plan to deal with these issues if we turn to simplistic explanations for the instigation of violence.

Secondly, the Seattle experience shows the capacity for disruption of the idea of swarming and of the leaderless organisation. We need to study the types of network structures involved in different types of demonstrations so that we can better control the streets to reach the often seemingly incompatible goals of allowing legitimate protest, reducing the probability of violence and ensuring the right of the organisations that are the object of the protest their right to carry on their lawful business.

Thirdly, Seattle shows the importance of getting the intelligence picture right. In many of the disturbances we have seen worldwide in the last two or three years getting sufficient accurate information is not the problem. It is a failure of analysis underpinned by wishful thinking and inability to comprehend the strategy that is unfolding that is the root of the problem. Too often, what passes for analysis is little more than hysterical claims of anarchist-led plots to cause extreme violence. Related to this is the absolute necessity for competent police operational planning and control of discipline. In the United States, Europe and Australia, police faced with the same sort of anti-capitalist protest have largely learned from the police tactical failures in Seattle to better prepare to adequately contain, disrupt and control the protesters.

The Seattle protests also introduced a new era in the use of alternative media to prepare for the demonstrations, to communicate during them and to effectively get the protest message out to the world at large and the mainstream media. Since the creation of the Independent Media Centre in Seattle, each subsequent anti-globalisation or related protest has spawned its own local 'indymedia' organisation, each with its own website. These sites are linked and carry information on organising protests, details about forthcoming events and general information about the issues of concern to the constituency. There are over forty sites worldwide, largely following the locations of major protest sites – including sites in Sydney, Melbourne, Brisbane and Adelaide.

A feature of Seattle and all of the subsequent global demonstrations of note was the eclectic nature of the groups that networked to form the protest movement. Groups cover the spectrum from anti-globalisation protesters *per se* to those interested in human rights, Third World debt, the environment, labour issues, immigration, race relations and gender issues. Such varied memberships will continue to characterise these protests, but will often take on a local flavour as well. For example, recent demonstrations in Australia have usually included a significant group of people concerned with the issue of immigration detention camps. The fact that such coalitions emerge makes it more likely that many demonstrations will be larger than they would otherwise be. The symbols of globalisation – multinational corporations, financial institutions, and international gatherings of political and other leaders will continue to be the focal point around which demonstrations are organised.

Small groups that prefer violent tactics will continue to be a major problem for police. Good intelligence and police tactics designed to track and contain them will be important tools. However, we should not either overestimate their contribution to such violence as does occur, nor underestimate the ability of non-violent protesters to marginalise the extremists. This latter trend has emerged strongly in the debates that accompanied the World Social Forum in Porto Alegre in January. This meeting – a sort of alternative World Economic Forum – was significant because of the number of groups who see themselves as reformers rather than rejectionists. They are not so much anti-globalisation as wanting it to take on a softer, more human form.

Leaders of the reformers seem to have decided that there are diminishing returns in summit street protest – especially after the death of a protester in Genoa – because the protest itself, rather than the reasons for the protest are all that is getting media attention. In addition the increasing willingness of international policy makers to listen to moderate anti-globalisation voices will encourage those groups to try to limit or distance themselves from violence. The only danger here is the possibility that the remaining protesters will turn more violent, especially as they see inclusion of the moderates as selling out to the very forces that are the problem.[12]

CONCLUSION

This very brief examination of just some of the features of anti-globalisation. com shows that there is a lot more we need to know about the developing nature of protest if police are going to be able to effectively balance their many responsibilities in maintaining public order and at the same time safeguard democratic principles of dissent. There is a real prospect of losing control of the streets if police do not better understand the evolving concepts of netwar. It is a challenge that requires much more than simplistic assertions of anarchist conspiracies.

NOTES

1. Inglehart, Ronald (2000), 'Globalisation and Postmodern Values', *Washington Quarterly*, Winter, 23/1, pp 215–28.
2. *Ibid.*, p 219.
3. *Ibid.*, p 223.
4. For an excellent discussion of the trends and the evidence for them, see Gergen, Kenneth (2000), 'The Self in the Age of Information', *Washington Quarterly*, Winter, 23/1, pp 201–14.
5. Harding, James (2001), 'Counter-capitalism. Inside the Black Bloc', *Financial Times*, 15 October.
6. Much of this discussion of the events in Seattle will draw heavily on the work of Paul de Armond, director of a US research network that studies militant movements, who has made a detailed analysis of the unfolding events in Seattle, their features and causes. For those who are interested in the detail, the RAND Corporation has reprinted it Arquilla, John and Ronfeldt, David (2001), *Networks and Netwars: The Future of Terror, Crime, and Militancy*, Santa Monica: RAND. His analysis is backed up by a number of other commentaries on the events from a range of ideological viewpoints and by the extensive television and video coverage that is available for analysis.
7. De Armond, Paul (2001), 'Netwar in the Emerald City. WTO protest strategy and tactics'. Online. Available: http://nwcitizen.com/publicgood/reports/wto/. 3 March 2003.

8.   De Armond (2001), 'Netwar in the Emerald City. WTO protest strategy and tactics'.
9.   See Arquilla, John and Ronfeldt, David (2000), *Swarming and the Future of Conflict*, Santa Monica: RAND.
10. As an intriguing aside it is worth quoting from Ronfeldt and Arquilla on the ideological debates these developments can cause. They report that a device called Tribal FloodNet can enable a lone, anonymous individual to mount a massive denial of service attack on a website, thus obviating the need to organise for many individuals to mount simultaneous attacks separately. However, 'the contrast between the two systems has led to an ideological controversy. Hacktivist proponents of FloodNet [the system requiring cooperation of individuals] ... prefer to assert "the presence of a global group of people gathering to bear witness to a wrong." They criticise the Tribal version for being undemocratic and secretive.' See Ronfeldt, David and Arquilla, John (2001), 'What Next for Networks and Netwars?', in Arquilla and Ronfeldt, *Networks and Netwars*, p 338.
11. De Armond (2001), 'Netwar in the Emerald City: WTO protest strategy and tactics', p 210.
12. Another of the paradoxes of the globalisation debate can be seen in a trivial example of co-option noted by author Naomi Klein in the Sony Play Station game 'State of Emergency', which features cool-haired anarchists throwing rocks at evil riot cops guarding a fictitious 'American Trade Organisation'.

4. The al-Qaeda Threat and the International Response

Rohan Gunaratna

When will fear, killing, destruction, expulsion, orphaning and widowing remain only limited to us while security, stability and happiness remains only limited to you? This is an unfair allotment. The time has come to share in these matters equally.

Just like you kill, you will be killed. And just like you bombarded, you will be bombarded. Be prepared to receive the glad tidings of what will be bad for you.

By the grace of Allah, the Islamic umma [community] has started to fire at you with its sincere youth, who have promised Allah to continue jihad with words and swords, in order to defend the truth and to extinguish the falsehood till the last drop of blood.

Osama bin Laden, 12 November 2002[1]

Al-Qaeda al-Sulbah (The Solid Base) is the first multinational terrorist group of the twenty-first century. While past and present terrorist groups generally have a national base, limiting their terrorist campaigns to a single theatre, al-Qaeda is an umbrella organisation waging multiple campaigns both against the West and Muslim regimes friendly to the West. In addition to its core force of 3,000 members, al-Qaeda has established linkages with twenty-four Islamist groups. Driven by the ideal of a universal jihad, al-Qaeda has been able to politicise, radicalise and mobilise Muslims both in the territorial communities of the Middle East and Asia as well as in the migrant communities of Europe, North America, and Australasia. As a group with a global reach, al-Qaeda presents a new kind of threat, hitherto unimagined by counter-terrorism practitioners and security and intelligence professionals alike.

Between pre-modern Afghanistan and post-modern continental United States via Europe and Asia, al-Qaeda has built a state-of-the-art terrorist network for moving funds, goods, and personnel to attack its targets.[2] It is the painstaking and steadfast construction of this network over many years that enabled al-Qaeda to mount the attacks of September 11. Al-Qaeda targeting reflects its sophistication as a professional terrorist group. After the East Africa bombing – a land suicide attack on a US diplomatic target – the US security community strengthened the security of all US missions overseas. However, instead of another land suicide operation, al-Qaeda mounted a sea-borne suicide operation. After al-Qaeda attacked USS Cole in October 2000, the US security community invested in preventing another land or maritime attack by strengthening perimeter security. However, al-Qaeda evaded security measures and struck America's most outstanding landmarks from the sky. Thereafter, al-Qaeda planned to strike the US once more with a radiological dispersal device using Jose Perdilla, an American Muslim, in an operation that was disrupted at the reconnaissance stage. In keeping with al-Qaeda's evolving doctrine, it is likely to attempt to destroy the third target, the US Congress, in the future.[3] As terrorist groups copy cost-effective tactics, al-Qaeda is likely to again utilise civilian infrastructure to attack Western targets.

In keeping with its founding charter authored by its then leader Sheikh Dr Abdullah Azzam in March 1988, al-Qaeda is the 'spearhead of Islam' or the 'pioneering vanguard of the Islamic movements'.[4] Because of the inspirational value, al-Qaeda's preference is to attack strategic targets usually resorting to suicide attacks (martyrdom operations). Attacking high prestige and symbolic strategic targets is difficult requiring extensive planning and preparation over a long period of time across several countries. Al-Qaeda expects the Muslims it instigates and the Islamic movements it inspires to strike at least tactical targets. To strengthen Islamic movements worldwide, al-Qaeda together with its erstwhile host – the Islamic Movement of Taliban, the de facto government of the Islamic Emirate of Afghanistan – and its previous incarnation – the Maktab al Khidamat lil Mujahidin al Arab – trained several tens of thousands of Western, Middle Eastern, African, Caucasian, Balkan, and Asian Muslims.

DECENTRALISATION

Al-Qaeda training infrastructure has gravely suffered as a result of US intervention in Afghanistan since October 2001. However, al-Qaeda began decentralising the organisation, opening new facilities for training its recruits in many of the regional theatres from Mindanao in the Philippines to Pankishi Valley in Georgia, much before September 11. In forming the 'World Islamic Front for Jihad Against the Jews and the Crusaders' in 1998, al-Qaeda networked with – and in some cases co-opted – the Moro Islamic Liberation Front (MILF) in Southeast Asia, the Islamic Movement of Uzbekistan in Central Asia and the Salafist Group for Call and Combat (GSPC) in North Africa. Despite the loss of Afghanistan, a massive blow to al-Qaeda's capabilities, both the support it enjoys in the tribal areas as well as the pre-

September 11 decentralisation is likely to ensure its survival. With focused targeting on the Afghan-Pakistan border where both al-Qaeda and Taliban (Mullah Omar Faction) are concentrated, the group will depend on its regional networks to continue the fight. Al-Qaeda's Southeast Asian network is an integral part of the terrorist organisation. The disrupted Singapore operation clearly demonstrates the group's intentions and the capabilities as well as the opportunities for attack in target-rich Southeast Asia. Therefore, the threshold for terrorism – both support for conducting attacks and attacks themselves – has clearly increased in Southeast Asia.

Al-Qaeda has adapted to dismantlement of its training infrastructure in Afghanistan. Although the organisation has neither physically nor ideologically abandoned Afghanistan, it is seeking to compensate for the loss of a state-of-the-art training infrastructure and operational base by continuing to work together with local groups. As much as such groups have depended on al-Qaeda in the past, the parent organisation has depended on local groups. Immediately after al-Qaeda bombed the US embassies in East Africa in August 1998 and Pakistan began to arrest key al-Qaeda operatives who used its soil for transit into landlocked Afghanistan, Osama bin Laden looked to the Philippines. Peshawar based al-Qaeda head of foreign operations Zein al-Abideen phoned the MILF leadership and requested them to open new training facilities for foreign recruits in February 1999. Until the Camp Abu Bakar complex was overrun, al-Qaeda recruits from Malaysia, Singapore and Indonesia trained in its satellite camps: Hodeibia, Palestine and Vietnam. Thereafter, the training facility moved to Poso in Sulawesi, and after its closure to Balikpapan in Kalimanthan, where al-Qaeda continued to train its Southeast Asian and other recruits until September 11.

Al-Qaeda's post-September 11 pronouncements – including Abu Gaith Sulayman's recorded message – reflect both its intention and will to attack western (especially US) targets. Although al-Qaeda has lost key leaders such as its military commander Mohommad Atef, its core and penultimate leadership that provides the strategic and tactical direction is still intact.[5] As long as the leadership of a group survives, the group itself will survive. Furthermore, the Islamist milieu both in the Muslim territorial and migrant communities continues to provide the bulk of the recruits, finance and other forms of support. As the focus of the coalition is largely military, the robust Islamist ideology of al-Qaeda that has gone unchallenged ensures the survival of the group. Al-Qaeda is replenishing its human losses (killed, captured, and arrested) and material wastage (weapons and other supplies) both inside and outside Afghanistan. As a result, al-Qaeda's global network – with members drawn from 46 countries and activities in 98 countries – is still functional, including its operatives in Europe.[6] Although al-Qaeda operational cells have been disrupted in France, the Netherlands, Belgium, Germany, Italy, Spain, and the UK, support cells disseminating propaganda, raising funds, recruiting, procuring supplies, and mounting surveillance on intended targets are still active. Its collaborators, supporters and sympathisers have filled the leadership vacuum created by the first wave of arrest of al-Qaeda leaders in Europe immediately after September 11. The post-September 11 al-Qaeda cells are more clandestine, compact and self-contained, thus hard to detect and disrupt. As such, western societies and their governments will face a long-term continuous threat from al-Qaeda.

THE EVOLVING THREAT

Post-September 11 al-Qaeda attempted, and failed, with a number of attacks. The targets included: US, UK, Australian, and Israeli diplomatic missions; a US warship off Singapore; US and British warships in the Straits of Gibraltar; the water supply to the US embassy in Rome. In addition to Richard Reid – the unsuccessful shoe bomber – al-Qaeda also attempted to bomb the US embassy and American cultural centre in Paris and attack the US base in Sarajevo. A Sudanese al-Qaeda member fired a surface to air missile at a US warplane taking off from the Prince Sultan airbase in Saudi Arabia in December 2001. Al-Qaeda suicide bombers also attacked both a French oil tanker off Yemen and US troops in Kuwait during October 2002. To instigate Islamists to strike worldwide Jewish targets, Nizar Seif Eddin al-Tunisi (Sword of the Faith) alias Nizar Nouar, ordered a suicide bomber in a Liquid Petroleum Gas vehicle to ram Ghriba Synagogue – Africa's oldest Jewish Synagogue – killing fourteen German tourists and five Tunisians in Djerba, Tunisia on 11 April 2002.[7]

Due to the difficulty of operating in the post-September 11 environment, al-Qaeda has delegated many of its responsibilities to other Islamist movements that operate under its umbrella. In a number of theatres, al-Qaeda is operating through a variety of groups that formally had shared training, financial, and operational infrastructure in Afghanistan. This phenomenon is most visible in Pakistan where twenty-four attacks by al-Qaeda and its associated groups have occurred. Beginning with the massacre of Christians in Bhawalpur in the Punjab district in October 2001, al-Qaeda launched a number of terrorist operations including the kidnapping and murder of the *Wall Street Journal* journalist Daniel Pearl and a church bombing in Islamabad, killing a US diplomat's wife and daughter. A suicide bomber of Harakat-ul Mujahidin-al-Aalami – an al-Qaeda associate group – killed eleven Frenchmen and twelve Pakistanis on 18 May 2002. The well-planned attack was conducted after mounting surveillance on the Sheraton Hotel and the bus route used by French naval engineers and technicians working on a submarine project in Karachi. The suicide vehicle bomb attack by an al-Qaeda associate group against the US Consulate in Karachi on 14 June 2002 injured a US marine and killed eleven Pakistanis. Using a similar tactic, they also targeted President Musharraf on 26 April 2002, but the remote control failed to detonate the explosives-laden vehicle.

While the Taliban operated as a guerrilla force, al-Qaeda remains a terrorist group. The Taliban operated somewhat openly and al-Qaeda functions clandestinely. The Taliban/al-Qaeda combined strategy is to install a regime that is either friendly to the Islamists in Pakistan, or to install a regime neutral to Islamists. They believe that the future survival of al-Qaeda and the Taliban along the Afghanistan-Pakistan border will depend on their ability to generate sustained support from Pakistan. As such, they are likely to target Musharraf repeatedly until he is killed or removed from office. Al-Qaeda also mounted at least two clandestine operations to assassinate Afghan President Hamid Karzai or his cabinet. After a traffic accident both an Afghan and a foreigner in an explosive-laden Toyota were arrested in the centre of Kabul on 29 July 2002. In September 2002, al-Qaeda mounted a second assassination operation that was disrupted by Karzai's US bodyguards. Immediately after, an unknown group positioned a claymore mine on a route usually taken by the Presidential motorcade.

THE PRIMARY TARGET: THE USA

The United States, the 'head of the poisonous snake', remains the principal target of al-Qaeda. This inclination was reflected when Osama said, 'the battle has moved to inside America. We will continue this battle, God permitting, until victory or until we meet God'.[8] Until the US intelligence agencies infiltrate terrorist groups, a task that cannot be accomplished in the short term, it is reasonable to assume that the US is as vulnerable as it was before September 11. The governments that have assisted the US in its campaign in Afghanistan as well as those governments that have disrupted al-Qaeda cells on their soil have also earned the wrath of al-Qaeda. For example, following the Singaporean disruption of cells of Jemaah Islamiyah (JI), al-Qaeda's Southeast Asian arm), the leadership relocated in Indonesia have vowed to crash a plane on Changi airport. Similarly, in retaliation for Pakistan's support for the US, several Islamist groups have attacked soft targets nationwide. For instance, Islamist terrorists killed four Pakistanis at a Christian school for children of foreign aid workers in Murree Hills on 5 August and three others in the church of a Christian hospital in Taxila on 9 August 2002. Several other revenge-motivated attacks have occurred. An explosion killed the Mayor and 12 others in Mindanao, Philippines on Christmas Eve 2002.

The current threat scenario shows that al-Qaeda is constrained from launching another attack on the scale of September 11. However, al-Qaeda is still able to conduct small, medium and large-scale attacks. With unprecedented security, intelligence, and law enforcement cooperation as well as with heightened public awareness, al-Qaeda have found themselves unable to engage in extensive and long-term planning and preparation across more than one country, a pre-requisite for conducting coordinated simultaneous attacks. Nonetheless, once al-Qaeda patiently identifies the gaping holes in the post-September 11 security architecture, its super cells may be able to plan, prepare, and execute mass casualty attacks. For the time being, due to the limitations of mounting large-scale operations, al-Qaeda is considering an assortment of options. They range from attacks on population centres, economic infrastructure, and symbolic or high prestige targets inside the US. While some of al-Qaeda's super cells are 'hibernating', others are preparing to attack opportunistic targets. Of the 36 large, medium and small-scale attacks conducted by al-Qaeda and its associate groups against US and Coalition targets worldwide only a fraction have been successful. They have failed due to tighter international security countermeasures and hurried planning. Nonetheless, al-Qaeda ideology ensures that the group is determined to strike back. As a result of a range of countermeasures, the danger is shifting, stretching the threat spectrum to include a wider range of targets as well as a change in *modus operandi*. Al-Qaeda is operating through other Islamist groups providing them with trainers and funds, consequently influencing their strategic and tactical direction. Al-Qaeda is likely to operate through associated group for as long as the threat to the organisation remains.

THE IMPORTANCE OF AFGHANISTAN-PAKISTAN

Developments in Afghanistan and Pakistan are central to the future survival of the Taliban and al-Qaeda. These two groups are adapting to the security environment and can be seen to have undergone three critical internal strategic changes. Firstly, Mullah Omar, the leader of the Taliban and the former head of the Islamic Emirate of Afghanistan, has assumed the principal responsibility to fight the US-led coalition forces in Afghanistan. In the fight, Osama bin Laden himself has pledged loyalty and allegiance to this leadership. With Osama in hiding, as 'leader of the Faithful', Mullah Omar spearheaded the regrouping and re-organising of the Taliban since September 11. After re-establishing communication with the scattered units of the Taliban, he regrouped them along secure areas of the 2,446 kilometres long

Afghanistan-Pakistan border. As they did during the Soviet period, their dream is to consolidate the strength of the Taliban and deepen their strategic influence in Afghanistan and Pakistan by preparing for a campaign of protracted guerrilla warfare. To rebuild support, the Taliban indoctrinates the Afghan people both directly by disseminating propaganda and through supporters and sympathisers scattered throughout Afghanistan.

Secondly, over the past year the Taliban and al-Qaeda have replaced losses in the rank and file by promoting middle level and junior leaders as well as by fresh recruitment. To compensate for the total loss of state support from Pakistan to the Taliban, Mullah Omar has established Lashkar-e-Omar – a covert network of support organisations in Pakistan – to sustain a low intensity campaign in Afghanistan. By instigating its associate groups in Kashmir such as Harakat-ul Mujahidin and Jayash-e-Mohommad to intensify the violence in Kashmir, the Taliban forced Pakistan to re-deploy its troops on the Afghan border along the 2,414 kilometres long India-Pakistan border. With the increase in the porosity of the Pakistan-Afghanistan border, the Taliban and al-Qaeda have re-established their lines of communication, supplies, and recruits into Pakistan. The Taliban, al-Qaeda, and associate groups all harness the Islamist milieu in Pakistan and overseas to ensure a revival in support (encouragement, funds, and supplies) necessary for survival and sustenance. Neglected conflicts where Muslims suffer – Palestine, Kashmir, Chechnya, Maluku, Mindanao, and Algeria among others – ensure continuity of support. Currently, there are no signs of mass desertion from the Taliban or al-Qaeda ranks, indicating the state of the morale.

Third, al-Qaeda's deputy leader Dr Ayman al-Zawahiri now plays a more substantial role in support and operational activities both inside and outside Afghanistan. To topple Karzai in Afghanistan and Musharraf in Pakistan, al-Qaeda has established networks of collaborators, supporters, and sympathisers in both countries. To coordinate and conduct operations and revive support, al-Qaeda is establishing linkages with its affiliate NGOs and other charities overseas. With the failure of al-Qaeda to strike tactical US, Allied, and coalition targets worldwide after September 11, the group is considering reverting to both tactical and strategic targets. The group is also considering revisiting maritime, as well as chemical, biological, radiological and nuclear (CBRN) scenarios, options al-Qaeda considered in the mid-1990s. For instance, Osama paid US$1.5 million to a Sudanese military officer to purchase a uranium canister from South Africa. Al-Qaeda was duped when the group was sold an externally radiated canister. Although suicide terrorism coupled with conventional attacks have proved to be most effective, al-Qaeda and its associated groups are likely to go down the road of chemical, biological, and radiological terrorism in the future.

Al-Qaeda has inspired and instigated a wider constituency of groups and individuals to take on the fight for Allah. As seen in a number of sporadic attacks in Europe, North Africa, Indonesia, Pakistan, and Kashmir, Islamist groups are considering a range of options – arson, shooting, grenade attacks, and improvised explosive devices against Jewish, Christian, and Hindu targets. The Islamists continue to inspire and instigate violence against 'the enemies of Islam', 'the infidels' and the 'unbelievers' both by word of mouth and on over 1,000 sites on the worldwide web. The Islamists thus operate across a wide spectrum, from low tech to high tech, stretching government resources and weakening security countermeasures. This demonstrates the success of al-Qaeda in educating a much wider constituency to challenge the West and Muslim regimes friendly to the West.

THE SOUTHEAST ASIAN NETWORK

The security and intelligence services, accustomed to collecting intelligence by technical methods, have limited high quality information about the Southeast Asian group.[9] Most public officials and academics find it difficult to understand al-Qaeda because the group functions both operationally and ideologically. In addition to dispatching its operatives to target countries (such as the September 11 team led by Mohammed Atta), it provides the experts, training, and resources to other Islamist political and military organisations to advance a common goal. Al-Qaeda repeated its strategy of penetrating Islamist networks worldwide in its contact with JI in Southeast Asia. JI is a regional organisation with overground and underground networks extending from Southern Thailand to Australia. Among the groups it has infiltrated and influenced in this region are: Kumpulan Mujahidin in Malaysia; Jashkar Jundullah in Indonesia; and the Moro Islamic Liberation Front (MILF) in the Philippines. When JI wanted to destroy US, British, Australian and Israeli diplomatic targets in Singapore, al-Qaeda dispatched four Afghan-trained Arab suicide bombers to Southeast Asia. In an interview, an al-Qaeda detainee told this author: 'We did not want to risk using Asian Muslims for a landmark operation'.[10]

Through physical and intellectual contact, al-Qaeda members and literature have physically and ideologically strengthened a dozen Islamist terrorist groups, political parties, charities, and individuals. In the region, it has shaped a mission and a vision for Islamists to construct a caliphate comprising Malaysia, Singapore, Brunei, Indonesia, Cambodia and Mindanao. To establish this Darulah Islamiah Raya, about 400 Islamists have been trained in facilities in: Afghanistan (Derunta and Khalden); Pakistan (Karachi, Lahore and Peshawar); Malaysia (Negri Sembilan and other locations); Mindanao in the Philippines (Camp Vietnam, Hodeibia and the Abu Bakr Complex); and in Indonesia (Poso, Sulawesi and Balikpapan, Kalimantan) throughout the 1990s. The regional leader, Indonesian national Riduan Isamuddin, alias Hambali, fought in the anti-Soviet multinational Afghan campaign and assembled the al-Qaeda network in the region from 1991. In addition to its plan to assassinate Pope John Paul II and President Clinton in Manila and explode 11 airliners over the Asia-Pacific in early 1995, al-Qaeda exploded a bomb injuring 11 and killing one Japanese passenger and nearly destroying a Tokyo-bound Philippine Airlines flight in December 1994. In addition to bombing the residence of the Philippine Ambassador in Indonesia, JI simultaneously bombed 30 churches killing 22 and wounding 96 in Jakarta, West Java, North Sumatra, Riau, Bandung, East Java and Nusatenggara on Christmas Eve 2000 and struck five targets in Manila on 30 December, 2000.[11] It has also played a pivotal role in the violence in Maluku that has killed over 5,000 people during the past five years. Further, al-Qaeda's Malaysian cell also hosted the USS Cole attack's planners and provided the critical cover and finances for Zacarias Moussaiou, an arrested September 11 suicide hijacker. Moussaiou even visited the Malacca Flying Academy in Malaysia to learn to fly. Finally, Moussaiou substituted for Ramzi bin al-Shibh of the Hamburg cell who tried but failed to get a visa to enter the US on three occasions. Hambali, who holds both al-Qaeda and JI membership and featured in all these activities, is alive and active. Recent recoveries from Afghanistan examined by the author include documents with extensive references to al-Qaeda's spiritual leader in Southeast Asia, Abu Bakar Bashir, Hambali and other directing figures of the network in the region.

As a result of a Spanish investigation into al-Qaeda, the Indonesian government has reluctantly admitted that al-Qaeda operated a training camp in Poso. The training camp led by Omar Bandon consisted of eight to ten small villages located side by side on the beach, equipped with light weapons, explosives and a firing range. Participants in the training are not only from the local people but also from overseas. The instructor of the physical training in the camp is Parlindugan Siregar, a member of the al-Qaeda network in Spain, reported Indonesian intelligence.[12] Both Nic Robertson of CNN in Afghanistan and the Special Branch investigating the al-Qaeda cell in Leicester recovered copies of videotapes of the Poso camp. With the exception of the ten church bombers, the government has failed to arrest and prosecute both the Poso trainees and the trainers, who remain free and active.

THREAT TRAJECTORY

Of all its associate groups, JI has been by far the most active. JI's overt support and covert operational infrastructure is enmeshed with the Muslim socio-economic and political fabric of Southeast Asia. As a closely-knit politico-religious organisation, it recruits from families, extended families, neighbourhoods, schools and universities. Even before September 11, JI mounted surveillance on US and Israeli diplomatic targets in the Philippines, US warships in the Straits of Malacca, and multiple targets in Singapore. After the JI operation to destroy diplomatic targets in Singapore was disrupted in December 2001, governments in the region targeted the JI infrastructure in Malaysia and the Philippines. The only governments that failed to take action were Australia, Thailand and Indonesia. Until the bombing in Bali on October 12, Indonesia denied that terrorists were operating on their soil. Instead of targeting Indonesia, governments within and outside of the region failed to work steadfastly with President Megawati and her ministers, officials and the public to prevent Islamism moving from the periphery to the centre. This threatens not only Indonesia, but also her neighbours and the wider Asia-Pacific region.

JI has used Australia to disseminate propaganda and raise funds, Thailand to plan, and Indonesia to prepare the strike on Bali. The choice of target was motivated by a number of factors. Due to the arrest of operatives, seizure of assets, and countermeasures enacted by Singapore, Malaysia and the Philippines, JI was constrained in mounting an operation in those countries. In Australia, JI cells were almost all support rather than combat cells. In Thailand, JI had important functionaries. JI infrastructure was fully operational in Indonesia. As both the structure and perimeter of US and other diplomatic targets were hardened in Jakarta, JI was driven to set its sight on a soft target in Indonesia. Kuta, on the island of Bali, was ideal because it was a predominately Hindu town that attracts around 22,000 Australian tourists annually. In mid-January 2002, JI operational commander Hambali met with Mohommad Mansour Jabarah, a 21-year-old Canadian al-Qaeda operative in Southern Thailand. Hambali, who trained and fought in Afghanistan, held dual membership both of the JI and al-Qaeda shura (consultative) councils. Hambali planned with Jabarah (who was dispatched to the region by Khalid Sheikh Mohommad, head of al-Qaeda's military committee) to bomb bars, nightclubs and restaurants frequented by westerners. The decision to strike Bali was made by Hambali in Bangkok, a city used by two September 11 hijackers, to enter the US in January 2000.

Based on the US debriefing of Jabarah (arrested in Oman and handed over to the Americans), the FBI issued a memo on 22 August 2002 to the regional intelligence community of JI's intentions. However, neither Australian nor

Southeast Asian intelligence agencies succeeded in developing the tactical intelligence to detect and disrupt JI's plans. After the September 11 attacks, al-Qaeda (and in particular JI) had identified Australia as an enemy but the Australian government declined to take the threat seriously. Despite the Australian Embassy in Singapore being identified as an al-Qaeda target, Osama bin Laden's statement that Australia has waged a 'crusade' against the Islamic nation and dismembered East Timor, credible intelligence that a number of Afghanistan-trained Australians were dispatched on missions to strike targets inside Australia, and Australia's high profile participation in the campaign in Afghanistan. A week before Bali, the Australian government announced that there was no significant threat of terrorism to Australia or to its interests overseas. The lessons of Bali are clear: countries that tolerate terrorists or are reluctant to act against them suffer. Even after the JI cells were detected and neutralised in Singapore, Malaysia and in the Philippines, President Megawati placed her personal and political career before national and regional security, and therefore was hesitant to target the al-Qaeda network in Indonesia. Even after Bali, Indonesia investigates only those JI members directly connected to the Bali bomb blast. Indonesia hesitated to target JI as an organisation or its political wing – the Mujahidin Council of Indonesia led by Abu Bakar Bashir, and its militia wing – Lashkar Jundullah, led by Agus Dwikarna. Lashkar Jundullah was responsible for bombing a McDonald's restaurant in Sulawesi, Indonesia on 6 December 2002. The bombing killed three Indonesians, including the bomber, and injured several.[13] As a result, JI and Lashkar Jundullah will be able to strike again both inside Indonesia and using Indonesia as a launching pad to attack neighbouring countries.

PROGNOSIS

Despite being the most hunted movement in history, al-Qaeda and its associated organisations constitute a significant threat in the short term (one to two years). Al-Qaeda itself will fragment, decentralise and regroup in five zones of the world. It will work with like-minded groups, select a wider range of targets, focus on economic targets and population centres, and conduct most attacks in the global south. Although the group will be constrained from conducting coordinated simultaneous attacks against high profile symbolic or strategic targets in the West, together with its regional counterparts al-Qaeda will conduct similar attacks in Asia, Africa, Middle East, and even in Latin America. Despite heavy losses, including the likely capture or death of its core and penultimate leaders, al-Qaeda's anti-western, universal jihad ideology inculcated among politicised and radicalised Muslims will sustain support for Islamism, Islamist political parties and Islamist terrorist groups. With the detection, disruption, and degradation of its human and material infrastructure, al-Qaeda may evolve and survive as a state-of-mind among Islamist territorial and migrant pockets. With a skewed US Middle Eastern policy, Islamist support for political violence will grow, prompting terrorist groups to conduct mass casualty attacks, especially suicide bombings of economic targets and population centres.

To compensate for the loss of its state-of-the-art operational and training infrastructure, al-Qaeda will alter its shape. Although its intention to attack has not diminished, its capabilities have gravely suffered. With the US working with several Middle Eastern and Asian governments, al-Qaeda's strength has depleted to a third of its rank and file, and the organisation has suffered the loss or capture of its key leaders and experienced operatives. Therefore, the group is increasingly probing targets that can be attacked with least effort and least cost. In keeping with its doctrine of repeating its successes, al-Qaeda and its associate groups are increasingly adopting the tactic of suicide terrorism against soft targets.

While al-Qaeda's priority will be to attack US targets, it only has the resources and opportunity to attack US allies and friends. With diminished al-Qaeda assets and hardened US and Israeli diplomatic targets, the group will attempt to mount attacks against British, French, German, Italian, Canadian, Australian and possibly other European and Japanese targets. Throughout 2002, al-Qaeda or its associate groups killed German tourists in Djerba, Tunisia; French naval technicians in Karachi, Pakistan; Australians and other Westerners in Bali, Indonesia; and Israelis in Mombasa, Kenya. Osama bin Laden's pronouncements in October and November 2002 will be the best guide to unfolding al-Qaeda events in 2003. As such more effort is needed to track and target al-Qaeda experts moving worldwide and disrupt them from coordinating attacks together with associate groups with which it shared ideology, finance and training during the last decade in Afghanistan and in other conflict zones.

Countermeasures, especially target hardening, by law enforcement and protective services of vulnerable government personnel and infrastructure have forced al-Qaeda to focus on economic targets and population centres. Hardening of government targets will displace the threat to softer targets making civilians more prone to terrorist attack. Economic targets especially the tourist and the hotel industry will suffer from terrorism. Churches, synagogues, and other non-Islamic institutions as well as trade and investment will remain particularly vulnerable. Similarly, hardening of land and aviation targets will shift the threat to sea targets particularly to commercial maritime targets. Due to the difficulty of hijacking aircraft, al-Qaeda will seek to acquire and employ hand-held Surface to Air Missiles (SAMs). If appropriate and immediate countermeasures are not taken to target the al-Qaeda shipping network, SAMs under al-Qaeda control held in the Pakistan-Kashmir-Afghanistan theatre, the Arabian Peninsula, and the Horn of Africa will find their way to the Far Asia and to Europe, and possibly even to North America. Moreover, associated groups operationally and ideologically unconnected to al-Qaeda will learn from al-Qaeda technologies, tactics, and techniques.

With US security forces and the intelligence community targeting al-Qaeda's nerve centre in Afghanistan and Pakistan, the organisation will decentralise even further. While its organisers of attacks will remain in Pakistan and its immediate region, its operatives will travel back and forth coordinating with al-Qaeda nodes in the south. To make its presence felt, al-Qaeda will increasingly rely on its global terrorist network of like-minded groups in Southeast Asia, South Asia, Horn of Africa, Middle East, and the Caucuses to strike its enemies. Already attacks in Kenya, Indonesia, India, Pakistan, Kuwait and Yemen seek to compensate for the loss and lack of space and opportunity to operate in Afghanistan. Its operatives will work together with JI and other groups in Southeast Asia, Al Ithihad al Islami in Africa, Chechen Mujahidin in the Caucuses and the trans-caucuses, the Tunisian Combatants Group and other groups in the Middle East, Jayash-e-Mohommad and other groups in South Asia. Al-Qaeda will rely on groups it trained and financed in the past decade to continue its fight. In addition to its own members, al-Qaeda will operate through the GSPC and Takfir Wal Hijra – two groups it has infiltrated in Europe and North America. With the transfer of terrorist technology and expertise from the centre to the periphery, the attacks by such associated groups will pose a threat as great as al-Qaeda itself.

Although attacking inside North America, Europe, Australasia and Israel remains a priority, the measures and countermeasures taken by these governments will make it difficult for al-Qaeda to mount an operation in the West. Al-Qaeda finds it less costly to operate in parts of Asia, Africa, and the Middle East where there is a lack of security controls. Therefore, most attacks will be against western targets located in the global south. While focusing on western targets will remain a priority, al-Qaeda will continue to conduct operations against Muslim rulers and regimes supporting the US-led 'war on terror'. Pakistani and Afghan leaders Musharaaf and Karzai will remain vulnerable to assassination and their regimes will come under sustained political challenge. Similarly, a number of Pakistani groups fighting in Kashmir will come under the control of al-Qaeda. The groups working together with the surviving elements of the Taliban will develop a clandestine network inside Afghanistan to conduct guerrilla warfare, terrorism, and political assassination.

Al-Qaeda has suffered with the arrest of nearly 3,000 organisers, operatives and supporters worldwide from October 2001. With the increase in pressure, the surviving operatives of al-Qaeda increasingly depend on its associate groups to conduct attacks. Traditionally, al-Qaeda with better trained, more experienced and highly committed operatives wanted to attack more difficult targets especially strategic targets and leave the easier and tactical targets to associate groups. Today, with al-Qaeda operatives working closely together, the lethality of the attacks conducted by the associate groups has increased. With attacks conducted by al-Qaeda's associated groups posing a threat as great as al-Qaeda, the theatre of war will widen. US assistance, presence and influence will grow in the Muslim world generating wide-ranging reactions.

With the loss of Afghanistan as a 'liberated theatre of jihad', Islamists will seek to create new theatres. Dr Ayman al-Zawahiri considers Afghanistan and Chechnya as the only two liberated theatres of jihad.[14] Already due to the difficulty of movement of recruits and flow of support from Islamist migrant pockets in the West and in the Middle East to Afghanistan, there has been a partial diversion of support to Chechnya. Although there is a significant reserve of Afghan trained active and sleeper terrorists in the West, terrorists entering the West to attack targets may be trained in a number of theatres, especially Chechnya. With al-Qaeda fragmenting, several other groups will take over the role of waging a universal jihad. More territorial Islamist groups will espouse universal agendas and more Muslim separatist groups will become vulnerable to penetration by Islamist groups.

Al-Qaeda will be operating across the technological spectrum but is likely to use low-tech, high impact attacks, especially utilising civilian infrastructure to attack civilian society and critical infrastructure. With greater border control, members and associate members of al-Qaeda will use what can be readily purchased off-the-shelf from pharmacies, chemistry shops, and hardware stores. Al-Qaeda members will live off the environment and turn commercially available material into weapons. An al-Qaeda Tunisian member conducted a suicide attack against a synagogue in Tunisia using an LPG truck; JI used a consignment of chlorate purchased from the port city of Surabaya in Indonesia against targets in Bali; and the September 11 hijackers used passenger aircraft against the World Trade Center and Pentagon. Using multiple identities, al-Qaeda members will travel to target countries, receive instructions, plan and prepare attacks through the Internet, and attack targets. They will generate support from low-level crime, organised crime, infiltrated charities, and from politicised and radicalised segments of their migrant and diaspora communities.

The thinking of Khalid Sheikh Mohommad will be reflected in new attacks. This will involve: mass casualty attacks; the abundant use of suicide terrorism; bombings; and assassination. As mass casualty attacks need a large number of operatives, greater resources and planning over a long period of time, al-Qaeda will be able to conduct fewer attacks but they are likely to become spectacular ones. Assassination will be used more frequently, although suicide bombings will be the predominant form of attack. As suicide attacks are very difficult to disrupt in the execution phase, 2003 will see the tactic of suicide terrorism being used more widely. As al-Qaeda maximises its successes and partial successes and minimises its failures, suicide attacks will become increasingly common. Although al-Qaeda's long-term and sustained interest in using chemical, biological, radiological and nuclear agents has not diminished, conventional terrorism will remain the preferred mode of attack.

STATE RESPONSE

The fight against al-Qaeda and its associate groups seriously began only after September 11. Although the JI network in Southeast Asia was detected in December 2001, only some countries acknowledged JI as a threat until the Bali bombing. Both Indonesia until Bali and Thailand after Bali denied the very existence of a regional terrorist network. Although al-Qaeda in Southeast Asia has a head start of ten years, government actions against both al-Qaeda and its associate groups have significantly damaged their capabilities. Largely due to the tireless efforts of the intelligence community, especially the Singaporean security service, the region is aware of the existence of a resilient terrorist network. Only about a fourth of the operatives have suffered arrest or death. Although parts of the network have received extensive damage, such as its Singaporean, Malaysian and Filipino components, the organisation's leadership, support (propaganda, recruitment, fundraising, procurement, transportation, safe houses), and operational (surveillance, attack) organs are fully functional. Only a regional approach involving all the countries of Southeast Asia acknowledging a pervasive group and its potentiality for harm can achieve comprehensive and sustained action. Since September 11, regional security and intelligence agencies are developing a reasonably good understanding of the terrorist network – its functionaries, its assets, its linkages, and *modus operandi*. Initially, some leaders did not wish to take an aggressive stand against al-Qaeda and JI, stating that the terrorists only targeted the US. However, political leaders in Malaysia and Indonesia have realised that the policy of appeasement with Islamists simply does not work.

As JI is a pan-Southeast Asian organisation operating across territorial borders, only the creation of a regional task force can cripple it. Whenever JI has been targeted in one country its operatives and assets have moved to a neighbouring country. For instance, when 240 JI members in Malaysia were targeted, the bulk of its operatives moved to Indonesia and Thailand. The nature of the JI organisation is such that no one single country can successfully fight and dismantle JI. The targeting of JI must therefore be intelligence driven, primarily based on human source intelligence, detainee debriefs and intercepted communication. While intelligence agencies provide the critical intelligence, law enforcement authorities must locate JI members, especially the leaders that provide strategic and tactical direction and the handful of experts who coordinate financial, logistical and other operations. The key to fighting JI is common counter-terrorism intelligence databases, exchange of personnel, transfer of expertise, joint operations, and most importantly, sharing of experience. While relentlessly targeting the core and penultimate leaders of JI, governments must develop robust political and economic responses to isolate their existing and potential supporters.

Prophylactic measures must prevent the JI support base from growing. When hunted, JI's resilience is dependent on its ability to replenish its human losses and material wastage. The milieu in which JI operates provides significant recruits and support at this point in time. As long as governments can prevent the socio-economic and political marginalisation of Muslim communities in their countries, JI will find it difficult to survive. Therefore, the highest priority must be given to preventing the demonisation of the Muslim community especially if they are migrants. As is the case with other religious communities, it must always be remembered that it is a miniscule proportion of Muslims who support violence.

The fight against JI must be comprehensive, not only a military one. That is, within the Muslim communities a clear message must be sent that JI is not Koranic but a heretical organisation. Like al-Qaeda, JI misinterprets and misrepresents the Koran to advance specific political aims and objectives. Unlike a military response, such an ideological response will take more time to take effect, but it is by far the most effective. It will not only disrupt the flow of recruits and reduce support but also generate high grade and high quality information about JI that could be exploited by governments to target its capabilities. As JI is a multidimensional organisation, the response must be multi-pronged. JI capabilities cannot be degraded and destroyed militarily alone. It is a multi-agency effort involving the customs, immigration, coast guard, police, military, intelligence services, community organisations, religious institutions, schools and the mass media. The average life span of a terrorist group is thirteen-and-a-half years.[15] It is a long fight, but with determination, commitment, and unity of purpose at all levels, especially at the political level, it is a fight that can be won.

As much as 2002 was, 2003 will be a year of experience and learning both for government law enforcement and intelligence agencies. With the wider acknowledgement that there is no standard textbook for fighting al-Qaeda, it will be a learning process where new structures and institutions will have to be built and shaped to fight a rapidly evolving cunning and ruthless foe, willing to kill and die. To win, governments will have to repeat their successes and build upon them. Past experience suggests that the fight against terrorism will be a prolonged battle requiring patience and commitment. Since September 11, the damage to al-Qaeda at all levels has only been partial. The global organisation has received significant damage, but the threat has not diminished.

Al-Qaeda has suffered gravely in Afghanistan and elsewhere, but the core leadership is alive and the group's ideology is intact. The dozen attacks and fresh propaganda indicate that the leadership and membership have not given up the fight. To nurture existing and rekindle new Muslim migrant and territorial support, al-Qaeda in September 2002 issued a 100-page document justifying the September 11 attack. Amidst security countermeasures the group has demonstrated its capacity to replicate, regenerate and reorganise.

In Southeast Asia, al-Qaeda cells probe the gaping holes in the post-September 11 security architecture to strike. Today, no one single country can protect itself from a multinational terrorist organisation. For instance, Malaysia, Indonesia, and Singapore cannot protect themselves as long as al-Qaeda has a robust presence in Indonesia. The first step towards reducing the immediate threat to Southeast Asia is to develop a regional task force to target al-Qaeda's support and operational infrastructure at home and in the immediate region.

CONCLUSION

With persistence and perseverance, al-Qaeda as a physical entity can be destroyed. However, as long as its ideology remains appealing, it will pose a continuous terrorist threat to governments and societies worldwide. Although al-Qaeda as a physical entity will be relegated to history, it has at least partially accomplished its primary role of 'showing the way' to other groups, especially the need to go beyond a limited territorial agenda and wage a universal jihad. Such an appealing ideology cannot be countered in the short term. The momentum al-Qaeda has so successfully unleashed will spawn and sustain a dozen existing and emerging Islamist groups at least in the mid term (five years).

US policies towards the Middle East, especially the US-led invasion of Iraq and the continuing Israeli-Palestinian issue will strengthen support for Islamism, Islamist political parties and terrorist groups. The US's skewed foreign policy will continue to pose a significant terrorist threat to western interests both at home and overseas. In many countries, Islamism will move from the periphery to the centre, making it difficult for many governments to openly support the US-led 'War against terror'. With support for Islamism rising, Islamists will campaign either politically or violently or both in Turkey, Pakistan, Indonesia, and other emerging democracies. In addition to well-organised groups, individual terrorists will mount operations, similar to the shooting at the El-Al counter at the Los Angeles Airport in July 2002. With more transnational Islamic media, the Muslim public will become more active globally. The number of Muslims directly supporting violence will remain small, but there will be more support for a Muslim way of life, especially the implementation of Sharia laws. Furthermore, the need to wage jihad in support of their suffering brethren will rise among politicised and radicalised segments of diaspora Muslim communities.

If the threat posed by Islamism is to be countered and the life span of Islamist terrorist groups is to be shortened in the long term (ten years), the current western (principally US) approach of 95 percent military and 5 percent ideological will have to be reversed. To reduce the space for the al-Qaeda to survive and grow, the international community must develop a multi-pronged, multi-dimensional, multi-agency, and multi-jurisdictional approach against terrorism. Failure to develop a comprehensive long-term strategic response will mean al-Qaeda changing shape, surviving and continuing the fight.

NOTES

1. Bin Laden, Osama (2002), distributed by Al-Jazeera Television, 12 November. Online. Islami Way. Available: http://johnw.host.sk/islamic_articles/to_the_people_that_are_allied. htm. 9 March 2003.
2. Al-Qaeda is able to build a state-of-the-art global network because it is a diverse group – it has recruited worldwide.
3. As al-Qaeda is a learning organisation, it studies all operations where it has suffered losses and improves the next time. Losing and learning doctrine is typical of sophisticated groups.
4. Azzam, Abdullah (1988) 'Al Qaidah al Sulbah', *Al Jihad*, 41, April, p 46.
5. Gunaratna, Rohan (2002), *Inside al-Qaeda: Global Network of Terror*, New York: Columbia University Press, pp 227–9.
6. CIA estimate.
7. Al-Qaeda's front, The Islamic Army for the Liberation of the Holy Sites, claimed the attack. A subsequent interview by Abdel Azeem Al Muhajir, an al-Qaeda military commander, confirmed it as an al-Qaeda operation.
8. Interview, Al-Jazeera's Kabul correspondent Tayseer Allouni, 21 October 2001.
9. As al-Qaeda continues to pose a threat, government intelligence agencies are reluctant to make information about the group public.
10. The author interviewed a number of al-Qaeda and Taliban detainees, including the American Taliban John Walker Lindh in US custody.
11. For more details see Gunaratna (2002), *Inside al-Qaeda*.

12. Al-Qaeda infrastructure in Indonesia, BIN, Jakarta, 2001.
13. 'Three Killed in McDonald's Blast'. Online. CNN.com, 6 December, 2002. Available: http://www.cnn.com/2002/WORLD/asiapcf/southeast/12/05/indonesia.bomb/index.html. 9 March 2003.
14. Ayman al-Zawahiri (2001), 'Knights Under the Prophet's Banner – Mediations on the Jihadist Movement', *AL Sharq al-Awsat* (in Arabic), 2 December.
15. Schmid, Alex and Jongman, Albert (1998–2000). Research conducted for PIOOM, The Netherlands.

5.   Islamic Extremism and Wahhabism

Clive Williams

Wahhabism links Saudi Arabia, Pakistan, the Taliban, al-Qaeda and offshoot Islamic extremist elements elsewhere, yet to many the concept remains a mystery.

In general terms, Wahhabism is an Islamic reform movement that had, until the past thirty years or so, been restricted mainly to the Saudi peninsula. Since that time, oil revenues have allowed Saudi Arabia to spread Wahhabism internationally through the building of mosques and funding of religious schools or *madrassas*. Wahhabism has sought to eliminate elements from the Muslim religion that have become popular over the centuries and corrupted its beliefs, and return Islam to the purity of its roots.[1]

WAHHABISM

Muhammad ibn Abd al-Wahhab (died 1792 AD) could be considered the first modern Islamic fundamentalist. He made the central point of his reform movement the idea that absolutely every new concept added to Islam after the third century of the Muslim era (about 950 AD) was false and should be eliminated.

The reason for this extremist stance, and a primary focus of his efforts, were a number of common practices that he regarded as regressions to the days of pre-Islamic polytheism. These included praying to saints, making pilgrimages to tombs and special mosques, venerating trees, caves, and stones, and using votive and sacrificial offerings.

In contrast to such popular superstitions, al-Wahhab emphasised the unity of God (*tawhid*). This focus on absolute monotheism lead to him and his followers being referred to as *muwahiddun*, or 'unitarians'. Everything else he denounced as heretical innovation, or *bida*.

He was further dismayed at the widespread laxity in adhering to traditional Islamic laws: questionable practices like the ones above were allowed to continue, whereas the religious devotions which Islam required were being ignored. This resulted in indifference to the plight of widows and orphans, adultery, lack of attention to obligatory prayers, and failure to allocate shares of inheritance fairly to women.

All of the above he characterised as being typical of *jahiliyya*, an important term in Islam. It refers to the barbarism and state of ignorance that existed prior to the coming of Islam. By doing so, he identified himself with the Prophet Mohammad and at the same time connected contemporary society with the sort of society Mohammad worked to overthrow.

Because, in his view, so many Muslims lived in *jahiliyya*, he accused them of not really being Muslims after all. Only those who followed the teachings of al-Wahhab were still truly Muslims, because only they still followed the path laid down by Allah.

Wahhabi religious leaders reject any reinterpretation of the Koran when it comes to issues settled by the earliest Muslims. In taking this position, they place themselves in opposition to a variety of Muslim reform movements that developed in the late nineteenth and twentieth centuries. These movements worked to reinterpret aspects of Islamic law in order to bring it closer to standards set by the West, particularly with regard to topics like gender relations, family law, and participatory democracy.

Today Wahhabism is the dominant Islamic tradition on the Arabian Peninsula, though its influence is limited in the rest of the Middle East. As Osama bin Laden comes from Saudi Arabia and is Wahhabi himself, Wahhabi extremist thinkers and radical ideas of achieving purity have influenced him considerably.

Even though Wahhabism is a minority position, it has nevertheless influenced other extremist movements throughout the Middle East. This can be seen by two factors, the first of which is al-Wahhab's use of the term *jahiliyya* to vilify a society which he does not consider pure enough – whether they call themselves Muslim or not. Today, Islamists use the term when referring to the West and at times even to their own societies. With it, they can justify overthrowing what many might regard as an Islamic state by essentially denying that it is actually Islamic at all.

Strict Wahhabi opposition to any reinterpretation of traditional Islamic law demonstrates a second factor. Although Wahhabism allows for new interpretations when it comes to issues never decided upon by early jurists (such as the relative morality of socialism or capitalism), many of the fundamental influences of the West do not touch upon them. Modern Islamists follow the Wahhabi example by opposing any attempt to reconcile traditional Islam with modern, western notions regarding issues like gender, family, and religious rights.

It is also worth observing that al-Wahhab was strongly influenced by the works of Ibn Taymiya, a medieval orthodox theologian. Taymiya argued against the excesses of mystical Sufism and favoured a return to more 'orthodox' beliefs 400 years before al-Wahhab.

THE INFLUENCE OF DR AYMAN AL-ZAWAHIRI

Dr Ayman al-Zawahiri, born in 1953, is a close confidante of Osama bin Laden and serves as al-Qaeda's ideological leader. He is the person most likely to lead al-Qaeda in the event of bin Laden's death.

Before he joined al-Qaeda, al-Zawahiri was the leader of the Egyptian Islamic Jihad (EIJ), now part of Osama bin Laden's 'World Islamic Front for Jihad Against Jews and Crusaders'. In recent years, he has been a major influence with regard to Osama bin Laden's religious thinking.

Al-Zawahiri's family was religiously conservative. He is remembered as having been a quiet and well-read student, but his attitude may have changed in 1967, when Israel defeated the combined armies of several Arab nations. This was a watershed time for many Muslims in the Middle East, and al-Zawahiri was no different. He joined the Muslim Brotherhood at the age of just fourteen, and in 1979, he joined the even more radical EIJ.

He eventually became one of the group's principal leaders and was active in recruiting new members to its underground anti-government operations. After the assassination of Egyptian President Anwar Sadat, the Egyptian government cracked down on religious extremists, and al-Zawahiri was one of hundreds who were arrested. He could not be directly linked to the assassination, but was convicted on weapons charges and sentenced to three years in prison. During this time he was beaten and tortured, experiences that further radicalised him.

After his release he tried to return to medicine again, but found that his radical background made him unwelcome, and he eventually moved to Afghanistan, which had by that time become a gathering point for Muslim radicals from all over the world. There he was able to put his medical skills to work treating Muslim fighters wounded in combat against the Soviet Army. It was at this time that he met Dr Abdullah Azzam, a Palestinian Islamist who had taught Osama bin Laden at the King Abdul Aziz University in Saudi Arabia.

Following the Soviet withdrawal from Afghanistan in 1989, al-Zawahiri returned to Egypt – now even more radical than before and, like many other Arab fighters, having learned how to use force and violence to create an Islamic state. He was responsible in the period 1989–1992 for bringing former mujahideen into the EIJ. Government pressure forced him to join Osama bin Laden in Sudan in 1992, and in 1996, he and bin Laden returned to Afghanistan.

Al-Zawahiri was sentenced to death in absentia by an Egyptian court in 1999 for his role in organising a variety of terrorist attacks in absentia. In particular, he has been held responsible for the massacre of 58 foreign tourists at Luxor in 1997.

OSAMA BIN LADEN AND WAHHABISM

Wahhabism is the faith that drives Osama bin Laden. The modern Saudi state is built on the eighteenth century alliance between the Wahhabi religious movement and the House of Saud. It was instrumental in creating the Saudi monarchy in the 1930s, and if sufficiently alienated, could tear it down. Many influential Saudis are sympathetic to bin Laden's approach of promoting Wahhabism through violence and contact continued between Saudi government officials and bin Laden until as recently as last year.

As noted earlier, throughout their history, Wahhabis have fiercely opposed anything they viewed as *bida* – that is, any change or modernisation that deviates from the fundamental teachings of the Koran. The telephone, radio broadcasts and public education for women were at one point condemned as innovations wrought by the Devil. Riots ensued over the introduction of television in Saudi Arabia in 1965, and were only quelled after police fired on demonstrators. Similar tensions exist today. A recent ruling suggested that the music option for mobile phone rings should be outlawed on religious grounds.[2]

Whenever the forces of change prevailed, it was usually with the argument that the novelty could help propagate the Koran. When that argument failed to convince, change stalled. So, for example, there are no movie theatres in Saudi Arabia – they would promote the unhealthy mingling of the sexes – and women are banned from driving. Above all this, the Wahhabis believe their faith should spread, not giving ground in any place they have gained a foothold.

The Saudi official focus has been on spreading Wahhabism peacefully, but many of the more extremist elements, such as those led by Osama bin Laden, feel that the outcome they seek can be achieved only through violence. The ferocity with which the Wahhabis fight for their cause is legendary. One historian of the Arab world described followers of the sect as they engaged in battle: 'I have seen them hurl themselves on their enemies, utterly fearless of death, not caring how many fall, advancing rank after rank with only one desire – the defeat and annihilation of the enemy. They normally give no quarter, sparing neither boys nor old men'.[3] This fanaticism was certainly true of the al-Qaeda 055 Brigade, which fought against the Northern Alliance in Afghanistan.

Wahhabis extolled the purist state put in place by the Taliban,[4] which is why the three states that recognised the Taliban were Saudi Arabia, and the United Arab Emirates and Pakistan – where Wahhabism also has considerable influence.

BIN LADEN'S GOALS

So what is it that bin Laden wants? His basic argument is that Muslims are currently suffering from political, social and economic deprivation for the simple reason that their governments have not fully implemented sharia, or Islamic law. Because their rulers have failed to do this, bin Laden no longer considers them to be truly Muslim.

Thus, he claims, rather than living in Islamic states, many Muslims in the Middle East and elsewhere are really living in *jahiliyya*, or pre-Islamic paganism, ignorance and barbarism. Muslims are forbidden to make war on each other, but they are allowed to make war on non-Muslims who are persecuting them – thus current rulers are made open to attack. However, they are not the only targets, because the leaders are not solely responsible for the current state of affairs, so the attacks may be extended to agents of the State.

In the minds of these radicalised elements, Muslims are victims of a centuries-long crusade by Jews and westerners (the US combining both elements) that has been driven by the goal of undermining and eventually destroying Islam. They colonised *Dar al-Islam* (the House of Islam – those lands under Muslim administration), divided it up into nation-states, and even left people there to rule over the Holy City of Jerusalem. This is the situation today with the sacrilegious Israeli occupation of Jerusalem and US military presence in Saudi Arabia.

Currently, according to bin Laden, they are attempting to impose their own secular values that are at odds with fundamental and traditional Islamic values and practices. They claim altruistic motives, but Muslims know the real purpose is to undermine their faith. Thus, the US and the West must be resisted and attacked. Some think that because the US is the bigger enemy, it should be attacked first, whereas others believe that the local Muslim rulers, being the closer enemy, should be the top priority. In fact, al-Qaeda's main priority until 1998 was support for the campaigns against Muslim rulers.

While Osama bin Laden has promoted the use of violence to further the cause of Wahhabism and Islam, many reports suggest that he is not an original thinker – being neither a religious scholar nor a political philosopher. Instead, he has tapped into a fully formed tradition, which has given him all the ideological tools he needs to both explain current problems and offer a solution. Muslims in the Middle East can accept these arguments because the ground has already been prepared by centuries of development.

Nevertheless, Osama bin Laden is probably the most influential and charismatic Muslim today, appealing particularly to youth and the latent anti-Americanism that exists in most Muslim societies. His skill has been in promoting his vision of a Caliphate of all Muslims following in the pure Wahhabi tradition. It is a vision that holds considerable attraction to many Muslims internationally, and provides a common thread in conflicts involving Muslims from Chechnya to Central Asia – to Australia's own strategic environment in Southeast Asia.

NOTES

1. For a good general explanation of Islam, see http://atheism.about.com/cs/islam/ that also covers related sub-topics. I have drawn from this and other sites to produce this chapter.
2. MacFarqhuar, Neil (2001), 'Wahhabis: Adherents to a Strict Form of Islam', *New York Times*, 7 October, p 9.
3. *Ibid.*, p 9.
4. The Taliban grew out of a radical fringe of Deobandism. The Deobandi movement developed in British-ruled India during the mid-1800s. It is an offshoot of the Sunni Hanafi legal school and takes its name from the Indian Himalayan town of Deoband, the location of an influential madrassa, or religious school. The Deobandi movement aims to reform and unify Muslims and has elements of anti-colonialism and anti-modernism. The movement found new adherents in Pakistan after India was partitioned. The Taliban mixed elements of Deobandism with their ethnic-Pashtun tribal traditions. The Taliban's religious code was further forged by its long isolation from the modern world and years of fighting the Soviets, followed by civil war. Under the Taliban interpretation of Islamic law, legal punishments include public executions and amputations and women are banned from education. (See Online. CNN, Available: http://www.cnn.com/SPECIALS/2001/trade.center/islam/deobandism.html. 23 March 2003).

PART II

Terror Tactics and Asymmetric Strategies –
New and Old

6.   Trends in the Development of Terrorist Bombing

Angus Muir

HISTORICAL TRENDS

Terrorism and bombing – both tools and techniques – have long had an intimate co-relationship. We need only look back to 1605 and the Gunpowder Plot to see that the potential for explosives in acts of mass political violence has long been appreciated. This particular event took place long before the words 'terror' and 'terrorism' were coined during the French Revolutionary period. In the nineteenth century the development of high explosives coincided with the development of leftist political ideologies that identified violence as a key element in changing the existing socio-political status quo. Anarchists and nihilists in particular celebrated explosives as a near miraculous vehicle for transforming society through violence. In Joseph Conrad's *The Secret Agent* (1907), we see this attitude displayed in contemporary fiction. Amongst the more historically important operational uses was the assassination of Tsar Alexander II in 1881 by dynamite-wielding members of the Russian anarchist group *Narodnoya Volya* (People's Will), an attack celebrated by anarchists throughout Europe – both for the significance of the target and the method used.

This intimate relationship has proved constant regardless of terrorist motivations, transcending the secular/religious divide in particular. Moreover, while the technique of bombing may be seen as a form of 'tactical conservatism' – it is a tried and true method that has been consistently applied by most groups over a long period of time – the trade of making and using bombs itself is highly innovative and progressive. Innovation and creativity are part of a cycle of method and counter-method whereby a tool or technique is reduced in effectiveness by countermeasures, these are then refined to bypass the countermeasures and so on.

Bomb making is also an eminently communicable skill, an important feature in an increasingly globalised world. Bomb making may be directly communicated through inter-group cooperation and state sponsorship. Good examples of the former include the transmission of ideas and techniques (particularly of suicide and vehicle bombings) from the Lebanese Hizbollah to Hamas and Palestinian Islamic Jihad in the early 1990s, and the more recent use of urban bombings and large improvised mortars by the Revolutionary Armed Forces of Colombia (FARC), apparently learned from the Provisional Irish Republican Army (IRA). Al-Qaeda's training camps in Afghanistan were an alarming development, well resourced and numerous, benefiting from a secure environment (at least until October 2001) and providing instruction not only to core cadre but also to other like-minded jihadists, many of whom returned to their countries of origin.

Although state sponsorship of terrorist groups has declined since the 1980s, the resources of a state provide an obvious and extensive source of bomb-making tools and techniques. The assistance given to Hizbollah by Iran is an important (and lingering) example in this regard, as was that granted to leftist groups by Eastern bloc states, or to Palestinian groups by various Arab regimes. Bomb-making can also be communicated through observation, either one group emulating another's tactics, learning from manuals, or more recently learning from Internet-based sources such as the well-publicised *Anarchist's Cookbook* or the more recent *Terrorist's Handbook*. Such sources, however, may be plagued by incorrect information and lack the important dimension of 'intrinsic' knowledge that only hands-on participation and experience can provide.

DEVELOPMENTS IN THE 'MODERN' AGE OF TERRORIST BOMBINGS

The most obvious and important process in the 'modern' age of terror (generally identified as the period from 1968 to the present) has been the development of technology itself. This applies to explosives, detonator and timer technologies, and is also related to the increasing commercial availability of raw materials and other components – for example, the use of commercial fertilisers as explosives, cellular phones as detonators and so on. Other technological advances in the areas of communications and transport have also had an effect. Transportation networks have extended the reach of terrorist bombing campaigns as well as providing a new variety of targets. Similarly the advent of television and the Internet have meant that the political message of terrorist bombings is far more widely disseminated.

State sponsorship for ideological reasons also extended terrorist bombing capabilities. The provision of military training and equipment, funding and the provision of international logistic support all contributed to greater reach and destructive capability. Moreover, as groups grew and matured, each developed their own specialised departments and personnel for conducting bombings, bending their minds to maximising efficiency and destructive power.

THE VARIETY AND MEANING OF TARGETS

The modern world also provides terrorist groups with a plethora of potential targets. These include commercial targets, diplomatic and military installations and premises, and the vast array of people and facilities associated with the burgeoning tourism industry. Ironically, all of these have been made more accessible by modern transportation systems and the development of the travel industry.

Another important dimension of targets is the ongoing historical importance of psychology and symbolism. The sociologist Clifford Geertz has coined the term 'cultural centres' to describe those elements of societies that are viewed as of symbolic importance (consciously or not).[1] These include centres of political, economic and military power, but also more esoteric locales linked to a national psyche such as significant landmarks. In many cases these areas overlap – the World Trade Center in New York, twice the target of attack, is an extremely potent example. Beyond the temporal, religious locations have long been important centres of culture, and attacks on these may have repercussions far beyond the mere physical destruction caused. A good example is the Muslim Dome of the Rock in Jerusalem. The Dome has frequently been a target for right-wing Jewish groups, given that it is believed to have been built on the site of the first Jewish Temple. The plot by the Jewish Underground to destroy it, uncovered in 1984, was one of the more dangerous and well planned. According to Jewish eschatological thinking, the Dome must be destroyed before the Third Temple can be built – an important event in the Jewish (and fundamentalist Christian) messianic timetable. Spiritual concerns aside, the destruction of the Dome (the third holiest site in Islam after Mecca and Medina and the supposed site of Mohammad's ascension to heaven) would certainly cause an unpredictable and extreme backlash in the Muslim world.

TERRORISM AND RELIGION

This last example brings us to perhaps the most important trend in modern terrorism, the decline of secular ideological groups and the rise of those motivated by a religious imperative. This ideological displacement has, amongst other implications, resulted in a move away from state sponsorship, and was initially poorly understood, particularly in the western world (one could argue this is still the case), because of its ideological differences to its predecessors.[2] Although the rise of religious violence occurred against a background of religious revival amongst all the world's major religions, the clearest and most dangerous manifestation has been in the Islamic world, both Shiite and Sunni. The year 1979 provided the most dramatic example of this militant revival with the Iranian revolution, and also one of the most important catalysts for future Islamic militance, the Soviet invasion of Afghanistan.[3] More recently the collapse of the Soviet Union and the subsequent weakening of other states with sizeable Muslim populations such as Indonesia have accelerated this trend. This trend is further fuelled by the provision of funding and conservative religious dogma from oil-rich Persian Gulf states.

In terms of bombings by religious groups, divine sanction for violence and a Manichaean outlook have meant that attacks have become less discriminate in nature and the category of potential targets much broader. The time when secular terrorist groups would send a warning message before an explosion now seems almost quaint by comparison. During the era of secular ideological terrorism the adage 'terrorists want a lot of people watching and not a lot of people dead'[4] largely held true. In the realm of religious terrorism this could be more accurately altered to 'terrorists want a lot of people watching, *and* a lot of people dead'. Religious groups have a full understanding of their audience, both internal and external, and the way the media can be exploited, what is different is their perception of a total, divinely defined struggle. Statistically the observable trend is one towards fewer attacks but greater lethality.

SUICIDE BOMBINGS/MARTYRDOM OPERATIONS

Suicidal terrorist attacks are not a historically new phenomenon, but explosives have given them a new and more destructive dimension. Nor are suicide attacks the sole preserve of religiously motivated groups – the secular Sri Lankan Liberation Tigers of Tamil Eelam (LTTE) have long engaged in this particular *modus operandi* with a great deal of success, with dedicated suicide units and highly refined methods and equipment. More recently the second Palestinian *intifada* has seen suicide attacks by the secular al-Aqsa Martyrs Brigade in the Occupied Territories. However, the suicide attack is a tactic far more prevalent amongst religious groups. The distinction between suicide and martyrdom may seem fine but it is an important one to make. The term 'suicide' is largely used in the West with its usual negative connotations. 'Martyrdom' however is viewed more positively in Islam (as in Judaism and

Christianity) as a valuable contribution to a just struggle, and one that has extremely resonant religious traditions and characters to support it. Suicide bombers are elevated into group martyrology (along with other dead members of the group who were not actively seeking death but instead had it thrust upon them) and often sanctified, while their families are frequently compensated with generous support in recognition of their 'sacrifice'.

On a practical level suicide bombing is an accurate method and one that has a much greater chance of circumventing existing security measures. On a psychological level there are important dimensions for both internal and external audiences. Internally there is the development of group martyrology mentioned above – the naming of operational units after martyrs, martyr statements, actions on the anniversaries of martyrs' deaths and so on. Externally this tactic generates a high degree of terror and becomes a measure of the group's commitment to its cause.

THE SPECTRE OF CHEMICAL, BIOLOGICAL, RADIOLOGICAL AND NUCLEAR BOMBS

One of the most worrying aspects of escalating terrorist bombings is the long-considered possibility that a group will employ some form of Chemical, Biological, Radiological and Nuclear (CBRN) device.[5] Following the collapse of the Soviet Union there were serious concerns (which linger today) that stocks of Soviet weaponry or specialised personnel would fall into terrorist hands. An enormous amount of money and effort continues to be expended to prevent this from happening. The fear of a CBRN attack was brought to the fore in dramatic fashion in 1995 when the apocalyptic Japanese group Aum Shinrikyo conducted a series of nerve gas attacks on the Tokyo subway system that killed twelve and injured thousands. Further investigations revealed that Aum had been engaged in experimenting with nerve agents and biological agents for some time and had even sought to procure nuclear materials and possibly even a Russian nuclear device, deepening existing concerns.[6] While not an actual bombing in the technical sense, this incident became a defining one for counter-terrorism policy, particularly in the US. In November of the same year, Chechen separatists aggravated these concerns further when they constructed a radiological bomb and deployed it in a Moscow park (it was not armed, but intended only as a warning).

More recently these fears have been revived by the recent anthrax mailings in the US and by the revelation that al-Qaeda has sought to procure CBRN materials. The anthrax mailings highlight the prime value of these weapons – their capacity to generate fear and cause disruption. The method used to disseminate the anthrax was primitive in the extreme and the number of casualties low but the results were more profound and widely felt. Al-Qaeda's exploration in CBRN weaponry is entirely more alarming. Evidence gathered in Afghanistan since the US-led intervention shows the group has experimented with toxins and poisons and researched the gamut of CBRN possibilities. In early January 2003, a group of North African men allegedly connected with al-Qaeda were arrested in a London flat in possession of the toxin ricin.[7] In a January 1999 interview bin Laden described the acquisition of CBRN weaponry as a 'religious duty' and that 'it would be a sin for Muslims not to try to possess the weapons that would prevent the infidels from inflicting harm on Muslims'.[8] In another interview almost three years later bin Laden claimed to actually have chemical and biological weapons.[9] Despite this rhetoric the available evidence suggests that al-Qaeda has only a rudimentary CBRN capability, and for the time being will probably prefer the use of conventional bombs.

There are serious constraints on developing such a capability, not merely cost and procurement, but also construction and weaponisation. Aum Shinrikyo,[10] for example, employed members with high levels of scientific training, lavished millions of dollars on its CBRN programme but failed to produce pure nerve agents or develop an effective delivery system – it is estimated the sarin used in the Tokyo subway attacks was about 30 percent pure and was disseminated by piercing plastic bags full of the liquid with sharpened umbrella tips. Due to fears of retaliation, the possibility of 'rational' state complicity is low – even the case of a dictator facing removal from power, such as Saddam Hussein, passing them on as a final act of defiance seems unlikely. Even if such a course were taken, those in receipt of such largesse would still be faced with the problems of effective storage and transportation, and developing a viable means of delivery.

There are, however, four main reasons why this issue is still of paramount concern. Firstly, some groups may consider growing public indifference or acceptance of conventional attack and decide that a larger scale, unconventional bombing with even more casualties is necessary. Secondly, security measures against conventional weapons may cause terrorists to adopt unconventional bombs. Thirdly, a group may achieve a level of frustration, or face a threat to its existence, that warrants the use of any means in the pursuit of their struggle. And fourthly, the prevalence of religiously motivated groups in the contemporary period, including messianic and apocalyptic groups such as Aum brings into play the divine imperative to utterly destroy an enemy, and also invoke associations of the use of CBRN weapons with a final, cataclysmic battle of the kind anticipated by scripture.

POST-SEPTEMBER 11

In the aftermath of the tragedy of September 11 a number of trends in terrorist bombing suggest themselves. There will be the continued impact of modern technology noted above and the availability of explosives and explosive components. The attacks of September 11 suggest a new phase in suicide bombings that use transportation systems. They also suggest a new phase in lethality (and response, particularly the US-led intervention in Afghanistan) that has considerably upped the stakes in terrorist campaigns. The attacks also represent a timely and stark reminder of the capacity of terrorist groups to adapt and innovate. The destruction of the World Trade Center was a relatively low cost operation that relied on patience and good organisational security and which took full advantage of the freedoms of an advanced society and the security preconceptions of the aviation industry. A by-product of the attack (if it was not in fact intended) is the realisation by religious groups of the economic damage (both direct and indirect) that attacks of this nature may cause. In October 2002 a statement by bin Laden warned that al-Qaeda would 'target key sectors of your [the US] economy'.[11]

In terms of transportation, September 11 has exposed obvious weaknesses and dangers in commercial aviation. These are further compounded by the long understood dilemma of security measures versus commercial viability. Enhancement of existing – and the introduction of new – security regimes is important and is happening, but these are only as good as the weakest links in the chain. The case of Richard Reid, the so-called 'shoe bomber', is an excellent example in this regard – despite increased security measures and the bomber's suspicious behaviour he was still able to board an aircraft. If Reid is assessed to be at the lower end of the professionalism spectrum his case is even more worrisome. Of greater concern is the ongoing unevenness of global airport and airline security.

Commercial shipping is also a major risk area. The attack on the French tanker *Limberg* off the coast of Yemen in October 2002 by a suicide boat may be the first in a wave of such attacks. Similar attacks on naval vessels such as that on the *USS Cole* in October 2000 are commensurably more difficult but have an important psychological impact. Given already high rates of maritime piracy it is not inconceivable that terrorist groups could adopt this method to create floating bombs – particularly using petroleum tankers. Tankers are extremely vulnerable and active pirate networks exist in areas with a terrorist/proto-terrorist presence. The destruction of a vessel in busy, narrow sea-lanes, such as the Straits of Malacca, could have a serious impact on world and regional trade. Port facilities with combustible storage facilities are equally vulnerable. Sea freight itself is also a possible conduit for terrorist bombs or bombers. It is estimated that only 2 percent of containers undergo physical security checks, and there have already been incidents of al-Qaeda suspects using containers to enter Canada en route to the US. To put the problem in perspective, in 2001 around eighteen million containers entered US ports.[12] The possibility of a CBRN device in a container is a particular worry.

More realistic than a terrorist group shipping a device to an intended target is a less expensive, more practicable approach using tried methods such as a vehicle-borne bomb or a hijacked aircraft as a detonator and the suicide driver or pilot as the guidance system. There are a large variety of facilities such as chemical factories and nuclear power plants that may be seen as tempting targets. Chemical facilities are more vulnerable and one only needs recall the horrors of chemical accidents such as the Bhopal disaster of 1984 which killed 2,000 people and injured tens of thousands to imagine the likely outcome of such an attack.[13] Chemicals, poisons and radioactive material are also potentially vulnerable to such an attack when they are in transit by sea, road or rail.

ESCALATION AND THE FUTURE

A few closing points should be made with regard to the future. Most importantly the cycle of terrorist bombing innovation will continue, as will the trend of mass casualty attacks. In terms of bombing targets there is a clearly discernible trend for attacking the softer vulnerabilities of liberal democratic states, primarily those of a social and economic nature, and certainly in the case of al-Qaeda making these attacks as spectacular as possible. The objective is not merely destruction and terror, but also an attempt to make liberal democratic societies subvert their core values through draconian security responses, and to polarise constituencies into 'them' and 'us' – in the current environment perverting the fight against terrorism into a struggle between Islam and the West. As always the key to these responses is international cooperation of the effective and not merely paper variety and hopefully an identification of the underlying causes of the struggle itself. Hunting down and destroying terrorists and their infrastructure is essential but so too is destroying their motivations and rationales.

Terrorist bombings require bombs and bombers, and locations where the two can become acquainted and operational plans figured out. Steps can be taken to limit the availability of bomb componentry but due to their ubiquitous nature such steps can never hope to usefully limit supply – as with terrorist financing it takes very little in the way of explosives to achieve the desired result. Greater success can be hoped for on the CBRN front but even there no set of deterrents can hope to completely eliminate the possibility of terrorist acquisition. The best coercive hopes of deterrence lie in denying terrorists safe operating environments and the elimination of key personnel. And this can only be achieved through effective intelligence and law enforcement structures – backed by the military when appropriate – and concerted efforts on the more prosaic but critical front of denying terrorist groups a sympathetic constituency.

NOTES

1. Geertz, Clifford (1977), 'Centres, Kings and Charisma: Reflections on the Symbolics of Power', in Ben David, Joseph and Clark, Terry (eds), *Culture and its Creators*, Chicago: University of Chicago Press, pp 150–71.
2. See Juergensmeyer, Mark (1993), *The New Cold War: Religious Nationalism Confronts the Secular State*, Berkeley: University of California Press.
3. In 1979 there was also a rare incident of Islamic messianic violence when the Grand Mosque in Mecca was occupied by a group of extremists who proclaimed one of their number to be the Mahdi.
4. Jenkins, Brian (1975), 'International Terrorism: A Balance Sheet', *Survival*, 1975, 17, p 158.
5. Literature on the subject dates back to the early 1970s. See for example Jenkins, Brian (1975), *Will Terrorists Go Nuclear?*, Santa Monica: RAND.
6. Reader, Ian (1996), *Poisonous Cocktail? Aum Shinrikyo's Path to Violence*, Copenhagen: Nordic Institute of Asian Studies Books; and Kaplan, David and Marshall, Andrew (1996), *The Cult at the End of the World: The Incredible Story of Aum*, London: Arrow Books.
7. Centre for Non-Proliferation Studies (2003), 'Ricin Found in London Flat: An Al Qaida connection?', Monterey, 23 January.
8. Yusufzai, Rahimullah (1999), 'Conversation with Terror', *Time*, 11 January.
9. Mir, Hamid (2001), 'Osama claims he has nukes', *Dawn* (Pakistan), 10 November.
10. Brackett, David (1996), *Holy Terror: Armageddon in Tokyo*, New York: Weatherhill Inc., p 142.
11. BBC (2002), 'Bin Laden tape: Text', 6 October. BBC Online. Available: http://news.bbc.co.uk/2/hi/middle_east/2751019.stm. 24 April 2003. The audiotape was originally aired on the Arabic Al-Jazeera satellite television station.
12. *The Economist* (2002), 'The Trojan Box', 7 February.
13. Figures for the disaster vary. These are taken from the US Chemical Safety and Hazard Investigation Board.

7. The Chemical, Biological, Radiological and Nuclear (CBRN) Threat – Exaggeration or Apocalypse Soon?

Gavin Cameron

INTRODUCTION

The acts of terrorism on September 11 2001 appeared to herald a new era of high-casualty and high-consequence terrorism, unmatched even by previous incidents such as Aum Shinrikyo's release of sarin in the Tokyo subway in March 1995. Although relying on a familiar tactic – 'skyjacking' – the attacks on the World Trade Center and Pentagon were unlike their predecessors in the 1970s: the terrorists were not intent on escaping after the attack. The hijacking was not the principal aspect of the terrorists' action, merely a means to the greater act of violence: crashing the planes and the passengers aboard into the World Trade Center and Pentagon.

Until relatively recently, Aum Shinrikyo's attack was regarded as being a watershed, itself supposed to be the start of a wave of high-consequence terrorist attacks with Chemical, Biological, Radiological and Nuclear (CBRN) weapons. Such pessimism was not borne out by events in the subsequent years. It is therefore important to consider whether the events of September 11 are really indicative of a greater likelihood of terrorists resorting to CBRN weapons.

Falkenrath et al. list a dozen such cases within the twentieth century, all of which resulted in over 100 fatalities.[1] The examples that they cite include only those incidents that might be considered to be terrorism by any definition; they do not include the many systematic massacres that are sometimes regarded as being terroristic, such as those that have occurred repeatedly in Algeria or Cambodia. Moreover, the majority of cases on Falkenrath's list are examples of attacks using a single weapon, usually a bomb containing conventional explosive, rather than being the results of assaults with multiple weapons. Of Falkenrath's examples, five were of planes that were destroyed in mid-air, the most destructive of which was the Air India bombing in 1985, in which 328 people were killed. All twelve examples involved conventional weapons, as did the attacks on September 11. On that occasion, the terrorists used two traditional tactics, hijacking and crashing a vehicle into a building. Their innovation was to combine these tactics and to use planes rather than trucks as the vehicle of destruction. In doing so, the September 11 terrorists killed over 3,000 people. By comparison, the most notable terrorist use of CBRN weapons, Aum Shinrikyo's March 1995 attack on the Tokyo subway, killed twelve people and injured thousands.[2] Given this, one key consideration should be whether September 11 is indicative of further acts of high-casualty terrorism or of terrorism with CBRN weapons. The two are not synonymous.[3]

In considering the implications of September 11 for subsequent terrorist uses of CBRN weapons, this chapter differentiates between the various types of these weapons, analysing the threats posed by each. It assesses the relative difficulties of effective acquisition, weaponisation, and delivery of CBRN weapons, and the potential impact of such weapons use, suggesting that this impact would have psychological, social and political ramifications, as well as the obvious potential for casualties. However, this discussion examines also, from a historical perspective, the record of previous examples of CBRN use by sub-state actors. I argue that many previous threats have used low-level agents or have used high-level agents ineffectively. Indeed, one suggests that there is a disconnection between those sub-state actors who have used CBRN weapons and those who one would most fear using such weapons. It then assesses whether this disconnection has continued analytical validity in the wake of September 11, the subsequent anthrax attacks in the United States and elsewhere, and the continued evidence of al-Qaeda, among others, seeking CBRN weapons.

CHEMICAL, BIOLOGICAL, RADIOLOGICAL AND NUCLEAR WEAPONS: SIMILARITIES AND DIFFERENCES

Chemical and Biological Weapons

Chemical and biological weapons carry a cachet and prestige for any group using them that could make them attractive to terrorist organisations. Chemical and biological agents are, rightly or wrongly, perceived as clever, covert and extremely dangerous. The last factor, the potential of such weapons, is appealing to many terrorists because it offers them a heightened level of power over their putative victims. It appears to offer the terrorists control not only over their own fate, but also over that of many others. Both chemical and biological weapons are likely to be invisible and may be odourless depending on the agent used, reducing the likelihood of detection while the attack is underway. The covert nature of the weapon is a particular factor with biological agents since the incubation time, between the release of the agent and the onset of symptoms in victims, may be hours or days, again depending on the type of agent used. Such a delay increases the chances that the group will be able to escape undetected, a vital factor in many terrorist organisations' tactical choice. However, the same characteristic of biological agents also reduces the immediate effect of an attack using such pathogens, and thus may be less attractive to groups that seek to achieve a quick impact. Finally, both chemical and biological weapons are perceived as difficult (and potentially dangerous) to acquire, manufacture, and weaponise, certainly when compared to conventional weapons. This means that the prestige and self-worth that a group feels for attaining any of these goals will be proportionately higher than it would be for conventional weapons. It should be noted that some of these same attractive characteristics of chemical or biological weapons, such as the difficulties associated with acquiring or using them, also diminish the likelihood of terrorists successfully doing so. This clearly might act as a deterrent to some terrorists. The likelihood of achieving a successful attack is also a factor in terrorists' tactical decision making and this may encourage technological conservatism, relying on weapons that have been used before, that are tried, tested and trusted.

Conversely, given the covert potential of chemical and biological weapons, terrorist use of non-conventional weapons ensures the group or individual widespread publicity for themselves and their cause. This is a vital part of many, but by no means all, terrorists' rationale. Attracting such attention proves that the group matters, exists and has to be dealt with and acknowledged. However, attracting this level of attention has grown increasingly difficult to achieve.[4]

Although both chemical and biological weapons have the potential to cause mass casualties, there are significant barriers to doing so, using either type of device. However, it is important to distinguish between chemical and biological agents. Chemical agents are synthetic and may either be inhaled (for example sarin), or absorbed through the skin (as is VX). Biological agents are naturally occurring microbes: bacteria, viruses, and toxins that are largely ingested or inhaled.

Another key difference lies with some biological agents – viruses such as smallpox or bacteria such as bubonic plague – that are contagious. Whereas most biological agents, such as the anthrax bacteria, and all chemical agents affect only those people who come into direct contact with the agent and so are to some extent limited, agents such as plague and smallpox have the potential to continue infecting people. This makes them fearsome weapons, but it also means that they are highly unpredictable, a problem not only for the responder, but also for the terrorist. This is particularly so since one of the central challenges to effective deployment of either chemical or biological weapons is the weaponisation and delivery. Chemical weapons would be relatively easy to deliver in an enclosed space, but much harder to disperse in a way so as to cause high levels of casualties in an open space. Effective delivery of biological agents is more problematic. Theoretically, there is a relatively small margin between the terrorist using plague or smallpox to cause a pandemic and having no discernible effect at all. The example of Aum Shinrikyo provides excellent evidence for this. Although they did not seek to cause a pandemic using biological agents, the group did conduct numerous experiments to release highly dangerous pathogens, but had very little success in doing so.[5] To be effective, biological agents would need to be dispersed in an aerosol cloud consisting of particles small enough (one to five microns) to be easily inhaled and retained in the lungs. This requirement poses significant hurdles on the terrorist attempting to use such pathogens to cause high casualties. Agricultural crop sprayers are sometimes cited as easily available examples of how agents could be dispersed. Although such a scenario might work to spread chemical weapons, provided that the terrorist were aware of the effect weather conditions might have (strong winds for example are likely to dissipate the agent), it is not an effective means of delivery for biological agents.[6] The efficacy of a biological agent would depend on several factors: the agent itself, the delivery system, the quantity of agent used, the efficacy of the aerosolisation of the agent and the weather conditions at the time of release. For example, strong winds may affect the dispersal of the agent, and bright light, significant heat or dryness may all adversely affect the time the pathogen remains infectious after release. Moreover, the degree to which a biological agent is affected by these factors varies: anthrax, for example, is relatively hardy, a significant advantage for a terrorist.

There is no doubt that state-sponsorship would help a terrorist group significantly in its acquisition and effective deployment of chemical or biological weapons. In addition, there have been concerns over the potential for expertise and technologies to leak from the weapons programme of the former Soviet Union. However, with the exception of Aum Shinrikyo, there is little available information that terrorist groups have been able to exploit this potential opportunity.

The acquisition of chemical and biological agents, without state sponsorship, varies enormously in difficulty. For example, smallpox is supposedly held in just two sites in the world, whereas other pathogens can be acquired through mail order, provided that apparently valid documentation for legitimate research accompanies the order. Some pathogens are commercial products: botulinum toxin is widely used for medical and cosmetic purposes.[7] Some other biological pathogens are even easier to acquire, notably ricin, for which the main ingredient is the bean of the castor plant, and for which a plethora of publications, many originating from the radical right in the United States, provide instructions on production. Both bubonic plague and anthrax are naturally available in some areas of the world in which they are endemic. However, a terrorist group would have to ensure that it held a virulent strain of the pathogen. Moreover, although the raw materials and production methods for making ricin are straightforward, and ricin is a highly lethal pathogen, this does not mean that producing a weapon capable of causing mass casualties is equally easy: there remains the issue of effective delivery. Several of the groups, such as the Minnesota Patriots' Council, that have produced ricin in this way have also produced only a very impure version of the pathogen.[8] The problem of quality control in producing a chemical or biological agent is well demonstrated by Aum Shinrikyo's attempts to produce sarin. Despite scientists from some of the best universities in Japan, a generous research budget, and scope for testing the sarin, the cult failed to produce anything other than an impure and only partially effective version of the agent.[9]

Both chemical and biological agents can be produced using dual-use technology, methods and equipment that have legitimate as well as illegitimate purposes. As mentioned, culture collections will provide seed stocks of pathogens, ostensibly for biomedical or biotechnological research, but which may also be grown into weapons-significant quantities of the agent, using the widely available nutrient media or broth. Other types of equipment for growing biological weapons are equally dual-use: fermenters can be used to grow pathogens but are also widely available for production in a range of legitimate industries from brewing and pharmaceuticals to biotechnology. Freeze-drying and milling machines, extremely helpful in the conversion of agents into a dry, finely ground powder – ideal for dispersion – are widely used in the pharmaceutical industry. Such usage makes it difficult to impose meaningful restrictions on access to weapons-usable equipment, particularly if the terrorist organisation operates behind a front company to make its purchases.

Chemical agents – being compounds – may be acquired as a series of precursors, rather than as an entire agent. For obvious reasons, acquiring precursors is an easier route, although tight controls exist on some of these as well, through the Chemical Weapons Convention and Australia Group. In spite of this, groups seeking such precursors can use front companies and other evasive measures to circumvent such restrictions, particularly if a complicit supplier can be found. This is the route taken by Aum Shinrikyo for several of its key purchases for both chemical and biological weapons programmes.[10] In other cases though, constituent chemicals are used so widely in industry that controlling them is all but impossible. Such chemicals can then be used to produce the chemical precursors or, ultimately, the chemical agent. Here, the problem for the terrorist lays not so much in acquiring most of the key ingredients, but in the process of manufacturing an effective agent from those ingredients. Although many 'recipes' are readily available, either in the open literature or on the Internet, the reliability of these recipes is often limited. However, as a general point, chemical agents can be produced using technology and methods that are widely published in the open literature. Although nerve agents, such as sarin or tabun, require more sophisticated techniques, some of the World War 1 agents such as phosgene, hydrogen cyanide or sulphur mustard, are relatively easy to produce. Such manufacture would necessitate the acquisition of equipment that is readily available and unlikely to be a signal of malevolent intent by a group.[11]

Even assuming that a terrorist group is able to obtain a chemical or biological agent that has the potential to cause widespread casualties, the barriers to the organisation being able to use the agent to inflict such injuries remain substantial. The effective weaponisation and delivery of such agents, in order to cause high levels of casualties, is a non-trivial task. Where the objective of the terrorist is low levels of casualties, production of credible agents is more straightforward since the requirements of delivery and purity for the agent are so much lower. Where the terrorist seeks simply to cause disruption, acquisition or delivery of an agent is unnecessary, as numerous incidents in the United States since 1998 show, since even a hoax that claims to use such agents has to be taken seriously enough by authorities to cause disruption.

Radiological Weapons

Most of the world's 440 nuclear power reactors would be highly vulnerable to a similar attack to those launched on September 11: a passenger aircraft laden with fuel being crashed into the building. The impact and fire caused by such an attack would likely compromise the containment system that surrounds reactors, increasing the risk of a radioactive leak. Many containment facilities are designed to withstand the impact only of a small plane.[12] The exact nature of the damage caused by such an attack would depend on the size of plane, amount of fuel it carried, speed and angle of impact. Although the emergency coolant systems would ordinarily prevent an explosion, it is possible that both primary and backup systems could also be severely compromised by such an attack, possibly leading to a steam explosion at the reactor.[13] It is unlikely to be feasible for existing reactors to be engineered to withstand the impact of such a plane, although new reactors might be planned with this as one criterion.

Truck bombs used against nuclear facilities have historically caused widespread concern, particularly in the United States. Other forms of frontal assault on reactors by terrorists have a low probability of success, particularly of creating a radiation release, largely because reactors are not only well defended but can also be shut down from several different locations. It is hard to envisage a scenario in which terrorists were able to capture an entire reactor before the process was shut down. If terrorists were to succeed in destroying or disabling both the backup and the primary coolant systems at a reactor, they might manage to cause a core meltdown, even if the reactor was shut down. This is because the decay heat generated by a reactor is so intense that cooling has to continue for days after the reactor has been shut down. Reactors are designed to withstand the failure of their primary coolant systems and have backup systems to cope with this problem. However, the simultaneous failure of both primary and auxiliary systems has potentially disastrous consequences. To ensure a radiological dispersal, the terrorists would also have to engineer the failure of the reactor's containment system. Although this can occur naturally, once the core melts, containment vessels are built with safety devices that hopefully ensure that its integrity is maintained for as long as possible, to minimise the consequences of such an incident. If terrorists were able to damage the containment system severely, particularly in the early stages of an attack, then that would greatly increase their chances of achieving an off-site radiological dispersal.[14]

Nuclear reactors are obviously not the only parts of the nuclear complex that are vulnerable to attack. Enrichment, storage and spent fuel reprocessing facilities are also potential targets for an assault, as is the transport between them. The most dangerous target at a uranium enrichment plant would probably be the containers of liquid uranium hexafluoride at the feed end. An explosion releasing the liquid would cause it to solidify and about half would vaporise, reacting with the atmosphere to form a mixture of uranium oxide and fluorine compound (UO_2F_2) and hydrofluroric acid, the products of gaseous uranium hexafluoride.[15] The opportunities to create an off-site radiation leak at a reprocessing facility may be limited. Although the radioactivity of the materials is considerable – and therefore potentially attractive for radiological terrorism – it also means that they are remotely handled and are inaccessible, even to operators, due to the necessity for extensive radiation shielding. Significant amounts of explosives might conceivably rupture the spent fuel storage pool, but the likelihood is that the radiation released by such a spill would be small since the gaseous fission products would mostly plate out on the interior of the building, or would be captured by the filtration system. Nonetheless, if not only the pools or tanks were ruptured, but also the fabric of the building, then the explosion has the potential to throw large quantities of highly radioactive material into the atmosphere. If a plane crashed into a reprocessing facility, the resulting fire as the fuel burned would add to the radiological release. If the cooling system was also compromised in the explosion, then, potentially, the radioactive material could overheat and further material would be propelled into the atmosphere.[16]

The transport of spent fuel is the part of the nuclear cycle where material is seemingly at its most vulnerable. However, it would be far from straightforward for terrorists to exploit this: spent fuel is shipped in casks that protect the public from radiation, so the construction of the casks is extremely robust. Even enormous truck bombs, detonated within feet of the cask, may not be capable of penetrating it. Shaped charges probably could do so but, by their nature designed to penetrate deeply rather than to do massive damage, they are likely to rupture only the fuel pins directly in their path. Therefore, as with several other forms of radiological terrorism, the public reaction would probably be out of proportion to the true physical danger.[17] Nevertheless, such an attack would be a highly effective means of creating fear and disruption amongst a population.

If the terrorist group's intention is a radiological attack, then destroying a reactor is only one way to achieve this goal. Radiological materials in this category can be more easily stolen from nuclear, industrial and research facilities than can weapons-grade material.[18] The International Atomic Energy Agency (IAEA) reports 380 incidents of radiological trafficking since 1993, only the minority of which involved 'high end material'.[19] Abel Gonzalez, the IAEA's director of radiation and waste safety reported in late October that 'Security of radioactive materials has traditionally been relatively light … There are few security precautions on radiotherapy equipment and a large source could be removed quite easily, especially if those involved have no regard for their own health.' Many such sources are presently without any regulatory control and are unaccounted for.[20] A radiological device would be extremely easy to construct (it need only be an aerosol can or a bomb with a radioactive coating or with a container of radioactive material next to it) and the materials for it are so widely available (caesium-137, for example, is commonly used in hospitals for X-rays). Even elements, such as cobalt-60 or caesium-137, which needs a fierce fire to disperse them, could be used effectively in radiological weapons if the material was surrounding a mixture of high explosive and incendiary material. A firebomb of this variety is technologically well within the reach of many terrorist organisations.[21]

The technical feasibility of radiological terrorism as a low-technology weapon means that it is by far the most likely form of nuclear device, as well as the least catastrophic. Despite this, it would still have considerable value as a terrorist weapon, since the mere fact of being nuclear would almost certainly ensure that it had a considerable impact on the public's imagination and fear, and thus on a governmental response. For the same reason, it conveys an added prestige and status on the perpetrators. Radiological terrorism would set a group apart and take its terrorism to a new level, and thus possesses considerable attraction. Furthermore, while the use of a radiological weapon would be more difficult than most 'off the shelf' weaponry, and would be an example of technological innovation for terrorist groups, the arguments that make a nuclear-yield device an unlikely, if highly dangerous, threat apply to a much lesser degree for radiological weapons. While a nuclear-yield bomb would be an extremely expensive and difficult mass-casualty weapon, a radiological device would be only moderately difficult (there might be material handling problems, for example).

It is almost impossible to generalise on the extent of the risk to the public from a radiological dispersal device: it depends on the means of dispersal, population density, weather conditions, and the period of public exposure. Above all though, the effects of a radiological weapon are dependent on the type of material used. While weapons-grade plutonium might cause limited damage, other elements, such as caesium or even radioactive waste, are potentially very rapidly lethal.

Where the cause is a radiological dispersal device rather than a disaster at a nuclear facility, the consequences appear substantially smaller. Radiological devices are not ideal for creating mass casualties because the quantities of highly radioactive material required to cause powerful results over even a moderate area are likely to be so great that it would pose considerable problems for terrorists to acquire and then work with the material.[22] To achieve widespread casualties, terrorists would probably be obliged to find a way of manufacturing very small particles of radioactive material, exacerbating the handling and production risks and difficulties, or finding an effective means of dispersion. Radiological weapons might therefore be used as weapons of terror, rather than as an effective means of causing mass casualties for which other types of non-conventional weapon might be used instead.

Despite reports of groups such as al-Qaeda or Chechen separatists planning attacks with radiological weapons, such attacks are not tactics that many terrorist groups have historically sought to use and remain unlikely tactics for the majority of groups. Radiological weapons would have a vast impact and could, potentially, pose a considerable problem for an extended period. Consequently, an incident that is not intended to cause mass casualties, but is intended to achieve political or economic extortion, is the most plausible type of radiological terrorism. Once aware of the problem, it would probably be possible to clean up the radiological effects of a device, but restoring public confidence would be more difficult.[23]

Nuclear Weapons

A nuclear-yield weapon is likely to be the hardest type of CBRN device for terrorists to acquire, but, with biological weapons, also has the potential to be the most devastating. Terrorists intent on acquiring a nuclear-yield device have three options: steal or purchase an intact weapon; steal or purchase a sufficient quantity of weapons-usable materials and build a crude nuclear-yield device; or enrich enough weapons-grade material to build a device. In reality, the second option to acquire enough weapons-usable material to build a nuclear-yield weapon is widely regarded as the most credible.

Most terrorist groups seem unlikely to follow the example of Aum Shinrikyo in attempting to enrich material to a weapons-usable state. The process is lengthy, costly and for many of the cruder forms of enrichment, potentially easily discovered. Success is also far from assured: many state programmes spend millions and take years trying to enrich enough material for a viable nuclear weapons programme. Many such programmes ultimately fail. Moreover, it is the methods of enrichment most likely to succeed for a novice proliferator that are likely to be most easily discovered due to the scale of facilities and resources required. This may not wholly preclude terrorist groups from pursuing this method of CBRN acquisition, but it does mean that such organisations would need a friendly state, as al-Qaeda had in Afghanistan, willing to host the group's enrichment programme. The alternative, and the one that Aum pursued, relies on the group being sufficiently wealthy to find and buy a secluded enough place for their programme. Aum bought a half-million acre ranch in Western Australia where they mined natural uranium. However, it was to be shipped to Japan for enrichment, using a laser isotope separation process. This is a poor choice for a novice proliferator. The process is very expensive, not an enormous barrier to the vastly wealthy Aum, but success is also far from assured. Aum's choice of enrichment method was more a reflection of Shoko Asahara's fascination with lasers than of the most practicable method available.[24]

A group unwilling or unable to enrich its own weapons-usable nuclear material would have to rely on buying or stealing it. Another pathway to nuclear terrorism is to acquire nuclear material to construct a device, but acquiring sufficient nuclear material is likely to prove difficult. In spite of reports of nuclear 'leakage' in the former Soviet Union, only a handful of cases involving weapons-significant materials are known. Never was the quantity involved sufficient to build a weapon. It would be unwise to assume that all terrorist groups would similarly fail, or that the Former Soviet Union is the only place to acquire nuclear materials.[25] However, the need to acquire a considerable quantity of fissile material would seem to preclude all but the most affluent or state-sponsored groups.

Whether through enrichment or acquisition of enough fissile material for a nuclear-yield weapon, terrorists seeking to build a nuclear weapon then have a number of design options: constructing a gun-type weapon using highly enriched uranium (HEU), or developing an implosion device using HEU or plutonium. In terms of design, the crude gun-type device is significantly the easier of the two, requiring between 50 and 60 kilograms of HEU. A less than critical mass of uranium is propelled down a tube, the 'gun-barrel', using conventional high explosive into another less than critical mass of uranium. The combined quantity of the uranium is greater than critical and a nuclear explosion follows. The implosion type of nuclear weapon uses a sub-critical quantity of fissile material (either plutonium or uranium, but more often the former), machined into a sphere and surrounded by shaped conventional high explosives. These explosives are detonated simultaneously to the microsecond that compresses the sphere of fissile material, increasing its density so that it becomes super-critical. Once that occurs, a fission chain reaction and nuclear explosion will follow. An implosion device would require around eight kilograms of plutonium. The key difficulties arise in two areas: the sphere of plutonium needs to be minutely engineered, and the shock wave has to be simultaneous to the millionths of a second. If either condition is not met, there is a substantial risk of an unpredictable nuclear yield or, more likely, a failure to reach super-criticality. The risk of having a 'fizzle' may not be a major deterrent to terrorist groups, since the effects would still be considerable, although less than that of a nuclear yield. A gun-type assembly would have a high probability of achieving some nuclear yield without requiring testing of components and using the open literature. An implosion device using close to eight kilograms of plutonium is likely to be more sophisticated, requiring a higher degree of technical competence. In each case, however, the crucial barrier is the acquisition of enough nuclear material for the device.[26]

The final method for terrorists to acquire a nuclear-yield device is to steal or purchase an intact weapon. Concerns over nuclear-yield terrorism heightened significantly after the Soviet Union's collapse, due largely to the fear over 'loose nukes' and the opportunities for nuclear materials and nuclear expertise to leave the country and be exploited by rogue states or terrorists. That terrorists could acquire an intact nuclear weapon seems far-fetched: states obviously have a considerable stake in protecting their mass-destructive weapons generally. Both Aum Shinrikyo and Osama bin Laden may have sought weapons in the former Soviet Union, but neither was successful in its efforts which, given the wealth and contacts each possessed, suggests that such acquisitions remain far from easy. Nor does it seem plausible to suggest that states might be willing to sponsor a client group to use a nuclear device against their enemies. Fear of retribution from the attacked state, potential loss of control over the client group, and the intrinsic difficulty of acquiring nuclear weapons and thus a reluctance to surrender them to any other party, are all significant factors that mitigate against such state-sponsorship. Therefore, the most plausible scenario for terrorist acquisition of an intact nuclear device is through theft, assisted by insiders, to overcome the difficulties involved in by-passing site security at the location of the nuclear weapons, taking possession of the device, and removing it from the site before state reinforcements can be deployed.[27]

The effects of a detonated nuclear-yield weapon depend on the device itself. While a stolen or acquired state-manufactured weapon might have a very high yield, the effects of a detonated crude nuclear-yield device are much more uncertain but likely to be a lower yield. Still, for terrorist purposes, the fact of a nuclear yield, even a small one, may be more significant than the size of it. It is also crucial to remember that even a small nuclear yield has the potential to be devastating across a wide area.

PREVIOUS USES OF CBRN MATERIALS BY SUB-STATE ACTORS

Radiological Terrorism

The most important sub-state use of radiological material occurred on 23 November 1995, when Chechen guerrilla leader, Shamyl Basayev, informed the Russian television network NTV that four cases of radioactive caesium had been hidden around Moscow. Basayev had repeatedly threatened to attack Moscow with nuclear or chemical weapons, and had already proved his ability to create 'terrorist spectaculars' by taking 1,500 people hostage in Budennovsk in June. Russian officials largely dismissed the nuclear threat, claiming that the material was caesium-137.[28] However, the truth about the material is less important than the credibility of the threat, as demonstrated by the precautions the Russian authorities took, sending emergency search teams out around the city with Geiger counters.[29] Basayev was intent on displaying capability and on ensuring that his threats to launch further attacks against Moscow unless Russia withdrew from Chechnya were taken seriously.[30] His warning was plausible because the state of the Russian nuclear industry made it impossible to rule out the possibility that the Chechens had indeed acquired dangerously radioactive material.

In 2000 there was a spate of letters sent to a range of Japanese government departments containing trace elements of monazite, which includes the radioactive element thorium. The letters were ostensibly to warn the government of a radioactive smuggling plot.[31]

In the wake of the September 11 attacks in the United States, it has also emerged that al-Qaeda may have sought the means to build a 'dirty bomb'.[32] Although there have been previous allegations relating to the organisation's attempts to acquire material to build a nuclear-yield bomb,[33] the claims over a radiological weapon represent a significant departure. British intelligence forces are currently investigating allegations, made by Bulgarian businessman Ivan Ivanov, that in April 2001 a middleman for bin Laden approached him, seeking to obtain radiological material. Ivanov allegedly had a series of meetings near the Pakistani border with Afghanistan, including one with bin Laden. He then met with a 'chemical engineer' near Rawalpindi, and was offered US$200,000 to help the scientist acquire spent nuclear fuel rods from the Kozlodui nuclear electricity plant in Bulgaria. The plan would have involved buying the rods legally, through a newly established environmental front company that would deal with nuclear waste. Ivanov declined the opportunity and reported the contact once he returned to Europe.[34]

Last year, customs officials seized ten lead-lined containers on the border between Uzbekistan and Kazakhstan. The containers held a substantial quantity of radioactive material, ostensibly intended for a company in Quetta, Pakistan. The precise type of materials remains unclear, but it seems unlikely to have been a legitimate shipment and it does seem possible that bin Laden's al-Qaeda was a potential end-user.[35] There must also be concerns that the main threat in this respect may not be leakage from the Former Soviet Union, but assistance to al-Qaeda from Pakistani sources. In October, two key former members of Pakistan's nuclear programme were detained as a result of their connections to the Taliban. Bashiruddin Mahmood was project director before Pakistan's 1998 tests and has since been running a relief organisation, Umma Tameer-I-Nau (UTN), sympathetic to the Afghan regime. Abdul Majid was a director of the Pakistan Atomic Energy Commission in 1999.[36] Allegedly, they planned to use finely milled uranium, obtained from Pakistan, around a core of explosives to create such a 'dirty bomb', delivered either as an artillery shell or a mortar round. However, there was no evidence that either Mahmood and Majid, or al-Qaeda more generally, had been able to acquire such radioactive material.[37]

Historically, relatively few groups have sought to cause a radiological release from a nuclear facility and such an attack provides an unlikely means of seeking to cause casualties. Where groups have actively sought to cause widespread casualties from their actions, they have attacked people directly. Crashing passenger-filled planes into the World Trade Center towers would certainly qualify as such an example. An attack on a reactor would be an indirect attack on people, one that sought to maximise the political, social and economic consequences of the attack without necessarily causing widespread casualties. Although the potential for inflicting such injuries is clearly present, the certainty is not. Any subsequent attack on nuclear facilities is therefore likely to continue this trend: its primary purpose will be to create terror and strike at an important symbolic target, rather than to cause casualties as such.

To date, threats against nuclear reactors can be readily divided into three motivations: those with an overtly anti-nuclear motivation; those that chose to attack a reactor because it was a high profile target; and those that chose a reactor because it was the most convenient target.

Anti-nuclear actions have been characterised by a preference for attacking property rather than people, a tendency common in single-issue terrorism. The majority of anti-nuclear campaigns are intrinsically demonstration actions, aimed at displaying the ineffective safety and security of nuclear installations and materials. Their purpose is to highlight the danger and interfere with the plant's operations. Consequently, such attacks are extremely unlikely to seek to threaten the integrity of the reactor, for fear of sparking the type of incident that anti-nuclear activists most fear. Groups whose primary motivation is environmental are also extremely unlikely to seek any results that would threaten the environment.[38]

Attacks in the second category, directed against a high profile target, have been motivated by both political and economic considerations. There are examples of incidents, both of attempts to extort financial gain from the threat and, alternatively, political gain.

As well as the greater opportunities for material diversion, the economic and political instability in the Former Soviet Union has also caused an increased threat of attacks on the nuclear facilities themselves. Since 1992, there have been at least six attacks or credible threats directed against reactors in the post-Soviet states. In the autumn of 1996, the Russian nuclear regulatory agency, Gosatomnadzor, received a warning that an armed group of Chechens was planning to target the Balakovo Nuclear Power Plant, a facility containing four VVER-1000 reactors.[39] The threat was credible though because, since 1991, the Chechens had consistently made threats against Russian nuclear facilities and, in March 1996 their field commanders allegedly agreed to launch a series of such assaults.[40]

Motivations for threats to reactors have also included economic objectives. On 4 November 1994, Kestutis Mazuika, a Lithuanian national in Sweden, threatened to destroy the facility at Ignalina unless a ransom of US$8 million was paid to a secret organisation (NUC-41 'W') which he claimed to represent.[41] Just a few days after the Mazuika incident, on 9 November, VATESI – the Lithuanian Nuclear Safety Inspectorate – was warned by the German Federal Ministry for Environment, Nature Conservation and Nuclear Safety of a further threat against the Ignalina installation. Georgy Dekanidze, a local mafia boss, threatened to destroy the plant if his son was sentenced to death for the contract murder he was then on trial for. However, no indication of sabotage was uncovered. Boris Dekanidze was sentenced to death on 10 November and his father denied all knowledge of the threat against Ignalina.[42] The threat caused the Ignalina to be shut down for three days and cost US$10 million, while the reactors were thoroughly inspected for possible sabotage.[43]

Nuclear Weapons

The most credible attempts by terrorist organisations to acquire nuclear weapons have been by Aum Shinrikyo and al-Qaeda. Both pursued a concerted multinational campaign to do so and both were apparently unsuccessful. Aum's mining of uranium in Australia and the plan to enrich that material have been discussed already, but the cult initially sought to acquire an intact weapon from the former Soviet Union. It attempted also to purchase dual-use equipment in the US and actively recruited employees of Russia's premier nuclear research facility, the I.V. Kurchatov Institute[44] and physicists from Moscow State University, to join the cult. In 1993 they sought, but were denied, a meeting with Russian Energy Minister Viktor Mikhailov to discuss the purchase of a nuclear warhead.[45] Aum failed to acquire a nuclear bomb, although it is possible that they negotiated with intermediaries for such a purchase, suggested by numerous entries, citing prices, in the diary of Kiyohide Hayakawa who made several trips to Russia on weapons-buying expeditions.[46] The cult also developed links with Russia's military, political and scientific elite. During 1992 and 1993, they also approached Russian scientists for help with both their laser and nuclear programmes.[47]

Similarly, Osama bin Laden purportedly went to contacts in the Former Soviet Union to attempt to acquire a nuclear weapon, although his contacts were in the Ukraine[48] and the Central Asian Republics. Israeli military intelligence claims that he paid around UK£2 million to an intermediary in Kazakhstan, believing that because of its substantial Muslim population, he had a better likelihood of acquiring a weapon there. The 1998 US federal indictment claims that 'at various times from at least as early as 1993, Osama bin Laden and others known and unknown, made efforts to obtain the components of nuclear weapons'.[49]

Like Aum, bin Laden's group also appears to have sought to build a nuclear-yield weapon.[50] In 1993, bin Laden's deputy, Mamdouh Mahmud

Salim, approved the attempted purchase of enriched uranium 'for the purpose of developing nuclear weapons', according to the criminal complaint lodged against Salim on 25 September 1998, although it is unclear whether the group succeeded in buying any nuclear material.[51] It appears that, as with several other prospective buyers of nuclear materials, al-Qaeda became the object of a fraudulent scheme to supply them with useless nuclear material that the vendors would claim was weapons-usable. In the case of al-Qaeda, the offered 'red mercury' turned out to be radioactive rubbish. They were also offered 'enriched uranium' that was really low-grade reactor fuel, unusable in a nuclear-yield weapon without extensive further enrichment.[52] This failure to acquire useful nuclear material is likely to have been a critical factor in al-Qaeda's increased short-term focus on chemical means as their weapon of choice.

In February 2001, Jamal Ahmed Fadl testified in the trial of the 1998 African Embassy bombers that al-Qaeda was trying to acquire nuclear material from the early 1990s onwards. Fadl said that a bin Laden lieutenant ordered him to buy uranium from a former Sudanese army officer, who offered to sell ore from South Africa for US$1.5 million. Fadl was unsure whether the material was authentic, although it was shipped to Afghanistan.[53] In November 2001, bin Laden told a Pakistani journalist from the Urdu-language *Ausaf* paper that his movement already had chemical and nuclear weapons. He stated 'I wish to declare that if America used chemical or nuclear weapons against us, then we may retort with chemical and nuclear weapons ... we have the weapons as a deterrent'.[54]

The discoveries after September 11 very clearly show, however, that al-Qaeda has continued to prioritise nuclear and radiological weapons and, it now appears, may be closer to the latter than to any other type of CBRN weapon. In August 2001, an Arab delegation met scientists from Kabul University and offered them financial assistance in exchange for help and advice in locating and mining uranium within Afghanistan.[55] Although al-Qaeda appears to have gained some material, usable in a nuclear-yield device, both the British and US governments believe that the organisation is incapable of producing such a weapon at present. However, they believe that al-Qaeda may have experimented with crude chemical weapons in Afghanistan.[56] In November, President Bush asserted that al-Qaeda continued to seek chemical, biological and nuclear weapons.[57]

Al-Qaeda's agents are thought to have spent over UK£1 million in the search for enough material from which to build a radiological weapon.[58] US intelligence reports noted a meeting in which an associate of bin Laden's wielded a canister allegedly containing radioactive material that could be disseminated with a conventional explosive. However, conclusive evidence that al-Qaeda has a radiological capability remains elusive. Although diagrams and documents relating to radiological weapons were found in facilities abandoned by al-Qaeda in Afghanistan, these were of a type readily available via the Internet and were apparently of an extremely poor quality that would be unlikely to work.[59] Likewise, detailed plans for a nuclear-yield device were discovered in one of the Kabul buildings abandoned by al-Qaeda. Written in Arabic, German, Urdu and English, the documents contained descriptions of how to use TNT to compress a sphere of plutonium into a critical mass, sparking a chain reaction.[60] However, these documents, although clearly showing an interest in nuclear-yield weapons, also contain information that is readily available in the open literature. The theory of such a weapon design is well known, yet the practical application of that information is more difficult, even assuming that the group could acquire the requisite quantity of fissile material.

Al-Qaeda and Aum Shinrikyo are by no means the only terrorist organisations to seek, or claim they possessed, nuclear weapons. Of the incidents that involve weapons, rather than simply nuclear material, the overwhelming majority have been hoaxes. The US Department of Energy's Nuclear Emergency Search Team has dealt with hundreds of such hoaxes in the thirty years since its creation. An example in the United States is the report of 'a nuclear bomb in a black briefcase' in Lompac, California in March 2000.[61] Other threats have been more serious: in 1974, 'Captain Midnight' attempted to extort money by threatening to detonate a nuclear device in Boston;[62] and in 1978, three men were arrested for attempting to steal a United States nuclear attack submarine, complete with weapons, and sell it to an organised crime syndicate.[63] Similar incidents, requiring action, have occurred beyond the United States. In January 1977, the Red Army Faction may have attacked a US army base in Germany with the intention of acquiring nuclear weapons.[64] More recently, in September 1993, reports appeared in the Russian press that several SS-20 missiles, with warheads, had appeared in a Chechen military parade in Grozny;[65] and in 1999 the Russian press reported that two individuals accused of threatening to carry out a nuclear strike against some twenty countries had been arrested. The pair had made their threats to force the payment of wages and to retaliate for the humiliation of the Russian military.[66] However, aside from plans to acquire nuclear weapons and hoaxes, threatening the use of such weapons, very few incidents have occurred that involve such weapons, certainly compared to chemical, biological or even radiological weapons.

Chemical and Biological Weapons

Chemical and biological weapons are not synonymous with weapons of mass destruction. The Database of Incidents Involving Chemical, Biological,

Radiological, or Nuclear (CBRN) Materials, 1900-Present at the Center for Non-proliferation Studies, lists around 680 incidents perpetrated between 1900 and 2002. Of those, only around half were classified as having been perpetrated by groups or individuals with political or ideological motivations (ideological being taken to include religious motivations), and which could thus be considered sub-state terrorism. The rest consist of criminally motivated acts for economic gain, or were judged to be false (apocryphal) cases. However, of these, the overwhelming majority of incidents are important not because they represent a significant threat, but rather because they show a growing interest in non-conventional weaponry amongst such groups and individuals. Of the incidents listed between 1995 and 2000, a third were hoaxes and pranks and many others involved the attempted acquisition of such weapons, so the number of incidents that genuinely involve CBRN weapons is significantly smaller than might initially appear.[67]

In 1999, 65 incidents involved the use or possession of an agent, and 113 incidents in 2000 involved the use or possession of an agent.[68] Of these, most incidents resulted in zero or very few fatalities and were intended to achieve such results. This is in large part due to the agents involved, the majority of which were non-warfare 'household' agents. In 1999 and 2000, these included agents such as acid, pepper spray, chlorine, insecticide or pesticides, and rat poison. A few incidents did involve military-grade agents such as ricin, capable of causing an extensive number of casualties. However, where an agent was used, it was likely to be a low-end or household agent. In 1999, for example, over half of the incidents of agent use involved tear gas. Although this cannot be considered a household agent, it is unlikely to cause fatalities and is certainly at the low end of the scale compared to anthrax, ricin or sarin, for example. Other uses of agents involved non-specific 'poisons' or cyanide, for example, neither of which should be regarded as 'high end'.[69] By contrast, the sole case involving ricin was an example of a threat with possession, rather than a use, of the agent. James Kenneth Gluck threatened to poison two Colorado judges using ricin. He was arrested in November 1999 and the raw materials for ricin were seized from his home in Florida.[70] The sole incident involving anthrax that was not a hoax was an example of alleged but unconfirmed possession of the bacteria. In April 2000, the Dagestani Interior Ministry stated that the Russian Special Services believed Chechen rebels possessed four containers of biological agent, presumed to be anthrax.[71]

The attempt, or even the threat, to cause widespread casualties using non-conventional weapons is unusual. For example, groups such as Dahm Y'Israel Nokeam (DIN or 'Avenging Israel's Blood') who, in 1946, contemplated killing nearly two million Germans by poisoning the water supplies of four major cities in revenge for the Holocaust are the exception rather than the rule. DIN did not carry out this attack, but rather a much smaller one.[72] If fatalities are the key factor in defining an incident as mass destructive, then we have yet to see a clear-cut example involving non-conventional weapons. The exception might be the case of DIN, who used an arsenic-based agent to poison the bread of thousands of German prisoners-of-war in April 1946, and may have killed hundreds.[73] If injuries are included in the equation, then Aum's attack on 20 March 1995, with estimates of injured people ranging up to 5,500, ranks as the most significant terrorist use of non-conventional weapons. In any case, as a possible indicator of future terrorist actions, Aum's action is widely regarded as the most important incident of this type. Other significant incidents involving chemical or biological agents include the Rajneeshees, a religious cult that used salmonella to contaminate salad bars in Oregon in 1984, with the intention of influencing a local election. In the process, the group made 751 ill.[74] The Covenant, the Sword, and the Arm of the Lord (CSA) a US group influenced by Christian Identity beliefs in the mid-1980s, acquired a barrel of potassium cyanide, a toxin with widespread industrial uses, with the intention of poisoning US urban water supplies to further the group's ideological and religious objectives. However, the CSA compound was surrounded and the group's members detained by the Federal Bureau of Investigation (FBI) before such an attack could occur.[75] RISE, like Aum Shinrikyo, had an existential purpose behind its members' scheme to destroy much of the human race. It was a group influenced by a radical and ecoterrorist ideology. In the early 1970s, it planned to kill off most of humanity to save the environment, using biological weapons delivered in an aerosol and by contaminating water supplies. However, the group aborted the attack when the microbial cultures were discovered.[76] Both the Kurdistan Workers Party (PKK) and Liberation Tigers of Tamil Eelam (LTTE) are alleged to have used chemical weapons on at least one occasion. It is important to note that in each case the use of non-conventional weapons was for a small-scale tactical attack, not to attempt an act of mass-destructive terrorism. On 28 March 1992, the PKK poisoned three water tanks of a Turkish air force base outside Istanbul. The water was foamy, later found to contain with cyanide. The tanks contained 50 mg of cyanide per litre, a lethal dose.[77] On 27 August 1996, detectives discovered a container of sarin and twenty containers of mustard gas in Istanbul. Emin Ekinci, a member of the PKK, was arrested for having the agents in his possession.[78] The group is also alleged to have used chemical grenades in an attack on Ormancik, a village in southeastern Turkey on 21 January 1994.[79] The LTTE have also resorted to non-conventional weapons. On 18 June 1990, the Sri Lankan Army reported that the group had attacked a Sri Lankan Army encampment with canisters filled with an unidentified poison gas, later identified as chlorine.[80] Allegedly, the group has perpetrated several other similar attacks. On 24 November

1995, Tamil rebels supposedly used poison gas during a siege of a Sri Lankan base where Tamil rebels were being held prisoner. On 26 November 1995, there was an attack by the Tamil rebels, allegedly using poison gas, on advancing Sri Lankan forces outside of Jaffna.[81] The Tamil Tigers also apparently attacked a police station with poison gas on 20 July 1995.[82]

Al-Qaeda appears to have attempted both to acquire chemical and biological weapons and to manufacture their own. The Paris-based Arabic paper *Al-Watan al-Arabi* suggested that bin Laden had had contact with Qusay, Saddam Hussein's younger son, and that Iraq was cooperating with al-Qaeda's efforts to acquire both chemical and biological weapons.[83] In 1997, the same newspaper claimed that the leader of the Sudanese government, Hasan al-Turabi, organised a meeting attended by bin Laden, amongst others, at which funding for a biological weapons facility was discussed.[84] The evidence for this remains tenuous: following the US attack on the al-Shifa plant in Khartoum, the British Defence Secretary, George Robertson, claimed that the British had independent evidence – based on intelligence – that bin Laden had sought to acquire both chemical and biological weapons.[85]

However, in March 1999, the London-based paper *Al-Sharq al-Awsat* revealed that associates of bin Laden, on trial in Egypt as part of the 'Albanian Arabs' case, had allegedly been offered anthrax and other biological agents from a factory in East Asia for US$3,695 plus freight charges.[86] They also supposedly received an offer from a laboratory in the Czech Republic to supply a deadly gas (possibly botulinum, although that is unlikely to be in a gaseous form) for US$7,500 per sample.[87] Ahmad Salama Mabrouk, a member of al-Jihad, the group to which the defendants belonged and part of bin Laden's coalition of organisations, gave an interview to the London paper *al-Hayat*. In it, Mabrouk claimed that over the past two years, the group had acquired chemical and biological agents from Eastern Europe and the former Soviet Union, and that al-Jihad planned to use them against US and Israeli targets.[88] Although the specific claims have been unverifiable, their general point was supported in June 1999 by anonymous US intelligence sources that told ABC News that 'there is mounting evidence that bin Laden's network has acquired ingredients for chemical or biological weapons through countries that were once part of the Soviet Union'. The same sources further claimed that bin Laden had set up two crude weapons laboratories in Afghanistan, one near Khoust and the other near Jalalabad.[89]

In the aftermath of September 11, it has become increasingly obvious that al-Qaeda's interest in CBRN weaponry has persisted. Amongst the finds have been: material relating to chemical, biological and nuclear weapons from the Tarnak Farms site near Kandahar; information on the dispersal of anthrax in a UTN house in Kabul; information on producing ricin in another house in Kabul; and the discovery of an al-Qaeda volume, distributed on CD-Rom, that contained chapters detailing the production methods for a range of chemical agents and the biological agents botulinum and ricin.[90] The organisation had a series of laboratories in Afghanistan, dedicated to the development of chemical and biological weapons. These used equipment that had been purchased abroad and then shipped to Afghanistan from countries such as the United Arab Emirates and Ukraine.[91] The organisation appears also to have sought the help of scientists within Afghanistan to promote its pursuit of such weapons. Delegations of Pakistani scientists visited Kabul University six times from 1998, offering to provide funding for chemical weapons-related research and asking for help to obtain large quantities of sodium cyanide and thionyl chloride, both dual-use chemicals, but capable of being used to create crude chemical weapons. Thionyl chloride is a possible precursor for mustard gas and several nerve agents and sodium cyanide is usable in the formation of a cyanide weapon.[92] Although al-Qaeda's interest in chemical and biological weapons is clear, the group's success in acquiring such agents is far less so. There have been some unverified finds, such as the supposed discovery of thirty boxes, each containing ten phials of a colourless liquid, with Sarin/V-Gas marked in Cyrillic lettering on the side of each box.

More ominously, groups linked to al-Qaeda and operating in Europe appear to have been plotting to use chemical or biological weapons in their attacks. In December 2000, German police broke up an alleged plot by the Salafist Group for Preaching and Combat (GSPC), an Algerian-based group operating in Europe and associated with al-Qaeda. It supposedly planned to attack the European Parliament in Strasbourg with sarin. In 2001, an Italian-based cell planned to launch an attack in France, before being interdicted by the Italian security services. For this attack, they discussed using 'a suffocating gas' although precise plans for the attack, including its location were never clarified. One possibility was Notre Dame in Paris, as the group discussed 'La Dame' as a potential target. The surveillance tapes made by the Italian security services reveal the cell's leader, 'Sabre', explaining his desire to acquire chemical weapons because plastic explosives are outmoded and gas is more effective because 'It's a liquid. As soon as it's opened, people suffocate'. However, it is also obvious that the cell has made little progress towards acquiring such a weapon: 'Sabre' tells other members that he needs a formula for the poison gas that has been developed by a Libyan chemistry professor.[93] Although there is an increased interest in chemical and biological weapons by al-Qaeda and associated groups, as shown by the finds in Afghanistan and the plots to attack targets in Europe, there appears still a major disconnection between the current position and an immediate threat. The evidence listed above suggests interest in such agents and plots for the possible use of CBRN, but offers little new evidence of a credible capability. The gap between desire and capability is a crucial one. Although it would be unwise to dismiss the concept that a well-organised, well-funded, and well-connected group, such as al-Qaeda, could successfully acquire chemical and biological weapons and keep the fact hidden, especially given the diffuse global nature of the group, nevertheless, the open source evidence revealed in the past six months does no more than indicate an interest in – and desire to acquire – such weapons, something that governments and analysts have known for several years.

THE IMPACT OF SEPTEMBER 11

This, then, was the situation on 10 September 2001. Despite the attempts to acquire CBRN weapons by groups such as Aum Shinrikyo and al-Qaeda, and the use of such weapons by several groups, no terrorist organisation had perpetrated a high casualty incident using CBRN weapons. When terrorist groups had sought to cause high levels of casualties, they did so using conventional weapons, such as explosives. The overwhelming majority of incidents involving CBRN materials were hoaxes or threats, particularly in the United States since 1998, and the instances of use of an agent tended to be examples of 'low end' or household products. It was questionable whether such uses had anything significant to do with terrorist use of CBRN weapons for high casualty events, except for maintaining the issue of CBRN terrorism in the forefront of public, media, academic and governmental awareness. The threat from high-end CBRN terrorism arose because groups, such as al-Qaeda, continued to seek such weapons which remained, at the very least, theoretically available to a well-financed and connected organisation, one that would likely be willing to use such weapons to cause high levels of casualties.

What changed on September 11? The attacks revealed al-Qaeda's organisational ability and the willingness of the group to commit attacks that resulted in thousands of casualties. In that respect, the attacks of September 11 were unprecedented, causing numbers of casualties that exceeded any previous terrorist attack by several orders of magnitude. However, al-Qaeda committed these attacks using conventional weapons, albeit in an unusual and highly innovative way, and the political and social effect of the attacks could scarcely have been greater if the group had used a CBRN weapon. On the other hand though, the group's attack raises the issue of whether other like-minded organisations could create the same effect without resorting to CBRN weapons. Assuming that an exact replication of al-Qaeda's attacks is not possible, hopefully because airline security has improved to preclude it for one, are there other ways a group could inflict similar levels of casualties or destruction? The answer is almost certainly that a destruction of a highly populated skyscraper, by whatever means, could have a similar effect in terms of casualties, but it is difficult to imagine many targets that would also be such a visible and overt strike against a country's prestige. The attacks had many effects and a variety of motivations but one of these was certainly symbolic: to strike the United States at its military and economic centres, in full view of the world's media. The attacks of September 11, against the Pentagon, but more particularly against the World Trade Center, have undoubtedly raised the bar for future terrorism. However, terrorism and attacks by terrorist organisations cannot be viewed as a linear process. The most obvious example of this is the aftermath of Aum Shinrikyo's sarin attack in Tokyo in 1995. Although not the first use of a chemical or biological weapon by a terrorist group, Aum's attack seemed different, using a high-end agent to cause indiscriminate casualties. Most analysts and those charged with countering terrorism assumed that Aum's attacker represented a harbinger of the future that other, increasingly lethal, attacks with CBRN weapons would follow and that terrorism was on an escalatory spiral. Such assessments were not supported by the experience of the following years: there was no wave of similar attempts. In spite of the increased knowledge of CBRN weapons and availability of weapons-usable technologies from a range of sources including the former Soviet Union, we did not see anything.

Moreover, in many countries heightened fear of attacks using these weapons increased the coercive power available for any terrorist group willing and able to make a convincing threat to use CBRN weapons. Al-Qaeda's attacks of September 11, far from being reliant on CBRN weapons, used a technological conservative weapon, dependent on variants of familiar tactics – hijacking and vehicle bombing – to cause carnage. Although al-Qaeda was undoubtedly interested in a range of CBRN weapons, and clearly investigated each for their potential value in committing an attack, ultimately the organisation chose a different route from the one implied by Aum's 1995 attack. The precise reason for this tactical choice is not currently certain, but it seems likely that al-Qaeda decided to use methods that its leaders believed had the best chance of success. Although CBRN weapons have supposedly grown increasingly accessible in the past ten years, there remain substantial technical difficulties in acquiring, weaponising and delivering an effective CBRN weapon. Although the wealth, resources and contacts of an organisation such as al-Qaeda would undoubtedly have helped to reduce such difficulties, the example of Aum Shinrikyo, also wealthy and well connected, but unable to deliver a successful attack with chemical or biological weapons, shows that such problems still exist. Al-Qaeda therefore, appears to have chosen a method that, as well as being cheaper and technologically less sophisticated, also had a better probability of causing mass casualties than an attack using CBRN weapons.

Shortly after the attacks of September 11, the United States was confronted by a second, equally disturbing set of incidents: the posting through the US mail of a series of letters containing anthrax. In these attacks, five people died from anthrax inhalation and eighteen people were infected.[94] Despite initial fears, it now appears that al-Qaeda was uninvolved with this wave of attacks, a fact supported by bin Laden himself.[95] Although there have been hundreds of incidents in the United States since 1998 involving threats or hoaxes of packages containing anthrax, the attacks of the autumn were significant because the letters genuinely did contain the pathogen. More worrisome still, the anthrax had been milled to a fine powder and processed with chemical additives to make them more readily airborne and inhaled into the lungs of victims. This suggests that the perpetrators had access to specialised knowledge and technology relating to the weaponisation of anthrax. It seems possible that the perpetrators may have acquired a small quantity of the powder on the black market. This is partially supported by early indications that the powder may have originated from a legitimate US laboratory in Iowa, where a similar strain was used for defensive research purposes. However, a more worrying alternative is that the perpetrators, who remain unidentified, have developed the means of manufacturing high-quality anthrax as a dried powder and could therefore launch further, possibly more widespread or effectively delivered attacks that endanger thousands of people. Yet another alternative, equally worrying, is that the perpetrators had state-sponsorship. This is suggested by the physical characteristics of the anthrax which have, to date, been replicated only in the sophisticated biological weapons programmes of states. Nonetheless, beyond that circumstantial evidence, there is no further indication of state involvement in the anthrax attacks.[96]

Although these attacks were small-scale, and certainly not intended to cause mass casualties, they were indicative of an extremely troubling potential for further action. The letters accompanying the anthrax warned that an attack had occurred and stated the agent involved.[97] The primary intention of the attacks was therefore clearly to cause fear and disruption, an objective in which they were successful. Moreover, the attacks had a significant economic and especially psychological impact on US society. It is this that may encourage further, unrelated groups to identify small, but genuine, uses of biological agents as the best means of attaining their goals. The attacks were especially effective psychologically, coming as they did so soon after the immensely traumatic attacks of September 11 and the possibility of further high-casualty terrorism. Moreover, the letters affected not only the intended recipient, but in some cases, a researcher responsible for opening mail or a postal worker who simply handled the letter in transit. Therefore, the number of people who might have been exposed to anthrax was much higher than might have been expected from such a crude form of weapon delivery. The disruption was increased because the heightened public fears increased the number of false alarms of further anthrax attacks. By mid-October, the FBI and other agencies had had to respond to 2,300 scares, the vast majority of which were either practical jokes or legitimate mistakes over 'suspicious' packages. The false alarms cost millions of dollars and huge amounts of investigative time, as each had to be thoroughly checked and then examined.[98]

However, without knowing the identity of the perpetrator or their specific motivation or objective, it is difficult to come to meaningful conclusions about the purpose of the letters containing anthrax. It is clear that the perpetrator exploited the widespread publicity from and fear of future incidents of bioterrorism within the United States. This has been a major subject of discussion in media, academic, and government circles since the mid-1990s, and has been widely identified as vulnerability within the country. As a result partly of Larry Wayne Harris's arrest in 1998 for suspected anthrax possession (he had only a harmless vaccine strain of anthrax), and partly of the subsequent hundreds of hoaxes, alleging anthrax possession or use, the American public's fear of bioterrorism was highlighted, as was the chaos each threat caused and the struggle the authorities had in dealing with such threats.

CONCLUSION

The likelihood of terrorist use of CBRN weapons in the wake of September 11 remains extremely uncertain. The scale of the attacks suggests that mass destructive terrorism is now a fact and it thus seems unlikely that, given the option, al-Qaeda would avoid using CBRN weapons to cause mass casualties. However, although discoveries in Afghanistan and the disruption of plots in Europe continue to show that al-Qaeda and its associated groups are interested in CBRN weapons, these discoveries do not indicate that the organisation has successfully acquired such weapons. Moreover, the evidence clearly shows that al-Qaeda has simply been trying to develop any type of weapon that might help its cause. The suggestion, therefore, would be that CBRN weapons are being pursued simply as part of a range of options, for instrumental purposes, rather than as an end in itself. The attacks of September 11 show that CBRN weapons are not necessary to cause mass casualties. Given the difficulty and expense of acquiring and effectively using such weapons, al-Qaeda may continue to seek CBRN weapons, but likely not to rely on doing so successfully. The attacks of September 11, and the subsequent discoveries, suggest a group that is pragmatic and has an instrumental approach to CBRN acquisition.

The implications of September 11 for other groups seeking CBRN weapons remain to be seen. Clearly, the level of fear and awareness of potential attacks with such weapons has risen to unprecedented levels. However, this does not necessarily equate to an increased likelihood of CBRN weapons being used by sub-state actors, except for disruptive purposes. The numbers of false incidents or hoaxes using anthrax in the United States reflect that. The attacks of September 11 raised the bar for terrorist violence, but also showed that innovative use of conventional weapons can achieve this purpose.

NOTES

1. Falkenrath, Richard, Newman, Robert and Thayer, Bradley (1998), *America's Achilles Heel: Nuclear' Biological and Chemical Terrorism and Covert Attack*, Cambridge: The MIT Press, p 47.
2. The initial number of injured, and the standard figure since, has been 5,500. It is worth noting though that the majority of the casualties were self-reported. Fred Sidell, a member of the US medical team that attended the casualties from the 20 March attack, reported that the group was told that there had been 5,510 casualties. Of these, twelve were fatalities, seventeen people were critically injured, thirty-seven severely, and 984 moderately. This leaves over 4,000 casualties who reported to medical facilities who appeared to have nothing wrong with them. Whether these 4,000 are counted as casualties depends on whether one is assessing the actual injuries caused by the attack or the impact of the attack both psychologically and in terms of the need for healthcare provision. See Sidell, Fred (1995), 'U.S. Medical Team Briefing', *Proceedings of the Seminar on Responding to the Consequences of Chemical and Biological Terrorism*, Sponsored by the U.S. Public Health Service, Office of Emergency Preparedness, Conducted at The Uniformed Services University of Health Sciences, Bethesda, 11–14 July, pp 2–32–2–33.
3. Cameron, Gavin (2000), 'WMD Terrorism in the United States: An Assessment of the Threat & Possible Countermeasures', *The Nonproliferation Review*, 7/1, Spring, pp 162–79.
4. Utley, Garrick (1997), 'The Shrinking of Foreign News; from Broadcast to Narrowcast', *Foreign Affairs*, 76, March/April, pp 2–10.
5. Leitenberg, Milton (1999), 'Aum Shinrikyo's efforts to produce biological weapons: A Case study in the serial propagation of misinformation', *Terrorism & Political Violence*, Special Edition – The Future of Terrorism, 11/4, Winter, pp 149–58.
6. Tucker, Jonathan (2001), 'The Proliferation of Chemical and Biological Weapons Materials and Technologies to State and Sub-State Actors', Testimony before the Subcommittee on International Security, Proliferation and Federal Services of the US Senate Committee on Governmental Affairs, 7 November.
7. *Ibid.*
8. Tucker, Jonathan and Pate, Jason (2000), 'The Minnesota Patriots Council', in Tucker, Jonathan (ed.), *Toxic Terror: Assessing Terrorist Use of Chemical and Biological Weapons*, Cambridge: MIT Press, pp 159–84.
9. It is worth noting though that the idiosyncratic nature and dynamics of the cult also played a role in this failure. See: Cameron, Gavin (1999), 'Multi-track Micro-proliferation: Lessons from Aum Shinrikyo and al-Qaeda', *Studies in Conflict & Terrorism*, 22/4, October–December, pp 277–309.

10. Guest, Robert (1995), 'Cult Germ was Claim as Police Find Bacteria', *Daily Telegraph*, 29 March, p 13; *Mainichi Daily News* (1995), 'Bacteria used in germ warfare found at cult site', 29 March; *Kyodo* (1995), 'Aum bought experimental cells before subway gas attack', 18 May.

11. Tucker (2001), 'The Proliferation of Chemical and Biological Weapons Materials and Technologies to State and Sub-State Actors'.

12. Rufford, Nicholas, Leppard, David, and Eddy, Paul (2001), 'Crashed plane's target may have been reactor', *Sunday Times*, 21 October, p A9.

13. Henderson, Mark (2001), 'Nuclear reactors vulnerable to attack', *The Times*, 24 September, p 4.

14. Pollack, Gerald (1987), 'Severe Accidents and Terrorist Threats at Nuclear Facilities', in Alexander, Yonah and Leventhal, Paul (eds), *Preventing Nuclear Terrorism: The Report and Papers of the International Task Force on Prevention of Nuclear Terrorism*, Lexington: Lexington Books, pp 66–72.

15. Mullen, Robert K. (1987), 'Nuclear Violence', in Alexander and Leventhal (eds), *Preventing Nuclear Terrorism*, p 240.

16. Edwards, Rob (2001), 'The nightmare scenario', *New Scientist*, 172/2312, 13 October, p 10.

17. Mullen (1987), 'Nuclear Violence', in Alexander and Leventhal (eds), *Preventing Nuclear Terrorism*, pp 241–2.

18. Freeh, Louis (1994), Testimony to US Congress, 103rd Congress 2nd Session, 'International Organized Crime and its Impact on the United States', US Senate Governmental Affairs Committee, Permanent Subcommittee On Investigations' Hearings Held 25 May, p 62.

19. Edwards (2001), 'The nightmare scenario', p 10.

20. Henderson, Mark (2001), 'Terrorists could make atom bomb by raiding hospitals', *The Times*, 1 November.

21. Barnaby, Frank (1996), *Instruments of Terror*, London: Satin Books, pp 172–4.

22. Falkenrath et al. (1998), *America's Achilles Heel*, p 15.

23. Author interview with Leonard S. Spector, Deputy Director of the Monterey Institute of International Studies' Center for Nonproliferation Studies.

24. Cameron (1999), 'Multi-track Micro-proliferation: Lessons from Aum Shinrikyo and al-Qaeda', p 277.

25. Stern, Jessica (1999), *The Ultimate Terrorists*, Cambridge, MA: Harvard University Press, p 57.

26. Cameron, Gavin (1999), *Nuclear Terrorism: A Threat Assessment for the 21st Century*, Basingstoke: Macmillan Press, pp 131–2.

27. Stern (1999), The Ultimate Terrorists, p 59.

28. Agence France Presse (1995), 23 November; Hibbs, Mark (1995), 'Chechen Separatists Take Credit For Moscow Caesium-137 Threat', *Nuclear Fuel*, 20/25, 5 December, p 5.

29. Reeves, Phil (1995), 'Moscow Tries to Play Down Radioactive Chechen Feat', *The Irish Times*, 25 November, p 11.

30. Orjollet, Stephane (1995), 'Nuke package raises fear of Chechen attacks – but how real are they?', Agence France Presse, 24 November.

31. Jiji Press (2000), 'Letters with Radioactive Substance Claim Japanese Person Selling Uranium to DPRK', 12 June; The Center for Nonproliferation Studies Database of Incidents Involving Sub-National Actors and Chemical, Biological, Radiological or Nuclear Materials.

32. Webster, Philip and Watson, Roland (2001), 'Bin Laden's Nuclear Threat', *The Times*, 26 October, p 1.

33. In September 1998, a deputy of bin Laden's, Mamdouh Mahmud Salim, was arrested in Germany, attempting to buy low-grade reactor fuel. He was supposedly the victim of a criminal sting operation, believing he was purchasing material more readily usable to build a nuclear yield weapon. According to US court documents, Jamal al-Fadl, a former associate of bin Laden's, told the FBI that a Sudanese intelligence officer had offered him

uranium for US$1 million. He also stated that other al-Qaeda associates had sought enriched uranium throughout the mid-1990s, for the same purpose, to build a nuclear yield weapon. See Cameron (1999), 'Multi-track Micro-proliferation: Lessons from Aum Shinrikyo and al-Qaeda', pp 287–9; McCloud, Kimberly and Osborne, Matthew, 'WMD & Usama Bin Laden'. Online. *Center for Non-proliferation Studies*. Available: http://cns.miis.edu/pubs/reports/binladen.htm. 13 October 2001.

34. Nathan, Adam and Leppard, David (2001), 'Al-Qaeda's men held secret meetings to build "dirty bomb"', *Sunday Times*, 14 October, p A5.
35. Pugliese, David (2001), 'Police suspect bin Laden making "dirty" nuclear bombs', *National Post*, 17 October.
36. Webster and Watson (2001), 'Bin Laden's Nuclear Threat', p 1; *The Times* (2001), 'Nuclear networks: the need for action against bin Laden is sharper still', 26 October, p 21.
37. Fielding, Nick, Laurier, Joe and Walsh, Gareth (2002), 'Bin laden "almost had uranium bomb"', *Sunday Times*, 3 March, Section 1, p 13.
38. Hoffman, Bruce (1993), 'An Assessment of the Potential Terrorist Threat to Canadian Nuclear Power Plants', Ontario Court (General Division), 25 April, p 5.
39. Potter, William (1997), 'Less Well-Known Cases of Nuclear Terrorism and Nuclear Diversion in the former Soviet Union'. Online. *The Nuclear Threat Initiative*. Available: http://www.nti.org/db/nisprofs/over/nuccases.htm. 23 February 2003.
40. Shargorodsky, Sergei (1995), 'Security Tightened at Nuclear Power Plant after Threat', Associated Press, 1 July.
41. Potter (1997), 'Less Well-Known Cases of Nuclear Terrorism and Nuclear Diversion in the Former Soviet Union'; BBC Summary of World Broadcasts (1994), 'Man threatening to blow up nuclear power station arrested in Sweden', November 13.
42. Potter (1997), 'Less Well-Known Cases of Nuclear Terrorism and Nuclear Diversion in the Former Soviet Union'; Martin, Seamus (1994), 'Mafia threatens to bomb power station', *The Irish Times*, 14 November, p 15; BBC Summary of World Broadcasts (1994), 'Alleged terrorist denies plans to blow up Ignalina: bomb search fruitless', 16 November; Sains, Ariane (1994), 'Ignalina Sabotage Deadline Passes Without Blow-Up', *Nucleonics Week*, 17 November, pp 1–2.
43. Associated Press (1994), 'Lithuanian Nuclear Reactor Closed after Terrorist Threats', November 15. Thely, Benoit (1994), 'Suspect held as threat forces closure of Lithuanian reactor', Agence France Presse, 4 November; Reuters (1994), 'Lithuanian reactor shutdown costs $10 million', 16 November. Deutsche Presse-Agentur (1994), 'Lithuanian reactor complex back on stream after bomb scare', 17 November.
44. BBC Summary of World Broadcasts (1995), 'Russian nuclear staff said to have contacts with Japanese sect', 25 May.
45. Kaplan, David E. and Marshall, Andrew (1996), *The Cult at the End of the World: The Incredible Story of Aum*, London: *Arrow Books*, pp 112, 190–2, 208; Falkenrath et al. (1998), *America's Achilles Heel*, pp 20–22; Brackett, David (1996), *Holy Terror: Armageddon in Tokyo*, New York: Weatherhill Inc., pp 92–3.
46. Kaplan and Marshall (1996), *The Cult at the End of the World*, pp 191–2; Brackett (1996), *Holy Terror*, p 92.
47. Brackett (1996), *Holy Terror*, p 92.
48. Ukraine has strenuously denied any involvement with bin Laden or his organisation and noted that the last tactical nuclear weapons left the state in 1992. See: Vassylenko, Volodymyr (1998), 'Bin Laden's weapons', *The Times*, 2 November.
49. Goldman, John and Ostrow, Ronald (1998), 'U.S. Indicts Terror Suspect Bin Laden', *Los Angeles Times*, 5 November, p A1; *New York Times* (1998), 'U.S. Indictment: "Detonated an Explosive Device"', 5 November, p A8.
50. Although enriched uranium can be used in a Radiological Dispersal Device (RDD), other radioactive materials – such as caesium-137 or cobalt-60 – are more likely to be used in an RDD. Therefore, al-Qaeda's attempted acquisition of enriched uranium is more likely to be indicative of a desire to construct a nuclear-yield weapon.

51. Grunwald, Michael (1998), 'US Says Bin Laden Sought Nuclear Arms; Complaint Cites Alliance with Sudan, Iran', *The Washington Post*, 26 September, p A19; Weiser, Benjamin (1998), 'US Says Bin Laden Aide Tried to Get Nuclear Weapons', *New York Times*, 26 September, p A3.
52. Waller, Douglas (1998), 'Inside the Hunt for Osama', *Time*, 152/25, 20 December.
53. McGrory, Daniel (2001), 'Al-Qaeda's $1 million hunt for atomic weapons', *The Times*, 15 November.
54. Woodward, Bob, Kaiser, Robert and Ottaway, David (2001), 'US Fears Bin Laden Made Nuclear Strides: Concern Over "Dirty Bomb" Affects Security', *Washington Post*, 4 December, p A1; Farrell, Stephen (2001), 'Bin Laden makes nuclear threat', *The Times*, 10 November.
55. Walker, Tom, Grey, Stephen and Fielding, Nick (2001), 'Al-Qaeda's secrets: Bin Laden's camp reveal chemical weapon ambition', *The Sunday Times*, 25 November.
56. Hussain, Zahid (2001), 'Bin Laden met nuclear scientists from Pakistan', *The Times*, 4 November.
57. CNN (2001), 'Bush: Bin Laden seeking nuclear bomb', 6 November.
58. Lloyd, Anthony (2001), 'Bin Laden's nuclear secrets found', *The Times*, 15 November.
59. Woodward et al. (2001), 'US Fears Bin Laden Made Nuclear Strides: Concern Over "Dirty Bomb" Affects Security', p A1.
60. Lloyd (2001), 'Bin Laden's nuclear secrets found'.
61. *Ventura County Star* (2000), 'Nuclear bomb report traced to Oxnard man', 30 March, B2; Blake, Catherine (2000), 'Suspect in nuclear bomb threat held', *Los Angeles Times*, 30 March, B3; The Center for Nonproliferation Studies Database of Incidents Involving Sub-National Actors and Chemical, Biological, Radiological or Nuclear Materials.
62. The Center for Nonproliferation Studies Database of Incidents Involving Sub-National Actors and Chemical, Biological, Radiological or Nuclear Materials.
63. Babcock, Charles (1978), 'Suspects in plot may have thought mafia wanted sub', *Washington Post*, 6 October, p A12; *Washington Post* (1978), 'Around the Nation, Addenda', 20 October, p A7. Center for Nonproliferation Studies Database of Incidents Involving Sub-National Actors and Chemical, Biological, Radiological or Nuclear Materials.
64. Center for Nonproliferation Studies Database of Incidents Involving Sub-National Actors and Chemical, Biological, Radiological or Nuclear Materials.
65. Dudnik, Vladmir (1993), 'Does the Chechen Republic Possess SS-20 Missiles?', *Moscow News*, 17 September; Official Kremlin International News Broadcast (1994), 'Djokhar Dudaev Indirectly Confirms Presence of SS-20s in Chechnya', 21 January; The Center for Nonproliferation Studies Database of Incidents Involving Sub-National Actors and Chemical, Biological, Radiological or Nuclear Materials.
66. *Kommersant* (1999), 'Russian "Terrorists" to be Tried for Nuclear Threat', November 6; The Center for Nonproliferation Studies Database of Incidents Involving Sub-National Actors and Chemical, Biological, Radiological or Nuclear Materials.
67. Figures to March 2002. I appreciate the assistance of Jason Pate of the Center for Nonproliferation Studies in Monterey, California, for these numbers, based on the CNS Database of Incidents Involving Sub-National Actors & CBRN Materials.
68. Pate, Jason, Ackerman, Gary and McCloud, Kimberly (2002), '2000 WMD Terrorism Chronology: Incidents Involving Sub-National Actors and Chemical, Biological, Radiological, or Nuclear Materials'. Online. *The Monterey Institute of International Studies*. Available: http://cns.miis.edu/pubs/reports/cbrn2k.htm. 12 March 2002.
69. Cameron et al. (2000), 'A Chronology of Substate Incidents Involving CBRN Materials, 1999', pp 157–74.
70. *Ibid.*, pp 172–3.
71. Pate et al. (2002), '2000 WMD Terrorism Chronology: Incidents Involving Sub-National Actors and Chemical, Biological, Radiological, or Nuclear Materials'.
72. Bar-Zohar, Michael (1967), *The Avengers*, New York: Hawthorne Books, pp 40–52.

73. Bar-Zohar, *The Avengers'* pp 40–52; Falkenrath et al. (1998), *America's Achilles Heel*, pp 33–4n.
74. Carus, W. Seth (2000) 'The Rajneeshees', in Tucker (ed.) (2000), *Toxic Terror: Assessing Terrorist Use of Chemical and Biological Weapons*, pp 115–38.
75. Stern, Jessica Eve (2000), 'The Covenant, the Sword, and the Arm of the Lord', in Tucker (ed.) (2000), *Toxic Terror: Assessing Terrorist Use of Chemical and Biological Weapons*, pp 139–58.
76. Carus, W. Seth (2000), 'R.I.S.E.', in Tucker (ed.) (2000), Toxic Terror: Assessing Terrorist Use of Chemical and Biological Weapons, pp 55–70.
77. Reuters (1992), 'Turks report attempt to poison Air Force unit', 28 March; Chelyshev, Alexander (1992), 'Terrorists Poison Water in Turkish Army Cantonment', TASS, 29 March.
78. Hurriyet (1996), 'Sarin gas reportedly among mustard gas containers seized in Istanbul', 27 August, p 18, cited in BBC Summary of World Broadcasts, 30 August 1996.
79. Xinhua News Agency (1994), 'PKK rebels kill 16 people in south-eastern Turkey', 22 January; Ersanel, Nedret (1994), 'PKK's chemical arms depots', *Nokta* (Istanbul), 30 January, pp 8–9. This may be the same incident as that cited by Purver, in which a chemical attack on a village in eastern Turkey in January 1994 killed twenty-one. See Purver, Ron (1995), 'Chemical and Biological Terrorism: The Threat According to the Open Literature', Online. Canadian Security Intelligence Service. June. Available: http://www.csis-scrs.gc.ca/eng/miscdocs/tabintr_e.html. 19 December 2002.
80. Hoffman, Bruce (2000), 'The Debate Over Future Terrorist Use of Chemical, Biological, Nuclear and Radiological Weapons', in Roberts, Brad (ed.) *Hype or Reality: The 'New Terrorism' and Mass Casualty Attacks,* Alexandria, VA: The Chemical and Biological Arms Control Institute; Pringle, James (1990), 'Tamil rebels face all-out war launched by Colombo', *The Times*, 19 June; Xinhua News Agency (1990), 'Sri Lankan Tamil Tigers use poison gas against government troops, says senior officer', 18 June.
81. *Washington Post* (1995), 'Sri Lanka Charges Rebels Use Gas', 26 November, p A31.
82. RAND-St. Andrews Chronology of International Terrorism.
83. Alam-al-Din, Riyad (1999), 'Iraq, Bin Ladin Ties Examined', *Al-Watan al-'Arabi,* 1 January, pp 16–8.
84. Salim, Jilad (1997), 'Secrets of al-Manshiyah', *Al-Watan al-'Arabi*, 31 October, pp 22–4.
85. Clare, Sian and Morris, Lucie (1998), 'UK Defense Secretary Claims Evidence Against Bin-Laden', London Press Association, 23 August.
86. It is worth noting that there is an important difference between weapons and agents. Until they are weaponised, agents are obviously substantially less dangerous as effective arms. The point is emphasised by Ken Alibek, a former Soviet bio-weapons scientist, who observed that: 'The most virulent culture in a test tube is useless as an offensive weapon until it has been put through a process that gives it stability and predictability. The manufacturing technique is, in a sense, the real weapon, and it is harder to develop than individual agents.' Alibek, Ken with Handelman, Stephen (1999), *Biohazard*, New York: Random House, p 97.
87. Sharaf-al-Din, Khalid (1999), 'Bin-Ladin Men Reportedly Possess Biological Weapons', *Al-Sharaq al-Awsat*, 6 March.
88. Agence France Presse (1999), 'Egypte: le Jihad affirme détenir des armes chemiques', 19 April; Deutsche Presse-Agentur (1999), 'Egyptian militant says Bin Laden's group possess deadly weapons', 19 April; Agence France Presse (1999), 'Le Jihad a obtenu des armes chimiques et biologiques d'Europe de l'est', 20 April; Buccianti, Alexandre (1999), 'Des extremistes musulmans detiendraient des armes chimiques et bacteriologiques, selon un dirigeant islamiste', Agence France Presse, 21 April.
89. McWethy, John (1999), 'Bin Laden Set to Strike Again?' Online. ABC News, 16 June. Available: http://www.abcnews.go.com/onair/WorldNewsTonight/wnt990616_binladen.html. 18 June; CNN (1999), 'Bin Laden feared to be planning terrorist attack'. Online. Available: http://cnn.com/US/9906/16/bin.laden.plot/. 16 June 2003.

90. *The Economist* (2001), 'In the house of anthrax: Chilling evidence in the ruins of Kabul'. Online. November. Available: http://www.economist.com/world/asia/PrinterFriendly.cfm? StoryID=876941. 23 November 2001; CNN (2001), 'Evidence suggests al-Qaeda pursuit of biological, chemical weapons'. Online. 14 November. Available: http://www.cnn.com/ 2001/WORLD/asiapcf/central/11/14/chemical.bio/index.html. 15 November 2001; Lloyd, Anthony and Fletcher, Martin (2001), 'Bin Laden's poison manual', *The Times*, 16 November.

91. CNN (2001), 'Evidence suggests al-Qaeda pursuit of biological, chemical weapons'.

92. Walker et al (2001), 'Al-Qaeda's secrets: Bin Laden's camp reveals chemical weapon ambition'.

93. Bremner and McGrory (2001), 'Bin Laden Cell Plotted French Poison Attack', *The Times*, 30 November.

94. Ali, Javed (2001), 'No clear pattern emerging in anthrax investigation', CNN, 25 December.

95. Hussain, Zahid (2001), 'Bin Laden met nuclear scientists from Pakistan', *The Times*, 25 November.

96. Ali (2001), 'No clear pattern emerging in anthrax investigation'.

97. Pate, Jason (2001), 'Anthrax and Mass-Casualty Terrorism: What is the Bioterrorist Threat After September 11?', *US Foreign Policy Agenda*, November. Online. Available: http://usinfo.state.gov/journals/itps/1101/ijpe/pj63pate-2.htm, 5 March 2002.

98. Whitworth, Damien (2001), 'America paralysed by 2,300 anthrax scares', *The Times*, 17 October.

8. The Asymmetric Character of the Evolving Chemical, Biological and Nuclear (CBN) Threat

François Haut

INTRODUCTION

The events of September 11 2001 have relieved us of the need to sensitise the public to emerging terrorist threats or developing theories regarding terrorist aims and methods. One was able to see the live reality of world chaos, in that this chaos was immediately followed by the discovery of letters containing a small amount of anthrax, killing several persons and revealing another type of threat many people feared, even if its origin remains unknown.

If today's terrorism has been able to change its nature or origins, it is also able to change its tools, adapting itself to more sophisticated techniques, according to their availability in the new world disorder.

Most alarming of these upgrading capabilities of terrorism, and not improbable today, is the use of so-called weapons of mass destruction (WMD) – Chemical, Biological and Nuclear weapons (CBN). If the use of such weapons becomes standard, like hijacking, various questions arise: what are these weapons? What are the limits of their use? Would they really be used as mass destruction devices by terrorists?

Academic Rodney Stark gives us an interesting definition:

> [CBN] terrorism is the purposeful or threatened use of politically, socially, economically or religiously motivated violence via nuclear, biological, or chemical weapons conducted by a terrorist group, whereby the primary mechanism to influence the target is through the inducement of fear, anxiety, and/or destruction.[1]

We know that the CBN terrorist threat exists. It is by nature asymmetrical, even more so than 'classical' terrorism. So, we have to, now more than ever, try and understand this threat and clarify the new parameters it induces.

THE CBN TERRORIST THREAT

We will first analyse potential CBN risks. The CBN threat comes, at least, from two different sides. Firstly, conventional attacks, like bombings, could hit CBN 'targets'. Secondly, terrorists could use CBN 'weapons', as we have already witnessed.

Conventional Attacks on CBN Targets

Many of these targets are quite weak, even if their security has been significantly reinforced. One might remember the tragedy of Sevezo, Italy, in the 1970s. In 1984, the catastrophe at Bhopal, India, killed at least 2,500 following a problem that occurred in a pesticide factory. That same year in Mexico City, an explosion of liquid gas tanks killed 4,248.

Most memorably, the nuclear accident at Chernobyl in 1986 demonstrated the structural vulnerability of some reactors. Terrorism was not the cause of any of these accidents, but these events demonstrate that modern societies contain many vulnerable targets.

What occurred by accident yesterday could be deliberately wrought tomorrow. Let us remember that one hundred years ago, it was necessary to enter each house to plunge a village in the darkness. Nowadays, it is enough to destroy an electric generator.

In becoming ever more complex and sophisticated, our world is also more vulnerable to sabotage. To date, the terrorists' *modus operandi* has utilised predominantly conventional weapons. These weapons, such as explosives, could be used against nuclear facilities. According to Bruce Hoffmann,[2] conventional terror strategies could be deployed to create hostage situations, to blackmail, to steal nuclear material, or to destroy facilities and even to attempt to recreate a Chernobyl-type situation. The Oklahoma City bombing illustrates what a truck bomb attack is capable of in terms of damage.

These potentials are further exacerbated by the development of suicide operations. This can be seen as having been developed by the Liberation Tigers of Tamil Eelam (LTTE), later by Hamas in Palestine and most notably by al-Qaeda. This method is also increasingly associated with Muslim fundamentalists and involves not only poor and desperate people but also educated ones, accustomed to a western way of life. This type of attack is becoming ever more conceivable, with the sort of elevating effects that one can easily imagine.

CBN Weapons and Examples of Use

In the 1970s, a laboratory located in a safe house of the Red Army Faction in Paris was found to have made quantities of botulinum toxin. It is believed that none was used. The first confirmed case of use of chemical agents by terrorists is recent. In March 1995, several groups of the Aum sect spread, in the Tokyo subway, bags filled with gas sarin – a total of six or seven litres, approximately 30 percent pure. There were more than 5,500 injured and twelve deaths. When police carried out the systematic searching of the buildings of the sect, they found various biological agents and a great quantity of chemicals dedicated not just to the manufacture of sarin, but also of VX and mustard gas.

The effects of poisonous gas attacks in confined surroundings have been studied in many countries. In France, the Paris metro was the subject of a detailed analysis. It was revealed that it is impossible to dominate the flow of air circulating in the underground areas of the network. For example, if a terrorist released a radioactive substance using the ventilation system (easily accessible from the outside), or used an aerosol to spray a chemical or biological substance inside the network, the contamination would be very quick. The only answer would be to stop the trains immediately and evacuate all passengers.

Approximately twenty-five attempts to use biological or chemical lethal agents are publicly known. Individuals with the motivation of blackmail rather than serious political motives are mostly responsible. This figure is thus a minimum that does not take into account similar actions that have not been revealed. Of the known cases, the most disturbing are:

- In 1972, a member of the right-wing extremist Order of the Rising Sun was arrested in Chicago in possession of 35 to 40 kilograms of typhoid bacteria cultures with which he planned to contaminate water tanks of the city, St Louis and other major Midwestern towns.
- In 1976, letters were mysteriously sent to mayors of various American cities. The adhesive on their envelopes contained deadly germs.
- In 1983, a police unit in the US arrested two brothers in possession of about ten grams of lethal biological agents.
- In 1984, a sect deliberately contaminated salads in the restaurant of an Oregon village to influence the result of a local election. 751 people suffered salmonella poisoning.
- In 1984, a bulb containing a culture of tetanus was defrosted and sent through the mail in the suburbs of New York.
- In 1989, an American scientific team showed that a fly of Mediterranean origin whose larva develops in orchard fruits, had been

voluntarily introduced into various places of California. The mayor of Los Angeles and some newspapers received a letter in which a group claimed responsibility for this act to express its opposition to Californian husbandries.

- In 1994, the British Animal Liberation Front sent by the mail various envelopes containing the remains of syringes infected by HIV virus.
- In 1995, four members of the Minnesota Patriots Council: Douglas Baker, Richard Oeirich, Dennis Henderson and Leroy Wheeler, were convicted of conspiracy charges under the Biological Weapons Antiterrorism Act of 1989 for planning to use ricin against Federal Agents.
- Also in 1995, the police intercepted the planning of an attack using neurotoxic agents in Disneyland.
- In 1997, the British police arrested five Islamists associated with the Armed Islamic Group (GIA) in possession of the formula of sarin gas and various products used for its manufacture.
- In 1998, there were unsubstantiated threats of contamination by anthrax spores of items bought in Great Britain.
- The first example of nuclear terrorism in the post-Cold War era occurred in November 1995 when Chechen rebels placed a package of radioactive material in a Moscow park. Chechen separatists placed a box containing some thirty pounds of caesium-137[3] at the entrance of the park. The perpetrators omitted explosives that, if used to detonate the box, would have spread radioactive material throughout the park, contaminating the blast area for some time.

THE LIMITS OF TERRORIST CBN THREAT

Clearly there are limits to the CBN threat. Terrorists cannot use the CBN means in the same way that States can. Firstly, they need to acquire these weapons and secondly they may have technical difficulties in using them.

If some States do possess some sort of CBN arsenal, it's unlikely that they would share it with terrorist groups that they do not control. When coupled with the increasing reality that state-sponsored terrorism is almost non-existent, at least for large-scale action in the western world, this mode seems highly improbable.

However, lessons learned from Afghanistan show that some groups could try and manufacture some of these weapons. Biological warfare agents are, for the most part, inexpensive and readily obtainable, and 'cookbooks' are readily available. One such book is *Silent Death*, by an author who calls himself Uncle Fester. Other titles from the same publisher include *The*

Poisoner's Handbook and *Crimes Involving Poisons*. As noted earlier, nuclear devices are considerably more difficult to produce, even if some handbooks exist – such as the *Poor Man's Nuclear Bomb*.

Similarly, the theoretical effects allotted to CBN agents should not be extrapolated and over-exaggerated as existing stabilising factors do exist. Two key points are crucial in this regard: the spreading or dispersion method; and the purity and volatility of the products.

The small number of deaths in the Tokyo metro attack was due to the poor choice of dissemination method. There were only vapours of sarin and not pulverisation by means of an aerosol, which would have had much more lethal results. The rescue teams worked very quickly and the system of ventilation in the Tokyo subway is particularly efficient when compared with that in Paris. A similar attack on the Paris subway would have had far higher casualties, with many more deaths.

At the end of May 1998, during a lawsuit against one of the leaders of the Aum sect, it was learnt that a team from this organisation had begun in April 1990 a biological attack against various American military bases in Japan by propagating germs of botulinum. Whereas this product is one of the most lethal, nothing happened. The Aum sect made a new attempt in 1993 using anthrax. The results here too were disappointing. The method of dispersal of these products was undoubtedly ineffective.

The spreading of the manufactured agent is the most delicate stage. It can be carried out in several ways: contamination of food or liquids; dispersion by using aerosols or vapours in either a confined or open area; and also by using either small or powerful explosive loads. Many experts consider attacks in closed areas the most threatening: subway stations or covered stadiums for example. Government buildings, national monuments or hotels are similarly viewed as 'privileged targets'.

However, specialists disagree on the capability of terrorist groups to poison the population of a city through reservoirs of drinking water. Significant quantities of polluting agents would be needed, and there is no clearly defined ratio between volume of water in the reservoirs and consumption of drinkable water by the urban community. Moreover, most systems of water treatment are very efficient (filtration, chlorination and so on). Some of the water will never be in contact with the population and may remain in the reservoir for several months (which is enough to dilute some biochemical agents) – and/or will mainly have everyday uses such as the watering of lawns.

POTENTIAL CBN TACTICS

According to the factors listed above, what would a potential CBN terrorist strategy involve? The events of September 11 have taught us many lessons. For instance, al-Qaeda has revealed its essentially protoplasmic nature. In this, one can see that each group linked to this fuzzy entity has autonomy to decide the way it will fight the jihad according to a general guideline. This implies that we cannot work out a pattern of action with any degree of logic and predictability. This is unlike the Middle Eastern terrorism of the 1980s.

Today's terrorism has no central planning and locating an operational scheme would be guesswork, unless based on reliable intelligence sources. In other words, nothing clearly indicates that these terrorists would use CBN weapons. Nevertheless, in the anthrax attacks after September 11, even if we don't know the authors or the origins of the germs, we have witnessed the disconcerting effects of such distinctive action.

On the basis of former experiences, we have to be proactive and work out how some groups may use CBN weapons. Such terrorism is clearly a threat for our societies but it has technical limitations. Ultimately, it is unlikely at the current time that these sorts of attacks could really generate massive destruction. One can reasonably figure out, however, that terrorists would prefer to create a 'CBN Damocles effect' that would be more appropriate to these weapons.

THE ULTIMATE TERROR?

Arguing about a definition of terrorism is useless. From the perspective adopted here, it is a criminal activity aimed at generating a situation of fear among people, using small, asymmetrical means to achieve political goals.

The key issue is, of course, the 'situation of terror'. When a nation-state is the target, this situation of terror makes people frightened every morning. If it is a terrorist group using an invisible threat, people are afraid to live. Everything is on the vector of terror: the air one breathes; the food one eats; the water one drinks.

In March 1989, the most intensive food safety investigation in US Food and Drug Administration (FDA) history took place when a terrorist threatened to poison the fresh fruit supply to focus attention on the living conditions of the lower classes in Chile. The terrorist delivered on his phone call to the FDA, as two grapes were found laced with small amounts of cyanide.

Fortunately no one was poisoned, but the incident cost millions of dollars to investigate and had a significant impact on Chile's national economy, where fruit and vegetable exports are second in importance only to copper. A biological toxin could have been used just as easily as cyanide in this instance. The amounts of toxin needed to obtain the desired effect are exceedingly small. For example, about thirty grams of ricin, easily concealed anywhere, would be sufficient to lethally poison one batch of 150 pounds of meat, enough to produce 1,500 hot dogs. The threat is real and the knowledge required is not esoteric.

As with the attacks on the World Trade Center and the Pentagon, the 2001 anthrax strikes were conducted using simple, unconventional methods converting America's communications infrastructure into a delivery method for bioagents. A few mailed letters have resulted in several thousand false alarms and hoaxes tying up police, fire, medical and hazardous material teams. The anthrax scare caused an immense amount of panic among the populace, interfering with mail delivery and worrying both politicians and the military.

This type of action could easily be replicated in numerous places, with or without warning calls, with or without demands, causing some deaths, before stopping. This could be randomly repeated in different ways, different places, with different products. One can easily assume that there is no need for large amounts of CBN products or a mass destruction of people to create a real panic.

Such behaviour is undoubtedly asymmetrical. These kinds of actions could really create a Damocles effect, where officials and people live in a permanent situation of fear and paralysis created by this 'psywar', fearing that anytime, as in the legend, the horsehair suspending the sword might break.

CONSEQUENCES

Consider the relatively small costs involved, huge troubles caused and the spending generated in preventive measures. Applying the principle of precaution would be massive, costly and disproportionate.

Nevertheless, the events of September 11 have created a need to carefully assess our defence needs and ensure that the resources we spend on security are aligned with the most pressing security threats. The elements summarised here show that the CBN threat is real, serious, and deserves vigorous response.

However, we must also face the brutal reality that no technological remedies can provide complete confidence that we are safe from CBN attacks. Terrorist groups might still find a way to use CBN weapons if their goal is to terrorise or kill innocent people and harass them. Equally, we now know that the new terrorists of the CBN age have no regard for their own lives. Thus, wouldn't CBN terrorism be the ultimate terror?

NOTES

1. Stark, Rodney (1999), 'Rads, Bugs and Gas: The Threat of CBN Terrorism', Department of Defense and Strategic Studies Southwest Missouri State University, 14 May. Master of Science in Defense and Strategic Studies thesis.
2. Hoffman, Bruce (1986), *Terrorism in the United States and the Potential Threat to Nuclear Facilities*, Santa Monica: RAND.
3. Caesium-137 is a radioactive material that causes cancer and other severe health problems when it comes into contact with human skin, is ingested, or is inhaled.

9. Information Age Terrorism and Warfare

Kevin A. O'Brien

The advent of new technologies, advanced means of communication and ever-more sophisticated ways of moving money around have already influenced the way terrorists operate and will continue to do so. Terrorist organisers and fundraisers no longer have to be in the same country as their target or indeed as each other. Their communications to each other can be encrypted. And there is the potential, if the right targets are hit (such as strategic computer systems running banking or air traffic control operations), to affect thousands or even millions of people.

Jack Straw, UK Home Secretary, 1998

INTRODUCTION

Defining the Problem: Asymmetric Actors and Threats – The Place of Cyber-War

Since the end of the Cold War, much has been made regarding the changing security agenda and the emergence of new threats. In reality, most – if not all – of these threats to national and international security are evolutions of pre-existing threats, which have undergone modification, brought about by numerous engines of change in today's world. The much-vaunted globalisation, new liberalisations in formerly autocratic states, increasing privatisation of state-functions, and, most importantly, the revolution in computing, telecommunications, and data-transference capacities – commonly referred to as the Information Revolution – have all impacted strongly on the international security agenda and on the nature of the threat-actors in today's world.

This has given rise, in the threat-perceptions environment, to the introduction of the term 'asymmetric threat' to refer to those threats which have gained prevalence since 1990 and present non-traditional threat-postures to (generally) western governments, defence and national security communities. Generally speaking, these threats do not present the danger of major conventional war to the developed world powers but do present equally (if not, in some cases, greater) dangers to the populations and governments of these states.

This chapter will discuss two of the key pillars of asymmetry: notably Information Operations and Terrorism, including the links between the two. While a great deal changed on September 11 2001, one thing that has not changed in substance is the challenge of protecting the Information Society, notably from cyber-threats. Although the immediate threat to our societies is from the physical and possibly bio-weapons favoured by al-Qaeda and its associates, it is time now to prepare for future threats to the information society, including cyber-threats. In essence, not much changed with the attacks on New York and Washington because the rise of increasingly lethal, unclaimed terrorist attacks designed to cause mass casualties has been evident for some time. Al-Qaeda has long been an exemplar of the 'new terrorism' identified by analysts. What has been striking recently has been the way in which terrorists have used the very infrastructures of modern, globalised society (air transportation, postal system) against the societies that rely on these infrastructures. This asymmetric strategy has enabled small groups with relatively limited resources to achieve a disproportionate effect, always the goal of terrorists. However, this asymmetric approach is not surprising. Numerous studies and scenarios undertaken by western security planners in recent years have identified this approach as the most likely one for the West's opponents.

The main change since September 11 2001, of course, has been in public and political perceptions of the threat. The attacks have raised awareness of the degree of hostility felt towards the US by some communities and of the vulnerabilities of contemporary societies. Consequently, there is greater political willingness to address the risks posed by the combination of an increased, yet diffuse, threat and extensive, yet hard to quantify, vulnerabilities. In relation to information assurance and dependability, there are three main developments since September 11 that influence efforts to protect the 'information society'. Firstly, a recognition that protective efforts should focus not only on low-level, day to day threats such as hackers and criminals but that mass disruption attacks by 'high-end' terrorists also need to be taken seriously. Secondly, a recognition that, whilst poor security does leave infrastructures wide open to attack, as in the US airline sector, good business continuity planning can mitigate risks, as in the New York financial sector. Thirdly, a recognition by governments and businesses that security and dependability need to be taken seriously and require concerted, international action.

Ultimately, however, terrorists will continue to prefer the very public means of destructive attacks in the real world, with the enhanced reaction that such attacks engender in the population; at the moment, carrying out similarly 'devastating' attacks in cyber-space (for example, the destruction of a networked computer infrastructure, along the lines of the cyber-war, anti-Serbian government activities NATO conducted during the Kosovo War) results in little public reaction beyond a curious concern, certainly far short of the fearful emotional panic that loss-of-life terrorist attacks induce in threatened populations. For this reason, so-called 'cyber-terrorism' remains an uncertain tool for real-world terrorists to use. However, the use of cyber-means to enhance, distract from, or otherwise support a real-world attack is becoming of increasing possibility and relevance to terrorist aims in today's world, as the 'target set' continues to evolve.

The proliferation of networked computers and telecommunications systems means that another layer is now overlying our physical infrastructure: the National Information Infrastructure (NII). The NII has been defined as 'that system of advanced computer systems, databases and tele-communications networks ... that make electronic information widely available and accessible. This includes the Internet, the public switched network and cable, wireless and satellite communications.' Given the reliance of modern society on this NII, any major disruption could impact on the national economy as well as on individual government departments or businesses. And yet, the NII has not developed with security in mind. Specific portions of it are highly secure, notably some internal networks within government or in some financial institutions. However, overall the NII is extremely vulnerable to disruption from either physical attack (arson, bombs, and so on) or logical attack (such as 'malware' and other software programmes).

The US government has taken the lead in studying threats to its NII from hackers, terrorists or foreign governments. Its Department of Defense warned last year that the insecurity of the NII had created a 'tunnel of vulnerability previously unrealised in the history of conflict'. The Central Intelligence Agency (CIA), meanwhile, has warned that it treats Information Warfare (a potential 'weapon of mass disruption') as one of the two main threats to American national security, the other being Nuclear, Biological, Radiological and Chemical Weapons (CBRN, all 'weapons of mass destruction'). Infrastructure attacks – or those perpetrated by 'mass casualty weapons' – are an off-shoot of both, since damage and destruction to infrastructures, and the concomitant loss of life that they can cause, as was clearly witnessed on September 11, can result from both.

This is asymmetric warfare – but it is not all that novel nor all that new: as US military analyst Colonel Charles J. Dunlap has stated, 'in a way, seeking asymmetries is fundamental to all war-fighting. But in the modern context, symmetrical warfare emphasises what are popularly perceived as unconventional or non-traditional methodologies'.[1] In its most basic form, asymmetric warfare is an approach that tries to focus whatever may be one side's comparative advantages against its enemy's relative weaknesses. Generally, an asymmetric threat implies that an opponent is incapable, due either to his own capabilities or the strength of the force opposed to him, of confronting an opponent (generally the developed world, although this could include multinational corporations, transnational financial communities, or an international organisation such as the UN) in a conventional manner using like means or weapons to his opponent. Therefore, he chooses an asymmetric approach, using means (including the element of surprise, weapons and tactics in ways that are unplanned or unexpected) that will foil, off-set, reduce or circumvent the technological superiority of his opponent, or even give him the advantage over the opponent. As asymmetric attacks generally avoid strength and exploit vulnerabilities, an opponent could design a strategy that fundamentally alters the battle-space within which a conflict (generally low-intensity but with high involvement) is fought.

These threats can manifest themselves in a number of different ways, forming part of both the ends to be achieved and the ways and means of achieving these. They can have tactical and strategic impacts. At the strategic level, they work to exploit the fears of the civilian population in order to either weaken support for the democratic process, undermine the government, or to compromise its alliances and partnerships. In this sense, the threats have a strong psychological, as well as physical, impact (for example, playing on the degree of comfort a population has with electronic commerce). In addition, the potential for attacks on international forces deployed regionally (witness the 1992–1993 UN operations in Somalia) or on citizens, property or territory of the major powers itself increases the requirement for a flexible and, sometimes, unconventional response to the security of deployed forces, peace support operations, and western interests abroad. At the tactical level, they can force an actor to change course or tactics (for example, by playing on the modern fear of casualties to western military forces), or carry out attacks that are difficult for western forces to confront and prevent (for example, through terrorist activities or attacks, both physical and electronic, on critical national infrastructures). Threats deriving from terrorist activity, complex emergencies and peace support operations, economic disruption, civil disobedience and organised crime all represent an asymmetric approach to confronting a more powerful opponent.

Not only is it likely that many of the conflicts facing the West will be of an asymmetrical and devolving nature, it is also likely that these threats will come from diverse, differing and simultaneous vectors. For example, the possibility that transnational terrorism will be accompanied or compounded by cyber/infrastructure attacks damaging vital commercial, military, and government information and communications systems are of great concern. In this sense, a major western country could suffer greatly at the hands of an educated, equipped, and committed group of fewer than fifty people. Such an attack could cause an effect vastly disproportionate to the resources expended to undertake it. It should be noted that one of the open questions regarding the attacks of September 2001 is why – as will be explored here later – did al-Qaeda not use the cyber-tools and knowledge at its disposal to cause additional destruction and chaos alongside its real-world attacks.

All of these threats present the requirement for a massively improved intelligence capability to warn against and provide support to operations against these threats. While the traditional intelligence process may not present the best options for timely and cost-effective collection, processing, analysis, assessment and dissemination of intelligence relating to these threats, it is clear that traditional intelligence-collection means – very technologically heavy and still driven by Cold War requirements – definitely do not present the best options for dealing with asymmetric threats. While these threats present clear technologically or technically-based profiles which will continue to be of use to the intelligence-collection process (such as through intercepted electronic and communications traffic, or the use of orbital assets to determine the location of transnational terrorist bases in Afghanistan or delivery-system testing in North Korea, Iran or Pakistan), the best asset for intelligence-gathering on asymmetric threats will be human and open-source.

Asymmetry and Information Operations

One of the central pillars of asymmetry is the use of Information Operations to counter your opponent; as will be noted throughout this chapter, the linkages between this pillar and another – terrorism – lead to concerns about the ways in which today's terrorists can use cyber-space[2] to both plan and conduct their attacks. These 'information age terrorists' present potentially the single greatest threat (in terms of the potential to render mass destruction and death) to today's information-age societies.

The UK Ministry of Defence recognises that 'our increasing dependence on high technology to provide our battle-winning edge – and the widening disparity between our military capabilities and those of potential adversaries – may lead potential aggressors to adopt alternative weapons or unconventional strategies [including] asymmetric warfare'. This is because 'integration of information systems into military operations offers significant advantages but also introduces new vulnerabilities'.[3] Under such a scenario, information warfare could be used to disable critical national infrastructures throughout western states through attacks on computer networks, paralysing communications, transportation, power systems, and industrial enterprises. Other information operations, including perception management operations and psychological warfare, would allow opponents to exploit the international news media to weaken the resolve of western decision-makers (as happened during the Kosovo Conflict).

The recent US Quadrennial Defence Review stated that a future adversary could 'employ asymmetric methods to delay or deny US access to critical facilities; disrupt our command, control, communications, and intelligence networks; or inflict higher than expected casualties in an attempt to weaken our national resolve'.[4]

Future asymmetric actors will have a number of tools at their disposal; these include the use of cyber-based warfare and the acquisition of selected high-technology sensors, communications, and weapon systems. This could be called the 'strategy of the niche player', where cyber-weapons and tools would be used to disrupt information technology (IT) military and civilian systems, as well as launching attacks on NII and critical national infrastructures (CNI) in order to disrupt and destroy the information-based economies and infrastructures of western states.[5] The threat is compounded by the selected acquisition of high technology sensors, communications and weapons systems by rogue states and non-state actors such as Transnational Organised Crime (TOC). The exploitation of civilian sources such as the Internet and commercial satellite imagery, as well as the proliferation of advanced weapons, permit better operational planning, more accurate targeting and greater damage by the asymmetric actor.[6] Most ironically, the developed world is making the asymmetric actor's job much easier through its over-reliance, increasing daily, on large volumes of information provided through a largely unregulated Internet. In most instances, the populations and governments of western countries rely almost entirely on national critical information infrastructures (NCII) consisting of government and corporate computer servers, telecommunications facilities and Internet Service Providers. All of these present ready targets for any type of asymmetric attack discussed here; responding to a potentially devastating cyber-based attack has become one of the key priorities of most developed world governments today.[7]

THE RELATIONSHIP BETWEEN CYBER-CRIME, CYBER-TERRORISM AND CYBER-WAR

One of the starting points for considering the growing threat from cyber-terrorism, as well as the user of cyber-space by transnational terrorist organisations is the legal basis for considering such activities. This provides not only a comparative international framework for understanding the approach that governments are taking to combating cyber-terrorism and cyber-based terrorists, but also an appreciation of how governments perceive the threat.

As noted in the UK government's 1998 'Legislation Against Terrorism: A Consultation Paper', the threat from cyber-terrorism as well as the significant use of cyber-space continues to grow exponentially:

> The advent of new technologies, advanced means of communication and ever-more sophisticated ways of moving money around have already influenced the way terrorists operate and will continue to do so. Terrorist organisers and fundraisers no longer have to be in the same country as their target or indeed as each other. Their communications to each other can be encrypted. And there is the potential, if the right targets are hit (such as strategic computer systems running banking or air traffic control operations), to affect thousands or even millions of people. Such technologies could not have been envisaged when the existing counter-terrorist legislation was framed over 20 years ago, but the powers made available in future must be adequate – and flexible – enough to respond to the changing nature of the terrorist threat both now and in the years to come.[8]

The UK's Terrorism Act (2000) designates 'terrorism' as 'the use or threat of action where ... (b) the use or threat is designed to influence the government or to intimidate the public or a section of the public, and (c) the use or threat is made for the purpose of advancing a political, religious or ideological cause [and the action] (e) is designed seriously to interfere with or seriously to disrupt an electronic system'. Significantly, the jurisdiction for such activities includes action 'outside the United Kingdom' and includes reference to any person or to property 'wherever situated', reference to the public includes 'the public of a country other than the United Kingdom', and reference to the government includes 'the government of the United Kingdom ... or of a country other than the United Kingdom'. Finally, section five states that 'a reference to action taken for the purposes of terrorism includes a reference to action taken for the benefit of a proscribed organisation'.[9]

Overall, for the purposes of cyber-terrorism, this means that any individual engaged in, for example, the e-Intifada that has been on-going between supporters of the Israeli government and supporters of the Palestinian self-determination cause since October 2000 when the real-world Intifada kicked off again – regardless of where in the world they are based – are subject to prosecution under this Act, whether a member of a proscribed terrorist organisation or not. Significantly, at the moment, no cyber-based group (such as known hacktivist groups, like the notable Pakistani hacker group 'G-Force Pakistan', a group active since February 2000 and which defaced nineteen different sites within three days of the Intifada recommencing) has yet been added to any listing of proscribed (or even noted) international terrorist organisations.

In the United States, the Uniting and Strengthening America by Providing Appropriate Tools Required to Intercept and Obstruct Terrorism Act – or USA PATRIOT Act, as passed on 24 October 2001 – includes an amendment to the Immigration and Nationality Act and US Code to state that:

> (iv) ENGAGE IN TERRORIST ACTIVITY DEFINED: As used in this chapter, the term 'engage in terrorist activity' means, in an individual capacity or as a member of an organization – (I) to commit or to incite to commit, under circumstances indicating an intention to cause death or serious bodily injury, a terrorist activity; (II) to prepare or plan a terrorist activity; (III) to gather information on potential targets for terrorist activity.[10]

This – in conjunction with all of the points raised throughout USA PATRIOT relating to 'electronic crime' – obviously alludes to the mounting evidence that al-Qaeda used the Internet to support its operations.

In Canada, the definition of 'terrorist activity' defines terrorism as an action 'taken or threatened for political, religious or ideological purposes and threatens the public or national security by killing, seriously harming or endangering a person, causing substantial property damage that is likely to seriously harm people or by interfering with or disrupting an essential service, facility or system'. The act must 'intentionally (C) cause a serious risk to the health or safety of the public or any segment of the public … or (E) causes serious interference with or serious disruption of an essential service, facility or system, whether public or private, other than as a result of advocacy, protest, dissent or stoppage of work that is not intended to result in … harm' – both of which clearly refer to cyber-terrorism.[11] This is applicable 'either within or outside of Canada' and is carefully circumscribed to make it clear that disrupting an essential service is not a terrorist activity if it occurs during a lawful protest or a work strike and is not intended to cause serious harm to persons. Canada will also sign the Council of Europe Convention on Cyber-Crime.

Finally, under Australia's Security Legislation Amendment (Terrorism) Act 2002, 'terrorism acts' are defined to include:

> An act, or threat of action, that is done or made with the intention of advancing a political, ideological or religious cause; and done or made with the intention of either coercing or influencing by intimidation the Government of Australia or of another country; or intimidating the public or a section of the public … (d) creates a serious risk to the health or safety of the public or a section of the public; or (e) seriously interferes with, seriously disrupts, or destroys, an electronic system including, but not limited to (i) an information system; (ii) a telecommunications system; (iii) a financial system; (iv) a system used for the delivery of essential

government services; (v) a system used for, or by, an essential public utility; or (vi) a system used for, or by, a transport system.[12]

Thus, it is clear that cyber-terrorism and cyber-based terrorist organisations are regarded in the same light as real-world terrorism. At the same time, national statutes and amendments to anti-terrorism laws are moving to confront the borderless nature of the cyber-terrorist threat – much in line with moves to deal with the transnational nature of the 'new terrorism'.

Threats and Actors: 'Information Age Terrorism'

The Federal Bureau of Investigation (FBI) defines terrorism as 'the unlawful use of force or violence against persons or property to intimidate or coerce a government, the civilian population, or any segments thereof, in furtherance of political or social objectives', while the US Department of Defense outlines 'the unlawful use of – or threatened use of – force or violence against individuals or property to coerce or intimidate governments or societies, often to achieve political, religious, or ideological objectives'. Refocusing the emphasis – from the Department of Defense's emphasis on the act – Bruce Hoffman, in *Inside Terrorism,* defined terrorism as 'the deliberate creation and exploitation of fear through violence or the threat of violence in the pursuit of political change', thus emphasising the results (the 'fear') over the act itself. When considering the potential for cyber-based terrorism to exploit such fear – versus the capability of real-world terrorism to do the same – this differentiation would be useful to keep in mind.

In the information age, terrorism has expanded its scope and found an increasingly prominent use for instruments such as the Internet to facilitate these efforts. Tim Thomas has coined the term 'information terrorism' for this process of exploiting the Internet for terrorist purposes, defining it as (1) the nexus between criminal information system fraud or abuse, and the physical violence of terrorism and (2) the intentional abuse of a digital information system, network, or component toward an end that supports or facilitates a terrorist campaign or action. Computer attacks are the most often cited example of 'the use of force or violence' in the information age because they are the attacks with which everyone has some familiarity.[13]

Amongst both governments and businesses, there is increasing concern that information security breaches and cyber-crime will undermine trust in the new economy and threaten the development of the Information Society. In the UK, then Foreign Secretary Robin Cook warned Parliament on 29 March 2001 that 'a computer-based attack on the national infrastructure could cripple the nation more quickly than a military strike'.[14] In the same month, the European Commission pointed out that 'the information infrastructure has become a critical part of the backbone of our economies. Users should be able to rely on the availability of information services and have the confidence that their communications and data are safe from unauthorised access or modification. The take up of electronic commerce and the full realisation of an Information Society depend on this.'[15]

INFORMATION WARFARE AND NETWAR

Information Dominance and Information Superiority

As the 'Information Spectrum' includes 'Data', 'Information' and 'Knowledge', in a manner of speaking 'information warfare' can include threats, protection and activities along each of these paths.[16] Information itself exists in different forms:

- Ground truth
- As sensed
- As perceived by an individual (direct or indirect observation)
- As shared by two or more individuals

Deriving from information, awareness and understanding are the results of cognitive processes with these inputs. Thus, by attacking each of these points – or, indeed, defending each of them – one is engaging in the most basic form of information warfare. By defeating your opponent's awareness of the situation while maintaining yours, or by modifying his understanding of the facts and truth while enforcing your own (or, indeed, the view which you want your opponent to have of a situation), one is succeeding in information warfare.

These concepts translate fluidly across the whole spectrum of information operations (including elements such as computer network operations, psy-ops and propaganda, 'netwar' or cyber-war): in any of these scenarios, you are attempting to change your opponent's awareness and understanding of the situation; even in circumstances where attack and defence parameters are used in support of cyber-terrorism, the aim is to defeat your opponent's systems – often by 'taking them down', eliciting information from them, or modifying their contents in order to create a different impression or make a statement – and thereby to defeat his understanding of reality.

This changes the ability of terrorists, organised criminal groups or other sub-state malicious actors to use the date, information and knowledge resources available in the Information Society to plan and organise, finance and communicate, and ensure command and control (C^2) over real-world operations; this was clearly demonstrated over the past eight years by al-Qaeda and other pan-Islamist terrorist organisations, and was not simply a realisation post-September 2001, as will be discussed later.

Even in these situations, however, the terrorists used the information and communications technology (ICT) resources both at their disposal and – most importantly – at the disposal of their opponents in both western and Asian intelligence services to defeat the opponent through 'spoofing' their real intentions.

Information Operations, Computer Network Operations and Netwar

With the West leading the world in information technologies and the Information Revolution sweeping large parts of the globe, the vulnerability of these states to cyber-based Information Operations (IO), as well as to the more 'traditional' aspects of IO such as psychological warfare and perception-management warfare, has increased markedly. Ironically, the more the world digitises, the more vulnerable it becomes. In the military and government fields, this is becoming all the more worrying: computerised weapons-systems are used for precision strikes, e-mail is used for military communications, and logistics processes have become digitised; insiders, rogue hackers, and foreign military jammers can exploit all of these. In addition, the use of such non-technological IO means deployed against a much more capable and technologically advanced conventional force was demonstrated more than adequately in the Kosovo Campaign, where Belgrade easily 'won' the psychological and perception IO war against the North Atlantic Treaty Organisation (NATO). In a more worrying sector – that of cyber-based IO – the West is becoming increasingly vulnerable as it becomes increasingly capable. This is not only in the military sector, but also in the civilian and commercial sectors, as was aptly demonstrated by both the Distributed Denial of Service (DDoS) attacks launched against the Internet-based companies Yahoo, Amazon and eBay during 1999–2000, and by the ILOVEYOU e-mail virus – estimated to have cost western businesses US$7 billion in damage – launched seemingly as a practical joke from the Philippines by college students in 2000.[17]

Information Operations are 'actions taken in support of objectives which influence decision makers by affecting other's information and/or information systems, while exploiting and protecting one's own information and/or information systems'.[18] Targets include the major elements of the national economy: the public telecommunications network; the financial and banking system; the electric power-grid; the oil and gas networks; and the national transportation system (including the air transportation system). The conduct of offensive IO poses a clear asymmetric threat to the West, with its increased reliance on information and information systems as a vital component of decision-making, presenting the possibility of organisations, or individuals, with hostile or malicious intent, taking action to deny, disrupt or destroy capabilities in this area. This could have devastating consequences combined with WMD or terrorist activities: for instance, taking down a city's emergency telephone system through a cyber-attack while setting off terrorist bombs and interfering with the media could produce an asymmetric synergy, making the individual attacks much more effective than they would have been alone.[19] IO has been used to infiltrate or disrupt military or civilian Information Technology systems, including those used for command, control, communications and logistics, to modify or manipulate data, or to attack the national strategic infrastructure (such as, disrupting critical systems like international air traffic control systems).[20]

Offensive IO can be divided into three principal categories:

- *Attacks on infrastructure*: 'activity that causes damage to information or information systems, or interferes with operations', involving a broad spectrum of operations – including activities such as computer network attack (CNA), electronic warfare and physical destruction – ranging from hacker vandalism of public Internet sites to coordinated reconnaissance, infiltration, data manipulations or DDoS on corporate or government information systems.
- *Deception*: 'designed to mislead an enemy by manipulation, distortion, or falsification of evidence to induce him to react in a manner prejudicial to his interests', including manipulation of the open media, such as propaganda operations through public communication channels including television, radio and the Internet, as well as misinformation and hoaxes, sometimes taking advantage of new video and audio manipulation technologies and computer animation.[21]
- *Psychological operations*: 'ability to influence the will of another society', involving political or diplomatic positions, announcements, or communiqués, as well as the distribution of leaflets, radio or television broadcasts, and other means of transmitting information that promote fear or dissension, with its message reinforced through acts such as hostage taking or the threat of mass casualties.[22]

Interestingly, cyber-terrorism is not only about damaging systems but also about intelligence gathering. The intense focus on 'shut-down' scenarios ignores other more potentially effective uses of IT in terrorist warfare: intelligence gathering, counter-intelligence and disinformation. In addition, conflict in the form of cyber-warfare that would blur conventional boundaries between crime and war might prove attractive to an opponent that sees no strategic benefit in a direct confrontation of the military of the West in a regional war.

Computer Network Operations and Cyber-War

As outlined by Andrew Rathmell,[23] Computer Network Operations (CNO) are 'a subset of a broader set of malicious computer-mediated activities'. British military doctrine states that CNO comprises three key elements:

a) Computer Network Exploitation (CNE), namely: 'the ability to gain access to information hosted on information systems and the ability to make use of the system itself';
b) Computer Network Attack (CNA), namely: the 'use of novel approaches to enter computer networks and attack the data, the processes or the hardware'; and
c) Computer Network Defence (CND), which is 'protection against the enemy's CNA and CNE and incorporates hardware and software approaches alongside people based approaches'.[24]

As outlined in a recent Center for Strategic and International Studies (CSIS) study, there is currently a lack of clarity as to the nature of cyber-war and what it means for those defending against such attacks. The CSIS study concluded that, in order to be able to defeat cyber-war, we need a clear picture of current and projected cyber-war options for attackers:

- Effective defence and response requires a full-scale net technical assessment of what attackers can really do, key vulnerabilities, and requirements for defence and response
- Exercising responses to assumptions about such attacks is not analysis or adequate planning
- Cyber-war can occur at a number of levels and in conjunction with other means of attack
- A covert cyber-war may be possible where the attacker cannot be identified quickly or at all
- Larger-scale cyber-war may involve clearly identifiable attackers[25]

CNO are one element of IO, another is 'Netwar'.

Netwar

David Ronfeldt and John Arquilla first introduced the term 'netwar' several years ago to refer to 'an emerging mode of conflict at societal levels, short of traditional military warfare, in which the protagonists use network forms of organisation and related doctrines, strategies, and technologies attuned to the information age'. The protagonists are likely to consist of dispersed small groups who communicate, coordinate, and conduct their campaigns in a networked manner, without a precise central command.[26] Ronfeldt and Arquilla believe that a network's strength depends on five levels of functioning: organisational (design level), narrative (story being told), doctrinal (strategies and methods), technological (information systems in use), and social (personal ties to assure loyalty and trust). As an example of 'netwar', the al-Qaeda network functioned on all of these levels during the planning and execution of the attacks on the WTC. The network also makes the group appear leaderless, and thus makes it harder to find those responsible.

During confrontations with Iraq – even as far back as Operation *Desert Storm* – it is believed that CNO capabilities (such as computer viruses inserted into the Iraqi Command and Control computers) were used. In addition, during Operation *Restore Hope* in Haiti, the US used hacking to exploit knowledge about Haitian government intentions and capabilities.[27] By the time of the 1999 Kosovo Conflict, NATO and its member-states were openly using CNO, distorting information perceived by Serbian air-defence systems on their screens. Hackers disrupted and defaced Serb and NATO websites, and jammed computer messaging systems with 'email bombs'. US hackers based in the CIA and National Security Agency (NSA) – following a *Presidential Finding* – burrowed into Serb government e-mail systems, while some infiltrated their way into the networked-systems of banks around the world in search of accounts held by the Serbian leadership.[28]

It is perhaps not surprising that the US military and government have advanced the furthest in developing concepts of netwar and IO for use in conflict. The US now includes IO as a key component of national security strategy and doctrine; this emphasis has only been heightened since September 2001. The US views Information Superiority (IS) as centring on three key areas: Intelligence; Command, Control, Communications and Computers (C^4); and IO, which builds on the traditionally narrower activities of Command and Control Warfare (C^2W) and Information Warfare. With components including Deception, Physical Destruction, Psychological Operations, Operational Security, and Electronic Warfare – underpinned and bound together by a foundation of Intelligence and Communications – CNO, supported by the Joint Task Force-Computer Network Operations (JTF-CNO), under US Space Command (USSPACECOM) – has recently been added as the ability to logically interfere with an information system has become of increasing relevance.

Outside the United States, IO is a relatively recent doctrinal construct not yet accepted by all NATO nations. Even within the US Armed Forces some view it with scepticism. In the UK, for example, the Ministry of Defence recently established the Land Information Assurance Group (Volunteers) comprising a forty-person-strong Territorial Army unit to develop effective counter-measures against cyber-attacks.

TRANSNATIONAL TERRORISTS AND CYBER-SPACE

In the wake of September 11, it is clear that terrorists are using cyber-space for their own means. Indeed, terrorist organisations had already – before the rise of the Internet – begun to appreciate the opportunities that threats to infrastructure, as opposed to human beings, could cause. In the early 1990s, the Provisional Irish Republican Army (IRA) used this concept very effectively, sufficiently occupying the resources of the British government through infrastructure attacks (as opposed to direct attacks against people). In the future, stock markets or other primary financial institutions might become high-profile targets and the most effective means of accomplishing a terrorist's goal. Indeed, taking the New York Stock Exchange offline for a few days rather than actually bombing a building would accomplish more damage.

According to February 2000 testimony to the US Congress by John Serabian Jr (Information Operations Issue Manager of the CIA), 'terrorists and other non-state actors have come to recognise that cyber weapons offer them new, low-cost, easily hidden tools to support their causes. The skills and resources of this threat group range from the merely troublesome to dangerous.' Groups such as Hizbollah, Hamas, and al-Qaeda are using computerised files, email, and encryption to support their activities. While terrorists and extremists have long been using the Internet to communicate, raise funds, recruit, and gather intelligence, cyber-attacks offer terrorists the possibility of greater security and operational flexibility. Theoretically, they can launch a computer assault from almost anywhere in the world without exposing themselves.[29]

The Internet has changed terrorist communications networks from those of strong central control to ones with no clear centre of control due to its networked nature. Indeed, transnational terrorist organisations have begun to appreciate the full opportunities that cyber-space offers for their activities: the use of new/Internet-based technologies for coordinating, communicating and supporting the planning of terrorist (cyber-based and real-world) activities; the ability to develop and support so-called 'virtual sanctuaries' where the full activity of the terrorists is conducted solely in cyber-space; and other means outlined below with particular regard to al-Qaeda. In this same sense, the Internet can be used for clandestine communications through Virtual Private Networks, posting messages on e-mail and electronic bulletin boards, as well as steganography (hiding messages within pictures and objects) and encryption.

In June 2001, the CIA's top advisor on technology matters, Lawrence Gershwin, stated that, while terrorists still prefer bombs, 'We anticipate more substantial cyber-threats in the future as a more technically competent generation enters the terrorist ranks'.[30] The capabilities and opportunities offered to terrorists include such things as using the Internet to gather detailed targeting information; gathering and moving about money to support activities – or even manipulating stocks to benefit the terrorist organisations (as is suspected from September 2001); coordinating and planning activities from around the world; and using it as a platform for propaganda and publicity (for example, terrorists leave messages of future or planned activities on websites or e-mail, while publicising accountability for acts of violence). In a similar manner, the Internet can be used for psychological terrorism and rumour mongering. It can also be used to conduct attacks against individuals, groups, or companies such as financial institutes, or to directly lobby decision-makers through extortion, brand-destruction, fraud and other means.

A number of leading terrorist organisations have made the migration to cyber-space, led by the Liberation Tigers of Tamil Eelam (LTTE) and, oddly enough, the Scottish National Liberation Army. Other examples include a group calling themselves the Internet Black Tigers who took responsibility for attacks in August 1998 on the e-mail systems of Sri Lankan diplomatic posts around the world, including those in the United States; third-country sympathisers of the Mexican Zapatista rebels who crashed web pages belonging to Mexican financial institutions – generating propaganda and rallying supporters; and others such as Kurdish separatists in Greece and Turkey, Kashmiri separatists in India, and Zapatista rebels in Mexico who have all also hacked official government web-sites and posted anti-government propaganda and pictures.

Perhaps the most widely known IT-advanced terrorist organisation is Aum Shinriyko, which even owns its computer/IT firms – the M Group – which has served some of the giants of Japanese industry and government, and was only discovered in March 2000 to be linked to Aum. According to a 2000 *Newsweek* report, 'Technology has always been Aum's secret weapon. In the 1980s its efforts to peddle bargain PCs through cult-owned electronics shops blossomed into a US$1 billion empire.' The group's founder, Shoko Asahara, lured engineers, chemists and computer scientists from Japan's elite universities to work developing weapons of mass destruction. There were also rumours that Aum's 1995 Tokyo subway attack was supposed to have been supported by hacking into the subway ventilation and train-control systems in order to maximise the causalities caused by the sarin gas – a rumour that was later denied by officials in Japan.

AL-QAEDA AND TERRORISM IN CYBER-SPACE

One of the ways in which officials world-wide will develop new methods for critical infrastructure protection (CIP) is through an understanding of how the terrorists carried out this attack. Until as recently as last year, bin Laden used high-technology means (such as satellite telephones) to communicate with his followers. This stopped abruptly as bin Laden realised the potential threat this presented him. However, although bin Laden may only use the lowest technology means – such as in-person communication with his subordinates – these subordinates are believed to use encrypted Internet messages to correspond with each other.

Currently, it is believed that al-Qaeda uses both high and low technology means to co-ordinate its activities: in organising for the attacks, the terrorists used active cyber-means – booking airline tickets online, exchanging hundreds of e-mails, using the Internet to learn about the aerial application of pesticides – to plan their attacks; they also protected their communications by using public computer terminals, anonymous e-mail services, and encryption or steganography on web-sites to relay information publicly. Much of this granted them the total anonymity that was essential to the preparations for these attacks. But it also left, in the aftermath, an electronic trail for investigators to follow.

In 2000, former FBI Director Louis Freeh highlighted this issue to the Senate: 'Uncrackable encryption is allowing terrorists – Hamas, Hizbollah, al-Qaeda and others – to communicate about their criminal intentions without fear of outside intrusion.' Indeed, bin Laden may actually have used technological means to 'spoof' western intelligence collection – such as signals intelligence (SIGINT) and imagery intelligence (IMINT) – into believing that he was planning an attack 'overseas' and not on the continental US, turning the West's intelligence means against it, and using human couriers to carry the real messages: according to Congressional sources, US intelligence intercepted communications discussing such attacks, and other warnings since May 2001 pointed towards an overseas attack on US interests, similar to the attack on the USS Cole in October 2000.

In the United States, the powers granted by the Foreign Intelligence Surveillance Act (FISA) has allowed officials to develop a clear picture of the terrorists' activities prior to the attacks: for example, one FISA search authorised authorities to monitor the Internet communications of a particular user, which has yielded hundreds of e-mails linked to the hijackers in English, Arabic and Urdu. According to the FBI, some messages have included operational details of the attack. Other officials have seized library log-in sheets and computer equipment, and issued search-warrants to AOL, Microsoft, Earthlink, Yahoo, Google, NetZero, Travelocity and many smaller providers. It is hoped that lessons will be learned from this that will contribute to future detection and deterrence of attacks.

In December 2001, the Canadian Office for Critical Infrastructure Protection and Emergency Preparedness (OCIPEP) released a report on the potential for al-Qaeda to regroup in cyber-space, based upon their long-demonstrated use of the Internet and IT to support their operations. Warning of 'a possible future cyber attack by agents or sympathisers of Osama bin Laden's al-Qaeda terrorist organisation', the report stated that 'bin Laden's vast financial resources would enable him or his organisation to purchase the equipment and expertise required for a cyber attack and mount such an attack in very short order'. While bin Laden himself may no longer have (assuming he is even alive) the ICT resources to call on which he has used over the past decade, the study does not rule out the possibility of al-Qaeda agents or sympathisers in other countries carrying out sophisticated and coordinated cyber-attacks against critical infrastructure facilities, such as the US telecommunications grid, electric power facilities and oil and natural gas pipelines.

Bin Laden demonstrated a sophisticated knowledge of ICT in the months between the August 1998 attacks in Africa and the September 2001 attacks in the US. A report released the day after the US attacks stated that bin Laden may have deliberately used the West's intelligence capabilities against it by 'spoofing' these intelligence services – and particularly their SIGINT assets – into believing that an attack was going to take place in Africa and not the US. Since May, there had been numerous warnings that bin Laden or another terrorist leader was preparing a major campaign against Americans, but all the intelligence suggested that any attacks would come overseas. Bin Laden appears to have used the communications he knew the United States was monitoring to throw America's spies off his trail, instead using human couriers to carry his real messages and money.[31]

The Threat: the Rise of Non-Traditional Sub-state Actors

The spectrum of cyber-threats is commonly taken to range from recreational hackers at the bottom end to national intelligence services and armed forces at the top end. In between, in terms of capability, come sub-state entities such as semi-organised crackers, hacktivists, organised criminals and terrorists.

Cyber-threats emanating from such groups can be defined as 'all forms of electronic attack as well as physical attacks and threats to system integrity'. The threats of concern surround both those that may cause observable disruption (such as direct action, terrorism) and those that may be clandestine (for example, espionage and crime). Such threats are both to the functioning of information infrastructures and to the information carried on such infrastructures (such as, the confidentiality, integrity and availability of information and information systems).[32]

In the study of international and corporate security, it has become axiomatic that organised sub-state actors, including terrorists and insurgents, organised criminals and activist movements, have become increasingly powerful actors in international affairs as a result of social, political and technological changes. As the authors of a Norwegian government study put it: 'The coercive power of sub-state actors (that is, the ability to influence state conduct through violence and sabotage or the threat to do so) is growing and will continue to grow in the future.'[33]

A number of authors have championed the idea that evolutionary changes have led to the emergence of a 'new terrorism' in the 1990s.[34] Proponents of the new terrorism thesis argue that political aims are being replaced by new motivations, ranging from those groups that aim to alter society at a fundamental level (millennialism) and those that are focused on single issues like abortion, the environment or animal rights.

New terrorism is also defined by its adoption of novel organisational structures and new patterns of group membership. One of the most common themes regarding this facet of new terrorism is that of flattened hierarchies. Traditional hierarchies have become increasingly unnecessary, as advances in information technology have made communications easier to arrange. Such leaderless resistance is the natural consequence of ever increasing levels of cellular disaggregation by sub-state actors. As Arquilla and Ronfeldt note, such organisations are a compromise between 'collective diversity' and 'co-ordinated anarchy', with modern communications technologies allowing discreet and minimal communications for consultancy and mobilisation. Under this system, 'subversive networking' undermines state power through the utilisation of 'semi-autonomous cellular structures'. Examples of such activity include the networking of Mexican Zapatistas and US 'hacktivists' and the cellular organisation of London's J18 anti-capitalist protests.[35]

Cyber-terrorism is not only about damaging systems but also about intelligence gathering. The focus on 'shut down' scenarios and analogies to physically violent techniques ignore other more potentially effective uses of IT in terrorist warfare: intelligence gathering, counter-intelligence and disinformation. In addition, concomitant cyber-attacks with real-world terrorist incidents (as alluded to in the September 2001 attacks) could potentially multiply the disastrous consequences massively. Attacking an information system would be a good way to either distract the target or otherwise enable the terrorist to perform a physical attack: for example, had Aum Shinrikyo been able to crack the Tokyo power system and stop the subways, trapping passengers on the trains, the number of casualties caused by their 1995 sarin gas attack might have been significantly larger.[36]

Competitor Governments and Cyber-War

Most interestingly, the perception that asymmetric threats are posed solely by those opponents of the West who possess little strength in any sector is quickly dismissed by the fact that the Chinese People's Liberation Army (PLA) has published recently a number of studies in which asymmetric warfare and tactics are seen as key in any future conflict, whether military or otherwise, with the West (particularly the US). Stating that 'hacking into websites, targeting financial institutions, terrorism, assassinating US financiers, using the media and conducting urban warfare' are among the methods considered by the PLA, these studies are driven by the efforts of the PLA to modernise their IW (Information Warfare)/IO capabilities. Recognising that it cannot match the West in either conventional or nuclear weapons, the PLA has begun to emphasise the development of new information and cyber-war technologies, including viruses and similar cyber-threats, to neutralise or at least erode any enemy's political, economic and military information and command-and-control infrastructures.[37] Designating this practice as Unrestricted Warfare, the PLA argue that China can outmanoeuvre western high-tech sensors, electronic countermeasures and weaponry by employing different methods entirely.

> If [China] secretly musters large amounts of capital without the enemy nation being aware of this at all and launches a sneak attack against its financial markets, … then after causing a financial crisis, buries a computer virus and hacker detachment in the opponent's computer system in advance, while at the same time carrying out a network attack against the enemy so that the civilian electricity network, traffic-dispatching network, financial-transaction network, telephone-communications network and mass-media network are completely paralysed, this will cause the enemy nation to fall into social panic, street riots and a political crisis.[38]

Indeed, the Chinese government and PLA may be behind the most sophisticated on-going cyber-war today. Known collectively as 'Solar Sunrise' (February 1998) and 'Moonlight Maze' (on-going since mid-1999), this series of increasingly sophisticated cyber-attacks and attempts at penetrating US government systems has been traced to sources in both China and Russia, but no clear perpetrators have come to light. While 'Solar

Sunrise' exploited lax computer security in the US Department of Defense (and was ultimately traced to two California teenagers under the orders of an Israeli hacker), 'Moonlight Maze' was suspected of links to both the Chinese PLA and the Russian Academy of Sciences. The hackers accessed sensitive Department of Defense science and technology information.

Such concerns were enhanced when – following the downing of the US EP-3 by Chinese fighters – a number of US government websites were taken over and defaced by suspected Chinese hackers in the days following the incident. On one site at the Department of Labor, a hacker posted a tribute to Wang Wei, the Chinese pilot who was killed in a collision with the EP-3 on 1 April. By the end of the week, the so-called 'Honker Union of China' – an informal network of Chinese hackers – claimed that they had defaced more than 1,000 US websites; one message said: 'Don't sell weapons to Taiwan, which is a province of China'. American hackers responded with their own methods: for example, web-portal Sina.com was struck by a series of denial-of-service (DOS) attacks on the evening before 1 May.[39]

Thomas has also noted that, with regard to the Internet, a terrorist attempts to succeed by using the Internet's open promise of an integrated and co-operative world to discredit governments, degrade user confidence, and corrupt or disrupt key systems through the insertion of data errors or by causing intermittent shutdowns. This produces, in many cases, fear or alarm and thus is a modern day supplement to traditional terrorism.[40]

One asymmetric response to military weakness is to seek to use international legal instruments to restrain vertical proliferation on the part of a rival. This might explain the Russian gambit at the UN. Russia's attempts to ban IO make strategic sense and mirror its efforts to restrict nuclear weapons in the early years of the Cold War. Russia recognises that, as it struggles to rebuild its economy, it is vulnerable to the advanced tools and doctrines of IO that its western rivals are developing. Unable to counter in kind, or to afford comprehensive defensive measures, Russia is seeking to use international law to reduce America's military advantage. In this sense, the West will need to pay particular attention to this most pressing of new concerns.

Cyber-Crime vs. Cyber-Terrorism

The 25 October 2000 crack of Microsoft's internal data-sharing networks by persons unknown and the alleged theft of various Windows code has highlighted more than ever the threat posed by cyber-crime. Often referred to as computer crime or e-crime, cyber-crime is growing more significant every week throughout the world. Exploited by traditional criminal organisations, such as the growing transnational organised crime (TOC) elements operating around the world today; terrorist groups, both domestic and transnational;

national governments and their intelligence services; and individuals, cyber-crime impacts on everything from banking systems to aviation authorities, security and customs organisations, telecommunications systems. Such TOC groups can be placed in different countries across the globe, all of which are linked by computer. In reality, cyber-crime can affect any individual or organisation that uses a computer and networked communications to conduct their affairs.

Cyber-crime is, quite strictly as defined by various national computer crime statutes, criminal activities that require knowledge of computers to succeed in the commissioning of offences such as hacking into a computer to alter or destroy files, or to gain information (known as cracking) for personal benefit. This is distinct from other types of computer and networking criminal activity, such as computer-related crime in which computers are used as tools, but knowledge of computers is not necessary for the successful commission of the offences. Cyber-crime's relationship with the Internet can be divided into crimes which use the Internet, but which are simply an electronic extension of traditional crime (such as fraud, theft, smuggling, and distribution of obscene or racist material); there are crimes which have developed because of the very existence of the Internet, including attacks on the Internet itself through such means as hacking, distributed denial of service (DDoS) attacks, and virus attacks, and there is the use of the Internet by the criminal as a means for communications or storage.

A February 2000 report in *Business Week* paints a vivid image of the damage that cyber-crime can inflict. In December 1999, 300,000 credit-card numbers were snatched from online music retailer CD Universe. The previous March, the Melissa virus caused an estimated US$80 million in damage when it swept around the world, paralysing e-mail systems. That same month, hackers-for-hire pleaded guilty to breaking into phone giants AT&T, GTE, and Sprint for calling-card numbers that eventually made their way to organised crime gangs in Italy; the FBI estimated the costs to be US$2 million.[41] According to a recent Australian Federal Police's Transaction Reports and Analysis Centre (Austrac) report, cyber-banking and crime will be the most important challenge of the twenty-first century. The Internet revolution has made money transfers across frontiers alarmingly easy, and the world's police forces have yet to catch up with criminals who are taking full advantage of the new information technology that is readily available in any neighbourhood computer store.

Cyber-crimes are perpetrated by a number of different actors. The overwhelming majority are carried out by internal sources (insiders), including past and present employees of companies and institutions. Some even estimate that up to 90 percent of economic crime in this area is attributable to insiders. Other actors involved include hackers/crackers, virus-writers, narcotics traffickers, paedophiles, fraudsters, organised criminal groups, terrorists, and foreign intelligence services. Increasingly, computers and the Internet are being used in a range of traditional crimes, including murder for hire and making criminal threats.

TOC is becoming more involved in cyber-theft and cyber-intrusion every month. In September 1999, the 'Phonemaster', an international group of criminals who penetrated the computer systems of MCI, Sprint, AT&T, Equifax, and even the National Crime Information Center, were convicted of theft and possession of unauthorised access devices, and unauthorised access to a federal interest computer. One suspect downloaded thousands of Sprint calling-card numbers, which he sold to a Canadian individual, who passed them on to someone in Ohio. These numbers made their way to an individual in Switzerland and eventually ended up in the hands of organised crime groups in Italy.[42] Even a number of transnational terrorist groups, such as the Peruvian Sendero Luminoso, are becoming more involved in cyber-crime to fund their activities. The Russian mafia and other groups are moving away from drugs into the more profitable business of computers.

There are a wide variety of cyber-crimes, most of which mirror similar activities in the 'real' world. These include computer and networking crimes such as:

- *Computer network break-ins*, where hackers use software tools installed on a computer in a remote location to break into computer systems to steal data, plant viruses (such as the ILOVEYOU virus, which crashed millions of computers world-wide and caused an estimated US$10 billion damage) or trojan horses, or work mischief of a less serious sort by changing user names or passwords;
- *Industrial espionage*, where networked systems provide opportunities for cyber-mercenaries to retrieve information regarding R&D and marketing strategies;
- *Software piracy*, where as much as US$7.5 billion worth of software may be illegally copied and distributed annually world-wide;
- *Child pornography*, where the acquisition of images of children in varying stages of dress and performing a variety of sexual acts through the Internet makes both the trading of such images and the establishment and networking of individuals involved in such activities much easier – and much easier to hide;
- *Distributed denial of service* (DDoS) attacks, in which computers are instructed to repeatedly send e-mail to a specified e-mail address, thereby overwhelming the recipient's account and potentially shutting down entire systems;

- *Password sniffers*, programmes which monitor and record the name and password of network users as they log in, jeopardising security at a site;
- *Spoofing*, in which one computer is disguised to appear electronically to be another computer in order to gain access to a system that would normally be restricted; and
- *Credit card fraud*, in which credit card information is stolen from companies' online databases and used over the Internet.[43]

With around 80 percent of a company's intellectual property in digital form today, spending on Internet security software has increased markedly: last year, companies in the US spent US$4.4 billion on such purchases, including firewalls, intrusion-detection programs, digital certificates, and authentication and authorisation software; by 2003, those expenditures could total US$8.3 billion. A 2000 FBI/Computer Security Institute survey noted that, of the 520 companies and institutions surveyed, more than 60 percent reported unauthorised use of computer systems throughout 1999, up from 50 percent in 1997, while 57 percent of all break-ins involved the Internet, up from 45 percent in 1998. Less than 15 percent of these cases were reported to the authorities.[44]

DDoS is particularly concerning, as it is not technically illegal in most countries. This was brought home when Yahoo! was taken down on 6 February 2000, then retailer Buy.com was hit the next day, only hours after going public. By that evening, eBay, Amazon.com, and CNN had all been struck. The following morning, online broker E*Trade and others were frozen out by attacks. The software to conduct these attacks is simple to use and readily available at underground hacker sites throughout the Internet. There are currently an estimated 1,900 web-sites that offer digital tools giving individuals the power to crash computers, hijack control of a machine, or retrieve a copy of every keystroke.[45]

In 2000, the UK's Serious Fraud Office noted that Internet and telephone fraud alone amounted to UK£30 million. More worrying is the increase in telephone-related hacking, in which an 0800 facility is used by crackers, who have the technology and general awareness to cross the telephone system and come out on a public telephone line. The average loss from this activity (from a Friday afternoon to a Monday morning) to the telephone bill of a company is about UK£12,000 a day. Ironically, one of the biggest victims of this has been the Metropolitan Police Service, who had their telephone system hacked into, with an estimated loss of approximately UK£500 million.[46]

In many senses, the Internet is already its own global state, with its own economy and finances. Direct Internet sales are expected to reach US$5 trillion in the US and Europe by 2005.[47] As e-commerce continues to grow, the Internet provides a seemingly helpful tool for investors due to its convenience and the inexpensive cost of researching investment opportunities. Unfortunately, it has also become an excellent tool for perpetrators of fraud.

Auctions were the most prevalent cyber-fraud in 1999, largely due to the fact that individuals run many online auctions. The National Consumer League's Internet Fraud Watch concluded that auctions constituted 87 percent of all online frauds in 1999 (up from 68 percent in 1998 and 26 percent in 1997); followed by general merchandising frauds at 7 percent; Internet access service frauds at 2 percent; company equipment and software frauds at 1.3 percent; work-at-home frauds at 0.9 percent; and advance-fee loans, magazines, adult services, travel/vacations, and pyramid scheme frauds at around 0.1–0.2 percent each. Consumers lost over US$3.2 million to cyber-fraud, with an average loss per consumer of US$580 for on-line purchases of computer equipment or software, and US$465 for general merchandise sales. The average loss per consumer to online auction sales was US$293.[48] The Federal Trade Commission, which responds to consumer complaints regarding Internet fraud, filed 61 suits in 1999, up from one in 1994. Thus far, these actions have resulted in the collection of more than US$20 million in payments to consumers and the end of schemes with annual estimated sales of over US$250 million.[49]

Total frauds reported rose from 689 in 1996 to 10,660 in 1999, with the Internet (at 90 percent) and e-mail (at 5 percent) being the primary contact method for initiating the fraudulent action. Examples of fraud include *pyramid schemes* in which participants attempt to make money solely by recruiting new participants into the programme; *pump and dump* schemes, in which readers are urged to buy a stock quickly before the price falls, following which the fraudsters sell their shares and stop hyping the stock, resulting in the price plummeting and the investors losing their money; and other investment schemes in which spectacular profits or a guaranteed return is offered, such as extraordinarily high bank deposit rates, promises of free stocks, getting-rich-quick e-mail opportunity, or stock that is artificially inflated. Interestingly, the overwhelming majority of fraudulent payments (93 percent) were made offline by cheque or money order sent to the fraudulent company.[50]

Attempts at cracking stock market and banking financial assets have also increased. An example was the attempt by Russian TOC to use crackers to make forty illegal transfers from Citibank in an attempt to steal US$10 million. In addition, online investment fraud is increasing. In the US, the Securities and Exchange Commission (SEC) receives around 250 complaints per day of suspected cyber-fraud, totalling more than 54,000 in one year, an increase of 50 percent from five years ago. Attempts to crack down on violators are difficult and appear to meet with little result; this may be partly because the number of investors trading online grew by 2.2 million to more than 5.2 million in 1999, with more than 25 percent of all stock-trades occurring over the Internet. Many of these individuals are new to online trading and thus prone to such frauds. One recent cyber-fraud took in US$6.3 million before the SEC was able to stop it.[51]

One famous example is of two individuals in Los Angeles, who were convicted in December 1999 of securities fraud for artificially inflating a company's stock price by posting false information about the firm on Internet bulletin boards. The pair, using public computers at the University of California which made tracing them much more difficult, made US$370,000 by purchasing shares of a company called NEI Web World at thirteen cents a share then selling them for as much as fifteen dollars after claiming on bulletin boards that LCG Wireless Inc. planned to buy NEI Web World. The case is similar to that of PairGain, believed to be the first instance of Internet-based stock manipulation, in which a former employee of PairGain Technologies Inc. directed bulletin board visitors to a false Bloomberg story that said the company was a takeover target. PairGain stock soared by 31 percent before dropping back down. The employee pleaded guilty in June 1999.

One of the biggest frauds ever perpetrated on the Internet was the fictitious 'Dominion of Melchizedek', in which a fake 'country' was established by California-based cyber-fraudsters as a 'tax haven', and offers made to incorporate banks, insurance companies, trusts and private corporations for a few thousand dollars. 'Melchizedek' claimed to have 'embassies' and other 'legations' in Washington, Canberra, Budapest, Lima and Sao Paulo, and 'trade centres and liaison offices' in Singapore and Lagos. The group were caught in 1998 and 1999 by international law enforcement efforts.[52]

Currently, the FBI estimates that cyber-crimes are running at approximately US$10 billion a year. More than 90 percent of all companies have reported breaches, while 74 percent reported theft of proprietary information, financial fraud, system penetration by outsiders, data or network sabotage, or DoS attacks. Information theft and financial fraud caused the most severe financial losses, at US$68 million and US$56 million respectively, while losses traced to DoS attacks were only US$77,000 in 1998, and by 1999 had risen to just US$116,250. This may be contributing to a decreasing confidence in e-commerce by the public. A Spring 2000 poll conducted by the Information Technology Association of America found that 61 percent of those surveyed said that rising cyber-crime made them less likely to do business over the Internet, while 62 percent said they did not believe enough was being done to protect consumers against cyber-crime.[53]

In March 2000, then-FBI Director Louis Freeh reported that cyber-attacks in the US had doubled in the last year.[54] In addition, there exists the threat that, during a foreign intervention, asymmetric opponents may use IO strategically (in both the cyber and psycho-political arenas) to cause mass disruption to civil society and introduce a cyber-war that would slow the decision-making process of the governments involved. While amateur hackers receive most publicity, the real threats are the professionals or 'cyber-mercenaries'. This term refers to highly skilled and trained products of government agencies or corporate intelligence branches working on the open market. The Colombian drug cartels hired cyber-mercenaries to install and run a sophisticated secure communications system, while Amsterdam-based gangs used professional hackers to monitor and disrupt the communications and information systems of police surveillance teams. While amateur hackers have little reason to move around, the professionals can be very mobile. For this reason, links with TOC groups are of great interest. The Russian and Eastern bloc governments produced numerous trained hackers as well as IW weapons. Bulgaria is notorious as a virus factory while portable Directed Energy Weapons (which will fry unshielded electronic circuitry) can be purchased openly in the Baltic states. Finally, an asymmetric opponent could also conduct a slow-motion strategic economic warfare campaign against private economic interests in the West, through attacks on a wide range of e-payments or electronic currency systems that facilitate the global transition to e-commerce by a high-performance criminal organisation. In these situations, there appears little – at first – that western governments and the international community can do to defeat these threats.

However, such attacks may not be as easy as it would (at first) seem. In order to launch a sophisticated attack against a hardened target, an actor will most likely have three to four years of practice in programming C, C++, Perl and Java (computer languages), general UNIX and NT systems administration (types of computer platform), LAN/WAN theory, remote access and common security protocols (network skills), and a lot of free time. On top of these technical nuts and bolts, there are certain skills that must be acquired within the cracker community.

Other forms of attack (in addition to penetration or 'cracking' attacks) are becoming more prevalent. Both DoS and DDoS attacks have grown in strength since the February 2000 attack on US-based e-commerce sites. At the moment, a coordinated attack to bring down a government's or a corporation's computer systems cannot be maintained long enough to be anything more than a nuisance. Yet while only annoying at the moment, as interconnectivity increases and the importance of the online economy becomes manifest, such exploits will have serious financial implications.

Cyber-terrorism is not only about damaging systems but also about intelligence gathering. The focus on 'shut down' scenarios and analogies to physically violent techniques ignore other more potentially effective uses of

IT in terrorist warfare: intelligence gathering, counter-intelligence and disinformation. In addition, concomitant cyber-attacks with real-world terrorist incidents (as alluded to in the September 2001 attacks) could potentially multiply the disastrous consequences massively. Attacking an information system would be a good way to either distract the target or otherwise enable the terrorist to perform a physical attack: for example, had Aum Shinrikyo been able to crack the Tokyo power system and stop the subways, trapping passengers on the trains, the number of casualties caused by their 1995 sarin gas attack might have been significantly larger.[55]

Other concerns include 'cracking' attacks whose aim are not to gather information but rather to erase or modify existing data within an information system. For example, UK and US interbank transactions are backed up daily with multiple remote tapes, so any cracker wanting to destroy the interbank market will cause the loss of at most one day's transactions. However, consequences could rebound on consumer confidence in the banking system were exploits to be publicised. Similarly, 'spoofing' – which includes attempts to create phoney records or phoney messages in a system (such as creating false bank accounts), or attempts to create phoney instructions to the processing system – can also cause systems to fail.

Defending against Cyber-Terrorism: Critical Infrastructure Protection and Information Assurance

By 2001, European and US policy makers at the highest levels were expressing their concerns that insecure information systems threatened economic growth and national security. President Bush's National Security Adviser, Condoleezza Rice, noted in March 2001 that: 'it is a paradox of our times that the very technology that makes our economy so dynamic and our military forces so dominating also makes us more vulnerable'. She warned, 'Corrupt [the information] networks, and you disrupt this nation'.[56] The European Commission warned in March 2001 that 'the information infrastructure has become a critical part of the backbone of our economies. Users should be able to rely on the availability of information services and have the confidence that their communications and data are safe from unauthorised access or modification. The take up of electronic commerce and the full realisation of an Information Society depend on this.'[57]

As a result of these concerns, a complex and overlapping web of national, regional and multilateral initiatives has emerged.[58] A common theme behind these initiatives is the recognition of the inadequacy of existing state-centric policing and legislative structures to police international networks and the importance of ensuring that private networks are secured against disruption.

One way of grouping these initiatives is to use the standard information security paradigm of deterrence; prevention; detection; and reaction.

- *Deterrence:* Multilateral initiatives to deter CNA include harmonising cyber-crime legislation to promote tougher criminal penalties and better e-commerce legislation.
- *Prevention:* Multilateral initiatives to prevent CNA centre around promoting the design and use of more secure information systems and better information security management in both public and private sectors. Other measures include legal and technological initiatives such as the promotion of security mechanisms.
- *Detection:* Multilateral initiatives to detect CNA include the creation of enhanced cooperative policing mechanisms. Another important area is the effort to provide early warning of cyber-attack through exchanging information between the public and private sectors.
- *Reaction:* Multilateral initiatives to react to CNA include efforts to design robust and survivable information infrastructures; development of crisis management systems; and improvement in coordination of policing and criminal justice efforts.

Overall, these initiatives involve significant investments of time and effort from a variety of government departments in many nations, from numerous international organisations and from numerous companies, large and small. Many initiatives are pre-existing, many are being pursued in isolation. Nonetheless, there has emerged a coherent and effective set of initiatives involving states and businesses – not to mention some NGOs – that are focused upon improving the security of the emerging global information environment.

NOTES

1. Evans, Michael (1999), 'Conventional Deterrence in the Australian Strategic Context'. Land Warfare Studies Centre Working Paper No. 103. Online. Available: www.defence.gov.au/lwsc/wp103.html. 1 May 2003.
2. The term 'cyber-space' is used here to refer to any and all aspects of the Internet and World-Wide Web (including communications and informational means), as well as any networked system or systems which are connected to other systems outside of themselves.
3. 'The Forward Look 1999'. Online. The Office of Science and Technology. Available: www.dti.gov.uk/ost/forwardlook99/states/mod/text.htm#section02. 1 May 2003.
4. Tucker, Jonathan (1999), 'Asymmetric Warfare'. Online. Available: http://forum.ra.utk.edu/summer99/asymmetric.htm. 1 May 2003.
5. Allen, Robert (1997), *Asymmetric Warfare: Is The Army Ready?*, Army Management Staff College, Seminar 14, Class 97-3. Online. Available: www.amsc.belvoir.army.mil/asymmetric_warfare.htm. 1 May 2003.

6. Government of Canada – Department of National Defence (2000), *Threat Definition: Asymmetric Threats and Weapons of Mass Destruction* (3000-1 (DNB CD) April), p 17.

7. *Ibid.*, p 18.

8. Presented to Parliament by the Secretary of State for the Home Department and the Secretary of State for Northern Ireland by Command of Her Majesty (December 1998). Online. Available: www.archive.official-documents.co.uk/document/cm41/4178/4178. htm. 1 May 2003.

9. Government of the United Kingdom and Northern Ireland, Terrorism Act (2000) s1 (1–5) 'Terrorism: Interpretation'. Online. Available: www.hmso.gov.uk/acts/acts2000/00011-b.htm#1. 1 May 2003.

10. Government of the United States (2001), Uniting and Strengthening America by Providing Appropriate Tools Required to Intercept and Obstruct Terrorism Act, 25 October, HR 3162 RDS (107th CONGRESS, 1st Session): SEC. 411. 'DEFINITIONS RELATING TO TERRORISM – Amendment to Section 212(a)(3) of the Immigration and Nationality Act (8 U.S.C. 1182(a)(3))'. Online. Available: http://frwebgate.access.gpo.gov/cgi-bin/getdoc. cgi?dbname=107_cong_public_laws&docid=f:publ056.107. 1 May 2003.

11. Government of Canada, Anti-terrorism Act, Bill C-36 (18 December 2001): s83.01 (1)(b)(ii). Online. Available: www.parl.gc.ca/37/1/parlbus/chambus/house/bills/ government/C-36/C-36_4/C-36TOCE.html.

12. Government of Australia, Security Legislation Amendment (Terrorism) Bill 2002 (13 March 2002) Part 5.3:100.1(2) 'Definitions'. Online. Available: http://scaletext.law.gov. au/html/comact/11/6499/top.htm. 1 May 2003.

13. Thomas, Timothy (2001), 'Deterring Asymmetric Terrorist Threats to Society in the Information Age'. Online. Available: http://www.waaf.ru/31.htm. 1 May 2003.

14. Online. Available: www.iaac.org.uk/actionplan.htm. 1 May 2003.

15. Online. Available: www.isodarco.it/files/trento02-Mauro.ppt. 1 May 2003.

16. Alberts, David (2000), 'Information Superiority & Network-Centric Warfare'. Online. The Information Warfare site. Available: http://www.iwar.org.uk/iwar/resources/info-superiority1999/. 1 May 2003.

17. The distinction between 'cyber-crime' and 'cyber-terrorism' is often said to be that surrounding criminal activities perpetrated using new technologies. That is, 'cyber-crime' is equal to old crimes (such as fraud) while 'cyber-terrorism' is equal to new crimes (such as criminal threats to the information infrastructures themselves). In this sense, the term 'cyber-terrorism' is not a very useful term, as this is substantially not – at this point – 'terrorism' that is being discussed; for this reason, the terms 'cyber-based IO', 'cyber-threats' or 'cyber-attacks' (alongside 'netwar') are used to denote activities carried out in cyber-space to threaten directly those information infrastructures which underpin both the Internet and all other critical infrastructures in today's advanced societies.

18. Government of Canada, Anti-terrorism Act, p 12.

19. Cyrulik, Joseph (1999), 'Asymmetric Warfare and the Threat to the American Homeland', *Landpower Essay Series*, 99-8, November.

20. Government of Canada, Anti-terrorism Act, p 12.

21. Cyrulik (1999) 'Asymmetric Warfare and the Threat to the American Homeland'.

22. Government of Canada, Anti-terrorism Act, p 12.

23. Rathmell, Andrew (1999), 'Controlling Computer Network Operations', *Information & Security Journal:* Special Issue on 'The Internet and the Changing Face of International Relations and Security'. Online. Available: www.nato.int/acad/fellow/99-01/rathmell.pdf. 1 May 2003.

24. Government of the UK – Ministry of Defence (2001), *Draft Doctrine for Information Operations; Joint Doctrine Pamphlet XX-01.* Joint Doctrine and Concepts Centre, Shrivenham, 1 March, p 8.

25. Center for Strategic and International Studies (2000), *Asymmetric Warfare and Homeland Defense*, 8 December. Online. Available: www.csis.org/burke/hd/reports/Transatlantic 1107.pdf. 1 May 2003.

26. Arquilla, John, Ronfeldt, David and Zanini, Michele (1999), 'Networks, Netwar and Information-Age Terrorism', in Lesser, Ian, Hoffman, Bruce, Arquilla, John, Jenkins, Brian, Ronfeldt, David and Zanini, Michele (eds), *Countering the New Terrorism*, Santa Monica: RAND, p 47.

27. Arkin, William (1999), 'The Cyberbomb in Yugoslavia', *The Washington Post*, 25 October.

28. 'Pentagon Sets Up New Center for Waging Cyberwarfare', *Military and C4I*. Online. Available: www.infowar.com/MIL_C4I/99/mil_c4I_1000999a_j.shtml. 1 May 2003.

29. Serabian Jr, John (2000), *Statement for the Record before the Joint Economic Committee on Cyber Threats and the U.S. Economy*, Online. Central Intelligence Agency, 23 February. Available: www.cia.gov/cia/public_affairs/speeches/archives/2000/cyberthreats_022300.html. 1 May 2003.

30. McDonald, Tim (2001), 'CIA to Congress: We're Vulnerable to Cyber-Warfare', *NewsFactor Network*, 22 June.

31. *Seattle Times* (2001), 'How al-Qaeda Spoofed the West – bin Laden may have tricked spies: Officials say their intelligence pointed to an attack overseas', 12 September.

32. As defined by the Information Assurance Advisory Council (IAAC) Threat Assessment Working Group – see: www.iaac.org.uk.

33. Brynjar, Lia and Hansen, Annika (1999), *An Analytical Framework for the Study of Terrorism and Asymmetric Warfare*, Kjeller: Norwegian Defence Research Establishment, p 10.

34. Hoffman, Bruce (1998), *Inside Terrorism*, New York: Columbia University Press; and Lesser et al. (eds) (1999), *Countering the New Terrorism*. Also see Laqueur, Walter (1999), *The New Terrorism: Fanaticism and the Arms of Mass Destruction*, Oxford: Oxford University Press.

35. Arquilla, John and Ronfeldt, David (1996), *The Advent of Netwar*, Santa Monica: RAND, pp 67–75; Reeves, Richard, Veash, Nichole and Arlidge, John (1999), *The Observer* (1999), 'Virtual Chaos Baffles Police', 20 June.

36. Ingles-le Nobel, Johan J. (1999), 'Cyberterrorism hype', *Jane's Intelligence Review*, 11/12, December.

37. Dean, Joshua (2002), 'National infrastructures key to military strategy, Defense official says'. Online. *Government Executive Magazine*. 11 February. Available: http://www.govexec.com/dailyfed/0202/021102j1.htm. 1 May 2003. 23 March 2003.

38. *Ibid*.

39. *The New York Times* (2001), 'Chinese Hackers Invade 2 Official U.S. Web Sites', 28 April; Reuters (2001), 'Hackers Report a Truce', 10 May.

40. Thomas (2001), 'Deterring Asymmetric Terrorist Threats to Society in the Information Age'.

41. Sager, Ira (2000), 'Cyber Crime: First Yahoo! Then eBay. The Net's vulnerability threatens e-commerce – and you', *Business Week*, 21 February.

42. Statement for the Record of Guadalupe Gonzalez (Special Agent In Charge, Phoenix Field Division, FBI) on Cyber-crime Before a Special Field Hearing Senate Committee on Judiciary Subcommittee on Technology, Terrorism, and Government Information, Washington, DC. 21 April 2000.

43. Voss, Natalie (1997), 'Crime on the Internet'. Online. *Jones Telecommunications and Multimedia Encyclopaedia*, 23 September. Available: http://www.digitalcentury.com/encyclo/update/crime.html. 1 May 2003.

44. Sager (2000), 'Cyber Crime: First Yahoo! Then eBay. The Net's vulnerability threatens e-commerce – and you'.

45. *Ibid*.

46. Detective Inspector James O'Connell (Metropolitan Police Computer Crime Unit), 'Strategies to Defeat Crime: Policing Cybercrime', *Cityforum Conference Transcripts*.

47. Center for Strategic and International Studies (2000), 'Cybercrime ... Cyberterrorism ... Cyberwarfare ...'. Online. Available: http://www.csis.org/pubs/cyberfor.html. 1 May 2003.

48. National Consumers League (2000), 'National Consumers League Warns Consumers Millions are Lost to Internet Fraud', 16 February.
49. Sager (2000), 'Cyber Crime: First Yahoo! Then eBay. The Net's vulnerability threatens e-commerce – and you'.
50. Internet Fraud Watch (1999), 'Going once, going twice ... scammed!', 23 February.
51. Fraser, Andrew (1999), 'Regulators Struggle to Keep Up with Explosion of Online Fraud', *The Wall Street Journal*, 1 March.
52. *The Nation* (1999), 'Cyberfraud – The Fictitious "Dominion Of Melchizedek"', 30 May.
53. Fields, Gary (2000), 'Poll: Cybercrime deters shoppers 61% say viruses, other attacks make them less likely to spend on the Net', *USA Today*, p 5A.
54. *Newsbytes* (2000), 'FBI Chief says Cyber Attacks Doubled in a Year', 28 March.
55. Ingles-le Nobel (1999), 'Cyberterrorism hype'.
56. AP (2001), 'National Security Adviser sees cyberterrorist threat', 26 March.
57. Council of Europe Treaty (2000), 'Creating a Safer Information Society by Improving the Security of Information Infrastructures and Combating Computer-related Crime', Online. Global Internet Policy Initiative. Available: http://www.gipiproject.org/cybercrime/. 1 May 2003.
58. An overview of such activities is included in Rathmell, Andrew and O'Brien, Kevin (eds) (2000), *Information Operations: A Global Perspective*, Coulsden: Jane's Information Group.

10. The Networking of Terror in the Information Age

Michele Zanini

INTRODUCTION

The information revolution has fuelled the longest economic expansion in US history and led to impressive productivity gains in recent years. Along with these benefits, however, has come the dark side of information technology – cyber-terrorism. The idea of terrorists surreptitiously hacking into a computer system to introduce a virus, steal sensitive information, deface or swamp a website, or turn off a crucial public service, seriously concerns computer security personnel around the world. The exponential increase in reported incidents over the last ten years (see Figure 10.1), along with recent high profile attacks – such as the denial-of-service (DOS) attacks against major e-commerce sites Yahoo and eBay in 1999 or the ongoing 'cyber-jihad' against Israeli and American websites being waged by Pakistani-based hackers in support of the Palestinian al-Aqsa Intifada – continue to raise the spectre of cyber-terrorism.

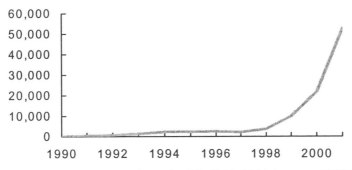

Figure 10.1   Computer attacks in the US, 1990–2001 (source: CERT)

Despite such publicity, the information age is affecting not only the types of targets and weapons terrorists might choose, but also the ways in which such groups operate and structure their organisations. Several of the most dangerous terrorist outfits are using information technology (IT) – such as computers, software, telecommunication devices, and the Internet – to better organise and coordinate dispersed activities. Like the large numbers of private corporations that have embraced information technologies in order to operate more efficiently and with greater flexibility, terrorists are harnessing the power of IT to enable new operational doctrines and forms of organisation. Just as companies in the private sector are forming alliance networks to provide complex services to customers, so too are terrorist groups 'disaggregating' from hierarchical bureaucracies and moving to flatter, more decentralised and often changing webs of groups united by a common goal.

The rise of networked terrorists groups is part of a broader shift to what Arquilla and Ronfeldt have called 'netwar'. Netwar refers to an emerging mode of conflict and crime at societal levels, involving measures short of traditional war in which the protagonists are likely to consist of dispersed, small groups who communicate, coordinate, and conduct their campaigns in an internetted manner, without a precise central command. Netwar differs from modes of conflict in which the actors prefer formal, stand-alone, hierarchical organisations, doctrines and strategies, as in past efforts, for example, to build centralised revolutionary movements along Marxist lines.

This chapter assesses the degree to which – and how – networked terrorist groups are using IT, particularly in the Middle East. The analysis reviews past trends, and offers a series of educated guesses about how such trends will evolve in the future. The first section discusses the organisational implications of netwar, especially the degree to which IT is enabling different forms of terrorist structures and Command, Control, Communications and Computers (C^4). The second section examines past evidence of terrorist use of IT for offensive netwar, such as destructive and disruptive attacks on information systems, and for perception management. The third section contains a speculative look at how future terrorist uses of IT could develop in the near to medium term. The final part concludes with implications for counter-terrorism policy.

ORGANISATIONAL NETWORKING AND TECHNOLOGY ACQUISITION

In an archetypal netwar, the protagonists are likely to amount to a set of diverse, dispersed 'nodes' who share a set of ideas and interests and who often are arrayed to act in a fully internetted 'all-channel' manner. The potential effectiveness of the networked design compared to traditional hierarchical designs attracted the attention of management theorists as early as the 1960s.[1] Today, in the business world, virtual or networked organisations are heralded as effective alternatives to traditional bureaucracies because of their inherent flexibility, adaptiveness, and ability to capitalise on the talents of all their members.

Networked organisations share three basic sets of features. Firstly, communication and coordination are not formally specified by horizontal and vertical reporting relationships, but rather emerge and change according to the task at hand. Similarly, relationships are often informal and marked by varying degrees of intensity, depending on the needs of the organisation. Linkages to individuals outside the organisation, often spanning national boundaries, usually complement second, internal networks. Like internal connections, external relationships are formed and wind down according to the life cycle of particular joint projects. Thirdly, both internal and external ties are enabled not by bureaucratic fiat, but rather by shared norms and values, as well as by reciprocal trust. Internally, self-managing teams conduct the bulk of the work, while external linkages comprise 'a constellation involving a complex network of contributing firms or groups'.[2]

THE EMERGENCE OF NETWORKED TERRORIST GROUPS IN THE GREATER MIDDLE EAST

What has been emerging in the business world is now becoming apparent in the organisational structures of the newer and more active terrorist groups, which appear to be adopting decentralised, flexible network structures. The rise of networked arrangements in terrorist organisations is part of a wider move away from formally organised, state-sponsored groups to privately financed, loose networks of individuals and sub-groups that may have strategic guidance, but which nonetheless enjoy tactical independence.

The Middle East is an example. There, terrorist groups have diverse origins, ideologies, and organisational structures, but can be categorised roughly into traditional and new-generation groups. Traditional groups date from the late 1960s and early 1970s, and the majority were (and some still are) formally or informally linked to the Palestine Liberation Organisation (PLO). Typically, they are also relatively bureaucratic and maintain a nationalist or Marxist agenda.[3] These groups have utilised autonomous cells as part of their organisational structure, but a hierarchy through clear reporting relationships and virtually no horizontal coordination guides the operation of such cells.

In contrast, the newer and less hierarchical groups, such as Hamas, the Palestinian Islamic Jihad, Hizbollah, Algeria's Armed Islamic Group, the Egyptian Islamic Group, and Osama bin Laden's terrorist network, al-Qaeda, have become the most active organisations.[4] In these loosely organised groups with religious or ideological motives, operatives are part of a network that relies less on bureaucratic fiat and more on shared values and horizontal coordination mechanisms to accomplish their goals.

The new and more active generation of Middle Eastern groups has operated both inside and outside the region. For instance, in Israel and the occupied territories, Hamas and to a lesser extent the Palestinian Islamic Jihad have demonstrated their strength over the last five years with a series of suicide bombings that have killed more than 100 people. In Egypt, the Islamic Group (also known as al-Gama'a al-Islamiya) carried out a 1997 attack at Luxor, killing 58 tourists and four Egyptians. Another string of terrorist attacks (and foiled attempts) has focused attention on the loosely organised group of 'Arab Afghans' – radical Islamic fighters from several North African and Middle Eastern countries who forged ties while resisting the Soviet occupation of Afghanistan. One of the leaders and founders of the Arab Afghan movement is Osama bin Laden, a Saudi entrepreneur based in Afghanistan.[5]

To varying degrees, these groups share the principles of the networked organisation – relative flatness, decentralisation and delegation of decision-making authority, and loose lateral ties among dispersed groups and individuals. Hamas, for example, is loosely structured, with 'some elements working clandestinely and others working openly through mosques and social service institutions to recruit members, raise money, organise activities, and distribute propaganda'.[6] The pro-Iranian Hizbollah in southern Lebanon acts as an umbrella organisation of radical Shiite groups and in many respects is a hybrid of hierarchical and network arrangements – although the organisational structure is formal, interactions among members are volatile and do not follow rigid lines of control.[7]

Perhaps the most interesting example of a terrorist netwar actor is Osama bin Laden's complex network of relatively autonomous groups that are financed from private sources. Bin Laden uses his wealth and organisational skills to support and direct al-Qaeda, a multinational alliance of Islamic extremists. Al-Qaeda seeks to counter any perceived threats to Islam – wherever they come from – as indicated by bin Laden's 1996 declaration of a holy war against the United States and the West in general. In the declaration, bin Laden specified that irregular, light, highly mobile forces wage such a holy war. Although bin Laden finances al-Qaeda (exploiting a fortune of several million dollars, according to State Department estimates) and directs some operations, he apparently does not play a direct command-and-control role over all operatives. Rather, he is a key figure in the coordination and support of several dispersed nodes.[8]

There are reports that communications between al-Qaeda's members combine elements of a 'hub and spoke' structure (where nodes of operatives communicate with bin Laden and his close advisers in Afghanistan) with a wheel structure (where nodes in the network communicate with each other without reference to bin Laden).[9] Al-Qaeda's command and control structure includes a consultation council (*majlis al shura*), which discusses and approves major actions, and possibly a military committee.[10] At the heart of al-Qaeda is bin Laden's inner core group, which sometimes conducts missions on its own. Most of the other member organisations remain independent, although the barriers between them are fluid. According to US District Court testimony in New York, al-Qaeda has forged alliances with Egypt's Islamic Group (leading to an alleged influx of bin Laden operatives into its structure), the National Front in the Sudan and with the government of Iran and Hizbollah. Media reports also indicate that bin Laden has ties with other far-flung Islamic armed groups, such as Abu Sayyaf in the Philippines, as well as with counterparts in Somalia, Chechnya and Central Asia.[11]

COMMAND, CONTROL, COMMUNICATIONS, AND THE ROLE OF IT

Lateral coordination mechanisms facilitate the operations of networked groups. In turn, such coordination mechanisms are enabled by advances in information technology – including increases in the speed of communication, reductions in the costs of communication, increases in bandwidth, vastly expanded connectivity, and the integration of communication and computing technologies.[12] More specifically, new communication and computing technologies allow the establishment of networks in three critical ways.[13]

Firstly, they have greatly reduced transmission time, enabling dispersed organisational actors to communicate and coordinate their tasks. This phenomenon is not new – in the early twentieth century, the introduction of the telephone made it possible for large corporations to decentralise their operations by establishing local branches.

Secondly, they have significantly reduced the cost of communication, allowing information-intensive organisational designs such as networks to become viable.[14] As Thompson observed, in the past organisations sought to reduce coordination and communications costs by centralising and co-locating those activities that are inherently more coordination-intensive.[15] With the lowering of coordination costs, it is becoming increasingly possible to further disaggregate organisations through decentralisation and autonomy.

Thirdly, new technologies have substantially increased the scope and complexity of the information that can be shared, through the integration of computing with communications. Innovations such as computer conferencing, groupware, Internet chat and World Wide Websites allow participants to have 'horizontal' and rich exchanges without requiring them to be located in close proximity.

Thus, information-age technologies are highly advantageous for a netwar group whose constituents are geographically dispersed or carry out distinct but complementary activities.[16] IT can be used to plan, coordinate, and execute operations. Using the Internet for communication can increase speed of mobilisation and allow more dialogue between members, which enhances the organisation's flexibility, as tactics can be adjusted more frequently. Individuals with a common agenda and goals can form sub-groups, meet at a target location, conduct terrorist operations, and then readily terminate their relationships and re-disperse.

The al-Qaeda network appears to have adopted information technology to support its networked mode of operations. According to reporters who visited bin Laden's headquarters in a remote mountainous area of Afghanistan, the terrorist financier has modern computer and communications equipment. Bin Laden allegedly uses satellite phone terminals to coordinate the activities of the group's dispersed operatives, and has even devised countermeasures to ensure his safety while using such communication systems.[17] Satellite phones reportedly travel in separate convoys from bin Laden's, the Saudi financier also refrains from direct use, and often dictates his message to an assistant, who then relays it telephonically from a different location. Bin Laden's operatives have used CD-ROM disks to store and disseminate information on recruiting, bomb making, heavy weapons, and terrorist operations.[18] Egyptian computer experts who fought alongside bin Laden in the Afghan conflict are said to have helped him devise a communications network that relies on the World Wide Web, e-mail, and electronic bulletin boards so that members can exchange information.

This is a trend found among other terrorist actors in the Middle East. Counter-terrorist operations targeting Algerian Armed Islamic Group (GIA) bases in the 1990s uncovered computers and diskettes with instructions for the construction of bombs. In fact, it has been reported that the GIA makes heavy use of floppy disks and computers to store and process orders and other information for its members, who are dispersed in Algeria and Europe. The militant Islamic group Hamas also uses the Internet to share and communicate operational information. Hamas activists in the United States use chat rooms to plan operations and activities. Operatives use e-mail to coordinate actions across Gaza, the West Bank, and Lebanon. Hamas has realised that information can be passed relatively securely over the Internet because counter-terrorism intelligence cannot monitor accurately the flow and content of all Internet traffic. In fact, Israeli security officials cannot easily trace Hamas messages or decode their content.

In addition, terrorist networks can protect their vital communication flows through readily available commercial technology, such as encryption programs. Examples from outside the Middle East point in this direction – according to one report, Animal Liberation Front cells in North America and Europe use the encryption program 'Pretty Good Privacy.' to send coded e-mail and share intelligence.[19] New encryption programs emerging on the commercial market are becoming so sophisticated that coded e-mails may soon be extremely difficult to break. In fact, strong encryption programs are being integrated into commercial applications and network protocols so that soon encryption will be easy and automatic.[20] Rumours persist that the French police have been unable to decrypt the hard disk on a portable computer belonging to a captured member of the Basque Fatherland and Liberty group (ETA).[21] It has also been suggested that Israeli security forces were unsuccessful in their attempts at cracking the codes used by Hamas to send a full range of instructions for terrorist attacks over the Internet.[22] Terrorists can also use steganography – a method of hiding secret data in other data such as embedding a secret message within a picture file.[23] Terrorists can also encrypt cell phone transmissions, steal cell phone numbers and program them into a single phone, or use pre-paid cell phone cards purchased anonymously to keep their communications secure.[24]

The latest communications technologies are thus enabling terrorists to operate from almost any country in the world, provided they have access to the necessary IT infrastructure. This affects the ways in which groups rely on different forms of sponsorship. Some analysts have argued that networked terrorists may have a reduced need for state support – indeed, governmental protection may become less necessary if technologies such as encryption allow a terrorist group to operate with a greater degree of stealth and safety.[25] Others point to the possibility that groups will increasingly attempt to raise money on the Web, as in the case of Pakistan's Lashkar-e-Taiba (Army of the Pure).[26]

NETWORKED ORGANISATIONS AND INFORMATION TECHNOLOGY: MITIGATING FACTORS

To be sure, there are limits to how much reliance terrorist networks will place on information-age technology. For the foreseeable future, electronically mediated coordination will not be able to entirely supplant face-to-face exchanges, because uncertainty and risk will continue to characterise most organisational choices and interactions among individuals.[27] Moreover, informal linkages and the shared values mentioned above – which are critical enablers of networked designs – can only be fostered through personal contact. As Nohria and Eccles argue, 'electronically mediated exchange can increase the range, amount, and velocity of information flow in a network organisation. But the viability and effectiveness of this electronic network will depend critically on an underlying network of social relationships based on face-to-face interaction.'[28]

Moreover, while IT-enabled communication flows can greatly help a network coordinate dispersed activities (thus increasing its flexibility and responsiveness), they can also present a security risk. Communication over the electronic channels can become a liability, since it leaves digital 'traces'. For instance, FBI officials have recently acknowledged that they used an Internet wiretap program called 'Carnivore' to track terrorist e-mail correspondence at least twenty-five times. According to *Newsweek*, Carnivore's ability to track Osama bin Laden e-mail was critical in thwarting several of his strikes.[29]

The case of Ramzi Yousef, the 1993 World Trade Center bomber, also provides a revealing example of how information-age technology can represent a double-edged sword for terrorists. Yousef's numerous calls to fellow terrorists during his preparation for the strike were registered in phone companies' computer databases, providing law enforcement officials with a significant set of leads for investigating terrorists in the Middle East and beyond. Prior to his arrest, Yousef unintentionally offered the FBI another source of information when he lost control of his portable computer in the Philippines. In that laptop, US officials found incriminating data, including plans for future attacks, flight schedules, projected detonation times, and chemical formulae.[30]

There are other examples of how electronic information belonging to terrorist groups has fallen into the hands of law enforcement personnel. In 1995, Hamas' Abd-al-Rahman Zaydan was arrested and his computer seized – the computer contained a database of Hamas contact information that was used to apprehend other suspects. In December 1999, fifteen terrorists linked to Osama bin Laden were arrested in Jordan; along with bomb-making materials, rifles, and radio-controlled detonators, a number of computer disks were seized. Intelligence analysts were able to extract information about bomb-building and terrorist training camps in Afghanistan.[31] In June of 2000 the names of nineteen suspects were found on computer disks recovered from a Hizbollah-controlled house. Finally, Japanese authorities retrieved several RSA-encrypted computer records belonging to the millennialist Aum Shinrikyo cult after an electronic key was recovered.[32]

Thus, the organisational benefits associated with greater IT must be traded off with the needs for direct human contact and improved security. This makes it likely that terrorist groups will adopt designs that fall short of fully connected, all-channel networks. Hybrids of hierarchies and networks may better reflect the relative costs and benefits of greater IT reliance – as well as further the group's mission.[33] Another important factor determining the adoption of IT by terrorist groups involves the relative attractiveness of high-tech offensive information operations.

NETWAR, TERRORISM, AND OFFENSIVE INFORMATION OPERATIONS

In addition to enabling networked forms of organisation, IT can also improve terrorist intelligence collection and analysis, as well as offensive information operations (IO).[34] The acquisition by terrorist groups of an offensive IO capability could represent a significant threat as the world becomes more dependent on information and communications flows.[35] We argue that information-age technology can help terrorists conduct three broad types of offensive IO. Firstly, it can aid them in their perception management and propaganda activities. Next, such technology can be used to attack virtual targets for disruptive purposes. Finally, IT can be used to cause physical destruction.[36]

Perception Management and Propaganda

Given the importance of knowledge and soft power to the conduct of netwar, it is not surprising that networked terrorists have already begun to leverage IT for perception management and propaganda to influence public opinion, recruit new members, and generate funding. Getting a message out and receiving extensive news media exposure are important components of terrorist strategy, which ultimately seeks to undermine the will of an opponent. In addition to the traditional media such as television or print, the Internet now offers terrorist groups an alternative way to reach out to the public, often with much more direct control over their message.

The news media play an integral part in a terrorist act because they are the conduits for news of the violence to the general population. As Bruce Hoffman has noted, '[t]errorism ... may be seen as a violent act that is conceived specifically to attract attention and then, through the publicity it generates, to communicate a message'.[37] Terrorists have improved their media management techniques to the point of using 'spin doctoring' tactics.[38] In fact, some groups have even acquired their own television and radio stations to take direct control of the reporting of events. Hizbollah has broadcast footage of strikes carried out by its operatives through its television station, and has a sophisticated media centre that regularly – and professionally – briefs foreign journalists. Hizbollah field units have even included specially designated 'cameramen' to record dramatic video footage of Israeli casualties that was then aired in Lebanon and usually rebroadcast by Israeli television.[39]

The Internet now expands the opportunities for publicity and exposure beyond the traditional limits of television and print media. Before the Internet, a bombing might be accompanied by a phone call or fax to the press by a terrorist claiming responsibility. Now, bombings can be followed – should terrorists so desire – by an immediate press release from their own websites (at little cost). The fact that many terrorists now have direct control over the content of their message offers further opportunities for perception management, as well as for image-manipulation, special effects, and deception.

An Internet presence could prove advantageous for mobilizing 'part-time cyberterrorists' – that is, individuals not directly affiliated with a given terrorist group who nonetheless support its agenda and who use malicious software tools and instructions available at a terrorist website. This scenario would closely resemble the initiatives taken by both the Israeli and Palestinian governments, which have encouraged private citizens to download computer attack tools and become involved in the conflict surrounding the al-Aqsa Intifada.

It appears that nearly all terrorist groups have a World Wide Web presence.[40] Websites can also be used to refine or customise recruiting techniques. Recording which types of propaganda receive the most browser hits could help tailor a message for a particular audience. Using some of the same marketing techniques employed by commercial enterprises, terrorist servers could capture information about the users who browse their websites, and then later contact those who seem most interested. Recruiters may also use more interactive Internet technology to roam online chat rooms and cyber cafés looking for receptive members of the public, particularly young people. Electronic bulletin boards and user nets can also serve as vehicles for reaching out to potential recruits. Interested computer users around the world can be engaged in long-term 'cyber relationships' that could lead to friendship and eventual membership.

Disruptive Attacks

Netwar-oriented terrorists can also use IT to launch disruptive attacks – that is, electronic strikes that temporarily disable, but do not destroy, physical and/or virtual infrastructure. If the ultimate goal of a terrorist is to influence his opponent's will to fight, IO offers additional means to exert influence beyond using simple physical attacks to cause terror. Disruptive attacks include 'choking' computer systems through such tools as e-bombs, fax spamming, and hacking techniques to deface websites. These strikes are usually non-lethal in nature, although they can wreak havoc and cause significant economic damage.

To date, disruptive strikes by terrorists have been relatively few, and fairly unsophisticated – but they do seem to be increasing in frequency. For example, in 1996, the Liberation Tigers of Tamil Eelam (LTTE) launched an e-mail bomb attack against Sri Lankan diplomatic missions. Using automated tools, the guerrilla organisation flooded Sri Lankan embassies with thousands of messages, thus establishing a 'virtual blockade'. Japanese groups have allegedly attacked the computerised control systems for commuter trains, paralysing major cities for hours. In 2000, a group of Pakistani hackers who call themselves the Muslim Online Syndicate defaced more than 500 websites in India to protest the conflict in Kashmir.[41] Finally, Pakistan's Lashkar-e-Taiba claimed to have attacked Indian military websites in early 2000.[42]

Disruptive rather than more fully destructive actions can take place for several reasons. For example, terrorists who rely on the Internet for perception management and communication purposes may prefer not to take 'the Net' down, but rather to slow it down selectively. In addition, groups may want to rely on non-lethal cyber-strikes in order to pressure governments without alienating their own constituent audiences. Terrorist groups may also follow the lead of criminal hackers and use the threat of disruptive attacks to blackmail and extort funds from private sector entities. For example, the ongoing 'cyber-jihad' against Israel may come to target commercial enterprises that do business with the Israelis.[43] This has already been seen in the early 1990s, where hackers and criminals blackmailed brokerage houses and banks for several million British pounds. Money can also be stolen from individual users who visit terrorist websites.[44]

Destructive Attacks

As mentioned earlier, IT-driven IO can lead to the actual destruction of physical or virtual systems. Malicious viruses and worms can be used to permanently destroy (erase) or corrupt (spoof) data and cause economic damage. In the worst case, these same software tools can be used to cause destructive failure in a critical infrastructure like air traffic control, power, or water systems, which can lead to casualties. It is likely that information operations that result in the loss of life may offer the same level of drama as physical attacks with bombs. Striking targets through electronic means does not carry the risks associated with using conventional weapons – such as handling explosives or being in close proximity to the target.

Offensive IO: Mitigating Factors

The extreme case where the use of IT results in significant human losses has yet to occur. The lack of destructive information attacks is arguably influenced by the relative difficulty of electronically destroying (rather than disrupting) critical infrastructure components – the level of protection of existing infrastructure may be too high for terrorists to overcome with their current IT skill set. In fact, a terrorist organisation would first have to overcome significant technical hurdles to develop an electronic attack capability. Concentrating the necessary technical expertise and equipment to damage or destroy targeted information systems is no easy task given the computer security risks involved. In developing and increasing their reliance on electronic attacks, a terrorist organisation may be assuming risks and costs associated with the relative novelty of the technology. Terrorists wishing to expand the scope of their offensive IO activities would have to continue upgrading and researching new technologies in order to keep up with the countermeasures available to computer security experts and systems administrators. This technology 'treadmill' would demand constant attention and the diversion of scarce organisational resources.

Another important determinant of the low IT skill level of netwar terrorists has to do with the fact that conventional weapons such as bombs remain more cost effective. Most terrorism experts believe that existing groups see their current tactics as sufficient and are not interested in branching into computer network attacks. Since current tactics are simple and successful, there is no built-in demand to innovate: bombing still works.[45] As long as current tactics enable these groups to accomplish their short-term goals and move toward their long-term goals, there will not be strong incentives to change behaviour. The fragility of computer hardware may make a physical attack on these targets more attractive because it is significantly less challenging from a technical standpoint than attempting a virtual attack.[46]

Disruptive attacks may be easier to carry out, but because of their very nature they do not produce the same kind of visceral and emotional reaction that the loss of human life does. Indeed, some terrorism analysts argue that it is unlikely that terrorist groups will turn to disruptive attacks as the primary tactic. Brian Jenkins points out those IT-enabled disruptive strikes:

> do not produce the immediate, visible effects. There is no drama. No lives hang in the balance ... Terrorist intentions regarding cyberterrorism are even more problematic. Linking the objectives of actual terrorist groups to scenarios of electronic sabotage that would serve those objectives is conjecture.[47]

In addition, many computer security experts believe that even disruptive attacks remain technologically challenging for most terrorist groups and too undervalued by the media to make them attractive for terrorists.[48]

EVALUATING PAST, PRESENT, AND FUTURE TRENDS

Given that information technology brings drawbacks as well as benefits, the terrorist groups examined here have not chosen to rely exclusively on IT in order to coordinate their operations and execute attacks. The available evidence suggests that netwar terrorists have embraced IT for organisational purposes, especially to facilitate C^4, but they have been either unable or unwilling to attempt more ambitious offensive IO. The benefits clearly outweigh the risks when it comes to utilising IT for perception management and propaganda. See Table 10.1 for a summary.

Table 10.1   Benefits and drawbacks of IT use for netwar terrorists (facilitating and mitigating factors)

IT Use	Facilitating	Mitigating
Organisational	Enables dispersed activities with reasonable secrecy, anonymity.	Susceptibility to wire and wireless tapping. Digitally stored information can be easily retrievable unless well protected.
	Helps maintain a loose & flexible network. Lessens need for state sponsorship.	Cannot by itself energise a network; common ideology and direct contact still essential.
Offensive	Generally lower entry costs. Eradication of national boundaries. Physically safer. Spill over benefits for recruitment/fundraising.	Current bombing techniques already effective. Significant technical hurdles for disruptive and destructive IO. Unique computer security risks impose recurring costs of 'technology treadmill'.

FUTURE DEVELOPMENTS IN INFORMATION-AGE TERROR

Were the trends described above to persist, one could speculate that future netwar actors will continue to consolidate their IT use primarily for organisational purposes, with some emphasis on perception management on the offensive IO side. Under these conditions, networked terrorists would still rely on traditional weapons such as conventional bombs to cause physical violence. But they will also transmit information on how to build such weapons in CD-ROMs or e-mail, use chat rooms to coordinate their activities, and use websites to publicise and justify their strikes to a global audience.

The al-Aqsa Intifada in the West Bank and Gaza highlights how protracted IO campaigns could be waged in conjunction with a campaign of conventional violence. Mirroring the real-world violence that has resulted in hundreds of casualties, a conflict has also been waged in cyberspace over economic and propaganda stakes. Palestinian hackers who support the al-Aqsa Intifada have been waging a cyber-jihad against Israeli government and commercial targets, defacing websites and conducting DOS attacks. More than forty Israeli sites have been hit, including the Tel Aviv Stock Exchange and the Bank of Israel. Israeli hackers have counterattacked, hitting more than fifteen different Palestinian targets, including Hizbollah, Hamas, and the Palestinian National Authority. As the disruptive attacks have escalated, individuals and groups have joined both sides, from professional hackers to 'script-kiddies' (relative amateurs who rely on off-the-shelf and easy-to-use tools).[49]

Having said that, the swift and unpredictable changes associated with technology suggest that other outcomes are possible. The question is, will terrorists have the desire and opportunity to significantly increase their reliance on IT – primarily for offensive purposes – in the future? Several factors could influence such a shift, including the degree to which new technology will serve their main strategic goals in a safe and effective manner.[50] For instance, the introduction of easy-to-use, 'unbreakable' encryption programs to support e-mail and file exchange will encourage netwar terrorists to adopt such techniques. Moreover, terrorist access to technologies that can be readily employed without extensive internal development efforts[51] – by group members and part-time 'volunteers' or through 'hackers for hire',[52] – will be a critical facilitating factor. Equally important, the relative vulnerability of the information infrastructure plays a role in this calculus.

These possible developments would likely prompt the evolution of current netwar terrorist groups towards greater reliance on IT for offensive purposes, and could also encourage the emergence of new and completely virtual groups that exclusively operate in cyberspace.

The Evolution of Current Groups

As Brian Jackson notes, the introduction of new technologies in an organisation follows a complex and often lengthy process. Not only does innovation have to be developed or acquired, but also organisational actors have to become familiar with new systems, and be able to use them effectively.[53] Given the challenge, terrorist groups are likely to channel their scarce organisational resources to acquire those IT skills that have the greatest leverage for the least amount of cost and effort.

This line of reasoning can help explain terrorists' recent emphasis on using communications technology for organisational purposes. Having access to the Internet and cellular telephones is not overly complicated, and it plays a significant role in enabling dispersed operations – a key goal of netwar groups. It also suggests that over time terrorist groups might begin to experiment more aggressively with information-age technologies for offensive IOs, as they become more familiar with such innovations. Indeed, some may follow a 'migration' pattern as illustrated in Figure 10.2: the knowledge of IT issues gained by relying on technology to facilitate interactions among group members, or to gain a Web presence, might eventually be expanded and harnessed for increasingly offensive uses.

The pace with which current groups move through such a path is also dependent on the degree of cooperation and information exchange among netwar terrorists. Such cooperation has often occurred in the past – for instance, Islamic radicals have organised 'terror conferences',[54] while European terrorist groups such as the Irish Republican Army (IRA) entered into joint ventures with counterparts across the globe in order to learn from one another and disseminate knowledge (such as designs of booby-traps and radio-controlled bombs).[55] Given the loose and reciprocal nature of ties between actors in networks such as al-Qaeda, it is entirely possible that those with IT skills would be leveraged globally and placed at the disposal of the organisation's various members.

Lastly, as leading-edge groups begin to move toward the upper-right quadrant of Figure 10.2, other groups may be tempted to follow suit: terrorists that hitherto had decided to adopt a low technology profile for their offensive operations could be emboldened by successful instances of IT attacks by others.[56]

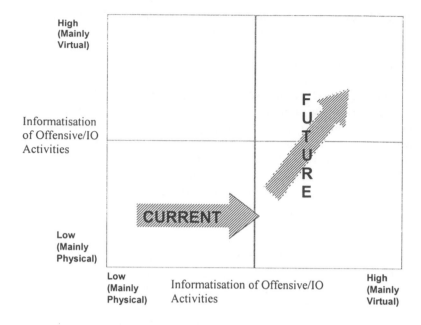

Figure 10.2   Possible shifts in the use of technology

The Emergence of New Groups

An alternative hypothesis to the notion that existing terrorist groups should be watched for signs of movement toward cyber-terror is that qualitative improvements in the informatisation of networked terrorists will only be witnessed with the emergence of newer, and more technologically savvy groups. Just as Hamas and al-Qaeda have overshadowed the Popular Front for the Liberation of Palestine (PFLP) and other Marxist groups formed in the 1960s, new-generation groups may take the trend toward networked and IT-reliant organisations a step further. New groups could even be led by individuals who are technically skilled, suggesting the rise of a hybrid breed of 'terrorists cum hackers'. Like hackers, they would undertake most of their attacks in cyberspace. Like terrorists, they would seek to strike targets by both disruptive and destructive means in order to further a political or religious agenda.

The possibility that innovation will only take place with the advent of new groups finds support in previous work by terrorism experts such as Hoffman, who describes most groups today as operationally conservative.[57] Aside from organisational inertia, current groups may also be hesitant to rely further on IT for offensive purpose because of large, 'sunk costs' in traditional tactics, training, and weapon stockpiles. Existing groups wishing to 'amortise' such capital cost may be unwilling to direct scarce resources toward the development of new and radically different offensive techniques.

POLICY IMPLICATIONS

The acquisition and use of information-age technology by terrorist groups is far from being a certainty. Indeed, the scenarios painted above are not mutually exclusive. It is conceivable that current groups will acquire new IT skills over time and adopt more offensive IT strategies. New hacker/terrorist groups may also emerge to compound this problem. Some terrorist networks may even become sophisticated enough to sustain and coordinate offensive campaigns in both the virtual and physical realms.

What is certain, however, is that counter-terrorism policy will only be able to counter the dangers associated with terrorist IT use if it becomes attuned to the information age. Counter-terrorist policies and tactics could even alter the speed with which terrorists become informatised – groups facing a robust counter-terrorism campaign may have less time and resources to acquire new technologies.[58] For such reasons, it seems advisable that counter-terrorism policy-makers and strategists bear in mind the following recommendations.

Firstly, they must monitor changes in the use of IT by terrorist groups, differentiating between organisational and offensive capabilities. Counter-terrorism policies will have to take into account the type of IT capabilities developed by each group, targeting their specific technological vulnerabilities. Evaluating how IT shapes a group's organisational processes and offensive activities will remain a critical component of the threat assessment. Monitoring the shift in capabilities for each type of IT use, and then examining trends in the aggregate, can also help forecast future terrorist behaviour.

Among the most significant trends to be carefully examined is the possible emergence of a new – and potentially dangerous – breed of terror, comprising those groups that are highly informatised along both the organisational and offensive axes. In this regard, a number of 'signposts' should be identified and tracked. These would include: significant increases in the level of technical expertise of known leaders and their subordinates; increases in the frequency of disruptive attacks; increases in the seizures of IT equipment owned by terrorists; the presence – and successful recruiting of 'hackers for hire'; and the availability of effective and relatively secure off-the-shelf information technologies (including those that facilitate hacking).

Secondly is the targeting of information flows. Since network designs are inherently information intensive, counter terrorism efforts should target the information flows of netwar groups. Intercepting and monitoring terrorist information exchanges should remain a top priority, and the implementation of Project Trailblazer by the National Security Agency – to develop a system that can crack new encryption software, fiber-optic cables, and cellular phone transmissions – represents a useful addition to America's SIGINT capability.[59]

Equally importantly, policy makers should consider going beyond the passive monitoring of information flows and toward the active disruption of such communications. To the degree that erroneous or otherwise misleading information is planted into a network's information flows by what are seemingly credible sources, over time the integrity and relevance of the network itself will be compromised. This in turn would breed distrust and further cripple a group's ability to operate in a dispersed and decentralised fashion – essentially eliminating a netwar group's key competitive advantage.

Increased emphasis on targeting information flows should not exclude non-electronic efforts to gather intelligence and undermine the network. Indeed, HUMINT will remain an important tool for intercepting (and injecting) information not transmitted through electronic means of communication.[60] This is an especially pressing concern, given that several intelligence observers have pointed to a lack of US capability in this area.

Thirdly, deterring IT-based offensives remains crucial. Changes in the vulnerability of critical infrastructures can significantly alter a terrorist's IT calculus. If such infrastructures, such as those that manage air traffic control, were to become relatively more vulnerable, they might become more attractive as targets: terrorists could strike at a distance, generating as much – if not more – destruction as would have been caused by the use of traditional weapons. US policy should identify specific vulnerabilities to expected threats and develop security techniques that mitigate each. An analysis of these issues is beyond the scope of the current chapter, but there are numerous studies that explore this process, including RAND's *Securing the US Defense Information Infrastructure: A Proposed Approach*.[61] The FBI's National Infrastructure Protection Center and other newly created organisations represent useful steps in this direction. Counter terrorist agencies may also want to consider the option of employing a large number of hackers and leveraging their knowledge for defensive and possibly even retaliatory purposes.

Lastly, the key is to beat networked terrorists at their own game. It takes networks to fight networks. Governments wishing to counter netwar terrorism will need to adopt organisational designs and strategies like those of their adversaries. This does not mean mirroring the opponent, but rather learning to draw on the same design principles of network forms. These principles depend to some extent upon technological innovation, but mainly on a willingness to innovate organisationally and doctrinally, and by building new mechanisms for inter-agency and multi-jurisdictional cooperation. The Technical Support Working Group (TSWG) is a good example of a non-traditional government interagency group with more than 100 member organisations from at least thirteen federal agencies and a growing number of local and state agencies. Its principal aim is to help develop and deploy technologies to combat terrorism.[62] Another example is the Counter-Intelligence 21 (CI-21) plan, a set of reforms that seek to increase the level of cooperation between counterintelligence personnel at the CIA, FBI, and the Pentagon.[63] If counter terrorism agencies become ready and willing to rely on networks of outside 'ethical hackers' in times of crisis, the need to coordinate beyond the boundaries of government will increase.[64]

Supporters of these initiatives rightly recognise that the information age and the consequent advent of netwar have blurred the boundary between domestic and international threats, as well as between civilian and military threats. This in turn demands greater interagency coordination within the counter terrorism community. As terrorist groups evolve toward loose, ad-hoc networks that form and dissipate unpredictably, so must counter terrorism forces adopt a more flexible approach that crosses bureaucratic boundaries to accomplish the mission at hand. While militaries and governments will never be able to do away with their hierarchies entirely, there is nevertheless much room for them to develop more robust organisational networks than they currently have – a change that may offset some, if not all, of the advantage now accruing mostly to networked terrorist groups.

NOTES

1. In 1961 Burns and Stalker referred to the *organic* form as 'a network structure of control, authority, and communication', with 'lateral rather than vertical direction of communication'. In organic structure, 'omniscience [is] no longer imputed to the head of the concern; knowledge about the technical or commercial nature of the here and now task may be located anywhere in the network; [with] this location becoming the ad hoc centre of control authority and communication'. Burns, Tom and Stalker, George (1961), *The Management of Innovation*, London: Tavistock.
2. Monge, Peter and Fulk, Janet (1999), 'Communication Technology for Global Network Organisations', in Desanctis, Geraldine and Fulk, Janet (eds), *Shaping Organisational Form: Communication, Connection, and Community*, Thousand Oaks: Sage, pp 71–2.
3. The traditional, more bureaucratic groups have survived partly through support from states such as Syria, Libya, and Iran. These groups, such as the Abu Nidal Organisation, the Popular Front for the Liberation of Palestine (PFLP), and three PFLP-related splinters –the PFLP – General Command, the Palestine Liberation Front, and the Democratic Front for the Liberation of Palestine, retain an ability to train and prepare for terrorist missions; however, their involvement in actual operations has been limited in recent years, partly because of successful counter-terrorism campaigns by Israeli and western agencies and the ongoing peace process.

4. Office of the Coordinator for Counterterrorism (2000), *Patterns of Global Terrorism: 1999*, Washington, DC: US Department of State, Publication #10687.

5. Bin Laden allegedly sent operatives to Yemen to bomb a hotel used by American soldiers on their way to Somalia in 1992, plotted to assassinate President Bill Clinton in the Philippines in 1994 and Egyptian President Hosni Mubarak in 1995, and played a role in the Riyadh and Khobar blasts in Saudi Arabia that resulted in the deaths of twenty-four Americans in 1995 and 1996. United States officials have also pointed to bin Laden as the mastermind behind the American embassy bombings in Kenya and Tanzania in 1998, which claimed the lives of more than 260 people, including twelve Americans, and in the bombing of the *USS Cole* in Yemen, in which seventeen American sailors were killed.

6. Office of the Coordinator for Counterterrorism (2000), *Patterns of Global Terrorism: 1999*.

7. Ranstorp, Magnus (1994), 'Hizbollah's Command Leadership: Its Structure, Decision-Making and Relationship with Iranian Clergy and Institutions', *Terrorism and Political Violence*, 6/3, Autumn, p 304.

8. It is important to avoid equating the bin Laden network solely with bin Laden. He represents a key node in the Arab-Afghan terror network. But the network conducts many operations without his involvement, leadership, or financing, and will continue to be able to do so should he be killed or captured.

9. Simon, Steven and Benjamin, Daniel (2000), 'America and the New Terrorism', *Survival*, 42/1, Spring, p 70.

10. See indictment testimony from United States District Court, Southern District of New York, United States of America vs. Osama bin Laden, 98 Cr. and S(2) 98 Cr. 1023 (LBS).

11. See, for instance: Kurlantzick, Joshua (2000), 'Muslim Separatists in Global Network of Terrorist Groups', *Washington Times*, 2 May; *Cairo Al-Arabi* (1997), 'Arab Afghans Reportedly Transfer Operations to Somalia', 10 March, p 1; *Paris al-Watan al-'Arabi* (1997), 'Afghanistan, China: Report on Bin-Laden Possibly Moving to China', 23 May, pp 19–20.

12. See Heydenbrand, I. (1989), 'New Organisational Forms', *Work and Occupations*, 3/16, pp 323–57.

13. Monge and Fulk (1999), 'Communication Technology for Global Network Organisations', p 84.

14. The current IT revolution has not only increased the capacity and speed of communications networks, but it has driven down telephone communication costs as well. The value and benefit of the Internet also rises as more servers and users link together online. Because the value of a network grows roughly in line with the square of the number of users, the benefit of being online increases exponentially with the number of connections (called Metcalfe's Law, attributed to Robert Metcalfe, a pioneer of computer networking). The number of users worldwide has already climbed to more than 350 million, and may reach 1 billion within four years. See *The Economist* (2000), 'Untangling e-conomics', 23 September.

15. Thompson, James (1967), *Organisations in Action*, New York: McGraw-Hill.

16. This is not to say that hierarchical terrorist groups will not adopt IT to improve support functions and internal command, control, and communications. Aum Shinrikyo was highly centralised around the figure of Shoko Asahara and its structure was cohesive and extremely hierarchical, yet the use of IT was widespread within the group. See Cameron, Gavin (1999), 'Multi-track Microproliferation: Lessons from Aum Shinrikyo and Al Qaida', *Studies in Conflict & Terrorism*, 22, p 283.

17. Afghanistan's ruling Taliban leaders have repeatedly claimed that Bin Laden's movements and access to communications have been severely restricted.

18. US intelligence agencies recently obtained computer-disk copies of a six-volume training manual used by Osama bin Laden to train his recruits. Kelley, Jack (2000), 'U.S. acquires reputed terrorism guide', *USA Today*, 18 September.

19. Iuris, Andre Pienaar (1997), 'Information Terrorism', in Humphreys, Amelia (ed.) (1997), *Terrorism: A Global Survey: a special report for Jane's Intelligence Review and Jane's Sentinel*, Alexandria: Jane's Information Group, p 64.

20. See Denning, Dorothy and Baugh, Jr, William (1997), 'Encryption and Evolving Technologies as Tools of Organized Crime and Terrorism', US Working Group on Organized Crime, National Strategy Information Center, Washington, DC.

21. *Ibid.*

22. Whine, Michael (1999), 'Islamist Organisations on the Internet', *Terrorism and Political Violence*, 11/1, Spring, p 128.

23. Denning and Baugh (1997), 'Encryption and Evolving Technologies'.

24. Cloned cell phones can either be bought in bulk (the terrorist discards each phone after use) or a phone number can be stolen and programmed into a single cell phone just before using it. A special scanner is used to 'snatch' legitimate phone numbers from the airwaves, for example, the Electronic Serial Number (ESN) and Mobile Identification Number (MIN). See Denning and Baugh (1997), 'Encryption and Evolving Technologies'.

25. Soo Hoo, Kevin, Goodman, Seymour and Greenberg, Lawrence (1997), 'Information Technology and the Terrorist Threat', *Survival*, 39/3, Autumn, p 142.

26. Lashkar and its parent organisation, *Markaz-e-Dawa wal Irshad* (Centre for Islamic Invitation and Guidance), have raised so much money, mostly from sympathetic Wahhabis in Saudi Arabia, that they are reportedly planning to open their own bank. See Stern, Jessica (2000), 'Pakistan's Jihad Culture', *Foreign Affairs*, 79/6, November/December, p 115.

27. In fact, ambiguous and complex situations are still better tackled through direct communications, as face-to-face interaction is generally faster at resolving outstanding issues and leaves less room for misunderstandings.

28. Nohria, Nitin and Eccles, Robert (1992), 'Face-to-Face: Making Network Organisations Work', in Nohria, Nitin and Eccles, Robert (eds), *Networks and Organisations*, Boston: Harvard Business School Press, pp 289–90.

29. *Newsweek* (2000), 'Tracking Bin Laden's E-mail', 21 August.

30. Reeve, Simon (1999), *The New Jackals: Ramzi Yousef, Osama Bin Laden and the Future of Terrorism*, Boston: Northeastern University Press, pp 39 and 97.

31. *Jane's Intelligence Review* (2000), 'Terrorist threats target Asia', 12/7, 1 July.

32. Denning and Baugh Jr (1997), *Cases Involving Encryption in Crime and Terrorism*.

33. In fact, strategy is likely to be an important driver of organisational form and therefore of the density and richness of communications among group members. For instance, any mission calling for quick, dispersed and simultaneous actions by several nodes simply could not be achieved without some IT support.

34. For example, IT improves intelligence collection because potential targets can be researched on the Internet. Commercial satellite imagery is now offered by several firms at 1-metre resolution and in January of 2001, the US government granted at least one commercial firm a licence to sell 0.5 meter imagery. Satellite photos can be used to identify security vulnerabilities in large targets like nuclear reactors. See Koch, Andrew (2001), 'Space Imaging Gets .5m Go Ahead', *Jane's Defence Weekly*, 10 January.

35. For more on the importance of information across the spectrum of conflict, see Arquilla. John and Ronfeldt, David (1997), 'Cyberwar is Coming!', in Arquilla, John and Ronfeldt, David (eds), *In Athena's Camp: Preparing for Conflict in the Information Age*, Santa Monica: RAND, p 28.

36. The following discussion draws from a variety of terrorist cases, some of which do not necessarily fit the netwar actor description (that is, they may not be networked, as in the case of Aum Shinrikyo). However, we believe they are all indicative of the trends that are starting to shape netwar terrorist offensive operations, and which will continue to do so in the coming years.

37. Hoffman, Bruce (1998), *Inside Terrorism*, New York, NY: Columbia University Press, p 131.

38. *Ibid.*, p 134.

39. On these points, see Nacos, Brigitte (1994), *Terrorism and the Media*, New York: Columbia University Press.

40. Examples of these websites include: Almurabeton, www.almurabeton.org; Al-Jama'ah Al-Islamiyyah, www.webstorage.com/~azzam/; Hizb Al-Ikhwan Al-Muslimoon, www.ummah.org.uk/ikhwan/; Hizbollah, www.hizbollah.org, www.moqawama.org/page2/main.htm and www.almanar.com.lb; *Harakat Muqama al-Islamiyya* (Hamas), www.palestine-info.net/hamas/.

41. See Hopper, Ian (2000), 'Kashmir Conflict Continues to Escalate', CNN, 20 March.

42. Jessica Stern, telephone interview by author, Santa Monica, September 2000.

43. A survey conducted by the Science Applications International Corp. in 1996 found that forty major corporations reported losing over US$800 million to computer break-ins. This example is cited on several websites including Don Gotterbarn's web site at http://www-cs.etsu.edu/gotterbarn/stdntppr. 1 May 2003.

44. A related criminal case reveals the potential for this threat. In 1997 a group known as the Chaos Computer Club created an Active X Control, which, when downloaded and run on the user's home computer, could trick the Quicken accounting program into removing money from a user's bank account. See 'ActiveX used as hacking tool', CNET News.com (1997), 7 February. Online. Available: http: http://news.cnet.com/news/0,10000,0-1005-200-316425,00.html. 1 May 2003.

45. As one scholar puts it, 'the gun and the bomb continue to be the terrorists' main weapon of choice, as has been the case for more than a century'. See Hoffman, Bruce, Roy, Olivier and Benjamin, Daniel (2000), 'America and the New Terrorism: An Exchange', *Survival*, 42/2, Summer, p 163.

46. Soo Hoo et al. (1997), 'Information Technology', p 146.

47. E-mail correspondence from Brian Jenkins (at RAND) who is quoting a forthcoming manuscript by Paul Pillar, October 2000.

48. Soo Hoo et al. (1997), 'Information Technology', pp 145–6.

49. Lemos, Robert (2000), 'Hacktivism: Mideast Cyberwar Heats Up'. Online. *ZDNet News*, 6 November. Available: http://www.zdnet.com.

50. From a strategic perspective, the more terrorist groups emphasise swarming doctrines to conduct dispersed and simultaneous operations, the greater will be the need for a sophisticated IT infrastructure.

51. One example is Netcat, a free hacking tool made available in 1996. See Soo Hoo et al. (1997), 'Information Technology', p 141.

52. Rumours persist that people proficient in network attacks are available for hire. Press reports indicate that anonymous users claiming to be terrorists have approached hacker groups and requested help gaining access to government classified information networks such as the Secret Internet Protocol Router Network (SIPRNET). One teenage hacker received a US$1,000 check. See McKay, Niall (1998), 'Do Terrorists Troll the Net?', *Wired News*, 4 November, http://www.wired.com. 1 May 2003.

53. Jackson, Brian (2000), *Technology Acquisition by Terrorist Groups*, Santa Monica: RAND Note.

54. Kushner, Harvey (1998), *Terrorism in America: A Structured Approach to Understanding the Terrorist Threat*, Springfield: Charles C. Thomas, p 41.

55. Wilkinson, Paul (1986), 'Terrorism: International Dimensions', in Gutteridge, William (ed.), *Contemporary Terrorism*, New York: Facts on File Publications, p 40.

56. Jackson (2000), *Technology Acquisition by Terrorist Groups*.

57. Hoffman, Bruce (1999), 'Terrorism Trends and Prospects', in Lesser, Ian, Hoffman, Bruce, Arquilla, John, Jenkins, Brian, Ronfeldt, David and Zanini, Michele (eds) (1999), *Countering the New Terrorism*, Santa Monica: RAND, p 36.

58. See Jackson (2000), *Technology Acquisition by Terrorist Groups*.

59. Kitfield, James (2000), 'Covert Counterattack', *National Journal*, 16 September.

60. After Osama Bin Laden noticed that his satellite phone connection was no longer secure, he began to use human couriers to pass information and instructions to his operatives.

61. See Anderson, Robert et al. (1999), *Securing the US Defense Information Infrastructure: A Proposed Approach*, Santa Monica, CA: RAND,

62. TSWG received US$48 million in 2000. Traditional terrorist threats such as bombs still generate the greatest concern and most of TSWG's budget covers needs such as blast mitigation. See Stanton, John (2000), 'A Typical Pentagon Agency Waging War on Terrorism', *National Defense*, May, p 24.

63. Kitfield (2000), 'Covert Counterattack'.

64. In some cases, hackers may be spontaneously driven to aid law enforcement officials in defending against particularly objectionable crimes. For instance, a group called Ethical Hackers Against Paedophilia has been created to identify and punish people who publish child pornography on the Internet. The government could take the lead in mobilising existing ethical hackers in the private sector to help in times of crisis. This would be different from deliberately organising a virtual militia composed of relatively unsophisticated citizens armed with off-the-shelf hacking tools – something the Israeli government has experimented with during the al-Aqsa Intifada. Given this option's potential to become a double-edged sword, as well as lack of information on its efficacy, more research on this topic is warranted.

PART III

Implications for the Asia Pacific

PART II

Implications for the State Public Law

11. Southeast Asia after September 11

James Cotton

Most narratives of Southeast Asia's place in the 'war against terrorism' begin with the arrests in Singapore, Malaysia and the Philippines of individuals suspected of links with al-Qaeda. However, the management of the terrorist problem by the various governments of Southeast Asia as well as the response of the region as a whole can only be understood in the context of a judgement on the contemporary condition of regional order. This topic will thus be considered first.

From 1997, the Association of Southeast Asian Nations (ASEAN) has been in disarray. Although the impact of the financial crisis of 1997 is the most visible cause, the organisation has also been challenged by developments internal to the region as well as by the outcomes of some specific policy choices. The 'haze' problem that derived from Indonesian land-use policies (or lack of them) caused serious environmental and health difficulties in the neighbouring countries, but did not elicit (though many meetings were devoted to the subject) an effective ASEAN response. Despite considerable disagreements among the member governments, the decision was taken in 1997 to 'enlarge' ASEAN to all of geographical Southeast Asia, even though this involved the group in comprehensive engagement with countries that were both at a much lower level of development and also the subject of adverse international scrutiny for their poor human rights records.[1] While tackling these and other problems, ASEAN was struck by the Asian financial crisis. The Thai economy suffered a serious reverse, and that of Indonesia – the core state of the organisation – has yet to recover. The lack of a concerted ASEAN reaction to the crisis underlined the shortcomings already apparent in the group's modalities.[2] With the support of (then) Malaysian Deputy Prime Minister Anwar Ibrahim, Thai Foreign Minister Pitsuwan proposed, at the annual Foreign Ministers' gathering in July 1998, the idea of a more interventionist role for the group in regional troubles – that of 'flexible engagement'. This innovation was also supported by the Philippines but rejected by the other states. Despite the new circumstances, ASEAN's consensus-based and non-interventionist modalities were to remain.

The financial crisis was the chief cause of political and social turmoil in a number of the member states. Having functioned as an organisation based upon elite accord, the coherence of the group was seriously challenged by pressures for democratisation and political succession. While democratic methods were retained or expanded in some states, in others the response of elites to economic and social fragility took the form of a resort to increasingly illiberal measures. Here the arrest in Malaysia of former Deputy Prime Minister Anwar Ibrahim was especially divisive, as it elicited extensive criticism in the now liberalised media in Indonesia and effectively a rebuke from (then) President Estrada in the Philippines. The advent of the war on terrorism and its extension to Southeast Asia took place in a local context that reflected profound uncertainties and regional incoherence.

SOUTHEAST ASIA AND AL-QAEDA

From the extensive – if decidedly uncritical and sometimes contradictory – press coverage of the events concerned, it is well known that there have been a number of arrests in Southeast Asia in 2001–2 of terrorists suspected of links with Osama bin Laden. According to the conventional media account, in Malaysia twenty-five Muslim militants were detained in December 2001 and January 2002. These arrests were linked to the earlier detention of alleged members of an Islamic fundamentalist group, Kumpulan Mujahidin Malaysia (KMM). At the same time in Singapore, fifteen members of a group reportedly calling itself Jemaah Islamiah (JI) were arrested. They were alleged to be plotting attacks on United States personnel and property in Singapore, as was revealed in videotape seized in Afghanistan and passed to the Singapore authorities. These developments in Singapore led to the detention in the Philippines of Fathur Rohman al-Ghozi, who was subsequently convicted for the possession of explosives. Al-Ghozi was also claimed to be responsible for the explosion of five devices in Manila in December 2000 that killed twenty-two people.[3] A number of Arab nationals were also detained in the Philippines, suspected of being part of a 'sleeper' terrorist cell. In Thailand, twenty-five foreign nationals were detained in November on suspicion of terrorist activities. There were further arrests in Singapore in September 2002 of nineteen members of JI and two militants with links to Philippine Muslim separatists.[4]

In various ways, those arrested in Southeast Asia were linked to the activities of al-Qaeda. A member of the initial Singapore group, Mohammad Aslam bin Yar Ali Khan was detained by the Northern Alliance in Afghanistan in November 2001, and the Singapore video was discovered in the ruins of the residence in Afghanistan of Abu Hafs (alias Mohammad

Atef), a close associate of Osama bin Laden. Eight of the Singapore detainees were purportedly trained by al-Qaeda in Afghanistan, and all were members of JI, a former senior figure of which was under detention in Malaysia. Ten of the Malaysian detainees were trained in Afghanistan, and one, Yazid Sufaat, had been filmed meeting in January 2000 with two al-Qaeda members who subsequently participated in the September 11 attacks. In the same year Yazid hosted a visit to Malaysia by Zacarias Moussaoui, later prosecuted in the US for his part in September 11. In the Philippines, the al-Qaeda links were traced back to the activities of Osama bin Laden's brother-in-law, Mohammad Jamal Khalifa, who had served as a benefactor for both Abu Sayyaf and Moro Islamic Liberation Front (MILF) in the early 1990s.[5] Al-Ghozi, having earlier studied in Pakistan and trained in Afghanistan, had spent some time at a MILF training camp in the southern Philippines. One of the detainees in Thailand was a Pakistani national who was identified as a member of a list of suspects wanted by the US.[6]

It was also maintained by the Singapore authorities that all these individuals were linked to JI, the leadership of which included Abu Bakar Bashir, an Islamic teacher who had been convicted in Indonesia in 1985 of subversion. As a young man, al-Ghozi had attended Bashir's school. The Indonesian connection underlined the fact that the missing element in this account was the absence of action by Jakarta to detain terrorist suspects, even though the leadership of JI was ascribed to Indonesian nationals. Decidedly mixed signals emerged from President Megawati's government. On her trip to Washington immediately after September 11 she spoke in support of the war on terror; very shortly afterwards her Vice-President, Hamzah Haz, made somewhat contradictory remarks.

On 16 December 2001, the National Intelligence Agency Chief of Indonesia (and State Minister) – Lt. Gen. A.M. Hendropriyono – stated that international terrorists had been training in Indonesia, having already claimed that al-Qaeda was behind communal violence in Sulawesi. According to a report by a Singaporean journalist, Indonesian intelligence was alleged to have obtained evidence of a plot, 'Operation Jihad in Asia', which outlined a campaign against US embassies and property across Southeast Asia. The leader of Laskar Jihad, a militant group implicated in attacks on Christian communities in Eastern Indonesia, Jaafar Umar Talib (himself an Afghan veteran), was allegedly offered money and training facilities by al-Qaeda, an offer he said that he had declined.[7] Subsequently, the prosecution and conviction of Agus Dwikarna for the possession of explosives in the Philippines led to claims of further evidence of al-Qaeda activity in Indonesia. Not only was Dwikarna alleged to have run a training camp for terrorists in Sulawesi, but he had acted as guide when senior members of al-Qaeda visited Indonesia in June 2000 as a prelude to 'shifting the base of

Osama Bin Laden's terrorist operations ... to South East Asia'.[8] In June 2002 Kuwaiti Omar al-Farouq was detained by Indonesian authorities and transferred to US jurisdiction in Afghanistan. Al-Farouq was identified as al-Qaeda's most senior operative in the region (after the elusive Hambali, alias Riduan Isamuddin), and was reported to have detailed plans to wage a terror campaign in Southeast Asia, including attacks on US targets and the assassination of President Megawati.[9] Evidence was accumulating that elements of a terrorist network were active in Indonesia.

As a result of these developments, Southeast Asia became the focus for what was sometimes described as a 'second front' in the war against terrorism. US policy makers who clearly enjoyed the closest cooperation with their Singaporean counterparts were unstinting in their praise both for what was represented as the resolute action of the Singapore security authorities as well as the outspoken approach of their political masters. In Malaysia, the fact that Yazid had been filmed at the request of US intelligence in 2000 confirmed that the government had long been cooperating with Washington in tracking the activities of groups both governments regarded as a threat. Nevertheless, perhaps because so many individuals had been placed under arrest, western praise for the government was tempered by apprehension that the political system was in some danger of being undermined. Prime Minister Dr Mahathir's alarmist statements about the alleged conspirators no doubt encouraged such a view:

> These groups are not happy with the government's success and they are trying to create trouble and resort to terrorism to topple the government ... If they succeed, this country will become a second Afghanistan.[10]

FBI Director Robert Mueller III stated that part of the planning for the September 11 attacks was prepared in Malaysia, as was evident from the role played by one of the Malaysian detainees in support of Moussaoui.[11] This theme was elaborated in the US popular media. *Newsweek* reported that it was in Malaysia that the September 11 attacks were planned. Not to be outmatched, *Time Asia* asserted that there was a definite linkage between the activities of the KMM in Malaysia, JI, and al-Qaeda.[12] Dr Mahathir's response was to delay the distribution of a number of international magazines carrying these stories. The assessment of the strength of the Malaysian connection was moderated in later US official remarks.

Within two months of the September 11 events, Philippine President Gloria Macapagal Arroyo visited the US. Impressing on her hosts the susceptibility of the Philippines to terrorism, and outspoken in her support for the air war then being conducted against the Taliban in Afghanistan, she obtained an extensive package of loans, grants, and military aid (the last amounting to US$92.2 million, equivalent to around 10 percent of the existing Philippine military budget).[13] The presence of al-Qaeda in the Philippines in the 1990s was already a matter of record. Ramzi Ahmad Yousef, responsible for the 1993 bombing of the World Trade Center, had been active in the Philippines after that event, and was implicated in the explosion of a bomb aboard a Philippines Airlines aircraft in 1994.[14] One of the groups in receipt of al-Qaeda money at that time was the Abu Sayyaf, and President Arroyo's government convinced Washington that this group, then holding two American citizens hostage on Basilan, were still agents of the international terrorist network.

Given Washington's continuing commitments in Central Asia, the US response was remarkably rapid. In February 2002, around 600 US troops, including 160 Special Forces soldiers, were sent to the southern Philippines in the Balikatan 02-1 exercise. Ostensibly present to train their Filipino counterparts, the US forces were nevertheless authorised to use their arms 'in self-defence', and there were soon fatalities as a result of a helicopter crash. This exercise then widened in scope to become 'Enduring Freedom', involving more than 4,000 US troops. US forces cooperated with their Philippine counterparts in tracking the Abu Sayyaf kidnappers, an exercise which ultimately destroyed the chief elements of the gang though at the cost of the lives of two of their three hostages. However, a bomb explosion in October 2002 in Zamboanga that targeted US personnel and killed one soldier was attributed to the Abu Sayyaf and indicated that the group was still active. US policy was not entirely focused on military means. In addition to a number of trading and financial concessions, a US$55 million package was offered for the development of Mindanao. In Thailand also, US specialists were committed in the training of counter-terrorism forces.[15]

The cooperation with US policy in Manila, Kuala Lumpur and Singapore, as well as in Bangkok, was not initially matched in Jakarta. The apparent inaction on the part of the Indonesian government in pursuing groups and individuals allegedly linked to al-Qaeda attracted adverse comments from policy makers in Washington. In a number of statements and interviews, Deputy Secretary of Defense Paul Wolfowitz warned of the dangers of 'ungoverned' regions as potential harbours for terrorists, and specifically mentioned Indonesia as a possible instance of this problem: 'you see the potential for Muslim extremists, Muslim terrorists to link up with those Muslim groups in Indonesia and find a little corner for themselves in a country that's otherwise actually quite unfriendly to terrorism'.[16] As to what action the United States should take, Wolfowitz was cautious, 'I would want to think long and hard before I said to the Indonesians that if you can't do the job we'll do it for you'. He did not rule out some form of direct US involvement. According to Wolfowitz, though the Indonesian government recognised the problem, the Indonesian leadership were hesitant:

> There's a will [to take action]. Restricted to some extent by their own fear of what
> some of these groups could do to them ... I think to the extent that they try to
> appease ['Islamic'] ... sentiment, my view is they're making a big mistake.[17]

It was then revealed in the US press that only pressure to suspend aid
finally moved the Indonesian government to seek to locate and freeze the
assets of terrorist suspects.[18] It also emerged that the perpetrators of an
aborted plot to bomb the US Embassy in Jakarta were permitted to leave the
country in July 2001 even though the Indonesian police had been advised of
their activities. Members of the Bush administration later modified their view
to suggest that the best way to achieve their anti-terrorist objectives in
Indonesia was through the re-establishment of cooperation with the
Indonesian military. However, such cooperation lay under Congressional
interdiction as a result of the outrages of the Indonesian military in East
Timor in 1999, and the failure (so far) of the perpetrators to be brought to
justice. Department of Defense officials then devoted their efforts to
overcoming or circumventing this obstacle, including exploring the
possibility of offering Indonesia counter-terrorism training under the
provisions of the program approved by Congress in December 2001. These
efforts produced at least modest results, with some terrorist suspects being
quietly transferred to US jurisdiction.

The bombing in Bali on 12 October in which 202 people were killed – 88
of them Australians – increased international pressure on the Indonesian
government. The fact that three bombs were detonated simultaneously in Bali
and one in Sulawesi (at the Philippine consulate in Menado) and that
Australians were apparently targeted seemed to indicate that al-Qaeda was
involved. However, the Indonesian government only began to take measures
to constrain the activities of JI after the United Nations took the decision to
add the organisation to its consolidated list of al-Qaeda-related terrorist
entities. Bashir was then detained for questioning by Indonesian police (a step
urged on President Megawati by George W. Bush himself in mid-September),
though on suspicion of connections with past sectarian violence and not in
relation to the Bali events.[19] Even this cautious response received a mixed
reaction from Muslim figures, who also expressed anxieties that new anti-
terrorism legislation would be used to constrain critics of the government.

The region's institutions were also stirred into action by the post-
September 11 developments. In November 2001 at the annual ASEAN Heads
of Government meeting, terrorism was roundly condemned, though no
additional measures beyond those already in existence were proposed.[20] Then
in February, ASEAN Foreign Ministers met to consider what practical steps
could be taken. The outcome was described as a 'watershed' in ASEAN's
cooperation, but in fact only Indonesia and Malaysia decided to join the
Philippines in an agreement to share information on terrorism. Thailand

decided the proposal merited further study, and Singapore refused to participate. The 'new' ASEAN nations – Vietnam, Myanmar, Laos, and Cambodia – were also missing from the accord. The real diplomatic action did not occur at the meeting, but consisted of 'noises off', with Indonesia issuing an official protest at the complaint of Singapore Senior Minister Lee Kuan Yew that the masterminds behind the attempted terrorist plot in Singapore (notably Abu Bakar Bashir) were still at large in Indonesia. Amien Rais, Speaker of the People's Consultative Assembly of Indonesia and presidential hopeful went further, stating that on this occasion 'Lee has acted like the mouthpiece of President Bush … He has intervened in other people's affairs'.[21]

International and Local Agendas in Southeast Asia

So far it is clear that crucial evidence for an al-Qaeda terrorist conspiracy in Southeast Asia derives chiefly from the testimony of individuals arrested in Malaysia and Singapore under the provisions of the Internal Security Acts (ISA) of those countries. This use of such powers is certainly consistent with the histories of these Acts, since they were originally artefacts of British colonialism introduced to counter the terrorist activities of the Malayan Communist Party and its supporters in the 1950s. More recently, however, the ISA has been used in both countries in ways perhaps not intended by its authors. In the absence of independent corroboration, this issue should be reviewed to gain a better understanding of the plausibility of information gained in this fashion.

In recent years, the ISA in Malaysia has been used on occasion to detain individuals apparently implicated in terrorist activities. In June 2000, twenty-nine members of an organisation calling itself al-Munah were arrested – a further thirty-three were detained in August. Members of this group who had seized military weapons were involved in a shooting incident with security forces in July 2000, in which two of the latter were killed. As a result, in December 2001, three were sentenced to death and sixteen to life imprisonment for 'waging war against the King'. However, eye witness testimony regarding the incident and differences between the police and military accounts of the activities of this group have left some unanswered questions. But this use of the ISA has not been typical of recent times, when it was more often employed against political opponents of the government. The ISA was used to detain former Deputy Prime Minister Anwar Ibrahim and twenty-seven of his followers in 1998, though it transpired that the employment of the Act was most convenient for the authorities at that time as it temporarily concealed the fact that Anwar had been seriously assaulted by the Malaysian Police Chief while in detention. In any event, in a trial that was a travesty of justice, Anwar was convicted of corruption and sodomy, conduct that even if it had occurred could hardly be described as sufficiently grave as to invoke an Act designed to counter communist subversion. Neither were the Anwar arrests at all unique. In April 2001, ten members of the Keadilan party, an opposition group founded by Anwar's wife, were also imprisoned under the ISA provisions. It was never explained how the latter posed a security threat, and indeed the testimony of those later released suggested that the interrogations they experienced at the hands of the authorities seemed only designed to elicit information about their personal lives and sexual proclivities.

Thus in June 2001 when five individuals who were described as members of the 'KMM' were reported as being held under the ISA, the government's motivation was not transparent. Hitherto, according to some analysts, militant Islam has not been very much in evidence in Malaysia.[22] In this instance, particular confusion was caused by the fact that of the sixteen eventually arrested, most were members of Parti Islam se-Malaysia (PAS), a party in opposition federally but in government in two of the Malaysian states. One of their number, in the earlier statements made by the authorities described as their leader, was Nik Adli, son of the Chief Minister of Kelantan state, Nik Abdul Aziz Nik Mat. Public confidence was also tested when the authorities, having designated the organisation as the 'Kumpulan Mujahidin Malaysia', then without explanation re-designated it as the 'Kumpulan Militan Malaysia' (Malaysian Militant Organisation), conveniently with the same initials.[23] The detainees were said to have committed a number of crimes and to have been plotting attacks on American targets in Malaysia, but no charges were brought to court. It is true that Nik Adli had once fought in Afghanistan in the era of the Russian invasion, but so had many other Malaysians and with explicit government encouragement. Meanwhile, with the events of September 11, the government began waging an extraordinarily ferocious campaign in the media linking PAS with the terrorist outrages in the US. This seemed to demonstrate that, throughout this episode, domestic politics was uppermost in the calculations of the political leadership. It should be recalled that PAS was and remains a major actor on the Malaysian political stage, having been in government at various times in the states of Kelantan and Trengganu, and even having been in the past a partner with the United Malays National Organisation (UMNO) Party in the ruling Barisan Nasional (National Front).

The political context for these events should be recalled. Prime Minister Dr Mahathir managed to defeat the challenge of his deputy, though only by resorting to the use of extraordinary state powers. In the elections of 1999, though his coalition was returned to office, the representation of his own party was severely reduced (from 94 to 72 seats), and perhaps for the first time in Malaysia's history more ethnic Malays backed PAS in preference to

UMNO, and the Barisan was only saved by the votes of ethnic Chinese and by support from indigenes in the Borneo states. Without labouring the point, it can be asserted that Malaysia, having been a semi-democracy,[24] has seen the progressive erosion of many of its quasi-democratic characteristics from the late 1980s. The press and media are now under almost exclusive government control, the electoral system is highly distorted, and the powers of the government to constrain the rights of the public to assemble and express their political views are unprecedented. Under the Police Act, all assemblies of as few as five persons must be licensed, and licences are often only granted to government-oriented parties or groups. Assembly without a licence is a serious offence, which is one explanation why the restaurant and coffee house sector of the economy is so buoyant. The character of the Anwar trial has been already noted. It should also be mentioned that the powers of the government to detain citizens without trial extend well beyond the ISA, and indeed more persons are held under the Emergency (Public Order and Prevention of Crime) Ordinance than under the ISA itself. In short, Malaysia's security forces and the legislation that empowers them are very much part of a no-holds-barred partisan political contest and their use in any particular instance is most likely to be intelligible in terms of that contest.

In retrospect, it can be hypothesised that the arrests of further alleged militants in December 2001 and January 2002 were separate developments, and indeed the authorities went so far as to describe these individuals as members of a 'second wing', albeit of the same subversive organisation. These arrests did appear to have some tangible connection with September 11. The al-Qaeda connection – which became a staple of the local and regional press – was then used to further blacken the reputation of the PAS. Thus, *The Straits Times* stated 'in Malaysia, al-Qaeda is believed to have political ties with PAS and military links with Kumpulan Mujahideen Malaysia'.[25] The campaign to discredit PAS had certainly been successful, with the opposition Democratic Action Party in 2001 leaving the alternative coalition that had campaigned against Dr Mahathir in the 1999 elections.

In Singapore, the politicisation of the security apparatus is just as apparent, though the government possesses a subtlety of control over the wider society of which its counterparts over the causeway can only dream. In recent years, the ISA has not been used at all extensively, with only six individuals held – generally for alleged espionage – in the 1990s. The government's domestic political opponents are normally dealt with through the courts, the strategy being to ruin any figure deemed a threat by suing them (always successfully) for libelling cabinet ministers. Thus in his career as a parliamentarian and party leader since 1981, J.B. Jeyaretnam has been fined almost US$1 million, and has been the subject of bankruptcy proceedings on two occasions. In the past the ISA has been a most successful disincentive against contesting the power of the ruling party, and there is every reason to believe that this disincentive still discourages opposition political activity to this day. It is worth noting that in executing its security powers the government does not always trust its own citizens. Important police powers are exercised by a contingent of Gurkha janissaries, whose lack of attachment to the society is considered a virtue. As their commander has observed, 'Not being influenced by the local scene is part of their concept in Singapore. They just don't get emotionally involved in anything they may get caught up in.'[26]

Between 1986 and 1988 the ISA was used to detain a group of youthful Catholic Church activists, who were subsequently exposed as Marxist conspirators bent on destabilising the city-state. It should be recalled that this was the time when Gorbachev was busy dismantling the Soviet Empire and his erstwhile Chinese comrades were proceeding vigorously down the capitalist path. Clearly neither Moscow nor Beijing had been in touch with the comrades in Singapore in some time. The ISA was also used against former Solicitor-General Francis Seow, who was acting for one of the incarcerated conspirators (but whose real offence was more likely to have been his besting of Lee Kuan Yew in a televised debate). The treatment of Seow has been well documented.[27] His alleged crimes were certainly serious. Not only was he serving the international communist conspiracy by seeking to act for the accused in the law courts, but he was simultaneously an agent of American imperialism by (allegedly) receiving funding from the US Embassy in Singapore intended to assist opposition candidates to run against the ruling party during elections and thus to revive Singapore's moribund democracy.

There are hints of the debilitating effects of this evident politicisation of the domestic security apparatus in the account given by the Singapore authorities of the December–January arrests. According to this story, the Internal Security Department (ISD) were informed on 29 November 2001 that a Singaporean, Muhammad Aslam bin Yar Ali Khan, had links with al-Qaeda. He left Singapore shortly afterwards. His capture in Afghanistan on 29 November prompted the arrest in Singapore of a number of his associates. A seizure of their effects showed that they were plotting acts of terror aimed at US personnel and facilities in Singapore. Afterwards, on 28 December the CIA provided a copy of a videotape found in Afghanistan that provided evidence of the precise targets of this terror campaign.[28]

On this version of events, Muhammad Aslam was already under suspicion as a result of information supplied by a Singaporean Muslim. When he left Singapore suddenly on 4 October, in the words of Senior Minister Lee Kuan Yew, 'the police did not stop him because [*sic*] they were hot on the trail of his associates'.[29] There is no way that this account can be verified, but given the powers of the Singapore authorities it is a little puzzling that he was not detained and his detention initially kept a secret. If this claim is false, then it may be the case that the ISD had no knowledge of the activities of JI, until the CIA supplied them with information obtained in Afghanistan. The Singapore government's statement of 11 January says that Singaporean JI members were travelling to Afghanistan by 1993, and that 'The surveillance activities of the first JI cell in support of terrorist targeting began as early as 1997', which is as much as to admit that this group was active for at least five years before it came to the notice of the ISD.

Prime Minister Goh Chok Tong revealed a further and even more serious failure on the part of the ISD in a speech in April. He stated that five militants who had been planning an attack on Changi Airport had fled to Thailand in January.[30] Clearly the authorities had not been aware of their activities at that time – otherwise they would have been detained. There is a final detail in the official Singaporean story that should be noted. According to the chronology of the investigation contained in the press release of 18 January, the contents of the videotape confirmed the story already told to the ISD by one of the suspects, Khalim bin Jaffar. On 24 January the authorities released a further statement that asserted that the same suspect had subsequently informed the ISD of a secret store where videotape was found that matched precisely the tape provided by the CIA. It is straining credulity somewhat to learn that though the detainee had confirmed in every detail the contents of the original video, it was not until later that he led the authorities to the incriminating evidence.

In the Philippines, direct US involvement has exposed the somewhat problematic nature of Manila's strategy. The exclusive target of the combined US-Philippine military operations, which formally concluded at the end of July, was the Abu Sayyaf group. Notwithstanding, if the objective of these operations was to destroy the local support network of al-Qaeda, they were most probably aimed at the wrong target. This argument requires some reference to the history of Muslim separatism in the Philippines. Such separatism is as old as Spanish and United States colonialism in the islands. The most important resistance movement traditionally has been the Moro National Liberation Front (MNLF), founded (with Libyan sponsorship) in 1968, and the Muslim interlocutor in negotiations in 1976 and again in 1996 to establish an autonomous regional government in the southern Philippines. At the present time elements of the MNLF are again in rebellion against Manila, its leader Nuar Misuari in the meantime having served as the local head of a regional administration. In an event with no connection to September 11, though as important a challenge as has been faced by Manila in the region concerned, 110 people were killed in November 2001 when former MNLF forces turned on government troops on the island of Jolo. At present, the MNLF is in disarray as a result of these events.

Attempts by MNLF leaders to develop an accommodation with the central government has proved unacceptable to some members, and in 1976 the Moro Islamic Liberation Front (MILF) split from the parent body. It should be observed that this split also reflected ethno-linguistic differences within the broader Moro community. The Abu Sayyaf represents a former faction of the MILF, independent from 1991.[31] While the MILF presently functions virtually as a government in parts of the Philippines, Abu Sayyaf has degenerated into a free enterprise outfit devoted to fund raising through such activities as kidnapping, bank robbery and extortion. According to most Philippine commentators, it is the MILF who represents the most substantial threat to the Manila government and it is they who are most closely linked to al-Qaeda. There appears to be evidence that the MILF maintained with al-Qaeda funding a training camp through which transited a succession of international terrorists. After his arrest it was claimed not only that al-Ghozi had perfected his pyrotechnic skills at this facility, but that he exploded the bombs in Manila in December 2000 in retribution for central government action against the MILF. But the Arroyo government was insistent that the MILF be quarantined in any US action. There had been a 'cessation of hostilities' with the MILF in 1997, a provisional peace agreement in 2001, and talks were continuing intermittently with the aim of arriving at a political solution that would meet the group's objectives.[32] In regional elections in 2001 the MILF scored some notable victories, indicating that they had a growing popular following.

However, if there was a doubt as to whether targeting the Abu Sayyaf was really a contribution to the campaign against al-Qaeda, it did serve to re-engage the US military in Philippine security. Ever since the loss of its bases in the Philippines in 1991, the US – despite its role as security guarantor for the country – found it difficult to realise security cooperation with Manila. In 1998 a Visiting Forces Agreement was negotiated that permitted US forces to visit from time to time, and a draft Mutual Logistics Support Agreement which was prepared in the aftermath of the Basilan commitment demonstrated that much augmented security cooperation with the Philippines was being contemplated in Washington. However, the Philippines Senate must approve any more permanent presence, or the commitment of troops for actual combat. Hence both sides insisted that Balikatan 02-1 was a training exercise, appearances to the contrary notwithstanding.

Despite the initial manifestations of internal discord, as the campaign against terrorism developed the leaders of ASEAN began to realise that the organisation itself might gain greater plausibility if it could play an appropriate part. Whatever other rationale ASEAN possesses, its most important function has been to provide diplomatic solidarity for the elites of the member states. A closer alignment with the US in pursuit of the current campaign could be turned to domestic advantage by those elites, being a potential instrument to be used against opponents, whether terrorist or not. Though there were some early misgivings on the part of states fearful that it might become a mechanism for later intervention in their internal affairs, the leaders of ASEAN decided to enter with Washington into a 'Joint Declaration for Cooperation to Combat International Terrorism'. The Declaration, which was adopted on 1 August 2002, provides principally for intelligence sharing and capacity building.[33] Though Secretary of State Colin Powell was careful to say at the time that the US had not abandoned its insistence upon upholding human rights standards in its dealings in the region, it was perhaps ironic that the agreement was initialled in Brunei, an absolute monarchy in which the Sultan has ruled under emergency powers since 1962.

OUTCOMES IN THE WAR ON TERRORISM

What will be the outcome of the US strategy of coalition building in Southeast Asia? The likely character and impact of US policy in each of the countries needs to be reviewed before offering an assessment of the overall pattern.

Malaysia

In many ways, Malaysia is an unlikely US ally. The illiberal trend in Malaysian domestic politics was a subject for adverse comment in the Clinton administration – witness Vice-President Al Gore's speech praising *reformasi* during the 1998 APEC meeting in Kuala Lumpur – and is still a concern. The Department of State's 2001 report on Malaysia's human rights record notes instances of extrajudicial killings, detention without trial, denial of counsel, torture of detainees, censorship of the media amongst other problems. Of the Anwar verdict it finds that his 'politically motivated convictions ... demonstrated the judiciary's lack of independence',[34] Because of this sorry record, Mahathir had not visited the US as an official guest since 1994, and prior to September 11 did not appear to have any prospect of an invitation.

Subsequent events led to a marked change in the diplomatic climate. On a visit to Malaysia in April 2002, Assistant Secretary of State James Kelly – while noting that Anwar's fate was still a matter for concern – praised Malaysia as a 'beacon of stability' and described Dr Mahathir as a strong partner in the war against terrorism. Defense Secretary Rumsfeld then lauded Malaysia's cooperation efforts in the war against terrorism.[35] Dr Mahathir's reward was an invitation to call at the White House during his visit to the United States on 13–15 May. Significantly, at the time a US official stated that the Anwar issue was best dealt with behind the scenes, and that Malaysia had not used the powers of the ISA for domestic political purposes since September 11.[36] In June the US military held joint exercises – codenamed CARAT – with Malaysia, their 1,400 strong force including a Muslim Imam. And in its account of the situation in Malaysia, the State Department's *Patterns of Global Terrorism 2001* described the KMM as 'associated with regional Islamic extremist groups with al-Qaeda links', thus unreservedly endorsing Dr Mahathir's domestic strategy.[37] Influential US analysts – despite the lack of any conclusive evidence – have echoed this assessment of the KMM.[38] If there has been any change in Malaysia's internal political climate in recent times, it has been towards greater repression. While in Kuala Lumpur, for all his positive remarks on the role of the Malaysian government, Secretary Powell was forced to concede that Anwar Ibrahim was a 'political prisoner'.[39] However, in the context of the anti-terrorist campaign, Malaysian cooperation has been sufficient for such issues effectively to be sidelined. The local outcome of the war against terrorism has therefore been to entrench illiberal forces.

Singapore

American criticism of 'the Singapore School', expressed by Samuel P. Huntington, in the publications of the National Endowment for Democracy, and by conservative US media commentators has been a constant of recent US–Asia relations. Singapore, while admired for its economic achievements, has also become identified as authoritarian and repressive. As the Department of State observes in its 2001 assessment of Singapore's record:

> The Government has wide powers to limit citizens' rights and to handicap political opposition. ... The Government continues to restrict freedom of speech and the press significantly and to limit other civil and political rights.[40]

As in Malaysia, an authoritarian trend has been much in evidence in the last few years. In the 2001 elections, the ruling PAP boosted its share of the popular vote to 75.3 percent (up from the 65.0 percent it gained in 1996). Once again opposition parties did not dare to field a sufficient number of candidates to displace the government even if all were elected, though this did not save some oppositionists from having their records very closely scrutinised for instances of libel once the elections had been concluded. Having long exercised complete control over the local media, in the last three years the government has extended its reach to the Internet, controlling the backbone through which all of Singapore's Internet traffic must pass and hacking into personal computers without permission to scrutinise files.[41] A change in the rules for the conduct of Internet chat rooms has seen a number of popular sites devoted to political and social comment close rather than risk prosecution. Since September 11, however, the closest cooperation between the American and Singaporean authorities has been in evidence. The fact that US personnel were being directly targeted in the plot uncovered by the ISD has undoubtedly contributed to a warming of bilateral relations. A Lee Kuan Yew visit to convene a leadership seminar at the White House was coyly described in the official statement as a visit by 'a Singapore official'. Once again the formation of the anti-terror coalition will discourage US critics of what is by any reckoning a profoundly illiberal regime.

Thailand

So far, Thailand's involvement in the war against terrorism has been marginal, though there have been claims that the country has been used as a transit point for al-Qaeda funds and personnel. Since the advent of the Thaksin government in 2001, there has been a pronounced authoritarian shift in the character of Thai politics, with the absorption of a number of political parties by the ruling Thai Rak Thai which clearly aspires to dominate the political landscape, restrictions on free comment in the media, and allegations of conflict of interest involving senior government figures. Initial Thai scepticism regarding the war was transformed to cooperation, but perhaps because it could be seen that the rulers of the neighbouring countries were able to turn this development to their advantage. In 2002, assassinations of police officers in Muslim-majority southern Thailand were ascribed to terrorists, though according to some accounts more orthodox criminals were involved.

The Philippines

US relations with the Philippines are in a distinct category, given the former colonial role of the US and continuing American security guarantees. For these reasons, the impact of US policy will be most evident in the military sphere. In the Philippines, the equipment and training of the military are in a very poor state due to lack of funds as well as misadministration. There is no doubt that US assistance will remedy some of these shortcomings, and the loyalty of the military to the present administration will also likely be enhanced. Nor has the US eschewed a contribution to the nation's wider problems, as is evident in the development package proposed for Mindanao. But in a system where state incapacity is often encountered, munificent support to one sector will enhance that sector's relative power and purchase. Thus may be repeated a classic problem of US strategy in the Cold War, when support for Third World militaries often spawned military-authoritarian governments.

Meanwhile, the impact of US intervention in Basilan may not address the root causes of lawlessness in that region. As Walden Bello observes, Basilan represents in microcosm many of the problems of the southern Philippines. As a result of in-migration of Christians in the last 100 years into a region almost exclusively inhabited by the Muslim Yakan ethno-linguistic group, Muslims constitute 71 percent of the population but Christians own 75 percent of the land.[42] The literacy rate is amongst the lowest in that part of the country and poverty is widespread. By itself, the eradication of the Abu Sayyaf, even if it is achieved, will not address the structural problems that breed discontent and rebellion. The US presence may even convince some of the inhabitants that the government in Manila is partisan in its treatment of local grievances. In short, according to some analysts, the re-engagement of the US in the Philippines may even restore American basing rights, but may also stimulate the same distrust of US motives and domestic divisions as was evident in the bases debate in the late 1980s and early 1990s.[43]

Indonesia

The impact of the US role in Indonesia is most difficult to judge, especially given the country's continuing institutional fluidity. It should be recalled that prior to 1992 military cooperation between the two states was vital for the prosecution of the war in East Timor. There may well be profound consequences for Indonesia's fledgling democracy if US pressure for action against militant Islamic groups is maintained. Megawati Sukarnoputri's government is dependent for its stability on the support of avowedly Islamic parties. Leaders of these parties, including the Vice-President and the Speaker of the People's Consultative Assembly, have been critical of the US regarding both its global strategy as well as its attempts to prompt the government in Jakarta to cooperate more closely in the prosecution of that strategy in Indonesia. It is surely noteworthy that one of the Indonesian citizens arrested in Manila in March 2002 and charged with possession of explosives had been, until the end of January, the Treasurer of Indonesia's National Mandate Party (PAN) led by Amien Rais.[44]

Suspicion of US motives in Indonesia is widespread. For many Indonesians, those linked by Washington to JI are respected members of a loose but very extensive network of Muslim charity and educational groups with no single leadership or identity.[45] Bashir's claim that the CIA were the instigators of the Bali bombing will be believed by many in this network, and US pressure on the Jakarta government to take stronger action against these individuals will be interpreted as yet more evidence of malign interference in the nation's internal affairs. Most Americans have quite forgotten (if they ever knew), that the CIA was actively campaigning to split the country in 1957–8, but for such Indonesians these events are a major determinant of their worldview.[46] Similarly, cooperation between Australia and Indonesia in the war against terrorism, the outcome of Prime Minister John Howard's official visit to Indonesia in February 2002, has probably also fed such suspicion, given that Australia is still blamed in many quarters for conspiring to separate East Timor from the Republic in 1999 (a claim explicitly affirmed by bin Laden himself). This belief is strengthened in light of the fact that Australia is not only the closest of US allies in the region but amongst the most enthusiastic supporters of the war against Iraq. If the Megawati government falls, this will be the second instance of a president removed during the initial cycle of the new democracy, and may mark the demise altogether of the democratic process.

Whether or not the Megawati government survives these pressures, if the US becomes more engaged in Indonesia the military's access to resources will undoubtedly be augmented. The Tentara Nasional Indonesia (TNI) was discredited by its role as principal pillar of Suharto's New Order, and the democratisation of 1998 envisaged a smaller and diminishing role for the military in politics. The responsibility of senior TNI officers for the East Timor débâcle of 1999 further undermined the status of the military. The prosecution in Jakarta of some of the officers responsible – though taking place through a decidedly flawed process – seemed to suggest that henceforth the military would not be above the law. Moreover it was understood, at least in some quarters, that credible prosecutions would be a necessary prerequisite for the re-establishment of Indonesia's international reputation.

Even prior to September 11, US Defence officials were keen to re-animate a program of military cooperation with Indonesia. This is a policy the Secretary of Defense then endeavoured to convince the Congress to accept, arguing, with respect to TNI outrages in East Timor, that 'they are addressing the human-rights issues in an orderly, democratic way'.[47] On this question, the consensus of commentators is that the trial of the military defendants has been a travesty. In July the Senate Appropriations Committee approved an assistance package of US$400,000 for the TNI (under the International Military Education and Training scheme), as part of a US$50 million package of assistance measures for Indonesian counter-terrorism proposed by the administration. Though Secretary Powell has endeavoured to link this support to an improvement in the accountability of the Indonesian armed forces,[48] there are few prospects of significant structural reforms in the military sector while Megawati is President. In short, if this rehabilitation of the TNI now proceeds without any accounting for the outrages of 1999 – an outcome rendered more likely given the absolving of military defendants in the trial relating to the Suai massacre[49] – the Indonesian military may be enabled to reoccupy some of the political space vacated since 1998. And given the fact that the Indonesian economy is still a long way from recovery from the crisis of 1997, as in the Philippines a military in receipt of external largesse may be positioned to prevail in some future possible contest with the civilian sector.

Indonesia's many problems include separatist movements in Aceh and West Papua, and religious and ethnic conflict in the Eastern provinces. In Aceh around 30,000 TNI troops are deployed in a continuing and bloody civil conflict, and in West Papua the appearance of East Timorese style militias portends a violent confrontation at some point in the future. In the past, international attention paid to these trouble spots may have had the effect of encouraging moderation and of stimulating the central government to pursue a form of provincial autonomy that would satisfy local demands and ameliorate grievances. Even while the prospect of US intervention may stir a xenophobic reaction on the part of Islamic militant movements in the mould of Laskar Jihad, Washington may nevertheless consider that Indonesian territorial integrity is vital for the prosecution of the war against terrorism. Interest in Washington in moderating Jakarta's policies in the regions may wane. And as security trumps human rights, United States scrutiny of Indonesia's human rights performance may become less critical.

ASEAN

Since 1997 there has been a struggle for the character of Southeast Asia's regional organisation. It is ostensibly committed to policies that would spread prosperity and eventually political openness, but its embrace of the democratic process, especially since its enlargement in 1997, is ambiguous. This is illustrated by the fact that while ASEAN sponsors an official NGO forum, in only three member states – Thailand, the Philippines and Indonesia – can it be said that civil society contributes to the political process without major political constraints. In Myanmar law prohibits an independent civil society. Prior to its espousal of the goal of prosperity, ASEAN's emphasis was upon the primacy of order; in the circumstances of post-September 11 there appears to be a return to this emphasis. Thus, if the current US approach to the war against terrorism is adopted by the organisation as a whole, it is likely that the illiberal tendency observed in some of the key member states will also be reflected in the methods and policies adopted by the group. And the outcome in ASEAN is bound to have wider consequences. The ASEAN 'modalities' have set the tone for APEC, and ASEAN is also the core group of the ASEAN Regional Forum. A small indicator of such a trend is the fact that the US-ASEAN Joint Declaration has made Myanmar a party to an international instrument with the United States, despite the former country's baleful human rights record.

CONCLUSION

The anti-terrorist campaign in Southeast Asia, as it unfolds, may produce contradictory results. Al-Qaeda and its supporters may be eradicated, though it must be recognised that groups who sympathise with its worldview are part of the mainstream of regional opinion. But in the process illiberal regimes and forces may well be strengthened. This is already the case in Malaysia, where international attention to the Anwar issue has largely subsided; it may occur also in Indonesia.

During the Cold War, local alliances were forged by the United States and the NATO powers in order to contain the Soviet bloc. The latter objective was paramount, and so the domestic governance of the allies in question was not generally a matter of concern. In some instances, US engagement had the consequence of entrenching profoundly authoritarian governments in Asia, Latin America and the Middle East. While the Republic of Korea and Taiwan, to take two notable examples, eventually democratised as a response to the new global climate in the late 1980s, this strategy became such a perennial of US policy that in some places its local political outcome survived the demise of the Cold War. The present US strategy is crucially dependent upon the cooperation of Saudi Arabia and Pakistan, the authoritarian rulers of which countries exercise considerable power over their populations by virtue of their linkages with Washington. The same point could be made in connection with some of the former Soviet Central Asian republics which, since September 11, have become new American allies and key players in the Afghanistan campaign.

This is not to suggest that – aside from the Philippines – any Southeast Asian country will become as enmeshed with the United States as is the case with Saudi Arabia and Pakistan, but it is to point to the lack of a comprehensive strategy to eradicate terrorism. Terrorism thrives in authoritarian and repressive political climates. If there is a perceived lack of connection between elites and masses, the former dependent upon external linkages, the latter enduring social pressures generated by adherence to globalising (and thus externally derived) state strategies, such conditions are especially propitious for the growth of terrorist groups. It should be recalled that Osama bin Laden, quite apart from his early relationship with US and Saudi intelligence, is very much a product of the tensions and contradictions of Saudi Arabian society.[50] Many of those responsible for the September 11 outrages were similar products.

Open societies, ruled by governments accountable to the rule of law, are the least likely to produce recruits for terrorist organisations. Democratic governance has made considerable strides in Southeast Asia, but liberalism is by no means the dominant trend. In this region perhaps the most important attempt ever to reconcile the teachings of Islam and the practice of democracy is in progress. A truly comprehensive approach to terrorism would place the first priority on encouraging such liberal trends as are in evidence, and resiling from cooperation and support that would have the contrary effect.

On the reluctance initially of the Indonesian authorities to detain such figures as Abu Bakar Bashir, FBI Director Mueller was quoted as saying 'Indonesia has special challenges in coping with this problem – the lack of resources, the large population size, the thousands of islands and the political distractions inherent in its new democracy'.[51] As Bashir's whereabouts were no secret at the time – being interviewed by a succession of journalists – none of the obstacles cited seemed relevant, except the last. Neither the Malaysian nor the Singapore government needed to worry about such 'distractions' in detaining terrorist suspects without trial. In the Philippines the elastic provisions of the immigration regulations took the place of the Malaysian and Singaporean ISA. While law enforcement officials are perhaps bound to take the short-term view, these remarks indicate a lack of regard for the full consequences of the present policy. If the US is not fighting the war against terrorism ultimately in defence of such guarantees of liberty as due legal process, then Washington lacks that global strategy that would eradicate the conditions that breed terrorism, in Southeast Asia much as elsewhere.

NOTES

1.   Funston, John (1998), 'ASEAN: Out of its Depth?' *Contemporary Southeast Asia*, 20/1, pp 22–37; Cotton, James (1999), 'ASEAN and the Southeast Asian "haze": challenging the prevailing modes of regional engagement', *Pacific Affairs*, 72/2, pp 331–51.
2.   Wesley, Michael (1999), 'The Asian Crisis and the Adequacy of Regional Institutions', *Contemporary Southeast Asia*, 21/1, pp 54–73.
3.   *Tempo* (2002), 'Al Qaeda, Made in Madiun?', 29 January–4 February; *Tempo* (2002), 'Judging Al-Ghozi', 12–18 March.
4.   *The Straits Times* (2002), 'Another 21 arrested here over terrorism plans', 17 September.
5.   Viyug, Marites and Gloria, Glenda (2000), *Under the Crescent Moon: Rebellion in Mindanao*, Quezon City: Ateneo Center for Social Policy and Public Affairs/Institute for Popular Democracy, pp 222–47.
6.   *The Asian Wall Street Journal* (2002), 'Thailand Arrests Foreigners on Suspicion of Terrorist Links', 11 March.
7.   *The Straits Times* (2002), 'Is there an Al-Qaeda connection in Indonesia?', 21 January.
8.   CNN (2002), 'Indonesian linked to al Qaeda cell', 19 July. Online. Available: http://asia.cnn.com/2002/WORLD/asiapcf/southeast/07/19/indo.alqaeda/index.html.   30 May 2002.
9.   *Time* (2002), 'Confessions of an al-Qaeda terrorist', 23 September, pp 28–35.

10. Associated Press (2002), 'Indonesia, Malaysia, Philippines draft agreement on Fighting terrorism', 21 February.
11. *The Washington Post* (2002), 'FBI Says Malaysia Was Site of September 11 Planning', 1 February.
12. Klaidman, Daniel and Liu, Melinda (2002), 'Malaysia: A Good Place to Lie Low', *Newsweek*, 4 February; Klaidman, Daniel and Liu, Melinda (2002), 'Indonesia: Asia's New Weakest Link', *Newsweek*, 4 February; Spaeth, Anthony (2002), 'Rumbles in the Jungle', *Time Asia*, 26 February; Zabriskie, Phil (2002), 'Picking a Fight', *Time Asia*, 26 February.
13. *The Philippine Star* (2002), 'The Philippines in America's New War: Reaping the Rewards', 22 April.
14. Bodansky, Yossef (2001), *Bin Laden: The Man Who Declared War on America*, Roseville: Forum, pp 112–14.
15. *The Asian Wall Street Journal* (2002), 'US will train Thai forces in combating terrorism', 18 March.
16. *The New York Times* (2002), 'Deputy Secretary Wolfowitz Interview with New York Times', 7 January.
17. *Ibid.*
18. *The Asian Wall Street Journal* (2002), 'Editorial: Indonesia's Timidity', 25 January.
19. *The Jakarta Post* (2002), 'Govt told to consult Muslim figures to avoid backlash', 28 October.
20. *ASEAN* (2001), '2001 ASEAN Declaration: On Joint Action to Counter Terrorism'. Online. Available: http://www.aseansec.org/view.asp?file=/newdata/2001_asean_declaration.htm. 20 May 2002.
21. *Dow Jones International News* (2002), 'Singapore: Indonesia Harbors Suspects Linked to Al-Qaida', 20 February; *The Straits Times* (2002), 'Jakarta protests to Singapore envoy', 22 February.
22. Barton, Greg (2002), 'Islam, Society, Politics. And Change in Malaysia', in Isaacson, Jason and Rubenstein, Colin (eds), *Islam in Asia. Changing Political Realities*, New Brunswick: Transaction, pp 91–164.
23. Funston, John (2002), 'Malaysia: Muslim Militancy – how much of a threat?', *Aus-CSCAP Newsletter*, May, pp 20–22.
24. Case, William (1996), 'Can the 'Halfway House' Stand? Semidemocracy and Elite Theory in Three Southeast Asian Countries', *Comparative Politics*, 28, pp 437–64.
25. *The Straits Times* (2002), 'Terrorism – Can S-E Asia be safe again?', 8 April.
26. Reuters Asia (2002), 'Gurkhas guard Singapore from terror', 17 April.
27. Seow, Francis (1994), *To Catch a Tartar. A Dissident in Lee Kuan Yew's Prison*, New Haven: Yale Southeast Asia Studies, Monograph 42.
28. Singapore, Ministry of Home Affairs (2002), *Press Statements*, 5, 11, 13, 18, 24 January.
29. *Forbes Magazine* (2002), Lee Kuan Yew, 'Lee Kuan Yew on the terror threat in Southeast Asia', 1 April.
30. *The Straits Times* (2002), 'PM reveals plan to crash jet into Changi', 6 April.
31. Viyug and Gloria, *Under the Crescent Moon: Rebellion in Mindanao*; Chalk, Peter (2002), 'Militant Islamic Extremism in the Southern Philippines', in Isaacson and Rubenstein (eds), *Islam in Asia. Changing Political Realities*, pp 187–222.
32. *The Wall Street Journal* (2002), 'Manila Suspends Talks with Rebel Group after Allegations of its Links to al Qaeda', 21 March; *The Bangkok Post* (2002), 'Manila refutes al-Qaeda links to southern rebels', 10 March.
33. US Department of State, 'United States of America – ASEAN Joint Declaration for Cooperation to Combat International Terrorism'. Online. Available: http://www.state.gov/p/eap/rls/ot/12428.htm. 5 August 2002.
34. United States Department of State (2002), *Country Reports on Human Rights Practices – Malaysia 2001*.

35. *Washington File* (2002), 'Transcript: State's Kelly Praises Malaysia for Aid Against Terrorism', US Department of State, 16 April; *Washington File* (2002), 'Transcript: Rumsfeld Hails Malaysian Anti-Terrorism Role', US Department of State, 2 May.
36. *The Far Eastern Economic Review* (2002), 'US Pragmatic Toward Malaysia', 6 June.
37. US Department of State (2002), *Patterns of Global Terrorism 2001*, Washington: Department of State, pp 123–4.
38. Gershman, John (2002), 'Is Southeast Asia the Second Front?', *Foreign Affairs*, 18/4, pp 60–65.
39. *Washington File* (2002), 'Transcript: Powell Discusses Human Rights, Middle East in Malaysia', US Department of State, 30 July.
40. US Department of State (2001), *Country Reports on Human Rights Practices – Singapore 2001*.
41. Rodan, Garry (1998), 'The Internet and political control in Singapore', *Political Science Quarterly*, 113/1, pp 63–99.
42. *The Bangkok Post* (2002), Walden Bello, 'Philippines as a second front', 5 March.
43. Wain, Barry (2002), 'Wrong Target', *The Far Eastern Economic Review*, 23 April.
44. *The Straits Times* (2002), 'Manila links 3 Indonesians to Al-Qaeda', 22 March. However, there have also been suggestions that this operation was a contrivance of Indonesian State Intelligence: Fealy, Greg (2002), 'Is Indonesia a Terrorist Base', *Inside Indonesia*, 71, July–September, pp 24–5.
45. International Crisis Group, 'Al-Qaeda in Southeast Asia: the case of the 'Ngruki Network' in Indonesia'. Online. Available: http://www.crisisweb.org/projects/showreport.cfm?report id=733. 20 February 2003.
46. Kahin, Gerorge Mct. and Kahin, Audrey (1997), *Subversion as Foreign Policy. The Secret Eisenhower and Dulles Debacle in Indonesia*, Seattle: University of Washington Press; Conboy, Kenneth and Morrison, James (1999), *Feet to the Fire. CIA Covert Operations in Indonesia, 1957–1958*, Annapolis: Naval Institute Press.
47. United States Department of Defense News Transcript (2002), 'Rumsfeld Media Availability with Indonesian Minister of Defense', 13 May; *The Jakarta Post* (2002), 'Rumsfeld urges US Congress to ease curbs on military ties with RI', 15 May.
48. *Washington File* (2002), 'Transcript: Powell Says US-Indonesian Military Fellowships to Restart', US Department of State, 2 August.
49. *The Jakarta Post* (2002), 'Former East Timor police chief acquitted of rights abuse charges', 'Five officers found not guilty of right abuses', 16 August.
50. Cooley, John (2002), *Unholy Wars. Afghanistan, America and International Terrorism*, London: Pluto Press.
51. Agence France Presse (2002), 'Full extent of al-Qaeda in Southeast Asia yet to be uncovered', 15 March.

12. The Persistence of Armed Muslim Rebellion in Southeast Asia: Implications after September 11

Andrew Tan

ARMED MUSLIM REVOLT IN SOUTHEAST ASIA

Armed separatist rebellions have continued to constitute serious challenges to the security of the Association of Southeast Asian Nations (ASEAN) states, notwithstanding the rapid economic development of the region as a whole since the 1970s until 1997 and the end of the Cold War. The persistence of armed rebellion demonstrates that some states in Southeast Asia are still relatively weak and continue to face a fundamental problem with legitimacy. There have been several significant armed separatist movements in the region. The ethnic separatist movements in Myanmar broke out in 1948 but appeared to be under control by 1999, especially with the defeat of the long-running Karen rebellion. Elsewhere, the Muslim rebellion in southern Thailand, which is irredentist in nature, has not made much headway and the situation has been relatively stable. The same cannot be said for the Moro rebellion in the southern Philippines as well as the Aceh rebellion in Indonesia. In these instances, the separatists have mounted credible challenges to the authority of the central government. Their persistence in these two countries demonstrates the failure of Indonesia and the Philippines in achieving legitimacy for their post-independence political structures as well as continuing internal weakness.

Apart from those armed separatist movements which have a strongly Islamic character, in that the protagonists aim to set up separate Islamic states, the growing worldwide resurgence of Islam, exacerbated by globalisation and the accompanying growth in the feeling of Muslim community (*umma*), have also resulted in the emergence of militant groups. These groups have also been influenced by militant pan-Islamic ideology initially propagated by the likes of Sayyid Qutb and Hassan al-Banna, and the activities of 'new' terrorist groups led by the likes of Osama bin Laden. They aim to overthrow the central government and establish a Muslim state governed by Islamic laws. These groups are also beginning to establish transnational links both within the region and also with international terrorist organisations.

Analysts such as Bruce Hoffman have explored the rise of this 'new terrorism'.[1] In recent years, globalisation and other factors have transformed the nature of terrorist groups. There has emerged new terrorist groups' that have less traditional nationalist or ideological motivations, embracing instead more amorphous religious and millenarian aims. In addition, they possess a more diffuse structure and membership. More significantly, these groups are potentially far more lethal than traditional terrorist groups given their attempts at mass casualty terrorist acts, using both conventional explosives or weapons of mass destruction (WMD). The implication of this is that such groups see violence as an end in itself, not just as a means to an end.[2]

Besides dramatic developments in telecommunications and information, the characteristics of increasing globalisation have provided new channels for transnational terrorism. The internationalisation of terrorism has become more pronounced as terrorist groups today operate in various countries, taking advantage of porous borders in a rapidly globalising world economy. These transnational terrorist are thus much more difficult to track. In addition, they have been able to exploit the new information economy and the Internet to reach out to a much wider base of support than was possible in the past. They are also much less dependent on the support of states in their terrorist cause since they have become more mobile and flexible. In short, a 'new' terrorism has emerged, alongside more traditional types. The international militant Islamic terrorist network, the al-Qaeda, led by Osama bin Laden, epitomises new terrorism.

There is evidence that some of the established Muslim rebel groups in the region have forged links with this international terrorist network. Militant Islamic groups not committed to any previous separatist agenda have also recently begun to emerge. The result is that the nature of armed Muslim revolt in the region is being transformed through contact with pan-Islamic militant ideology and the new terrorism. Old and new terrorism exist side by side, with links being established between the two.

In both Malaysia and Indonesia, the response to modernisation and globalisation has been a retreat towards Islamisation, with schisms separating moderate, modernist Muslims and the more pious fundamentalists. The Islamic resurgence and the resultant rise in political Islam in turn has put pressure on governments of both countries to respond to the demand for Islamic values and practices. In turn, this has raised doubts over their ability over the long term to maintain their multiracial secular orientation. Moreover, the spectre of Islamic extremism cannot be dismissed, if the experience of the

Middle Eastern states is any guide. Muslims in Southeast Asia are not immune to developments in the Middle East and the broader Muslim community. Indeed, there have been a number of disturbing incidents of Islamic extremist violence in both countries in recent years.

The economic crisis which gripped the region from 1997, and from which it has not fully recovered, has also exacerbated existing socio-economic inequalities and worsened the effects of poverty, corruption and lack of development which are evident in the more rebellious of provinces, like Aceh and Mindanao. The rise of political Islam in both Malaysia and Indonesia in recent times, particularly in the latter, can also be attributed in part to dissatisfaction with the current political, social and economic order. The retreat into fundamentalism and violent extremism to radically change the existing order has been the result.

THE PERSISTENCE OF MUSLIM SEPARATIST REBELLIONS

The Problem of Legitimacy

The persistence of the Moro and Aceh Muslim separatist rebellions demonstrates both the failure of Indonesia and the Philippines to achieve legitimacy for their post-independence political structures as well as continued internal weakness.

The fact that the ASEAN states (except for Thailand) were artificially cobbled together by departing colonial powers has meant that some have relatively underdeveloped institutions and lack national cohesion. The ASEAN states exhibit the classic feature of many decolonised developing countries, that is, the lack of a close fit between nation and state. They are in fact multinational or multi-ethnic states, where the dominant ethnic group holds the reins of power over other significant ethnic minorities that are often located at the periphery. There are also further complications due to differences in religion, geography and historical experiences. The nation-building efforts of the dominant group, however, often require the subordination of the minorities, creating grievances that tend to find expression in demands for separatism.

These separatisms are not merely based on territorial grounds alone, but must have as their basis a sense of community that provides a network of communications and a source of leadership. Some of the most serious and persistent separatist movements have depended greatly on a consciousness of past importance as a state. The fact that the Muslim sultanates of Aceh, Sulu (in the southern Philippines) and Pattani (in southern Thailand) were historical power centres, enduring until recent times, provided self-confidence and a network of leaders who have retained their prestige.[3]

In all cases of separatism, one can detect a clash between the dominant national elite and its cultural values and the subordinate minority with its own religious-cultural identification. The national identity is invariably defined in terms of the dominant group's values and culture, with other groups on the periphery tending to be left out. Thus, Thai nationality – which revolves around Buddhism, Thai culture and language, and the Thai monarchy – is alien to the Malay minority in southern Thailand, who subscribe to Islam, have their own royal traditions, language, history and culture.

Similarly, in the southern Philippines, the Muslim Moros are an anomaly in a country dominated by Catholics heavily influenced by Spanish and American culture. The Malay Muslims of both Pattani and Mindanao have been historically autonomous and distinct peoples, with the persistence of the separatist movements an indicator of their will to survive, with their struggles for independence characterised by periodic resurgence depending on internal and external factors.[4]

In Aceh, the sense of separateness is also very strong, given the local identity which has been infused with Islam, the proud historical heritage of having being an important Islamic kingdom in the past, the sense of bitterness generated by the brutality of counter-insurgency operations by the Indonesian armed forces, and what is seen as discrimination and rapaciousness on the part of the central Javanese government. In addition, there is also a clash of ethnic and religious difference. The Acehnese resent the Javanese, who dominate the bureaucracy and the armed forces. Moreover, the Acehnese adhere to a much stricter form of Islam compared to the traditionally more *abangan* or nominal Muslim lifestyle of the Javanese.

In all three states, the presence of large numbers of the dominant group in territory traditionally populated by these minorities coupled with heavy-handed, often insensitive attempts by the central authorities to impose 'national' values on the minorities, has resulted in resentment. Accentuating the problem is the attitude of members of the dominant group, who see minorities as inferior. Thus, Catholic Filipinos see the Muslims as inferior, and have proceeded – with the assistance of corrupt local officials and the police – to occupy vast tracts of land in Mindanao. Muslims rarely recorded land titles for the purpose of agriculture and plantation activities, thus depriving the local population of their land, rights and livelihood. In Aceh, the Javanese-dominated central government has kept the bulk of natural gas revenues, reducing the province to widespread poverty. Random brutality by the Indonesian armed forces, who have acted more like an occupation force, has also alienated many Acehnese. Not surprisingly, this has fuelled anti-Jakarta sentiment. It is therefore not surprising that armed separatism occurs as a means of expressing frustration and redressing the situation through the use of force.

Paribatra and Samudavanija have thus noted that:

> In post-colonial Southeast Asia ... it has been conveniently forgotten by central governments that the constructing of what is more accurately a state-nation, merely means that external or western imperialism had been replaced by an internalised one, which is potentially more brutal and enduring.[5]

Since peaceful secession is virtually out of the question in centralised nationalistic states such as Thailand, the Philippines and Indonesia, armed separatism is the only solution.

THE MORO REBELLION IN THE PHILIPPINES

The Moro rebellion in the Philippines has been the largest and most persistent of the armed separatist movements in the region since 1975. The roots of the conflict go back to the colonial period when the Spaniards, who arrived in 1565, halted the Islamisation of the Philippine islands. Despite repeated attempts, the Spaniards were never able to completely subdue Muslim Moros in the south. The Moros subsequently disputed the handover of all the Philippine islands, including Moro lands in the south, to the United States in 1898 following the Spanish-American War of that year. Anti-American resistance was crushed in a brutal campaign of pacification. After that, the situation was aggravated by a massive influx of Catholic settlers from the north.[6]

By the 1960s, the Moros had become a minority in many parts of their traditional homeland, losing their land to immigrant settlers through dubious legal transactions or outright confiscation. Indeed, Catholics outnumber Muslims in most provinces in the south today. The problem of growing Moro landlessness was compounded in the 1970s by the settlement of many surrendered communist Huk rebels who were given land in the south. Violent confrontations between Muslims and Catholics became so serious that President Marcos imposed martial law in 1972.[7]

Exacerbating the problem has been the well-documented cases of human rights abuses by militia groups, specifically the Citizen Armed Forces – Geographical Units (CAFGU), which became a key element in the government's counter-insurgency campaign after 1988. Some of the 90,000 men who have joined have dubious criminal backgrounds and have in fact contributed to the atmosphere of lawlessness. Indeed, according to a Human Rights Watch report, 'the presence of militia in many communities appears not to have quelled local conflict, but served to stimulate fear, mutual distrust and communal violence'.[8]

The grievances of the Moros were reinforced by a growing sense of Muslim identity associated with the worldwide Islamic resurgence. From the late 1960s on, new mosques were built and contacts with Islamic organisations in the Middle East, Indonesia and Malaysia were established. In 1969, the Mindanao Independence Movement (MIM), the Union of Islamic Forces and Organisations (UIFO) and Ansar El Islam were established.[9] Overseas sympathisers in the Middle East – notably Libya – also established an Islamic Directorate of the Philippines to coordinate overseas assistance. The goal of the Moros is independence. This was clearly stated in the MIM Constitution, which said that 'the policy of isolation and dispersal of the Muslim community by the government ... has been detrimental to the Muslims and Islam' and that 'Islam being a communal religion and ideology, and at the same time a way of life, must have a definite territory of its own for the exercise of its tenets and teaching, and for the observance of its *sharia* and *adat* laws'.[10]

In 1969, a group of Muslims from the MIM and the UIFO began military training in camps in the Malaysian state of Sabah, where they received the support of its then Chief Minister, Tun Mustapha, with the tacit agreement of the Malaysian government.[11] Another group also apparently trained in Malaysia in areas close to the Thai border.[12] This support from Malaysia has been crucial to the formation of the Moro rebel armies, for the Malaysian trainees returned and went on to organise and lead separatist guerrilla armies. One of them – Nur Misuari – a former student at the University of the Philippines, founded the Moro National Liberation Front (MNLF) in 1972. The MIM was dissolved in its favour, and the MNLF also succeeded in obtaining the support of the Islamic Conference of Foreign Ministers (ICFM), the Organisation of Islamic Conferences (OIC) and Libya.[13] Large numbers of Muslims joined the MNLF as it launched a jihad against the central government. Over 100,000 deaths occurred in the ensuing huge civil war, with over 500,000 fleeing as refugees.[14] In short, the Moro conflict has been a huge but under-reported civil war.

A subsequent split within the MNLF saw the setting up of the Moro Islamic Liberation Front (MILF). The MNLF has since been affected by a number of setbacks, with top leaders defecting to either cooperate with the government or to join the MILF. The MILF has been critical of the leftist orientation of the MNLF, and has sought instead to emphasise its Islamic credentials and identity. Its eventual objective is an independent Muslim Moro state. Led by Hashim Salamat, a religious leader trained at Cairo's al-Azhar University, the MILF had, by the 1990s, become the main Moro rebel movement. It is well organised and has several imams or Muslim religious leaders as its members. Its armed wing, the Bangsa-Moro Islamic Armed Forces (BIAF) has eclipsed the MNLF.

The BIAF is also militarily proficient, led by officers trained by ex-British Special Forces in Sabah in the 1960s, and bolstered by large periodic shipments of arms such as Russian-made RPG-2 rocket-propelled grenade launchers, mortars and machine guns, and allegedly US-made Stinger anti-aircraft missiles that were originally supplied to the Afghan mujahideen in their war of resistance against the Soviet Union in the 1980s. Many members of the BIAF also gained combat experience in Afghanistan as volunteers fighting alongside the anti-Soviet mujahideen resistance forces. These links with the mujahideen and with Muslim volunteers from different parts of the world has helped to build transnational ties with like-minded militants elsewhere. Indeed, the MILF established links with al-Qaeda in the early 1990s.[15] It has also received funding from al-Qaeda, particularly through Mohammad Khalifa, Osama bin Laden's brother-in-law. Moreover, while the MNLF is confined to isolated Sulu and draws its support from the Tausug ethnic group there, the MILF has the support of 1.6 million Maguindanaos who live on the larger island of Mindanao, as well as the largest Muslim ethnic group, the 1.9 million Maranaos.

The MILF wisely avoided major clashes with the government, and has thus been able to concentrate on building up its strength throughout the 1980s and the early 1990s. Western military intelligence estimates put its standing army at 35,000.[16] An effort on this scale stems from the MILF's ability to obtain funds from sympathetic Islamic organisations abroad, in Malaysia, Pakistan and the Middle East, and the fact that it has the support of Moro religious leaders. The MILF today is in control of large swathes of at least seven provinces in Mindanao, with the present Philippines government unwilling or powerless to challenge the movement. In fact, local officials have little choice but to actively cooperate with it, given its control on the ground. The MILF has its own 80-strong Consultative Assembly and draws popular support from Muslims throughout Mindanao. In short, the MILF acts as a de facto government overseeing large areas in Mindanao.

In contrast, the MNLF is more secular in orientation and more willing to compromise. Faced with evident decline in its strength and under pressure from the OIC to compromise, the MNLF accepted a peace agreement in August 1996, under which Nur Misuari and the MNLF eventually ran an Autonomous Region of Muslim Mindanao, a truncated area of five provinces where Muslims are in a majority. Ominously, however, the MILF denounced the agreement and declared that it was taking over the revolutionary movement. To underline their aspirations, some 60,000 Muslims gathered in the southern town of Sultan Kudarat and issued a call for an independent Islamic state. This does not augur well for a lasting and durable peace.

The MILF subsequently took advantage of the ceasefire to build up its own strength, to the point that it is now the dominant Moro rebel group. The perceptible failure of Nur Misuari to bring about any development to the Autonomous Region of Muslim Mindanao has also enabled the MILF to exploit pent-up frustrations and recruit even more members into its ranks. The Philippines government has tacitly acknowledged the strategic reality by refraining from challenging the MILF on the ground, with local authorities making their own arrangements with MILF officials and commanders.

Mediation by the OIC and the Muslim World League resulted in formal peace negotiations with the MILF in October 1999. Encouraged by East Timor's independence in 1999, the MILF demanded an independent Islamic state. Maintaining a hardline stance, the MILF declared that 'the same demand will be aired, twenty years or even 100 years from now because the Bangsamoro people believe that independence is the ultimate solution to the Mindanao problem'.[17] However, the main stumbling block to this was not merely the central government's opposition to an independent Moro state, but the fact that Catholics outnumber the Muslims in most provinces in Mindanao. The Catholics are not likely to acquiesce to this and would most certainly take up arms to oppose such an eventuality.

In recent times, rising concern over the activities of al-Qaeda in the region has led to investigations that link MILF with international terrorism. These links have come to prominence in the aftermath of September 11 2001. It is a well-known fact that Osama bin Laden provided funding and training to the MILF, funds were channelled through his brother-in-law, Mohammad Jamal Khalifa, who lived in Manila in the 1990s, where he ran a Muslim charity.[18] There is also evidence that MILF chairman Hashim Selamat was in regular contact with the al-Qaeda leadership. At the military level, al-Qaeda also imparted specialised training to MILF and other Southeast Asian Islamists at Camp Abubakar in Mindanao.[19] The MILF itself declared in early 2000 that ten Saudi 'military consultants' had arrived to help its cause.

But the events of September 11, rather than galvanising the MILF into revolutionary action, actually provided a boost to the peace process as the MILF leadership retreated from its links with al-Qaeda.[20] The MILF seems to be increasingly amenable to negotiations with the central government, although it has also made clear that it will not compromise over the goal of Moro independence. Indeed, after September 11, the MILF has been keen to distance itself from al-Qaeda to avoid being targeted by the US. Significantly, US Special Forces deployed in the southern Philippines after September 11 have targeted only the more radical Abu Sayyaf Group, not the MILF. It seems that while Moros have been caught up with radical Islamic ideology due to al-Qaeda indoctrination and the spread of pan-Islamic radicalism, the MILF is also aware that its *raison d'être* is to redress the fundamental grievances that underlie Moro rebellion and that, ultimately, its objectives are nationalistic and territorial.

There has also been the added complication of considerable sympathy from co-religionists elsewhere, particularly from Malaysia. There is evidence that certain Islamic groups in Malaysia have been involved in aiding the Moros, and it appears that the Malaysian government had not actively prevented them from doing so, in recognition of the potentially serious domestic political fallout from its own local Muslim constituency. Large numbers of Filipino Muslims have settled in Sabah, and received Malaysian citizenship in an attempt to maintain Malay Muslim dominance over the state. The Malaysian government had also turned a blind eye to the anti-Philippine activities of these exiles.

Philippine-Malaysian relations have, therefore, been strained. Nonetheless, recent developments have changed the way the Malaysian leadership views Islamic militants. The hostage crises, in which militant Moro rebels belonging to the radical Abu Sayyaf seized twenty-one hostages, including nine Malaysians, from the Malaysian resort island of Sipadan in April 2000, highlighted the new security threat. Moreover, the Sauk arms heist in July 2000 by a militant Islamic group in Perak, Malaysia, as well as the subsequent discovery of another separate militant Islamic group, the Kumpulan Mujahidin Malaysia (KMM), which had been behind several terrorist attacks, has flagged to the Malaysian leadership the internal threat posed by such groups.

Thus, when Nur Misuari of the MNLF reneged on his peace agreement and rebelled against the Philippine government in 2001, he had little sympathy from Kuala Lumpur, which arrested him and offered to hand him back to the Philippines. Indeed, Malaysian Prime Minister Mahathir stated that it was an internal matter for the Philippines. A more serious complication has been the activity of the extremist Islamic Abu Sayyaf Group. Founded by Amilhussin Jumaani and Abdurajak Abubakkar Janjalani in 1991, this armed terrorist group is opposed to any religious accommodation with the Christians and believes that violence is the only solution. Although it is estimated to be only about 500 strong and does not control territory or a regular army, it is well led by Muslim veterans of the Afghanistan conflict. In addition, it has proven skilful in waging urban terrorism. The Abu Sayyaf has been able to attract the sympathy and active support of a number of ex-MNLF supporters disillusioned with Misuari's leadership.

More seriously, the Abu Sayyaf itself is an expression of the rise of pan-Islamic militant violence worldwide, and indeed appears to have strong connections with international Muslim terrorist groups. Its founder, Janjalani – himself a veteran of the Afghan conflict – had brought back with him enthusiastic fellow veterans fired up by pan-Islamic militant ideology. In fact, the name Abu Sayyaf is a tribute to Osama bin Laden's ally Rasool Sayyaf, with whom he fought during the Afghan War.[21] Bin Laden also sent Ramzi Yousef to train the Abu Sayyaf in the use of sophisticated high explosives. Yousef had achieved notoriety with daring terrorist acts, such as bombing the World Trade Center in New York in 1993. Bin Laden also helped to bankroll the activities of the group. With training and money provided by international Islamic terrorists, and through the use of extortion and kidnapping for ransom, the Abu Sayyaf was thus able to wreak havoc in the southern Philippines.

Demonstrating its links with international terrorist groups, the Abu Sayyaf has made repeated demands that the United States government release Islamic militants jailed for terrorist activities in the West. They included Ramzi Yousef and Sheik Omar Abdel Rahman, a Muslim cleric jailed for plotting to bomb various targets in New York. Abu Sayyaf stated that American citizens would be targeted if these demands were not met.

The failure to provide development and to alleviate fundamental grievances centring on poverty, unemployment and landlessness in the Philippines has helped to fuel discontent and the resort to arms. It is therefore important to note that the Abu Sayyaf is a symptom of underlying problems centred on poverty. It has capitalised on Moro despair, and it is in this context that Islamic radical ideology appears attractive. In addition, given its international connections to militant Islam abroad, it is also a reflection of growing globalisation and the resultant emergence worldwide of the new terrorism.

It was the daring raid on Sipadan Island in April 2000 that gained Abu Sayyaf worldwide notoriety. At one stroke, the Abu Sayyaf put the separatist agenda before a worldwide audience. It demanded a separate Islamic state in the southern Philippines and a probe into alleged maltreatment of Filipinos in Sabah as conditions for the release of the hostages. At the same time, by involving the Malaysian government (since the act of terrorism took place on Malaysian territory) and foreign tourists, the Abu Sayyaf hoped that foreign pressure could be brought to bear on the Philippines government to stop its offensive against both the Abu Sayyaf and its close ally, the MILF. The Abu Sayyaf also gained from its higher profile since embarking on a policy of kidnappings. Not only did it obtain large ransoms, it also attracted new recruits, lured by the success of the group.

Apart from kidnappings, a number of bomb attacks in May 2000 on shopping centres, the airport and a cinema, caused widespread apprehension within Manila. The Philippine Embassy in Jakarta was also the target of a bomb attack on 1 August 2000. A previously unknown Indonesian group linked to the Moro rebels claimed responsibility for this attack. Cities in the southern Philippines have also suffered a number of terrorist bombing attacks.

The Moro problem demonstrates all the classic characteristics of a civil war.[22] The severity of it is beyond doubt. Similarly, the duration of the conflict is troubling – the MNLF launched its struggle for independence in the late 1960s. Yet after almost three decades of fighting, the Moro problem has remained as intractable as ever. Indeed, a third characteristic – that of resistance to negotiated settlement – appears to be present as well. Although the MNLF under Nur Misuari signed a peace accord with the government, the MILF – the larger of the two organisations – has appeared determined to achieve the objective of an independent Moro state.

Given the gravity and intractability of the situation, the Moro problem is thus likely to continue to bedevil Philippines domestic politics and constitute a serious domestic security challenge for the foreseeable future.

THE ACEH REBELLION IN INDONESIA

Armed separatism in Indonesia has been a significant internal security threat to that country. The Aceh rebellion has been significant for its duration, resistance to negotiated settlement and sympathy from abroad, especially from co-religionists from Malaysia, southern Thailand and Libya.

Although the rebellion is Islamic in nature, there are also historical, nationalistic and economic factors at work as well. Aceh has historically been an independent kingdom, with Islam as a focal point for nationalist sentiments. Indeed, it was the last part of the Indonesian archipelago to fall to Dutch rule, which was not effectively consolidated until the early twentieth century. Despite that, however, local sentiments and pride have remained strong. This was reflected in 1953, when Aceh joined the abortive Darul Islam rebellion which spread from West Java to the outer islands and sought the creation of an Islamic state of Indonesia. More significantly, there has been resentment over what the local Acehnese see as Javanese domination, corruption and rapaciousness. The poverty, unemployment and backwardness of the province contrasts with the presence and exploitation of huge gas deposits by the Mobil Oil Company, which has benefited mostly non-Acehnese, with the bulk of the revenue siphoned off by Jakarta.[23] The resentments were exacerbated by the differences between the pious Muslim culture of Aceh, which contrasted with the more secular, *abangan* culture and lifestyles of the Javanese who dominate the armed forces and bureaucracy. In addition, the transmigration program had also resulted in Javanese settlers establishing themselves in Aceh, much to the resentment of the local Acehnese.

The strong local Islamic identity and resentment against Jakarta contributed to the founding of the Free Aceh Movement (GAM) in 1976. Its founder, Tengku Hasan di Tiro, is of impeccable pedigree. He is descended from the hero of the Acehnese struggle against the Dutch, Tengku Chik di Tiro. While GAM appeared to have been crushed by the Indonesian authorities by 1979, resentment at the brutality of the Indonesian army, with many allegations of widespread atrocities, resulted in its revival. In 1989, GAM separatists launched a series of attacks on police posts and army installations, demonstrating its continued ability to threaten internal security. Hasan di Tiro has been able to effectively use economic and religious discontent to increase support for his cause. In addition, he also obtained the support of Libya, which provided military training for up to 600 Acehnese.

The Indonesian armed forces reacted swiftly and brutally. The military regarded civilian Acehnese to be possible sympathisers, and employed a disproportionate level of force. The army destroyed homes and executed all those suspected of aiding the rebels. In 1991, public executions of suspected rebels were held, and Acehnese refugees fled to Penang in Malaysia as a result of this crackdown. Malaysia's refusal to surrender those accused of rebelling against the Indonesian government indicated considerable sympathy in Malaysia for its Acehnese co-religionists. This has raised suspicions in Indonesia of Malaysia's passive complicity in the troubles in Aceh.

By 1992, the rebellion appeared to have been more or less contained, at a cost of some 2,000 lives. However, the underlying nationalist, religious and economic factors that fuelled strong separatist sentiments have remained intact. Sporadic clashes since then demonstrated that separatist sentiments remain alive.

What has enraged the Acehnese and kept alive separatist sentiments has been the acknowledged brutality of the army's actions, which has embittered relations with Jakarta and alienated the local populace. In August 1998, Indonesia's own National Human Rights Commission reported that 781 people in Aceh had been victims of military atrocities. An independent inquiry reported to Parliament in 1999 that it had uncovered 5,000 cases of human rights abuses committed by the military in Aceh.[24]

The end of the Suharto regime in May 1998 opened the way for more democratic expressions of dissent and emboldened the advocates of secession in various parts of Indonesia, especially in East Timor and Aceh. Sensing that perhaps the time had come to press their claim for independence, the separatists intensified their activities from early 1999, carrying out kidnappings, murder of military personnel and ambushes. In May 1999, heightened expectations of independence following the agreement to hold a referendum for self-determination in East Timor by the new Habibie government resulted in GAM campaigning for a similar referendum. The armed forces responded by killing some 41 civilians. In retaliation, GAM stepped up its armed campaign, which included attacks on soldiers and the burning of hundreds of buildings. The spiralling violence led to a refugee crisis involving some 100,000. This in turn led to a predictably heavy-handed military response, including the massacre of civilians. Indeed, it was the discovery of mass graves and allegations of casual executions of civilians in Beutong Ateuh in West Aceh that prompted an outcry and the despatch of a special investigation team by President Habibie.

Demonstrating the enhanced influence and power of the Free Aceh Movement, local government in Aceh was shut down in October 1999. The burning of the state parliament on 2 November 1999 followed this. On 4 November, some 100,000 people attended a mass rally for independence. On 8 November, 500,000 people rallied for independence. Dismissing calls for dialogue, Hasan di Tiro stated that it was 'stupid' because 'Indonesia will become at least five different countries'.[25]

Indeed, given East Timor's successful bid for secession, there were widespread fears within Indonesia that Acehnese independence would lead to a break-up of the Indonesian state, with others, in Riau, Maluku and Irian Jaya demanding their independence in such an eventuality. Thus, the Indonesian Parliament on 18 November rebuffed President Wahid's proposal for a referendum in Aceh, even if it was only on autonomy.

In response, GAM began targeting oil and gas installations belonging to Exxon Mobil in early 2001. This resulted in the military sending more troops to Aceh (now numbering 50,000, many with Special Forces training), amidst expectations that the conflict was now moving towards a renewed phase of violence.[26] Such moves could well worsen the situation, given the experience of past abuses and sheer mismanagement by the military. The fact that the Indonesian military is actively training Javanese migrants in Aceh has led to accusations of encouraging ethnic conflict, a recipe for more violence not less. Indeed, the military has been pressing President Megawati Sukarnoputri to allow it to use force to crush the rebellion. The President herself is not averse to the idea but has insisted that peaceful negotiations be given a chance first, although Acehnese independence is clearly out of the question.

The Free Aceh movement has never really had the numbers or ability to hold on to large swathes of territory, unlike the much larger Moro rebel movement in Mindanao. In 1999, the Free Aceh rebels were estimated to number anywhere from 800 to 5,000. It has only thus far been able to undertake sporadic terrorist attacks and has been mostly on the run from the Indonesian armed forces. However, there has been an external dimension similar to the Moro rebels, in that there exists Muslim support and sympathy from outside Indonesia. Libya helped Hasan di Tiro in founding the movement and also trained the initial group of fighters.

In recent years, there have been various allegations and reports of arms smuggled in from Thailand and Malaysia. Indeed, Acehnese sympathisers in southern Thailand and Malaysia are believed to fund the rebellion. The Malaysian connection was also dramatically highlighted by the assassination of a leader of a breakaway GAM faction, Teuku Zulfahri, in a Kuala Lumpur restaurant in June 2000. In December 1999, the Indonesian Home Affairs Minister publicly stated that Aceh rebels were smuggling in weapons from Malaysia.[27] This brought an immediate denial from the Malaysian Deputy Prime Minister Abdullah Badawi.

There have also been allegations of links between GAM and the Afghan mujahideen and al-Qaeda. Indeed, the US has been reported to be investigating such links. Prisoner interrogations and documents captured in the Afghan war against the Taliban in 2001 yielded information concerning recruitment centres and training facilities in Aceh and Maluku in Indonesia. Up to 3,000 al-Qaeda followers are said to have trained in these camps.[28] To date, however, it is the external links with Malaysian-based sympathisers and with Libya that have been much better documented and proven. GAM is also on record as opposing the presence of militant religious groups in Aceh on the grounds that the Aceh struggle is against Indonesia, and is not a religious war. Indeed, like the MILF, its leadership is keen to distance itself from al-Qaeda after September 11.

The conflict in Aceh has been characterised by durability, resistance to negotiated settlement and growing severity. Moreover, there is an external dimension present, in the form of a relatively stable arms supply and financial support from sympathisers abroad. More significantly, there has been growing popular support, with wide sections of Acehnese society, including students, merchants, peasants, workers, civil administrators, village headmen and religious leaders, joining in the independence cause in the wake of the heightened expectations generated by East Timor's own independence in 1999, as well as continued anger and bitterness over the brutality suffered at the hands of the Indonesian military.

The newly elected civilian democratic government under President Megawati in Indonesia has vacillated in its approach to Aceh. The passing of an autonomous law and the promulgation of *sharia* law in Aceh have not resulted in independence sentiments abating, given the presence of underlying grievances, such as socio-economic disparities and the search for justice over the human rights abuses of the military.

The military, which sees itself as the natural guardian of Indonesia's sovereignty and integrity, has also been apprehensive about any concessions, fearful that it could lead eventually to Acehnese independence and the break-up of Indonesia. Indeed, it has advocated the use of force, and has been pressuring the government to declare martial law and send more troops into the troubled province.[29] Nor is there any support from the international community for an independent Aceh. Indonesia's fellow ASEAN states fear an unstable, balkanised Indonesia should that happen, and will thus not support an independent Aceh, or, for that matter, an independent Moro homeland.[30]

Finally, in December 2002 – through Swiss mediation – GAM and the central government signed a peace settlement, which would involve maximum autonomy following a referendum. However, the depth of hostility between GAM and the armed forces was such that the agreement collapsed in May 2003. Subsequently, Jakarta effectively decided to resolve the struggle by force.

THE PATTANI REBELLION IN SOUTHERN THAILAND

Another Muslim separatist movement exists in the southern Thai provinces of Pattani, Yala, Narathiwat and Satun, which have predominantly Malay Muslim populations. These provinces are contiguous with the predominantly Muslim states of Kelantan, Terengganu and Kedah in Malaysia, from which the 1.4 million Malays in southern Thailand derive their aspirations and succour. The difference from the Muslim separatism in Mindanao and Aceh, however, is that the aspiration is irredentist in nature, with the objective being union with Malaysia, and not the establishment of a separate state.

Seat of the ancient Malay kingdom of Pattani, the southern Thai provinces have been ruled indirectly by Siam since 1785. In 1909, the Anglo-Siamese Treaty demarcated the border between Siam and British Malaya, thus achieving for Siam a measure of international recognition for its rule over the area. The Malays, however, viewed this British recognition of Thai authority and sovereignty as arbitrary and unjust, and have since viewed Bangkok as an occupying colonial power.

Malay resistance to Thai integration had some support from the Malay rulers of Kelantan. During the Japanese Occupation of 1941–5, the southern provinces were briefly united with Malaya, and the end of the Second World War saw hopes of Pattani being integrated into the Malayan Federation. A Malayan-based movement called the Gabungan Melayu Pattani Raya (GAMPAR or Association of Malays of Greater Pattani), and the local, religiously led Pattani People's Movement (PPM) were formed for the express objective of irredentism. The Thai government, however, succeeded in crushing the rebellion when the leader of the PPM, Haji Sulong, was arrested and executed by Thai police in 1954.[31]

The fears of the Malay community were heightened by the policies of the Thai government, which sought to centralise the bureaucracy of the southern provinces, taking away power from the traditional royal and religious elite. Secular education was introduced, and the Thai language actively promoted.

Thai local officials aggravated communal relations by their corruption and anti-Malay prejudices. More significantly, the Thai government's policy of assimilation raised fears of an erosion of Malay culture and values. The Thai government in fact refused to appoint Malay Muslims to the bureaucracy, a policy that was reversed only in 1977. The Muslim problem was also accentuated by the low economic status and poverty of the Malay populace, who occupied the bottom rung of society.

The geographical contiguity with Malaysia provides an important explanation for the impetus to armed irredentism among the Thai Malay Muslims. The visible economic development in neighbouring Malaysia, where kindred Malays are dominant politically and are also reaping the economic benefits of the pro-*bumiputra* (indigenous) New Economic Policy, provided an unwelcome comparison. Moreover, the free flow of people and information across the Thai-Malaysian border has enabled Thai-Malay Muslims to reinforce their cultural, ethnic and religious identity in the face of concerted attempts at assimilation.

The Muslim separatists in southern Thailand are currently grouped around three guerrilla movements: the Barisan Revolusi Nasional (BRN), the Barisan Nasional Pembebasan Patani (BNPP) and the Pattani United Liberation Organisation (PULO).

The BRN, founded in 1960, is leftist in orientation and in fact developed close links with the Communist Party of Malaya. However, confrontation in the 1960s split the movement between those supporting Indonesia and those supporting Malaysia. The BNPP, a splinter movement from the BRN, was formed in 1971. It is well organised and has support in Kelantan and from Middle Eastern organisations such as the Arab League and the Palestine Liberation Organisation (PLO). PULO was formed in 1968, and is led by intellectuals educated in the Middle East and Pakistan. PULO, like the MNLF in the southern Philippines, has achieved a measure of international recognition. Since 1977, PULO has attended the World Muslim League Conference as an observer. PULO claims to have over 10,000 guerrillas and has been the most active of the Islamic separatist movements.[32] In September 1977, PULO attempted to assassinate the Thai king during his visit to Yala Province. While the attempt failed, it highlighted the real danger from the Muslim separatists.[33] Guerrilla attacks have since targeted Thai military personnel, and the sabotage of public utilities.

PULO continued to launch sporadic attacks in the 1980s and 1990s. Responding to a series of terrorist attacks in 1993, the Thai Fourth Army commander responsible for security in the south, Lieutenant-General Kitti Rattanachaya, admitted that the attacks were launched by a younger generation of radicals who were motivated by hatred and bitterness against the injustice that prevailed in the south, and had thus resorted to terrorism. In

January 1998, a huge security operation against the separatists was launched in response to a wave of bomb attacks. In addition, security in Bangkok was increased amidst fears that the insurgents were planning terrorist attacks on the capital.

Thailand's Malay Muslim separatist problem remains as intractable as ever. No easy or quick solution is possible, given the pull of kinship via a porous border with Malaysia and the presence of sympathisers in that country, who could provide the succour and financial contributions necessary to sustain the separatists.

There are some similarities between the Muslim separatism of southern Thailand and that elsewhere in the region, namely in the southern Philippines. Both identify strongly with Islam as a focal point for their identity. There have also been problems of economic disparity, poverty and lack of development. In both cases, the fear of losing their cultural, ethnic and religious identity in the face of a dominant group belonging to another religion and with an alien culture, coupled with assimilationist policies and outright discrimination by the central government, have also provided the impetus for rebellion.

In comparison to Mindanao, however, the scale of the fighting has been much less severe. Unlike the Moros, the Muslim separatists are not fighting for an independent state but have an irredentist agenda. Recognising the socio-economic basis for rebellion, the Thai government has engaged in a battle for hearts and minds, focusing on measures to win over the Malay Muslim population. Principally, these measures have involved a more sensitive approach to questions of religion, language and culture, as well as generous funding for development projects in the south. The Thai government has even set up an Islamic bank to serve the needs of the six million Thai Muslims. The Thai royal family, especially the King and the Crown Princess, have taken a deep interest in development projects in the south as well, putting moral pressure on local officials. Indeed, there appears to be a positive effect emanating from the presence of a widely accepted moral authority in the form of the much-respected monarchy. The general prosperity of the south and the greater capacity to deliver on development also reflects the economic strides Thailand as a whole has made over the past two decades, in contrast to the much worse economic situation in both Indonesia and the Philippines.

In addition, a measure of cooperation by the Malaysian government, which has not supported the separatists, has also helped to ameliorate the severity of the conflict. Strategic cooperation against the Communist Party of Malaya (CPM) had made the Malaysian government wary of assisting the guerrillas. The surrender of the CPM in 1989 shifted the focus uncomfortably to the question of counter-insurgency against the Thai Malay Muslim separatist guerrillas in southern Thailand. Malaysian defence minister Datuk Sri Najib Tun Razak pledged in 1993 that the Malaysian armed forces would patrol the border more tightly to prevent the separatists from using the heavily forested areas in Kelantan and Perak as hideouts, and declared that Malaysia would not protect or cooperate with the separatists. As a result, the situation in southern Thailand is well under control. In contrast, the Moros have been able to achieve virtually a de facto government in many parts of Mindanao.

Yet, there is undoubtedly considerable sympathy and support for the Malay separatists in Malaysia. The opposition fundamentalist PAS, which controls the state government of Kelantan, has openly declared that it has offered refuge to Muslim separatists, stating that 'PAS has to offer this help because our Muslim brothers are being discriminated against in all aspects of life in southern Thailand'.[34] Indeed, PAS's strong showing in the Malaysian general elections in 1999, in which it retained Kelantan and Terengganu as well as capturing the majority of the Malay vote, has led to dismay in Thailand, which fears that this could fuel the irredentist aspirations of the Malay Muslims in the south.

Some of the characteristics of civil conflict can be found in the Muslim separatist movement in southern Thailand – those of duration and resistance to a negotiated settlement. However, the severity of the Malay Muslim separatist movement has been limited. Even so, an external element is present in three forms. The first is the sympathy from co-religionists in neighbouring Malaysia. The second is the link with other Muslim secessionists in the region.[35] The third is the most worrying of all – potential links with international militant Islam. Thai police have reported the emergence of a new terrorist group, known as Bersatu, which consist of Muslim fighters trained in the Middle East. This group has been linked with two bomb attacks in southern Thailand in April 2001. This emergence is inevitable given the worldwide Muslim revival and its radicalisation, a process also evident in neighbouring states of Indonesia and Malaysia. There are also reports that local Muslim militants have established contacts with militant Muslim groups in Afghanistan.[36] Still, the situation in southern Thailand has clearly been much better controlled than that in Mindanao and Aceh.

BEYOND SEPARATISM: THE NEW TERRORISM IN SOUTHEAST ASIA

The Emergence of Militant Islam

The rise in Islamic consciousness has raised fears in the region that extreme forms of Islam may develop, if the experience of the Middle Eastern countries is any guide. In this context, Islam is a potent mobilising symbol in harnessing political opposition to nationalist government. The Islamic factor has already proved to be a focal point for the rallying of armed resistance against the government in regions such as Aceh and Mindanao. Moreover, as the Algerian and other Middle Eastern examples show, economic distress and inequalities could lead many to seek solace in more extreme forms of Islam. This is especially true in the wake of the regional economic crisis of 1997, and deepening socio-economic disparities that have been a consequence of globalisation.

An emerging concern in recent years is increased evidence of Islamist militant terrorism. These groups are in the process of forging links with similar international militant Islamic groups, in particular, al-Qaeda. They may also have gained a following among armed separatists in the region. Indeed, they are prepared to use force to achieve their objective of achieving an Islamic realm embracing much of Southeast Asia.

In Malaysia, there have been a series of violent incidences involving militant Islamic groups dating back to 1980.[37] They culminated in an incident in Sauk, Malaysia, in July 2000, when the al-Ma'unah militant group staged a raid on a military armoury. The fifteen men involved took three hostages and fled into the Perak jungle, where army commandos overpowered them after two of their non-Muslim hostages were killed. In follow-up operations, a further thirty-nine members of the group were arrested under the Internal Security Act.

What is worrying for Malaysia's neighbours has been the current political situation, with its deepening division within the Malay polity between moderate and fundamentalist Islam. At its roots has been widespread poverty in oil-rich Terengganu, as well as a yearning among many Malays for more emphasis on spiritual, as opposed to secular, developmental goals. In particular, whilst they want modernity, they do not want to compromise the values and practices of Islam. Indeed, the government's model of modernisation has not resonated well with significant sections of the Malay community. Indeed, the current economic recession has simply made matters worse by exacerbating socio-economic disparities among Malay Muslims, between the elite ruling class and the rest of the Malay Muslim population. In addition, there remains widespread anger and a sense of injustice over the arrest and imprisonment of the former Deputy Prime Minister, Anwar Ibrahim, seen in many circles as the standard bearer for Islam in the government.

The impressive showing of the fundamentalist Parti Islam (PAS) in the 1999 general elections, when it won 20 parliamentary seats and took control of state governments in Kelantan and Terengganu, is indicative of the growing influence of political Islam in Malaysia. Given the competition to become more Islamic as well as the lack of any space for debate on religious matters, the trajectory of Islam in Malaysia can only be in one direction – towards even greater fundamentalism. PAS itself has taken a more fundamentalist anti-American stand in the wake of 11 September as conservative clerics take advantage of the sense of solidarity shown by Muslims to increase their influence at the expense of the moderates, with calls for jihad and proposals to send volunteers to Afghanistan to fight the United States.[38] Accompanying the rise of fundamentalism has been the emergence of an extremist fringe, in the form of violent groups such as al-Ma'unah and the KMM. Indeed, Nik Adli, son of the PAS President and a former Afghan mujahideen, is currently under detention for his alleged role in the KMM.

In Indonesia, there has been a similar rise in political Islam and the emergence of Islamic extremist groups. Under the Suharto regime, arrests and investigations were carried out in 1994 and 1995 over alleged attempts to overthrow the government and establish an Islamic state. Militant Islamic opposition to the Suharto regime also manifested itself in widespread street violence, particularly against the Christians, many of whom are ethnic Chinese. In June 1996, for instance, frustration at the Suharto regime saw Muslim mobs take to the streets. They destroyed twelve Christian churches, with the armed forces doing nothing to stop them. In October 1996, 3,000 Muslims in Situbondo set fire to twenty-five churches, killing five Christians.

The 1997 regional economic crisis hit Indonesia the hardest. The unsustainability of the corrupt, cronyistic system built by Suharto was cruelly exposed by the crisis. The more democratic environment following Suharto's ouster has led to greater political involvement by Islamic groups, whose voice had been long suppressed under the Suharto government. Severe economic stress, social strains, political instability and the crisis of governance in Indonesia have driven many to more extreme forms of Islam.

There have also been a number of recent terrorist attacks, including the Christmas bombings in Jakarta in 2000. Subsequent investigations pointed to the involvement of Malaysians belonging to the KMM and also revealed links with Moro militants.

Evidence of rising Islamic militancy can also be found in the Christian-Muslim violence in the Malukus, which broke out in the aftermath of Suharto's fall. There, dormant ethnic and religious animosities have emerged. Violence between Christians and Muslims resulted in violent rioting in 1999, fighting that has descended into a civil war since then. On 14 January 2000, 300,000 angry Muslims marched in Jakarta, stoked by newspaper accounts about alleged genocide against Muslims. Many vowed to join the fight in the Malukus and others threatened to launch a jihad or holy war in Jakarta itself.[39] In May 2000, hundreds of fundamentalist Muslim jihad volunteers belonging to the extremist Islamic organisation, the Laskar Jihad, began to arrive in the Malukus to assist their fellow Muslims in the civil conflict against the Christians. Volunteers from other parts of Indonesia, veterans of the Afghan War, and Arab and other Muslim volunteers from abroad, arrived to help in the war against the Christians. By mid-2000, the death toll had passed the 4,000 mark without any let-up. By mid-2002, the toll stood at some 9,000. The bitterness engendered by the conflict will not be easy to dissipate, given the scope of the violence, even if some order is finally restored. The scope of the violence is such that the number of refugees has reached 500,000.

The religious conflict in the Malukus has implications far beyond the islands, given the calls for jihad by prominent Muslim leaders such as Amien Rais and Islamic organisations such as the Indonesian Ulamas Association. The conflict in the Malukus has already shown worrying signs of spreading. Protests over the conflict in the Malukus by Muslims in Lombok led to a number of serious riots between Christians and Muslims on the tourist resort island, resulting in the evacuation of tourists and the collapse of the tourism industry. Fighting between Christians and Muslims has since broken out in Central Sulawesi.

The radicalisation of Islam as a result of religious conflict is a development that will only engender greater divisiveness and violence in the Indonesian archipelago. More seriously, the events of September 11 and the international pressure on Indonesia to take action against its own militants allegedly involved in al-Qaeda-supported terrorist activities in the region, as well as the continuing conflict in Palestine, have had the effect of moving the Islamic discourse towards fundamentalism. Indeed, there are today growing fears that extremist ideology is spreading rapidly among urban Muslim youth, and that Laskar Jihad is infiltrating mainstream Muslim organisations, such as the Muhammadiyah.

The Emergence of Transnational Terrorism

Increased globalisation and the growing ease of communication have made possible cross-border linkages and networks. These have facilitated the spread of a pan-Islamic militant ideology throughout Southeast Asia and the subsequent emergence of the new terrorism in the region. There also appear to be growing transborder links between the various Islamic extremist/separatist groups, a not unsurprising development. In Indonesia, bomb attacks during Christmas 2000 highlighted a transnational element in that Malaysians and Filipino Muslims were said to be involved. Indeed, the Malaysian government has uncovered evidence of transnational cooperation among militants involving the smuggling of weapons to trouble spots such as Aceh and Ambon.

The arrest of a Malaysian in Jakarta for attempting a bomb attack on a shopping mall revealed the extremist KMM. Surprisingly, it involved Nik Adli, son of the PAS leader Nik Aziz. Nik Adli had served as a mujahideen volunteer in Afghanistan in the 1980s. Another interesting discovery was KMM's links with Afghanistan and the Afghan mujahideen, and, by extension, sympathy with al-Qaeda's brand of pan-Islamic militancy. Members of the KMM had attended mujahideen training camps in Afghanistan run by al-Qaeda, and had links with Muslim extremists in Indonesia, Pakistan, Eygpt and elsewhere. The KMM has also been responsible for a string of terror activities in Malaysia, including bank robberies, the murder of a Christian State Assemblyman and bombings of a church and a Hindu temple. Yet, the KMM, al-Ma'unah and the recently uncovered Jemaah Islamiah (JI) have no links, indicating that other extremist Muslim cells or groups probably remain undiscovered.

This has raised the issue of the 'intelligence gap'. Currently, an estimated 1,500 Malaysian Muslims study in religious schools or madrassas, in Pakistan.[40] Many of these are influenced by pan-Islamic ideologies, particularly those of the dogmatic, Wahhabi-type, and have established transnational links during their stay in Pakistan or Afghanistan. Undoubtedly, some have gone to Afghanistan at some stage to train in al-Qaeda camps.

The Sauk incident involving the militant al-Ma'unah, and the discovery of the KMM have served as a wake-up call regarding the intelligence gap on the activities of militant groups. The actions of September 11 and the danger of the brand of militant Islam propagated by al-Qaeda have also dramatically highlighted the security threat. The Malaysian government has taken belated measures to track down students who went to Pakistan and Afghanistan.

The presence of Malay Muslim minorities in Thailand, Singapore and the Philippines, three of Malaysia's immediate ASEAN neighbours, makes domestic political developments in Malaysia of special significance for the region. Indeed, Lee Kuan Yew openly articulated his fears just days before September 11, voicing concern that the threat of rising Islamic militancy in Malaysia could spill over to neighbouring countries, including Singapore.[41]

Thus, the growing links between local militants and international Islamic terrorist groups have been of increasing concern. Bin Laden has helped to fund the MILF, currently the largest Muslim separatist group in the southern Philippines, and the Abu Sayyaf Group. There have been increasing concerns over the activities of al-Qaeda cells in the region. In this regard, the presence of veterans of the Afghan conflict, the volunteer mujahideen who fought the Soviets in that conflict, is a source of concern, given that they are found in the ranks of the Moro rebels, the Abu Sayyaf, and the KMM. Given the general resurgence of Islam in Southeast Asia, and political instability in Indonesia, it is not surprising that Bin Laden has turned his attention to building up his network in the region. In fact, he is reported to be infiltrating Muslim non-government organisations, sending out extremist preachers and taking extremist leaders to Afghanistan for training. In the past two years, he has even been reported to have visited Indonesia on several occasions, where al-Qaeda terrorist cells exist.

The existence of an al-Qaeda affiliated network in the region was dramatically highlighted by the arrest in Singapore in January 2002 of thirty-two members of the extremist JI group. The smashing of the group stemmed from the recovery of videotape from an al-Qaeda house destroyed by US bombing in December 2001. The tape revealed that the group planned to attack American military personnel at a local subway station and also US naval vessels at Singapore's Changi Naval Base. It was also later uncovered that the JI had also planned similar attacks on US embassies in Singapore, Jakarta and Kuala Lumpur, to take place on 4 December 2001.

It was soon subsequently established that more than fifty militants arrested in Malaysia since December 2001 belonged to the Malaysian wing of JI, had links with the Singapore group, and had assisted it in the procurement of explosives to make truck bombs.

Also of interest are the regional links with Indonesia and the Philippines. The directing figures of JI are alleged to be three Indonesian preachers, Hambali, Abu Bakar Bashir and Mohamad Iqbal Rahman (Abu Jibril). Whilst Hambali has disappeared, Abu Jibril has been under detention in Malaysia since June 2001 and Bashir was arrested in Indonesia following the 12 October 2002 Bali attack. Acting on information provided by Singapore, Philippine police discovered a tonne of explosives in Mindanao, and arrested four men connected to al-Qaeda, including the Indonesian bomb-maker and trainer of the JI, Fathur Rohonan Al-Ghozi. The JI thus had a very clear regional mode of operation, operating in some four countries in Southeast Asia.

The arrest in June 2002 by Indonesian authorities of Omar al-Farouq (subsequently handed over to the US), provided a much clearer picture of al-Qaeda's terrorist plans for the region. A senior al-Qaeda representative in Southeast Asia, al-Farouq confessed under interrogation and was able to provide information on planned attacks after September 11, on western embassies, US navy ships and Christian churches, as well as a plot to kill President Megawati, resulting in a heightened security alert in the region.

But this did not prevent the bomb attack on the Sari nightclub in Bali on 12 October 2002, which killed 202 people. The Bali attack was directed explicitly at western citizens. Symbolically, the attack on 12 October also coincided with the anniversary of the USS Cole attack in 2000. Indeed, the arrests of several of those connected with the bombing appeared to confirm the strong JI links.

It is thus clear that the region cannot avoid the globally interconnected activities of transnational terrorist groups. Indeed, extremist Islamic ideology, together with the training in Afghanistan of local militants, appears to be having the effect of radicalising at least some groups in the region and laying the ground for more devastating terrorist attacks in the future.

CONCLUSION

Implications of the New Terrorism

A few concluding observations regarding the implications of the new terrorism for Southeast Asia would be pertinent, given the global effects of September 11. Certainly, the devastating attacks on the World Trade Center in New York and the Pentagon are a watershed. The attacks demonstrated that mass casualty terrorist acts are possible and that they have major political, economic and psychological impacts.

Rising Islamic Militant Violence

The implications for Southeast Asia are immense. Al-Qaeda has demonstrated what can be achieved, even against the most powerful state in the world. The al-Qaeda model serves as an inspiration as to what can be done to maximise the impact of terrorist acts. For many, Osama bin Laden has even become a hero and role model. September 11 might thus galvanise militant Islamic terrorism throughout Southeast Asia. The 'new' militant terrorists may be more dedicated, better trained and carry out more lethal attacks, possibly involving the use of biological and chemical weapons. For instance, the use of biological or chemical weapons in the not too distant future against Philippine cities by Moro extremists to press their claim for a separate Muslim state would not be a far-fetched scenario. American installations and personnel, both civilian and military, throughout the region, may face increased risks of attack by local Muslim extremists. There is also a danger that extremists could, in time, launch vastly expanded urban terrorist campaigns. This could potentially strike the Philippines, Thailand, Malaysia and Indonesia. This would spread terror and contribute to a loss of confidence in security, with negative impacts on regional economies.

The Impact of Economic Recession

The region has already been suffering badly from the effects of the 1997 regional economic crisis. Economic recovery had been patchy and problematic at best. However, the events of September 11 have had a devastating impact, resulting in a global recession that has affected Southeast Asia. Already showing signs of an economic slowdown, the lingering effects of this event are likely to affect the economies in the region, as consumers avoid flying for fear of hijackings, and cut back on travel and holidays. In Southeast Asia, the rise in Islamic consciousness has been noted by the US corporate sector, which may have a dampening effect on net foreign investment into the region. This in turn would exacerbate regional economic recovery. Prolonged economic stress will have unforeseen consequences for political stability in countries such as Indonesia, the Philippines and Malaysia. In particular, it will contribute to even larger numbers flocking to fundamentalist Islam for solace. In turn, many will be easy prey to extremist preaching, with the result that extremist and separatist Muslim groups will have much greater opportunities for recruitment.

In the Philippines, the spate of urban attacks as well as the continuing fighting in the south has affected business confidence and hit the economy, slowing growth and raising the prospects of a recession. Compared to 4.9 per cent growth in the first quarter in 1999, the Philippine economy recorded 3.4 per cent growth in the first quarter in 2000. Much of this slump was attributed to the poor performance of the agricultural sector, given that it accounts for just over 20 per cent of the country's Gross Domestic Product, with 60 per cent of the country's rice and corn output coming from the three Mindanao provinces at the centre of the conflict.

In Indonesia, the Aceh situation has a serious economic dimension, given that Aceh produces a third of Indonesia's liquefied natural gas exports. The political uncertainties have already affected long-term contracts and operations at the Exxon Mobil natural gas facilities in Aceh, which GAM has been targeting, affecting foreign currency earnings at a time of major economic stress in Indonesia.[42]

Transnational Counter-Terrorism Cooperation

The growing links between Islamic militants in the region as well as with international Islamic terrorist groups are also areas of increasing concern. Globalisation has facilitated the movement and activities of transnational terrorists, making them much harder to track. Globalisation has also resulted in the imposition of modern, secular values, often originating from the West, upon traditional cultures and communities, leading to fragmentation and much stress. Much has been said about the conflict between McWorld and Jihad,[43] but the point here is that the disaffected and those who have been left out have struck back at the perceived injustices by joining radical movements and extreme causes. Hence, while the worldwide Islamic resurgence is an understandable response to the challenge of global, western values and systems, there has been an extreme fringe that espouses violence as a means of redress. The spread of communications and information has also opened up new avenues of recruitment and helped to spread the pan-Islamic militant ideologies that have spawned the new terrorism.

The emergence of the new terrorism has been recognised and has been met with increasing evidence of a coordinated response by states in Southeast Asia. The infrastructure in Southeast Asia for transnational regional cooperation in countering terrorism is currently rather weak, consisting in the main of measures to counter piracy.[44] Yet, the growing links between militants in the region and their links with international militant groups mean that enhancing regional cooperation is an urgent imperative. The agreement to further counter-terrorist cooperation between Malaysia and Indonesia in August 2001 has been followed by a joint ASEAN statement condemning terrorism and agreeing to cooperate to combat it following the events of September 11. ASEAN also agreed on common measures in an action plan against terrorism, such as strengthening national mechanisms, enhancing intelligence exchange and supporting the UN in playing a bigger role in combating it. Significantly, ASEAN intelligence chiefs met in January 2002 and discussed the threat in the region posed by militant Islamic groups.

There is also evidence that the pace towards regional counter-terrorist cooperation has gathered momentum. Previously sympathetic to the Moros, the Malaysian government deported renegade Moro leader Nur Misuari back to the Philippines in January 2002 to face charges of armed rebellion. Malaysia and Indonesia also agreed to exchange intelligence information to combat terrorism. Multilateral cooperation in intelligence sharing, establishing uniform laws and counter-terrorism was stepped up under an Action Plan adopted by the ASEAN states in May 2002. The ASEAN Regional Forum (ARF) meeting in July 2002 also agreed on a set of financial measures to cut off terrorist funding.

In the aftermath of the Bali attack, APEC leaders in October 2002 agreed to a raft of measures to counter terrorism, such as enhancing security in trade, expanding the Container Security Initiative (involving pre-screening of cargo containers), choking off terrorist financing and promoting cyber-security.[45]

Despite all these pronouncements, however, it is also clear that the presence of mutual suspicion and differing national interests among the ASEAN states has hampered regional cooperation. There has, for instance, been palpable reluctance on the part of Indonesia to take action against militant groups due to domestic political sensitivities. As the Indonesian Foreign Minister declared in January 2002, Indonesia would act 'in our own time and according to our own routines'.[46] The Bali bombing did result in enormous pressure on the Indonesian government by Australia, the US and

Britain to rein in the militants. In response, Bashir was finally arrested but domestic political sensitivities have prevented a more extensive crackdown on the thousands of militant activists involved in the JI, or other groups that have been involved in much violence, for instance, in the Maluku Islands. With an eye to the presidential elections in 2004, none of the major political players wants to risk a Muslim backlash as those votes could be crucial in determining the election outcome.

New Counter-Terrorist Strategies

New doctrines and strategies are required to deal with the new terrorism. Draconian Internal Security Acts allowing for preventive detention exist in Malaysia and Singapore, a legacy of communist insurgency in the 1950s. These are now ironically proving useful against Islamic militants, especially in Malaysia. In addition, any effective counter-terrorist strategy must involve a battle of hearts and minds, to ensure that the extremist groups are kept on the run and on the fringe of society. In particular, it is important to try to counter extremist ideology by providing alternative, moderate viewpoints and encouraging debate within Islam. In many Islamic schools in the region, for instance, very narrow and dogmatic interpretations of Koranic concepts such as jihad are taught, but progressive Islamic scholarship can provide a useful counter. In addition, there is a need for development and socio-economic equity to ensure that the root causes of terrorism and insurgency are adequately addressed.

Such measures recall some of the successful counter-insurgency strategies used in dealing with communist subversion and rebellion in the decades after independence. A coherent counter-terrorist strategy emphasising political, psychological, economic and military/police measures is required to deal with terrorism. Such a strategy can be effective if assisted by modern surveillance and reconnaissance technology, as well as implemented by dedicated and well-trained professionals, for instance, in the way the Special Branch successfully defeated communist rebellion in Malaysia.

Recent events involving militant Islam have had a clear impact on both Malaysia and Singapore. Even before the events of September 11, Malaysian Defence Minister Tun Najib had called for the need for the Malaysian armed forces to be able to meet a full spectrum of threats, ranging from conventional warfare to low-intensity conflict and urban warfare, the latter needed to deal with possible terrorist violence mounted by Islamic militants.[47] Indeed, he publicly identified religious militancy as Malaysia's greatest internal security threat, stating that 'we must be on guard as any wrong teaching of Islam, or any inflammatory instigation by certain elements can wreak havoc on our internal stability'.[48]

More tellingly, fears have been expressed that the rank-and-file of the security forces might not be prepared to carry out orders to suppress fellow Muslims should more extreme groups mount a serious challenge to the government.[49] Another scenario would be the declaration of a State of Emergency (which has occurred four times since independence) in response to a rise in power by PAS. In today's context of the rise in the consciousness of the Muslim community, it can no longer be assumed that rank-and-file Malay Muslim soldiers would obey orders to use force against fellow Muslims, despite the much vaunted professionalism of the Malaysian Armed Forces. The government itself has expressed fears over the growing influence of deviant and extremist teachings among members of the police and the armed forces.

Singapore's response has been the promulgation of 'homeland security', which, according to Defence Minister Tony Tan, would be worked out over the next few years to protect Singapore from the new terrorism. Tan stated that the September 11 events demonstrated that the traditional division between external and internal threats no longer held, and added that a Security Policy Review Committee would coordinate the building of a new security architecture to deal with the new terrorism, which is likely to entail much closer cooperation between the armed forces, police and the Ministry of Home Affairs.

The Philippines has welcomed substantial military assistance from the US in combating the Moro rebellions in the southern provinces. These include transport aircraft, helicopters, patrol craft, armoured personnel carriers, assault rifles and anti-terrorism training. In return, the Philippines is likely to ratify a Mutual Logistics Support Agreement with the United States. After September 11, US Special Forces have also arrived to assist the Philippine Armed Forces against the Abu Sayyaf. The Philippine government itself has promulgated a Fourteen Point Plan to combat terrorism, but this plan emphasises military measures, paying scant attention to tackling the underlying grievances that have spurred the Moro rebellion.

New Attention to Root Causes

Whilst there are increasing numbers of Muslims in the region who now adhere to radical pan-Islamist ideologies, local Muslims have home-grown political, economic and social concerns that have long predated September 11 and al-Qaeda. While they may derive satisfaction and be galvanised by al-Qaeda'a actions, it is important to remember that fundamental grievances underlie armed Muslim rebellion in Southeast Asia. The long-term solution therefore is to deal with the fundamental causes of such militancy. Armed rebellion, including separatist rebellion, has its root in socio-economic issues and grievances, which cannot be redressed through the use of force alone.

The Indonesian armed forces have botched their operations in Aceh, making the situation worse, not better. By their use of random brutality, they have in fact alienated the local populace, which today sees them as an army of occupation. There is clearly a need to address fundamental socio-economic issues through equitable growth and development, given widespread anger at the way the province's oil and gas revenues have been siphoned off to Jakarta by Javanese elites. There is, in particular, a need to rein in rampant corruption and severe socio-economic disparities. In Mindanao, for instance, many Moros have lost their traditional lands due to greedy landlords and corrupt local officials. There is much poverty, unemployment and despair in the face of corruption, discrimination and lack of development.

In contrast, the much more sensitive socio-economic approach taken by the Thai government has ensured that the Thai Muslim separatist movement has been kept relatively quiet compared to the worsening situation in Aceh and Mindanao. The success of its 'Development as Security' approach points to the need to pay attention to the root causes of terrorism and insurgency. This will isolate local militants and make it easier to contain them. It will also make it harder for international terrorist groups to make inroads into the region. Indeed, progress in the war against terror does not consist of a series of tactical military victories but requires a broad, comprehensive political strategy designed to win hearts and minds in the Muslim world.

Addressing fundamental causes are vital tools in this battle. The problem of Muslim alienation and rebellion in Southeast Asia is also clearly a complex one. Yet, it is sobering to remember too that the problem of Muslim rebellion in Southeast Asia predated al-Qaeda and will continue to exist long after al-Qaeda is defeated. Al-Qaeda may also have succeeded in demonstrating the efficacy of new and more lethal forms of terrorism. In the final analysis, therefore, the war against terrorism is likely to be a long, drawn-out affair, with containment, not victory, being the most realistic outcome.

NOTES

1. Hoffman, Bruce (1997), 'The Confluence of International and Domestic Trends in Terrorism', *Terrorism and Political Violence*, 9/2, Summer.
2. *Ibid.*, pp 8–9.
3. McVey, Ruth (1984), 'Separatism and the Paradoxes of the Nation-State in Perspective', in Joo-Jock, Lim and Vani, S. (eds), *Armed Separatism in Southeast Asia*, Singapore: Institute of Southeast Asian Studies, p 12.
4. Man, W. K. Che (1990), *Muslim Separatism: The Moros of Southern Philippines and the Malays of Southern Thailand*, Singapore: Oxford University Press, pp 178–9.

5. Paribatra, Sukhumbhand and Samudavanija, Chai-Anan (1984), 'Factors Behind Armed Separatism: A Framework for Analysis', in Joo-Jock and Vani (eds), *Armed Separatism in Southeast Asia*, p 41.
6. Mercado, Eliseo (1984), 'Culture, Economics and Revolt in Mindanao: The Origins of the MNLF and the Politics of Moro Separatism', in Joo-Jock and Vani (eds), *Armed Separatism in Southeast Asia*, pp 168–75.
7. *Ibid.*, pp 160–61.
8. See Human Rights Watch (1992), *Bad Blood: Militia Abuses in Mindanao, the Philippines*, New York: Human Rights Watch, p 1.
9. Mercado (1984), 'Culture, Economics and Revolt in Mindanao: The Origins of the MNLF and the Politics of Moro Separatism', pp 156–7.
10. *Ibid.*, pp 156–7.
11. Hawkins, David (1972), *The Defence of Singapore: From the Anglo-Malayan Defence Agreement to ANZUK*, London: United Services Institute for Defence Studies, pp 50–2.
12. Mercado (1984), 'Culture, Economics and Revolt in Mindanao: The Origins of the MNLF and the Politics of Moro Separatism', p 157.
13. *Ibid.*, p 157.
14. Rivera, Temario (1994), 'Armed Challenges to the Philippines Government: Protracted War or Political Settlement?', in *Southeast Asian Affairs 1994*, Singapore: Institute of Southeast Asian Studies, p 260.
15. Bergen, Peter (2001), *Holy War Inc. Inside the Secret World of Osama bin Laden*, London: Weidenfeld & Nicolson, p 237.
16. Tiglao, Rigoberto (1995), 'Under the Gun', *Far Eastern Economic Review*, 24 August, pp 23–6.
17. *The Straits Times* (1999), 'Philippine Rebels Want Islamic State in the South', 25 October, p 26.
18. Reeve, Simon (1999), *The New Jackals: Ramzi Yousef, Osama bin Laden and the Future of Terrorism*, London: Andre Deutsch, pp 72–3.
19. Gunaratna, Rohan (2002), *Inside al-Qaeda*, London: Hurst, pp 183–4.
20. *Ibid.*, p 185.
21. Bergen (2001), *Holy War: Inside the Secret World of Osama bin Laden Inc*, pp 237–8.
22. Kegley Jr, Charles and Wittkopf, Eugene (1999), *World Politics: Trend and Transformation*, New York: Worth, p 369. According to Kegley and Wittkopf, the main characteristics of civil wars since 1945 have been their severity, duration and resistance to negotiated settlement.
23. Leifer, Michael (1995), *Dictionary of the Modern Politics of Southeast Asia*, London: Routledge, p 45. See also Kell, Tim (1995), *The Roots of Acehnese Rebellion, 1989-1992*, New York: Cornell University.
24. *Straits Times* (2000), 22 February, p 45.
25. *Straits Times* (2000), 12 November, p 27.
26. *Straits Times* (2001), 'Unrest in Aceh Enters New Phase', 9 April, p A9. Indeed, more recent developments have seen a breakdown of negotiations and military 'invasion' of Aceh in May 2003.
27. *Straits Times* (1999), 'Aceh Rebels Smuggling Weapons from Malaysia', 24 December, p 2.
28. *Straits Times* (2001), 'US Looking at Possible Post-Osma Targets', 10 December, p 42.
29. *Straits Times* (1999), 'Military Awaits the Order to Return Troops to Aceh', 11 December, p 46.
30. As Singapore's Senior Minister Lee Kuan Yew warns, 'if the Acehnese do get a referendum and have independence, then I think Indonesia is at risk ... nobody wants that to happen'. Quoted in Barber, Richard (ed.) (2000), *Aceh: The Untold Story*, Bangkok: Asian Forum for Human Rights and Development, p 76.
31. May, R.J. (1992), 'The Religious Factor in Three Minority Movements', *Contemporary Southeast Asia*, 13/4, p 403.

32. Alagappa, Muthiah (1987), *The National Security of Developing States*, Dover: Auburn House, pp 211–12.
33. *Ibid.*, p 212.
34. *Asian Defence Journal* (1994), 'Thai Separatists Offered Sanctuary', October, p 94.
35. For instance, PULO has helped arm the Aceh rebels. *Far Eastern Economic Review* (1999), 'Worse to Come', 29 July, p 18.
36. *Straits Times* (2001), 'New Rebel Group to Blame?', 9 April, p A1.
37. See Tan, Andrew (2001), 'The Rise of Islam in Malaysia and Indonesia: An Emerging Security Challenge', *Panorama*, 1/2001, pp 84–8.
38. According to Professor Mohamad Abu Bakar, Head of International and Strategic Studies at Universiti Malaya, the sense of the Muslim community or *ummah*, has clearly grown (personal interview in November 2001).
39. *Newsweek* (2000), 'Warriors of Red and White', 17 January, p 20 and *Time* (2000), 'Chaos in the Islands', 17 January, p 14.
40. *Far Eastern Economic Review* (2001), 'Malays Study in Pakistan: Schools Cast a Wide Net', 27 September, p 22. The 'intelligence gap' was mentioned by a number of analysts the author interviewed in Malaysia in November 2001. In January 2002, Prime Minister Mahathir himself referred to the problem.
41. *Straits Times* (2001), 'Islamic Militancy Worries SM', 4 September, p 1.
42. *Straits Times* (2001), 'Gas Plant Caught in Middle of Aceh's Explosive Face-Off', 11 December, p 47.
43. See Barber, Benjamin (1996), *Jihad vs McWorld*, New York: Ballantine.
44. See Chalk, Peter (1998), 'Low Intensity Conflict in Southeast Asia: Piracy, Drug Trafficking and Political Terrorism', *Conflict Studies*, January/February, pp 20–22.
45. APEC Leaders' Statement on Fighting Terrorism and Promoting Growth, Los Cabos, Mexico, 26 October 2002. Online. Available: www.apec.org.sg. 1 May 2003.
46. *Straits Times* (2002), 19 January, pp A22–3.
47. Najib, Mohamad and Razak, Abdul (2001), *Defending Malaysia: Facing the Twenty-First Century*, London: ASEAN Academic, pp 83–5, 97.
48. *Straits Times* (2000), 'Muslim Militants: Military Must be on Guard', 11 November, p A29.
49. The professionalism of the Malaysian Armed Forces, instilled by the British during colonial days, has remained largely intact at the senior officer level. The question is the rank and file (personal interviews with analysts in Malaysia in November 2001).

13. Organised Crime and Terrorism in the Asia Pacific Region: The Reality and the Response

John MacFarlane

Much has been written over the last decade on the emerging problem of transnational organised crime, which has become identified as one of the key new issues challenging international stability and security. The United Nations Secretary General, Kofi Annan, summed up the situation in the following words:

> The benefits of globalisation are obvious: faster growth, higher living standards, new opportunities. Yet a backlash has begun, because these benefits are so unequally distributed, and because the global market is not yet underpinned by rules based on shared social objectives ... In this New World, groups and individuals more and more often interact directly across frontiers, without involving the State. This has its dangers. Crime, narcotics, terrorism, pollution, disease, weapons, refugees and migrants: all move back and forth faster and in greater numbers than in the past.[1]

The events of September 11 have dramatically demonstrated that highly-motivated and capable non-state actors, employing carefully planned and targeted terrorist operations – facilitated by criminal activities involving drug trafficking, financial crime and covert money movements, identification fraud, and so on – have been able to seriously challenge the global strategic order and precipitate a major rethink of national and international defence, security and law enforcement priorities. Those who predicted that September 11 would be just a nasty blip on the global security radar screen have been proven wrong: the War against Terror has fundamentally changed United States strategic priorities causing it to adopt a hard-line unilateralist approach (albeit couched in 'coalition' terminology) which will have a major impact on the global security outlook and, inevitably, risks upsetting the security relationships with other states. This is the era of the *post*-post-Cold War.

Although not so obvious, transnational crime also possesses the potential to severely destabilise states through the illicit trafficking in arms, people and drugs. Similarly, there may be attacks on critical databases and systems through cyber-crime, impacting on the economies of states through fraud, white-collar crime, money laundering or capital flight. Indeed the potential to upset public confidence in governance through endemic graft and corruption must also be considered.

All of this is particularly relevant to the Asia Pacific region. This chapter will consider the nature and capacity of transnational organised crime in the Asia Pacific, its links to terrorism in the region, and the regional and international measures that are being developed to deal with these threats.

TRANSNATIONAL ORGANISED CRIME IN THE ASIA PACIFIC

Factors Facilitating the Growth of Transnational Organised Crime in the Region

The global developments that have encouraged economic growth and diversification in recent years have also facilitated the development of transnational organised crime.[2] These developments include:

- The dramatic advances in and decreased costs of international travel and the transportation of goods; the removal of external travel restrictions in many countries that previously controlled overseas travel for their citizens; and the removal of visa requirements for entry into many countries.
- The changing nature of state sovereignty due to the emergence of regional associations and trading blocs. Related to this is deregulation, the internationalisation of business corporations, and networking across national boundaries.
- The dramatic developments in technology and communications, including the so-called 'CNN factor' and the emergence of the Internet.
- The social, economic, and political changes that have occurred with globalisation and the adoption of the market economy and western democratic values, which have led to increased levels of unemployment and untenable systems of state welfare and public health services in both developed and developing countries. This, in some cases, leads to crime becoming a means of survival for disadvantaged people.
- The uneven development between 'Northern' and 'Southern' states (especially African and South Pacific states).

- Increasing levels of education and rising expectations of people in many developing countries, possibly leading to mass population movements internally and illegal immigration externally in search of a better life.
- The increasing sophistication of criminal organisations, which are becoming significant players in international economic activity.
- The potential for transnational organised crime groups (particularly from the former Soviet Union) to acquire and sell chemical, biological, radiological or nuclear agents or technology to criminal or terrorist groups, or to so-called 'rogue states'.
- The apparent increase of corruption, which facilitates crime at both the national and international levels.
- The inability of most countries to allocate increasing resources to the criminal justice system and law enforcement.
- The difficulty that the law enforcement agencies of many countries have in developing and maintaining the technical skills required to keep pace with banking and financial methodologies, developments in computers, technology and communications, and the increasing complexity of national and international law.[3]

Definition of Organised Crime

With the signing by 154 nations of the *United Nations Convention Against Transnational Organised Crime* in Palermo, Italy,[4] in December 2000, for the first time there is an internationally accepted definition of organised crime.[5] The Convention states, at Article 2(a), that:

> [An] organised criminal group shall mean a structured group[6] of three or more persons, existing for a period of time and acting in concert with the aim of committing one or more serious crimes[7] or offences established in accordance with this Convention, in order to obtain, directly or indirectly, a financial or other material benefit.

Many other authorities and writers have also attempted to describe the attributes of organised crime. For example, Howard Abadinsky defines the concept in a more conventional way as:

> A non-ideological enterprise involving a number of persons in close social interaction, organized on a hierarchical basis with at least three levels/ranks, for the purpose of securing profit and power by engaging in illegal and legal activities. Positions in the hierarchy and positions involving functional specialisation may be assigned on the basis of kinship or friendship, or rationally assigned according to skill. The positions are not dependent on the individuals occupying them at any particular time. Permanency is assumed by the members who strive to keep the enterprise integral and active in pursuit of its goals. It eschews competition and

strives for monopoly on an industry or territorial basis. There is a willingness to use violence and/or bribery to achieve ends and maintain discipline. Membership is restricted, although non-members may be involved on a contingency basis. There are explicit rules, oral or written, which are enforced by sanctions that include murder.[8]

However it is defined, organised crime is intent on using its power to make money, and it will do so, legally and illegally, trading in whatever commodity will provide maximum profit for the lowest possible risk of detection and prosecution. At both the national and international levels, organised crime is likely to be involved in varied and nefarious activities. Among these activities are trafficking of arms and narcotics, crimes of violence, racketeering, money laundering, pornography and prostitution, computer and ecological crimes, and many others. As organised crime infiltrates these various sectors of the economy, its activities are often supported by accountants, lawyers, financial advisers, bankers and chemists, as well as corrupt or compliant politicians, judges, local government officials, law enforcement officers, members of the military, media executives, professional people, businessmen,[9] and even community activists and priests. The underlying motive for this criminality, in most cases, is quite simply power and money.[10]

The signing of the Convention was the culmination of six years of intensive effort by the Vienna-based Office of Drug Control and Crime Prevention (ODCCP).[11] This process began with the *Naples Political Declaration and Global Action Plan Against Organised Transnational Crime*, which the United Nations General Assembly adopted in 1994, to deal with the increasingly insidious threat of transnational crime. Accompanying the Convention are three important Protocols: the *Protocol to Prevent, Suppress and Punish Trafficking in Persons, especially Women and Children;* the *Protocol Against the Smuggling of Migrants by Land, Sea and Air;* and the *Protocol Against the Illicit Manufacturing of and Trafficking in Firearms, Their Parts and Components and Ammunition.* The ODCCP is now working on a draft treaty or protocol on corruption and some additional work on cyber-crime.[12]

Transnational Organised Crime in the Asia Pacific

In the interests of brevity, and to maintain the focus on the Asia Pacific region, this chapter will consider the impact of transnational and organised crime on the security and stability of five countries in the region: China (including, for the purpose of this discussion Hong Kong, Macau and Taiwan[13]); Japan; the Republic of Korea (ROK); the Democratic People's Republic of Korea (DPRK); and the Russian Far East.

Although the nature of the transnational organised crime threat differs with each of the countries concerned, the threat posed by these groups presents a significant problem for the countries of the Asia Pacific. Not only has organised crime presented a serious internal challenge for the governments of the region, but also it is inextricably linked to corruption which is a serious issue in most Asia Pacific countries (including Australia), and which undermines the conduct of good governance and frequently leads to community reactions involving public order issues.

In the case of the DPRK, the evidence available suggests that the regime has, at the least in the past, turned a blind eye to criminal activities, such as drug production and trafficking, and the counterfeiting of and trafficking in foreign currency, involving DPRK officials and diplomats abroad.

Impact of Transnational Organised Crime

National and transnational organised crime can have very significant impacts at the political, military, economic, societal, environmental, and, of course, human security levels. These impacts clearly extend to national and international security concerns and to questions of stability and predictability in international relations.

Simply put, Williams states that 'insidious, pervasive and multifaceted' transnational crime threatens: sovereignty; societies; individuals; national stability and state control; democratic values and public institutions; national economies; financial institutions; democratisation and privatisation; development; and global regimes and codes of conduct.[14]

Many of the crime trends now evident are not new to Asia, but the frequency and sophistication of these trends are increasing. In addition, almost all the significant crime problems of the Asia Pacific and other regions are transnational rather than domestic in scope. What is also new to the region is the way in which the increasing crime trends are intersecting with other social and economic problems to destabilise individual nations, and therefore, the entire region. Furthermore, transnational organised crime groups in the Asia Pacific are proving to be more resilient, sophisticated, and international in both their activities and outlook. They have been able to take advantage of weak governments, corruption, and nepotism, cultural and ethnic links spreading far beyond individual countries, the growth of materialism, and the proximity of cheap supplies of drugs (both natural and synthetic). This is only further compounded by the desire of many of the people of the region to settle elsewhere in pursuit of economic or personal security, and, above all, by the increasing gulf between the rich and the poor, the successful and the unemployable, the educated and the uneducated, and the well-fed and the hungry. These are all serious dichotomies for the people of the Asia Pacific region, and many of them are precursors to systemic and serious crime and long-term social instability.

Such has been the impact of transnational crime over the last decade that many countries now regard transnational crime, in its various manifestations, as a national security issue.[15] Consequently, law enforcement efforts in this area are strongly supported by national intelligence community taskings, and the whole of government approach to national security also encompasses prioritising and resource allocation to combat transnational crime. President Clinton of the United States took the lead in this area in 1995 when he issued Presidential Decision Directive 42 (PDD-42),[16] but other major industrialised countries such as the United Kingdom, Germany, France, Italy, Canada and Russia have adopted a similar approach and tasked their Intelligence Services and agencies accordingly. Unfortunately, with the exception of a greater emphasis on countering illegal immigration, the Australian government has not yet incorporated the wider threats from transnational crime or the higher level of offences against Commonwealth law, into the national security agenda.

Strategies for Dealing with Transnational Organised Crime

New strategies need to be developed to deal with the threat of transnational organised crime. Such strategies are varied and might include:[17]

- Encouraging the development of compatible laws between nations to facilitate the exchange of intelligence, the application of mutual assistance arrangements, simplify extradition arrangements between states, enhance investigations into and recovery of the proceeds of crime, and generally speed up the process of handling transnational criminal matters.
- Encouraging states to accede to the major United Nations and other international Conventions, such as the three United Nations *Drug Conventions* (1961, 1971 and 1988),[18] supporting the *Naples Political Declaration and Global Action Plan Against Organised Transnational Crime,*[19] supporting the implementation of the eleven point plan to combat transnational crime, agreed at the first Association of South East Asian Nations (ASEAN) Conference on Transnational Crime in Manila, the Philippines, in 1998[20] and the seven strategies agreed at the G-8 meeting in Birmingham, England, in May 1998,[21] the adoption of the *40 Recommendations of the G-7 Financial Action Task Force (FATF),*[22] and enacting the OECD recommendations on combating bribery of foreign public officials,[23] and the ratification of the new

United Nations Convention Against Transnational Crime and its various protocols.

- Encouraging bilateral and multilateral cooperation and information flows between law enforcement agencies, including supporting the role of such organisations as INTERPO, ASEANAPOL, EUROPOL and the Customs Cooperation Council.
- Encouraging a greater level of coordinated cross-border and transnational cooperation through regional coordination meetings and operational targeting, multilateral police training programs and technical exchanges (including employing compatible computer databases).

Transnational organised crime – and terrorism – can no longer be written off as 'boutique' regional security issues. These problems have become central to security and international policy concerns in the post-Cold War era, extending far beyond the scope of conventional law enforcement. The response to these transnational threats has resulted in a blurring of the traditional demarcation between diplomatic, military, law enforcement, and intelligence roles of nations.

Countering the threat of transnational organised crime calls for the development of appropriate resources, professional skills, regulatory regimes, highly developed criminal intelligence and analytical capabilities, a dynamic and modern criminal justice system, and close cooperation between the law enforcement community and the relevant professions. However, no state can defeat a criminal threat that is generated from outside its jurisdiction without developing sound working relations and cooperation with neighbouring states and adopting international 'best practices'. For this reason the answer to the transnational crime threat requires new, imaginative and constructive regional and international responses.

TRANSNATIONAL CRIME AND TERRORISM

Traditionally, terrorist activities have been financed from a variety of sources. Firstly, one often saw some degree of state sponsorship, from, say, Libya, Iran, Iraq, Syria and, in the past, the former Soviet bloc. Secondly, there is non-state sponsorship, which is an increasing feature of modern terrorism and appears to be a major characteristic of al-Qaeda, which has provided funding, training and infrastructure support to a network of groups sympathetic to its own aims, apparently on a scale much wider than previously estimated. Thirdly, one can see drug production and trafficking (or narco-terrorism). This has been a major source of income for al-Qaeda, which has used its international links on a commission basis (10 to 15 percent). Many other terrorist groups also use drug production or trafficking as a major source of income. Similarly, other illicit activities, such as diamond sales, have been evident. Al-Qaeda is assessed as having reaped hundreds of millions of dollars over the last three years from the illicit sales of diamonds mined by its allies, the Revolutionary United Front (RUF) in Sierra Leone.

In 2001, the FATF identified the following major sources of terrorist funding:

- Drug production and trafficking;
- Extortion, such as extortion of businesses, building companies, social clubs, and wealthy individuals;
- Kidnapping for ransom, such as hostage taking to extort money or political concessions (accompanied by the threat of execution);
- Robberies, especially bank robberies;
- Fraud, especially credit card fraud;
- Illicit gambling operations;
- Smuggling and trafficking in counterfeit goods;
- Direct sponsorship by states;
- Contributions and donations;
- Sale of publications (legal and illegal);
- Legitimate business activities.[24]

To this list could be added:

- Illicit trafficking in firearms and diamonds;
- Human smuggling and sex trafficking;
- Manipulation of the stock market.

It should be remembered that the funds generated from these criminal activities might not flow directly into supporting terrorist operations, but may be invested in legitimate sources to generate a long-term cash flow for the group concerned. Frequently, these means of generating money are so successful that they may continue, as conventional criminal activity, after the political campaign has been concluded.[25]

When he established al-Qaeda in the early 1990s, Osama bin Laden provided it with substantial 'seed money' – assessed at about US$150 million – from his personal wealth and the profits of his business enterprises. In addition, al-Qaeda has benefited (and apparently continues to benefit) from donations from wealthy supporters from Saudi Arabia, the Gulf States, and other Middle Eastern countries. In addition, al-Qaeda derives funds from a number of lucrative legitimate business enterprises established by bin Laden and others in the Sudan, the Middle East, and elsewhere. Al-Qaeda also appears to have made significant profits on the stock market, particularly through the exploitation of hedge funds, and the 'short selling' of shares in insurance and airline stocks just before September 11 2001.

The investigation of the sources of funding for the people involved in the incidents on September 11 have been based on international intelligence exchanges; the exploitation of documentation recovered from post-September 11 investigations in the US and elsewhere, and documents and videotapes recovered in post-action searches in Afghanistan; from the interrogation of well over 1,100 suspects in the US and elsewhere; and from substantial support from the international banking sector, leading to the freezing globally of the funds of some 74 organisations and individuals said to be associated with al-Qaeda and related terrorist activities. About 150 countries now have blocking orders in place to freeze terrorist funds and 200 countries have expressed their support in the fight against terrorist financing. Already, the money frozen is said to exceed US$100 million. Regardless of the issue of terrorist funding, criminal money laundering on a global scale is a massive problem. Michel Camdessus, the former Head of the International Monetary Fund (IMF), has assessed the annual volume of money laundering worldwide at US$600 billion, or between 2 to 5 percent of global GDP.

The International Response to Money Laundering and Terrorist Financing

A number of major initiatives have been taken to counter money laundering and trace the sources of terrorist finances. These initiatives, and the organisational structures supporting them, include: the FATF; the Egmont Group of Financial Intelligence Units; the Wolfsberg Group of (Private International) Banks; the Basel Committee on Banking Supervision; and the G-20 forum of Finance Ministers and Central Bank Governors.

The FATF[26] was established by the G-7 in 1989, and is administered by the Organisation for Economic Cooperation and Development (OECD). Since its creation the FATF has spearheaded the effort to adopt and implement measures designed to counter the use of the financial system by criminals. It established a set of forty Recommendations that set out the basic framework for anti-money laundering efforts and are intended to be of universal application. Indeed, the forty Recommendations are now the principal standard in this field. The FATF reviews its members for compliance with the forty Recommendations. There are currently thirty-one members in the FATF, including an Asia Pacific Group on Money Laundering (APG) which has an office in Sydney, and which covers the countries in the Asia Pacific region.

To reduce the vulnerability of the international financial system to misuse by criminals, the FATF is also involved in examining and identifying the serious systemic weaknesses in the anti-money laundering programs of certain jurisdictions, known as Non-Cooperative Countries and Territories (NCCTs). On June 22 2001, the FATF listed 19 NCCTs, including the following Asia Pacific countries: the Cook Islands; the Marshall Islands; Nauru; the Philippines; Indonesia; Myanmar; Niue; and Russia.

The FATF called on all its members to request their financial institutions to give special attention to transactions with persons, companies and financial institutions in these countries and territories.

On December 31 2001, the FATF declared that further counter-measures should be introduced, on a gradual and proportionate basis, to cover the recording of financial transactions from NCCTs. These additional counter-measures were: stringent requirements for identifying clients and enhancement of advisories to financial institutions for identifying beneficial owners before business relationships are established; enhanced relevant reporting mechanisms for suspicious transactions; a review of the requests for the establishment in any FATF country of branches or subsidiaries of banks for NCCTs; warning the non-financial sector that business with entities within NCCTs might run the risk of being associated with money laundering.

Terrorists frequently finance their operations through criminal activity, or they may also use funding from legitimate sources. In either case, terrorist groups utilise financial networks in the same way that other criminal groups do. That is, they move funds and hide connections between the source of their funding and the perpetrators, organisers, and sponsors of their activity. The FATF's work on underground banking (*hawala*) and alternative remittance systems, laundering mechanisms that play a role in some criminal and terrorist laundering operations, is also given a high priority.

In October 2001, the FATF promulgated eight Recommendations to deny terrorists and their supporters access to the international finance system. In brief, these recommendations were:

1. Immediately take steps to ratify the *United Nations Convention on the Suppression of Terrorist Financing, 1999*;
2. Criminalising the financing of terrorism, terrorist acts and terrorist organisations;
3. Freezing and confiscating terrorist assets;
4. Requiring financial institutions to report suspicious transactions that may be linked to terrorism;
5. Assisting other countries' investigation of terrorist financing networks;
6. Improving money laundering requirements on alternative remittance systems;

7. Strengthening customer identification requirements for domestic and international wire transfers;
8. Taking steps to ensure that non-profit organisations are not misused to finance terrorist groups.

The FATF met in Hong Kong between 30 January and 1 February 2001 to review progress in this area, and to begin to identify countries that are not taking appropriate measures to counter terrorist financing. These countries will be expected to be compliant by June 2002, or they may face sanctions.

The *Egmont Group of Financial Intelligence Units*[27] was formally established in 1995 to provide a forum for national Financial Intelligence Units (FIUs)[28] to improve support to their respective national anti-money laundering programs. This support includes expanding and systematising the exchange of financial intelligence, improving expertise and capabilities of the personnel of such organisations, and fostering better communication among FIUs through the application of new technologies. FIUs play a key role in identifying and tracking terrorist finance.

The *Wolfsberg Group*,[29] established in October 2000, consists of twelve leading international private banks, operating in collaboration with Transparency International, a Berlin-based NGO dedicated to increasing government accountability and curbing both international and national corruption. The Wolfsberg Group is currently examining such issues as: practical measures to investigate lists of terrorists, terrorist organisations, and so on, provided by governments or law enforcement agencies, to determine the whereabouts of their funds and the measures necessary to freeze them; issues related to correspondent banking, particularly as it concerns 'shell banks' in NCCTs; record-keeping on foreign bank ownership; exchanging information on suspicious broker-dealer activities; and examining measures to identify and deal with non-traditional funds transfer methods.

The Wolfsberg Group met last in Wolfsberg on 9–11 January 2002 to develop a set of best practice guidelines for traditional finance institutions investigating the financing of terrorism. As an example of the seriousness of this work, it was recently established that twenty-two United States securities firms surveyed had more than 45,000 off-shore clients with an estimated US$140 billion in assets in their accounts. Obviously sophisticated computer analysis is playing a key role in tracking money laundering and terrorist financing in this area.

The Central Bank Governors of the Group of Ten Countries established the Basel Committee on Banking Supervision[30] at the end of 1974. Its objective is to formulate broad supervisory standards and guidelines, and recommend best practice in the expectation that individual authorities will take steps to implement them through detailed arrangements – statutory or otherwise – which are best suited to their own national systems. Its work in the area of 'due diligence' is of particular relevance to countering money laundering and the funding of terrorist organisations. The Committee's Secretariat is provided by the Bank for International Settlements (BIS) in Basel.

The G-20, established in Washington on 25 September 1999, comprises the Finance Ministers and Central Bank Governors of nineteen countries, the European Union and the Bretton Woods Institutions (the International Monetary Fund and the World Bank). The G-20 promotes discussion, and studies and reviews policy issues among industrialised countries and emerging markets, with a view to promoting international financial stability.

On 17 November 2001, the G-20 promulgated a comprehensive plan of multilateral cooperation to deny terrorists access to their financial systems, through a number of concrete steps designed to combat terrorist financing and money laundering.

United Nations Initiative

Prior to September 11, only four countries had ratified the *United National International Convention for the Suppression of the Financing of Terrorism, 1999*. This Convention establishes that it is an offence where a person 'by any means, directly or indirectly, unlawfully and wilfully, provides or collects funds with the intention that they should be used or in the knowledge that they are to be used, in full or in part, in order to carry out' a terrorist act.[31]

However, with the huge increase in international concern about terrorist financing, the Convention came into force on 10 April 2002, by which time 132 countries had signed the Convention and twenty-six had ratified it, four more than the twenty-two required. The Convention calls for stepped-up efforts to identify, detect and freeze or seize funds earmarked for terrorist acts and urges states to use such funds to compensate victims and their families. It also calls on financial institutions to report to their governments any unusual or suspicious transactions. States that are party to the Convention must prosecute offenders or extradite them to nations that suffered from their illegal acts. They must cooperate in investigations and may not, for example, refuse a request for assistance on grounds of banking secrecy. They must also update their laws to comply with the provisions of the Convention.[32]

In addition to the above, an ad hoc committee of the Legal Committee of the United Nations General Assembly is developing a draft *International Convention against Terrorism* that will codify the outlawing of the financing of terrorism. However, at this stage, the committee has been unable to agree on a definition of terrorism, to find a way to distinguish a terrorist from a freedom fighter, and unable to agree on excluding state forces from anti-terrorism provisions (such as the problem of 'state terrorism'). Also, at the initiative of the Russian Federation, the Legal Committee is working on a new convention or protocol to address the suppression of nuclear terrorism.[33] Also, the G-7 Finance Ministers and Central Bank Governors met on 9–10 February 2002 to discuss the global economy, the importance of fostering development and ongoing efforts to combat the financing of terrorism. At the end of the meeting, they issued a progress report on combating the financing of terrorism.[34]

CONCLUSION

The international response to the need to track and freeze terrorist finance and counter conventional money laundering, since September 11 2001, has been most impressive. It also complements other international measures against both transnational terrorism and transnational crime. However, much of this is still 'work in progress' at both the national and international levels.

The measures taken as a result of the investigations following the events of September 11 have flowed on to facilitate the investigations of money laundering and money movements relating to more conventional criminal issues, such as major drug cases and the investigation of fraud, white collar crime, capital flight, and more generally the nexus between the legitimate and illegitimate business practices undertaken by transnational organised crime groups.[35]

The Response to Terrorism

Transnational terrorism requires a multi-faceted response:

1.   Law enforcement response:

a.   Requires large resources to be diverted from normal law enforcement;
b.   Requires high priority and enhanced intelligence exchanges;
c.   Utilises joint operational activities;
d.   Relies on extradition and mutual support;
e.   Must attack and neutralise the terrorist financial base.

2.   Military response:

a.   Is not generally regarded as a core military war-fighting task;
b.   Can only be used selectively;
c.   It is very hard to neutralise the target through military means alone;

d.   Any foreign direct military intervention is generally unacceptable.

3.   Intelligence community response:

a.   It is a very difficult target to attack. Imagery is of limited value if there are few fixed bases; communications intelligence (COMINT) is of limited value if conventional communications channels are not used; money movement is of limited value if non-conventional banking methods employed.
b.   Needs real-time data, involving processing a large volume of material that may need deciphering, translation, analysis and dissemination.
c.   Must overcome traditional cultural introversion and elitism of the intelligence community to facilitate exchange with the law enforcement community and overseas intelligence and law enforcement agencies. Transnational crime and terrorism are global threats that can only be neutralised by a global response.

4.   Political/strategic response:

a.   Needs to attack the root causes of terrorism. Why are people doing this? Why are people so angry? Why are they prepared to kill themselves for the cause? Is this a religious problem or are there other causes (and therefore solutions) of a much broader nature?
b.   Needs to recognise that we are living in a very complex and changing global environment. Has our thinking moved on to embrace these changes? Do our national strategies reflect these changes?
c.   Should take notice of the consistent line of criticism from a very broad spectrum of the international Islamic community that the United States and its allies have mishandled the Israel/Palestine situation; they are concerned at the continuing presence of foreign military forces in Saudi Arabia; and they criticise the overwhelming dominance of United States military power and its deployment where civilian casualties are suffered. We may not agree with these propositions, but if we do not try to understand them and make such adjustments as may be necessary to accommodate at least some of these concerns, we should not be surprised if we face the trauma of further attacks, only possibly next time employing much greater risks, such as the use of weapons of mass destruction.

NOTES

1. *Millennium Report to the General Assembly of the United Nations* (2000), 'We the Peoples', 3 April. Online. Available: http://disarmament.un.org/rcpd/pdf/plen2d.pdf. 24 March 2003.
2. Andre Bossard, former Secretary-General of the International Criminal Police Organization (Interpol), defines 'transnational crime' as 'an offence which implies crossing at least one border before, during, or after the fact'. Bossard, Andre (1990), *Transnational Crime and Criminal Law*, Chicago: University of Illinois and Office of International Criminal Justice, p 3.
3. McFarlane, John (1999), 'Transnational Crime as a Security Issue', in Hernandez, Carolina and Pattugalan, Gina (eds), *Transnational Crime and Regional Security in the Asia Pacific*, Manila: Institute for Strategic and Development Studies and Council for Security Cooperation in the Asia Pacific, pp 24–5. For a more detailed discussion, see MacFarlane, John (2001), 'Transnational Crime and Asia Pacific Security: Beyond 2000', in Simon, Sheldon (ed.), *The Many Faces of Security*, Lanham: Rowman and Littlefield.
4. It was highly symbolic that the meeting was held in Palermo, long the centre of power of the Sicilian mafia, the most feared and successful of the Italian criminal organisations, and the site of the murders, in 1992, of two anti-mafia judges, Giovanni Falcone and Paolo Borsellino, and the subsequent arrest of the Sicilian mafia boss of bosses, Toto Riina.
5. The Convention will have the status of international law when forty governments ratify it. See *Jane's Foreign Report* (2001), 'Organised Crime in 2000', No. 2623, 11 January, pp 1–2.
6. The Convention describes a 'structured group' at Article 2(c) as 'a group that is not randomly formed for the immediate commission of an offence and that does not need to have formally defined roles for its members, continuity of its membership or a developed structure'.
7. The Convention describes a 'serious crime' at Article 2 (b) as ' ... conduct constituting an offence punishable by a maximum deprivation of liberty of at least four years or more serious penalty'.
8. Abadinsky, Howard (1994), *Organized Crime*, Chicago: Nelson-Hall Publishers, p 8.
9. It is worth noting that the relationship between entrepreneurial crime and legitimate business is often very close. Many leading criminal entrepreneurs have come from a legitimate business background.
10. McFarlane (2001), 'Transnational Crime and Asia Pacific Security: Beyond 2000'.
11. Vlassis, Dmitri (1998), 'Drafting the United Nations Convention against Transnational Organized Crime', *Transnational Organized Crime*, 4/3–4, Autumn/Winter, pp 356–62.
12. 'Corruption to be Central Theme of Upcoming United Nations Crime Commission Meeting', SOC/CP/234, 7 May 2001. More than 100 countries met in The Hague in May 2001 for the Second Global Forum on Fighting Corruption and Safeguarding Integrity to commence work on a draft UN Treaty to control corruption. The next meeting of the Global Forum will be held in Seoul, South Korea, in 2003. See online. Available: http://www.unfoundation.org/unwire/archives/UNWIRE010531.asp#19. 1 June 2001.
13. The inclusion of Taiwan in this context has nothing to do with the question of sovereignty: it is due to the common ethnicity of the Chinese organised criminal groups involved.
14. Williams, Phil (1995), 'The New Security Threat: Transnational Criminal Organizations and International Security', *Criminal Organizations*, 9/3, Summer, pp 15–18.
15. See Naylor, R.T. (1995), 'From Cold War to Crime War: The Search for a New "National Security Threat"', *Transnational Organized Crime*, 1/4, Winter, pp 37–56; Lupsha, Peter (1996), 'Transnational Organized Crime versus the Nation State', *Transnational Organized Crime*, 2/1, Spring, pp 21–48; Rosenau, William, Gay, Kemper and Mussington, David (1997), 'Transnational Threats and US National Security', *Low Intensity Conflict and Law Enforcement*, 6/3, Winter, pp 144–61; McFarlane (1999), 'Transnational Crime as a Security Issue', pp 23–57.

16. Signed by President Clinton on 21 October 1995, PDD-42 specifically addresses the nation's fight against international crime. PDD-42 recognises that such criminal activity threatens US national security and directs the federal agencies to combat international crime from the criminal barons sheltered overseas to the violence and destruction they deliver to our streets. PDD-42 also provides continuity to earlier Administration policy, complements other presidential directives on alien smuggling, drug trafficking, terrorism and nuclear materials, and mandates intensified federal efforts against international criminals. Online. Available: http://www.usdoj.gov/criminal/press/Xoptim.htm. 17 June 2001.

17. See also: Kendall, Raymond (1998), 'Responding to Transnational Crime', *Transnational Organized Crime*, 4/3–4, Autumn/Winter, pp 269–75; Godson, Roy and Williams, Phil (1998), 'Strengthening Cooperation against Transnational Crime: A New Security Imperative', *Transnational Organized Crime*, 4/3–4, Autumn/Winter, pp 256–62; Williams, Phil (1998), 'Transnational Organized Crime: Threat Assessment and Strategic Response', in Anthony, Mely and Jawhar, Mohamad (eds), *Confidence Building and Conflict Reduction*, Kuala Lumpur: ISIS-Malaysia, pp 193–220.

18. United Nations Drug Control Program (1997), *World Drug Report*, Oxford: Oxford University Press, pp 168–73.

19. *Naples Political Declaration and Global Action Plan Against Organised Transnational Crime* (1995), *Transnational Organized Crime*, 1/1, Spring, pp 118–27.

20. ASEAN (1997), *ASEAN Declaration on Transnational Crime*, 20 December. Online. Available: http://www.aseansec.org/5640.htm. 24 March 2003.

21. *The Birmingham Summit: Final Communique*, 17 May 1998. Online. Available: http://www.mofa.go.jp/policy/economy/summit/1998/fin_comniq.html. 24 March 2003.

22. Financial Action Task Force on Money Laundering (1990), *FATF-I Report*, 7 February. Online. Available: http://www.fatf-gafi.org/FATDocs_en.htm. 24 March 2003.

23. Organisation for Economic Cooperation and Development (1997), *Convention on Combating Bribery of Foreign Public Officials in International Business Transactions*. Online. Available: http://www.oecd.org/pdf/M00017000/M00017037.pdf. 24 March 2003. See also the United Nations General Assembly (1997), *Declaration Against Corruption and Bribery in International Commercial Transactions*, December. Online. Available: http://www.un.org/documents/ecosoc/res/1997/eres1997-25.htm. 25 March 2003.

24. Tupman, Bill (2001), 'The Business of Terrorism'. Presentation made to a Conference on Terrorism and Finance at the Institute of Advanced Legal Studies, University of London, 29 November.

25. According to Schmid, there are a number of similarities and differences in relation to transnational crime and terrorism that need to be noted to better understand these two phenomena. The similarities include: members are generally (but not always) rational actors; both use intimidation and ruthlessness; both use similar tactics – drug trafficking, kidnappings, extortion, bank robberies, assassinations et cetera; both operate in secrecy; both are criminalised by the ruling regime; both usually (but not always) oppose the state; and both place heavy demands on individual members. The differences include: terrorist groups are usually ideologically rather than profit motivated; terrorists usually admit their guilt in court; terrorists seek media coverage for their cause; terrorist victimisation is less discriminate than criminal victimisation; terrorists compete with governments for legitimacy; criminal groups are more competitive and territorial. See Schmid, Alex (1996), 'The Links between Transnational Organized Crime and Terrorist Crimes', *Transnational Organized Crime*, 2/4, Winter, pp 40–82.

26. *Financial Action Task Force on Money Laundering*. Online. Available: http://www.fatf-gafi.org. 24 March 2003.

27. *The Egmont Group of Financial Intelligence Units*. Online. Available: http://www1.oecd.org/fatf/Ctry-orgpages/org-egmont_en.htm. 24 March 2003.

28. As at 4 February 2002, there were 58 countries with FIUs that participate in the Egmont Group.

29. *The Wolfsberg Group of Banks*. Online. Available: http://www.wolfsberg-principles.com. 24 March 2003.
30. The Basel Committee on Banking Supervision. Online. Available: http://www.bis.org/bcbs. 24 March 2003.
31. *United National International Convention for the Suppression of the Financing of Terrorism* (1999), Article 2. Online. Available: http://untreaty.un.org/English/Terrorism/Conv12.pdf. 24 March 2003.
32. UN Wire Report (2002), 'Terrorism: Treaty on Suppression of Financing to Enter into Force'. Online. Available: http://www.unfoundation.org/unwire/current.asp#25381. 24 March 2003.
33. *The Federation of American Scientists*, 'Suppression of Nuclear Terrorism Convention'. Online. Available: http://www.fas.org/nuke/control/nt/. 24 March 2003.
34. A full copy of this report can be found at: http://www.g-7.ca/final_com_e.html. 19 May 2003.
35. For example, in January 2002, the United States Department of Treasury Financial Crimes Enforcement Network published an *SAR Bulletin* (Suspicious Activity Report), which examined five significant cases of terrorist financing, and provided twenty-three very useful indicators, most of which are applicable to both terrorist and transnational crime investigations.

14. The Politics of the Southeast Asian Heroin Trade

Peter Chalk

With the collapse of the Soviet bloc in Eastern Europe in the late 1980s/early 1990s it appeared that the international system could be on the threshold of an era of unprecedented peace and stability. Politicians, diplomats and academics alike began to forecast the imminent establishment of a new world order, increasingly managed by democratic political institutions. These, it was believed, would develop within the context of an integrated international economic system based on the principles of the free market.[1] As this new world order emerged, so it was assumed that serious threats to international stability would decline commensurably.

However, the initial euphoria that was evoked by the end of the Cold War has now been replaced by a growing sense off unease that non-military threats at the lower end of the conflict spectrum – the so-called grey area phenomena (GAP) – may soon assume greater prominence. Such concern has been stimulated largely by the remarkable fluidity that now characterises international politics in which it is no longer apparent exactly who can do what to whom and with what means. As Richard Latter observes, the establishment of a new global security structure may reduce inter-state conflict only at the expense of an increased resort to sub-national violence that falls below the intensity level of conventional war.[2]

Stated more directly, the geopolitical landscape that now faces the global polity lacks the relative stability of the linear Cold War division between east and west. There is no large and obvious equivalent to the Soviet Union against which to balance the United States, the world's sole remaining superpower. Indeed, few of today's dangers have the character of direct military aggression emanating from a clearly defined sovereign source. By contrast, security, conflict and general threat definition have become more diffuse and opaque, lacking the simple dichotomies of the Cold War era. The challenges that will face the global community into the twenty-first century are likely to evolve as 'threats without enemies', with their source internal, rather than external to the political order that the concept of 'national interest' has traditionally represented.[3]

Such perceptions are certainly evident in Southeast Asia where few, if any, of the region's actors view the end of the Cold War as an unmixed blessing. Although visibly relieved by the decline of global tensions and the settlement of east-west ideological conflict at the international level, policy makers have, nevertheless, begun to express increased concern about the strategic uncertainties that are now seen to exist at the regional level. While many of these misgivings emphasise traditional military threats, a number focus on the contemporary challenge posed by non-military transnational security issues.[4]

One specific threat that has assumed greater prominence on Southeast Asia's broadened security agenda due to the diffusion of the post-Cold War power structure has been transnational organised crime (TOC). The increased salience of this particular issue stems, in many ways, from the region's over-riding predilection with financial power and influence. Combined with the existence of severe and widespread disparities in economic wealth, situations have increasingly arisen where people have been motivated more by the need to possess dollars and less by considerations of the means used to acquire them. The net result has been the gradual evolution of a parallel underground economy, which is currently being powered by syndicates dealing in everything from humans to drugs, gems, timber and weapons.[5]

This chapter shall discuss one prevalent manifestation of TOC in contemporary Southeast Asia: the heroin trade. It first examines opiate production in Burma, outlining major trafficking routes and markets for the trade, regionally and internationally. The chapter then analyses the issue of 'narco-terrorism' and assesses the prospect of this type of nexus emerging in Southeast Asia.

THE SOUTHEAST ASIAN HEROIN TRADE

Scope and Dimensions

The bulk of Southeast Asia's heroin originates from Burma, particularly the Shan hills of the country's northeast which form the apex of the trade. In 2001, Burma produced 865 metric tons of opium gum, a base that converts to approximately 72 metric tons of refined heroin (assuming all the gum was processed).[6] Overall production is expected to increase in 2002 in response to the disruption of opiates flowing out of Afghanistan, which since 1998 has remained the international system's main supplier of refined heroin.[7] According to the United Nations International Drug Control Program (UNDCP), the US-led war on terrorism post-September 11 has substantially impacted on cultivation and refining operations in the South Asian nation, creating an international export void that Burma is well placed to fill. Thai authorities agree, with Bangkok's Narcotics Control Board (NCB) speculating that overall heroin output levels could be as high as 250 tons by the end of 2002.[8]

The principal heroin warlord in Burma for many years was Chang Qifu, more commonly known as Khun Sa. During the 1960s, 1970s and 1980s he developed an increasingly powerful opium-heroin 'empire' thanks largely to the backing he received from both the Rangoon government and the CIA. By the 1980s, over 50 percent of the heroin that was produced in the country was refined by Khun Sa (the remainder being largely accounted for by Chifu's main rival, Lo Hsiung-Han, who also benefited from Burmese and US backing). He used the extensive profits from his drug trade to finance his own private militia, the 15,000 strong Mong Tai Army (MTA) as well as a thriving Shan 'capital' in Ho Mong.[9]

Over the past few years, however, control of the Burmese/Southeast Asian heroin industry has become increasingly diffuse. In 1996, Khun Sa voluntarily disbanded his MTA militia, stepping down as a major player in the country's drug trade in exchange for an official guarantee of immunity from criminal prosecution. His departure created an immediate void that has since been filled by a new generation of ascendant drug-trafficking armies, many of whom have set up refining and trafficking operations in Burma's northeast Shan border regions.[10]

Facilitating this devolution has been the complicity of Rangoon's ruling State Peace and Development Council (SPDC), which has permitted known drug traffickers to establish themselves as leading business figures in the country.[11] Indeed, by 1998, it is thought that as much as 60 percent of private investment in Burma was drug related.[12] Beyond this active indifference, the SPDC has also been prepared to negotiate ceasefire agreements with ethnic rebel armies that allow them to continue with their narcotics and trafficking activities in exchange for a cut of the proceeds generated by subsequent sales. According to Alan Dupont, there is concrete evidence to show that the government financed much of its arms build-up during the 1990s from mutually agreed taxes levied on heroin refineries in the northeast of the country.[13] This particular area constitutes the main locus of several tribal minority rebel groups, including the United Wa State Army (UWSA), which is rapidly emerging as one of the key players in the evolving Asian heroin and amphetamine trade.[14]

While the SPDC may have viewed its strategy of co-option as a viable means to secure the country's internal security, the policy has come back to haunt the regime in recent years. In particular, it has availed groups such as the UWSA with sufficient latitude to consolidate control over fortified 'no-go' zones, many of which have since been transformed into de-facto drug fiefdoms on the back of opiate-derived dollars. This lack of centralised control has not only led to a fragmented state structure in which the government can no longer claim to posses a true monopoly of coercive violence, it has also sharpened Rangoon's regional relations with increasingly frustrated states such as Thailand.

Markets and Trafficking Routes

Given the potential profits that can be earned through international sales, much of Burma's heroin tends to be trafficked to the West, particularly the United States, Canada and Australia. Traditionally, most opiates were smuggled across the Thai border, transported to Bangkok, Malaysia or Singapore, and trafficked from here to overseas markets in shipping containers or on board commercial and passenger flights. More concerted border security and interdiction in Thailand, however, has led to the emergence of increasingly used secondary paths. Considerable quantities are now moved through the southern Chinese provinces of Yunan and Guangxi to Guandong and then taken either overland or by boat to neighbouring Hong Kong where local triad gangs operate sophisticated transit routes to Oceania and North America.[15] An alternative route runs through Laos to transit points in Cambodia and Vietnam. From here opiates are shipped to international markets in Taiwan, Japan and, increasingly Australia either in shipping containers or via human couriers.[16]

In addition to the mainland Southeast/East Asian channel, significant quantities of heroin are trafficked through Nigeria, which acts as an intermediary transhipment point for heroin bound for both Africa (most of which goes to South Africa) and the US. Rampant corruption at virtually all levels of government administration have ensured that this country is now playing an increasingly pivotal role in the international distribution of Southeast Asian heroin, especially to the North American market.[17]

While the West continues to act as the favoured destination for Burmese heroin, increasing volumes are now being trafficked to local markets in Asia, which, as a whole, accounts for two-thirds of the world's heroin users. Indicative of this is the rapidly rising number of addicts throughout the region. Thailand is estimated to have at least 500,000 heroin addicts, which is more on a per capita basis than the US. Burma itself has between 400,000 and 500,000, while Vietnam has at least 200,000. Beyond Indochina, the effects have been just as dramatic. Malaysia has an addict population of around 160,000, a figure eclipsed by the half million regular heroin users that are now thought to exist in Indonesia, where an estimated 50 kilograms of opiates are illegally shipped into the country every month. Even more serious has been the impact on China, which according to official statistics has 745,000 heroin addicts – a figure that most commentators agree considerably underestimates the scale of the problem in the country.[18]

Several factors account for the proliferating heroin trade from and within Southeast Asia. Burma is characterised by near perfect geographical and topographical conditions for the growth of the opium poppy – the raw product for heroin. New road, river and air routes have allowed traffickers to move their products to local and international markets with relative ease. Extensive hinterlands, made virtually impenetrable by dense jungle and deep valleys, have allowed drug lords to establish concealed and naturally fortified bases of operation. Weak legal systems have permitted organised syndicates to bypass official arrest and prosecution procedures as well as to corrupt the very highest levels of political and judicial power. Finally, the Asian financial collapse has also had a direct bearing on the Southeast Asian heroin trade. With unemployment soaring, many have turned to narcotics trafficking as a means of economic survival. At the same time, reduced budgets have reduced the money available for drug interdiction, poppy eradication and cooperative law enforcement efforts.[19]

The Southeast Asian Heroin Trade and Terrorism

An interconnection between terrorism and drugs – so called 'narco-terrorism' – has existed for many years, typically manifesting itself in two ways. Firstly, there has been the use of terrorist violence by drug syndicates to elicit specific political objectives. Examples would include bombings carried out by the Medellin Cartel in 1993 to prevent twelve of its members from being extradited to stand trial in the United States or more recent attacks by Mafiosi gangs in the former Soviet Union to intimidate law makers and judges seeking to institute a crackdown on organised crime in Russia.

Secondly, one has seen the trafficking of drugs by terrorist organisations to raise operational and logistical capital. Prominent examples of groups that have engaged in such activities include: the Kurdish Workers' Party (PKK) in Turkey; Sendero Luminoso (also known as Shining Path) in Peru; the Revolutionary Forces of Colombia (FARC) in Colombia; (allegedly) the Liberation Tigers of Tamil Eelam in Sri Lanka; the Islamic Movement of Uzbekistan in Uzbekistan; the United Tajik Organisation in Tajikistan; the Kosovo Liberation Army in Albania and Kosovo; and al-Qaeda in Afghanistan.[20]

It is the latter dimension of narco-terrorism that has been most apparent in the international system, largely because drug syndicates, like business enterprises in general, require a stable (if co-opted) political environment in order to carry out their illicit designs. Terrorist organisations, by contrast, have an active interest in engaging in organised crime given the limited resources at their disposal. Such considerations have become even more relevant over the last decade given the curtailment of financial support from traditional state sponsors such as Libya, Syria, Cuba and even Iran – most of which are now working on an open political and economic agenda to which an association with terrorism would be entirely counter-productive.

In terms of weight and availability, there is still no commodity that is more lucrative than drugs, offering increasingly large profits to everyone along the grower-user chain (except, of course, to the consumers themselves).[21] In 1992, a single kilogram of heroin worth between US$1,200 and US$1,400 immediately after being processed in Burma, would typically double in price by the time it reached Chiang Mai in Thailand, triple again in Bangkok and eventually sell for between US$20,000 and US$60,000 in New York.[22] Today the profit margins are even greater, with the mark-up on heroin between production and street sale currently estimated to be as much as 20,000 percent.[23] Given profits of this magnitude, it is little wonder that narcotics have emerged as the income generator of choice for many organisations in the modern world.

The possibility of an 'unholy' confluence emerging between drugs and terrorism is one that cannot be ignored in Southeast Asia. Not only is an entrenched heroin (as well as a stimulant) trade already established, radical religious extremism is gaining an increasingly firm foothold throughout the region. Indeed, radical Islamic movements now exist in several member states of the Association of Southeast Asian Nations (ASEAN): including Indonesia – Laskar Jihad, Islamic Defenders Forces, the Islamic Youth Movement, Laskar Jundallah; the Philippines – Moro Islamic Liberation Front (MILF), the Abu Sayyaf Group; and Malaysia – Kumpulan Mujahidin Malaysia (KMM).

More seriously, there is growing evidence to suggest that cross-border linkages have developed between many of these groups and that these ties have been deliberately fostered by al-Qaeda. An alarming indication that a regional Islamic network was operating in Southeast Asia emerged in December 2001 when a major international terrorist plot was uncovered in Singapore. Subsequent investigations revealed plans to attack several high profile targets in the island nation: including the deep-water Navy port at Changi; the Ministry of Defence; a shuttle bus serving the Sembawang Wharves and Yishun subway; the US and Israeli Embassies; the British and Australian High Commissions; and commercial complexes housing American firms. The plot first came to light following the seizure of videotape and notes detailing reconnaissance of potential targets in Singapore from an al-Qaeda leader's house in Afghanistan.[24]

The Singapore attacks were allegedly to have been carried out under the auspices of Jemaah Islamiah (JI), a hitherto largely unknown entity created in the early 1990s by Abdullah Sungkar and now identified as al-Qaeda's main associate group in Southeast Asia. The organisation is currently believed to be under the central control of Abu Bakar Bashir and Riduan Isamuddin (who are thought to have taken over the leadership following Sungkar's death in 1999) and is alleged to be seeking the creation of a hard line Islamic state comprising the southern Philippines, southern Thailand, Malaysia, Indonesia and Brunei (to be known as Daulah Islamiya Nusantara). JI cells have been identified in several Southeast Asian countries, including the Philippines, Indonesia and Singapore.[25] However, it appears that the most concerted presence has been in Malaysia, where the movement is claimed to have its main leadership consultative council.[26] According to Zachary Abuza, it is also this sub-grouping that forms the principal logistical conduit for al-Qaeda operations between South and Southeast Asia.[27]

While most of the militant Islamic organisations in Southeast Asia exhort a strict Muslim ethos – which specifically prohibits the use or consumption of intoxicants and involvement in criminal behaviour – one cannot assume they will draw the line at drug trafficking and production if it is seen to be in their own best pragmatic interests. Certainly this did not occur in Central or South Asia, two regions similarly characterised by a mix of heroin and Islamic extremism and the inspirational source for many of the radical militants currently existing in Southeast Asia. Indeed, according to the Paris-based *Observatoire Géopolitique de Drogues*, the Taliban routinely collected around US$20 million a year from the heroin trade in Afghanistan, using this money to purchase weapons, ammunition, food, fuel, clothes and transportation.[28]

In Southeast Asia, several groups have already ventured directly into the criminal world. The MILF, for instance, has been directly connected to the activities of the Pentagon Gang, a kidnap, robbery and extortion syndicate that has been operating in Mindanao for the past three years.[29] More explicit has been the Abu Sayyaf, which in May 2001 staged an audacious raid on a beach resort in the Southwest Philippines, abducting seventeen tourists including three Americans. Just over a year previously, the group had conducted a similar operation on the Malaysian island of Sipadan, seizing twenty-one captives who were eventually released after a ransom payment (negotiated by Libyan leader Colonel Ghaddafi) estimated at US$20 million dollars was paid.[30]

Although the Abu Sayyaf example shows that kidnappings can be lucrative, drug trafficking is a far more effective and reliable means of quickly generating cash for arms, foreign expertise, communications and logistics, and also recruits. It is also an inherently less risky option: since

2000, the Abu Sayyaf has been subjected to concerted military hostage-rescue offensives that have seriously impacted on the group's overall operational capabilities, particularly in traditional strongholds such as Basilan (where numbers are currently thought to amount to no more than 100 hardcore activists).[31]

The existence of multiple channels for transferring illegal funds with minimal risk of disclosure or prosecution is a further factor that could avail the rapid development of a terrorist-narco nexus in Southeast Asia. The region remains particularly vulnerable to major money-laundering schemes largely as a result of severe institutional weaknesses that are endemic throughout many of the ASEAN states. Not only do many of these countries lack effective legislative and regulatory frameworks for dealing with financial crime, little (if any) cash transaction reporting actually takes place within the overall banking sector.

Compounding the situation are human susceptibilities stemming from the low pay received by bureaucrats – which greatly exacerbates their 'openness' to bribery – inadequate police resources and the low priority that is generally given to fighting money laundering.[32] This latter problem is something that has been especially marked in states such as Cambodia (which lacks even a rudimentary regulatory system for the banking sector), Thailand (on account of its well-established financial sector, bank secrecy laws, a free-wheeling stock exchange and weak stipulations governing corporate formations) and, until recently, the Philippines.[33] As Dupont notes, these factors combine to provide a highly conducive environmental context both for moving and 'hiding' hot money as well as concealing the source and purpose of transactions needed for weapons purchases and other logistical requirements.[34]

A well-established informal remittance system also exists throughout Southeast Asia. Known as *hawala* in South Asia, this procedure relies entirely on trust between families, secret societies and ethno-religious groups, operating through a multi-dimensional network of gold shops, pawn-brokers, trading companies and moneylenders. Financial exchanges typically rely on coded messages, handwritten chits or symbols that guarantee a high degree of personal security and anonymity in addition to allowing bulk transmissions of funds in a very short period of time.[35] The system has been used extensively by Burmese, Thai and Chinese drug syndicates and is a modality that is perfectly suited to networked terrorist organisations such as al-Qaeda that frequently bear in on and exploit personalised ties across borders. Indeed, *hawala* transfers are known to have formed a crucial fiscal conduit for availing bin Laden's international terrorist operations (including the 1998 US Embassy bombings in Kenya and Tanzania as well as the September 11 attacks in New York and Washington) when he was based in Afghanistan.

The interspersion of narco-funds with extremist organisations would significantly detract from the overall stability of the ASEAN security environment. On one level, it would provide terrorist groups with the necessary means to operate on a higher, more lethal level than would otherwise be the case. Secondly, it could lead to the emergence of 'degenerate' radical elements that deliberately foster armed campaigns of civil violence in order to sustain drug-related activities. Such groups obviously pose enormous obstacles to the institution of viable peace agreements and ceasefires on the ground. Reflecting these concerns, the Council for Security Cooperation in the Asia Pacific (CSCAP) and the Transnational Crime Working Group (TNCWG) now routinely refers to the (drug-induced) criminalisation of terrorism as potentially one of the most serious non-state challenges likely to confront governments of Southeast Asia into the new millennium.

CONCLUSION

Burma remains one of the most prolific heroin producing and exporting countries in the world, generating an illicit trade that has had an insidious, far-reaching and corrosive impact.[36] As this chapter has argued, the possibility of a highly destabilising interface occurring between narcotics and religious extremism cannot be discounted in Southeast Asia, something that will greatly exacerbate what is already a highly complex security milieu in the region.

If Southeast Asian governments are to effectively deal with the twin scourges of drugs and terrorism in the region, it is essential that they develop an effective and rigorous framework for coordinating collaborative action. The ASEAN Regional Forum, which remains the pre-eminent multilateral security regime in the Asia Pacific, represents the logical mechanism through which to achieve such institutionalised cooperation.

Thus far, however, the Forum has proven to be less than effective in terms of security deliberations, largely because it continues to reflect the ASEAN preference for unanimity and non-interference in decision-making. While these types of institutions may be conducive to furthering (the illusion of) harmonious regional relations, they are hardly suited to the type of frank and honest discussion needed for effectively dealing with amorphous 'grey area' influences – particularly in a region where internally based actors can so easily transcend and impact across national frontiers. Confronting the non-state challenges of the twenty-first century – of which the heroin trade is but one manifestation – will require the region's polities to move away from these dysfunctional collaborative predilections and accept normative patterns that are no longer tied to, or embedded in what is rapidly becoming a largely irrelevant nineteenth-century conception of national sovereignty.

NOTES

1.   A detailed survey of these proposed changes can be found in the *World Economic Outlook* (1991), Washington, DC: IMF. See especially pp 26–37.
2.   Latter, Richard (1991), *Terrorism in the 1990s*, Wilton Park Papers 44, London: HMSO, November, p 2.
3.   Abshire, David (1996), 'US Foreign Policy in the Post-Cold War Era: The Need for an Agile Strategy', *The Washington Quarterly*, 19/2, Spring, pp 42–4; Dalby, Simon (1995), 'Security, Intelligence, the National Interest and the Global Environment', *Intelligence and National Security*, 10/4, October, p 186; and Prins, Gwyn (1990), 'Politics and the Environment', *International Affairs*, 66/4, October, pp 711–30.
4.   Acharaya, Amitav (1993), *A New Regional Order in Southeast Asia: ASEAN in the Post Cold War Era*, Adelphi Papers 279: London: IISS, p 12.
5.   Chalk, Peter (1997), *Grey Area Phenomena in Southeast Asia*, Canberra: Strategic and Defence Studies Centre, pp 6–7, 15–16.
6.   Bureau for International Narcotics and Law Enforcement Affairs (2002), *International Narcotics Control Strategy Report, 2001*, Washington, DC: US State Department, March. Online. BINLEA. Available: http://www.state.gov/g/inl/rls/nrcrpt/2001. 1 March 2003.
7.   74 tons of opium gum was produced in Afghanistan in 2001, compared with 3,656 tons in 2000. Between 1998 and 2000, roughly 70 percent of all known illicit heroin production originated from the South Asian nation, with Burma making up most of the remaining 30 percent. See Bureau for International Narcotics and Law Enforcement Affairs, *International Narcotics Control Strategy Report, 2001* and *The Associated Press* (2001), 'Myanmar is World's Top Opium Producer', 20 December.
8.   *The Associated Press* (2001), 'Myanmar is World's Top Opium Producer', 20 December; *The Bangkok Post* (2002), 'Golden Triangle Likely to Yield More Drugs', 23 January.
9.   See, for instance, *The Economist* (1996), 'The Shan Connection', 1 January; *The New York Times* (1995), 'Burmese Lead in Heroin Supply and US Tries to Respond', 12 February; *The South China Morning Post* (1996), 'Former MP Turned Over to US on Drug Charges', 27 January.
10. Bureau for International Narcotics and Law Enforcement Affairs (2002), *International Narcotics Control Strategy Report, 2001*.
11. See, for instance, *The Economist* (2002), 'Rush to Market', 16 February.
12. Lintner, Bertil (1998), 'Drug Asian Crisis', *Asia-Pacific Magazine*, 13 December.
13. Dupont, Alan (2001), *East Asia Imperilled. Transnational Challenges to Security*, Cambridge: Cambridge University Press, pp 199–200.
14. The UWSA controls a large swath of territory in the Mong Yawn Valley, which lies adjacent to Thailand's northwestern border. Similar to FARC in Colombia, the group provides protection for the drug caravans that operate in the tri-border region of Burma, Thailand and Laos (commonly known as the Golden Triangle), using narco-profits to equip itself with a wide variety of weaponry that now includes mortars, rocket-propelled grenades, heavy machine guns and, allegedly, Russian-made SA-7 surface-to-air missiles.
15. One worrying trend that has occurred in the Burmese/Chinese border area is the development of 'suicide traffickers' – porters with explosives strapped to their inner thighs that are detonated in the event of an impending arrest. Australian intelligence officials believe the tactic is largely in response to the draconian counter-drug laws that are now in place in China, which in the case of heroin trafficking carries a mandatory death sentence. Author interview, Hawaii, February 2002.

16. Chalk, Peter (1998), 'Heroin and Cocaine: A Global Threat', *Jane's Intelligence Review*, Special Report No. 18, July; Bureau for International Narcotics and Law Enforcement Affairs (2002), *International Narcotics Control Strategy Report, 2001*; *The Washington Post* (2000), 'AIDS Outbreaks Follow Asia's Heroin Traffic', 6 March; *The Sydney Morning Herald* (1998), 'Slaying the Dragon', 17 October; *Far Eastern Economic Review* (1995), 'Medellin on the Mekong', 23 November.

17. Bureau for International Narcotics and Law Enforcement Affairs (2002), *International Narcotics Control Strategy Report, 2001*.

18. Dupont (2001), *East Asia Imperilled*, p 205; Chalk, Peter (2000), *Non-Military Security and Global Order. The Impact of Extremism, Violence and Chaos on National and International Security*, London: Macmillan, pp 45–6.

19. See, for instance, Metz, Steven (1994), 'Insurgency after the Cold War', *Small Wars and Insurgency*, 5/1, pp 71–9; Dupont, Alan (1999), 'Transnational Crime, Drugs and Security in East Asia', *Asian Survey*, XXXIX/3, pp 448–9.

20. See Chalk (1997), *Grey Area Phenomena in Southeast Asia*, pp 52–6; Blank, Stephen (2001), 'Narcoterrorism as a Threat to International Security', *World and I Magazine*, 1 December.

21. Bureau for International Narcotics and Law Enforcement Affairs (2002), *International Narcotics Control Strategy Report, 2001*.

22. Dupont (2001), 'Transnational Crime, Drugs and Security in East Asia', p 440; Kelly, Edward (1992), 'Cooperative Efforts in Combating drug Trafficking', in Lodl, Ann and Longguan, Zhang (eds), *Enterprise Crime: Asian and Global Perspectives*, Chicago: Office of International Criminal Justice, p 151.

23. *Weekend Australian* (1999), 'War on Drugs Lost to Market Forces', 6–7 March. The Financial Action Task Force estimates that the overall compound growth of drug money will have topped US$15 billion by 2004 (roughly equivalent to today's value of global gold stocks). See Raufer, Xavier (1999), 'New World Disorder, New Terrorisms: New Threats for Europe and the Western World', paper presented before the Future Developments in Terrorism Conference, Cork, Ireland, March, p 4.

24. *The Washington Post* (2002), 'Singapore Arrests Suspected Militants' (2002), 6 January; *The New York Times* (2002), 'Qaeda Moving Into Indonesia, Officials Fear', 23 January; *Associated Press* (2001), 'Exclusive: Terror Plot on US Carrier Foiled', 28 December; *The New York Times* (2002), 'Singapore Accuses Islamists of Bomb Plan', 7 January.

25. All four groups were allegedly involved in the Singapore plot. According to Philippine intelligence, they operate in much the same way as the al-Qaeda operational cells that carried out the US African embassy bombings in 1998 and the suicide attacks on the World Trade Center and Pentagon on September 11. Author interview, Hawaii, February 2002.

26. Author interview, Jakarta, March 2002.

27. Abuza, Zachary (2002), 'Tentacles of Terror: Al Qaeda's Southeast Asian Linkages', *Contemporary Southeast Asia*, December, 24/3, p 449.

28. The Taliban has traditionally imposed a tax of between 10 and 20 percent on all dealers moving opiates out of the country. The group has justified the practice, even though the Koran forbids the consumption of psychotropic or narcotic substances, on the grounds that the money is used to buttress poppy farmers (that is, it is a form of wealth redistribution) and that opium and its derivatives are consumed by *kafirs* (unbelievers), not Afghans or Muslims. See Rashid, Ahmed (2000), *Taliban: Militant Islam, Oil and Fundamentalism in Central Asia*, New Haven: Yale University Press, p 118; and *The Washington Post* (2000), 'The Paradox of the Poppy', 9 March; and *The Economist* (2000), 'Inhalable Exports', 28 October.

29. Author interview, Manila, February 2002.

30. Gunaratna, Rohan (2001), 'The Evolution and Tactics of the Abu Sayyaf Group', *Jane's Intelligence Review*, 13/7, July, p 29; *The Philippine Star* (2002), 'Abus Insist on $2 Million Ransom for US Hostages', 6 February; *The Economist* (2000), 'A Hostage Crisis Confronts Estrada', 6 May.

31. Author interview, Manila, February 2002.
32. Dupont (2001), *East Asia Imperilled*, p 203.
33. In September 2001 the government enacted anti-money laundering legislation, which meets certain requirements of the Financial Action Task Force (FATF) mainly by criminalising any person or institution – including banks, trust entities, insurance companies, investment houses, salesmen and securities brokers – that knowingly attempts to 'hide' the true origin of proceeds obtained via illicit means. In addition, the new law significantly waters down the country's notoriously tough Bank Secrecy regulations by establishing an Anti-Money Laundering Council that is specifically empowered to monitor banks and probe accounts of more than four million pesos (approximately US$78,000) and can, if requested, act on behalf of foreign governments. For further details see Anti-Money Laundering Act of 2001, Philippines Senate and House of Representatives, September 2001. Online: http://www.bspgov.ph/regulations. 20 May 2003.
34. Dupont, Alan (2002), 'Transnational Violence in the Asia-Pacific: An Overview of Current Trends', paper presented before the Transnational Violence and Seams of Lawlessness in the Asia-Pacific: Linkages to Global Terrorism Conference, Honolulu, Hawaii, 19–21 February, pp 6–7.
35. Chalk, Peter (2000), 'Southeast Asia and the Golden Triangle's Heroin Trade: Threat and Response', *Studies in Conflict and Terrorism*, 23/2, pp 95–6; Dupont (2002), 'Transnational Violence in the Asia-Pacific: An Overview of Current Trends', p 7; Gaylord, Mark (1992), 'Money Laundering in Asia', in Lodl and Longguan (eds), *Enterprise Crime: Asian and Global Perspectives*, pp 82–3.
36. For a detailed analysis of the various negative socio-economic effects associated with the Burmese heroin trade see Chalk, Peter (2000), 'Commercial Insurgency and the Southeast Asian Heroin Trade', *Studies in Conflict and Terrorism*, 23/2.

PART IV

Towards a Conclusion

15. Post-September 11 Legislative Responses to Terrorism

Mark Weeding

INTRODUCTION

In the immediate aftermath of the September 11 2001 attacks on the United States, governments worldwide sought to re-evaluate their legislative regimes in relation to terrorism. This chapter examines briefly the key legislative responses of four liberal democratic states: Australia, the United States, Canada and the United Kingdom.

All four states acted quickly to introduce counter-terror legislation into their respective parliaments. The US President signed the USA PATRIOT Act on 26 October 2001. In the UK the Anti-Terrorism, Crime and Security Act 2001 obtained Royal Assent on 13 December. In Canada Bill C-36, the Anti-Terrorism Act came into effect on 24 December 2001. Australia's legislative response was slightly delayed by comparison, but legislation was passed by July 2002. The notable exception here is the Australian Security Intelligence Organisation Amendment (Terrorism) Act 2002 that remains before the Senate at the time of writing.

Four clear trends emerge from an examination of the responses of these states to the increased terrorist threat since September 11. Firstly, the governments of these states have sought to increase judicial, law enforcement and intelligence powers in relation to terrorism. This suggests an immediate post-September 11 perception that legal frameworks were inadequate to properly counter this threat. Secondly, most legislation passed through the respective parliaments extremely quickly. This can be explained in part by general public and political support for rapid action, but raises questions regarding the long-term effects of hastily drafted legislation. While the events of September 11 demonstrated that the threat from terrorism was real, legislation could also have been passed during a continued and global psychological state of fear out of balance with that existential threat.

This approach poses significant challenges to civil liberties. Thirdly, all states considered here have sought to define terrorist events, and the organisational structures supporting them, as a qualitatively different type of crime, and proportionally more serious than the common criminality with which such events had previously been considered. In adopting this approach states reverse their prior approach of treating terrorism as 'normal' crime, and in so doing run the risk of elevating both terrorists and their causes to a higher philosophical plane. Linked to this is the fourth point: that post-September 11 states are adopting an intelligence-driven prevention strategy rather than a judicial/prosecutorial approach to terrorism.

Each state's primary legislative responses to terrorism are examined below. Significant elements of the legislation are discussed in the context of the above four themes. In conclusion, this chapter signals the potential issues arising from those responses, and, in particular, argues that they represent a fundamental shift in counter-terrorism strategy.

LEGISLATIVE RESPONSES TO SEPTEMBER 11

United States of America

Unsurprisingly, the United States reacted swiftly to the September 11 terrorist attacks. The Uniting and Strengthening America by Providing Appropriate Tools Required to Intercept and Obstruct Terrorism Act of 2001 was signed into law by President Bush on 26 October 2001. This convoluted title, reverse engineered from its more familiar acronym USA PATRIOT Act, refers to an Act 342 pages in length that made changes to over fifteen different statutes. The stated purpose of the Act is 'to enable law enforcement officials to track down and punish those responsible for the attacks and to protect against similar attacks'.[1] The legislation thus seeks to both strengthen criminal law and expand the remit of intelligence. In seeking to achieve both ends the Act blurs the boundaries between law enforcement and intelligence collection.

The USA PATRIOT Act grants wider powers to law enforcement and intelligence agencies in communications interception, strengthens anti-money laundering laws, tightens immigration laws, creates new federal crimes and institutes procedural changes. Many of its features are contentious and in response to reservations the Act contains sunset clauses in relation to wiretapping and foreign intelligence amendments.

Prior to 2001, US federal law regarding communications interception was governed primarily by Title III of the Omnibus Crime Control and Safe Streets Act of 1968. Title III generally prohibited electronic eavesdropping on conversations, whether face-to-face or electronic, except as a last resort in serious criminal cases. A court order was required to capture conversations concerning any of a statutory list of offences.[2] Below Title III the next tier of privacy protection covered matters beyond the reach of the Fourth Amendment protection such as telephone records and e-mails held in third party storage.[3] Below this still was a procedure that governed court orders approving the use of trap and trace devices and pen registers, which identify the source and destination of calls.

The USA PATRIOT Act modifies each of these three levels in significant ways. Briefly, it expands pen register and trap and trace to computer communication (such as e-mail), adds terrorist and computer crimes to Title III's list of statutory offences, reinforces protection for those who execute orders under the above three tiers and encourages cooperation between law enforcement and foreign intelligence personnel. In terms of safeguards against the misuse of these powers it provides redress for some communications privacy violations by government personnel and terminates the authority of many provisions on 31 December 2005.[4]

Foreign intelligence gathering in the United States has been governed by the Foreign Intelligence Surveillance Act (FISA), which is amended by section 902 of the PATRIOT Act to include international terrorist activities. Other amendments ease some of the restrictions on the domestic gathering of intelligence related to terrorism and to foreign powers and their agents. They extend the length of FISA court-approved search and surveillance orders and extend pen registers and trap and trace devices to investigations to protect against international terrorism rather than just the international terrorists themselves. This considerably expands the remit of such orders by subtly shifting the focus away from the perpetrator of terrorism to the *idea* of terrorism. FISA authority to collect intelligence is also increased from situations where the suspicion that a person is the agent of a foreign government is the sole purpose of surveillance to anytime this is a 'significant purpose' of the surveillance.

The Act also responds to September 11 by easing the processes for law enforcement and intelligence officials to share information related to terrorists and their activities. This has been clearly identified as an issue affecting the United States capacity to manage the terrorist threat in the past.[5] Additionally, the Act allows disclosure of matters before a grand jury to law enforcement and intelligence officers among others. The role of a grand jury is to decide if a crime has been committed, and if so by whom. 'Its probes may begin without probable cause or any other threshold of suspicion.'[6]

A number of border protection provisions have been added through the legislation including appropriations to triple Border Patrol, Customs Service and Immigration and Naturalization Service staff along the US-Canada border. Section 411 adds 'espousing terrorist activity, being the spouse or child of an inadmissible alien associated with a terrorist activity, and intending to engage in activities that could endanger the welfare, safety or security of the United States' to the list of terrorism related categories of inadmissibility.[7] On certification that he has reasonable belief that an alien is engaged in conduct threatening to national security, or is inadmissible or deportable on grounds of terrorism, espionage, sabotage or sedition, the Attorney General is permitted to detain alien terrorist suspects for up to seven days. Within seven days the Attorney General must initiate removal or criminal proceedings, or release the person. If a person is held, the determination must be reviewed every six months to ascertain whether release would continue to constitute a threat. This appears in conflict with the President's Military Order of 13 November 2001 that allows the Secretary of Defense to detain alien terrorist suspects, within the United States or elsewhere, such as Guantanamo Bay, without express limitation beyond basic needs.[8]

The Act also creates an array of new crimes related to terrorism such as biological weapons offences, harbouring terrorists and fraudulent charitable solicitation. In some cases these changes supplement existing law, filling gaps and increasing penalties.[9] In a draft of the Act, the Justice Department sought to include a maximum penalty of up to life imprisonment for anyone convicted of an offence designated as a terrorist crime. A trigger mechanism could not be identified and the Act simply adopted increased maximum penalties for various terrorism-related offences. This is a clear example of a move towards treating terrorist crime as something qualitatively different to 'normal' crime.

The most vocal critics of the Act have attacked the potential for new powers to be used to stifle legitimate protest and dissent, and the threats to privacy made theoretically more possible by relaxation of surveillance, communications interception and information sharing laws. In light of the above comments three issues emerge. Firstly, it is likely that the legislation is not entirely new. The speed with which the legislation was drafted and passed, within just six weeks of the September 11, suggests it contains 'bottom drawer' proposals that had been drafted earlier, perhaps even under previous administrations. While undermining some of the arguments regarding hasty legislation this indicates political opportunism in relation to some powers. Secondly, the line between law enforcement and intelligence collection has become more, rather than less blurred through this Act. While the transnational nature of networked terrorism has created this quandary, intelligence collection and policing have been fundamentally different tasks. There is no doubt that the two must cooperate more effectively to counter terrorism, but amendments such as those to FISA significantly break down the wall very deliberately established between the CIA and the FBI in the 1970s to protect privacy and civil liberties. Thirdly, terrorism is now special. The USA PATRIOT Act is entirely predicated on the concept of an existential threat. The emergency mindset will recede. Yet, notwithstanding sunset clauses, the legislation will most likely remain.

Canada

Canada's Bill C-36, The Anti-Terrorism Act, came into force on 24 December 2001. Announcing the commencement of the Act the Canadian Attorney General and Minister of Justice, Anne McLennan, noted that 'the Government of Canada is following through on its commitment to ensure that law enforcement and national security agencies have the tools they need to protect the security and safety of Canadians from terrorist activity'.[10]

Mechanisms in the Anti-Terrorism Act which seek to achieve these ends include defining and designating terrorist groups and activities, and creating new offences in the Criminal Code in relation to terrorist activity, strengthening investigative tools including allowing for investigative hearings and preventative arrest, and comprehensive financial provisions.

The Canadian government initially argued that its definition of terrorism was 'carefully circumscribed to make it clear that disrupting an essential service is not a terrorist activity if it occurs during a lawful protest or work strike and is not intended to cause serious harm to persons'.[11] This was amended to delete the word 'lawful' to ensure that unlawful protest activity would not be considered a terrorist act.

The amendment to the Criminal Code defines terrorist activity as 'an action that takes place either within or outside of Canada' that:

- is an offence under one of 10 UN anti-terrorism conventions and protocols; or
- is taken or threatened for political, religious or ideological purposes and threatens the public or national security by killing, seriously harming or endangering a person, causing substantial property damage that is likely to seriously harm people or by interfering with or disrupting an essential service, facility or system.[12]

One aspect of the Canadian legislation that deserves comment is the review mechanism. The Attorney General is required to report annually to Parliament on the use of the recognisance with conditions and investigative hearing provisions. The Solicitor General is required to report on the number of arrests without warrant in relation to the recognizance provision. The first annual reports under these provisions were tabled in Canada's Parliament on 1 May 2003. Neither provision was used during the first twelve months of the legislation being in place.[13]

The recognizance with conditions provision is designed to allow a person, with the consent of the Attorney General, to be brought before a judge to impose restrictions upon that person's activities, in order to prevent a terrorist act. 'In exceptional circumstances a peace officer may make an arrest without a warrant in order to bring the person before a judge to have the application of these restrictions considered.' Under the investigative hearings provision, if a judge is satisfied that there are reasonable grounds to believe a terrorist offence has been, or will be, committed a witness can be compelled to give evidence. Witnesses have the right to legal representation, and information they provide to the court cannot be used against them in a criminal proceeding.[14] Both of these sections of the legislation have caused some consternation within the Canadian community. They focus upon a preventative approach where guilt or innocence is not the key focus, and are similar to the US ability to impose preventative detention and to compel information from material witnesses.

Canada has boosted its electronic surveillance tools also, through eliminating the need to demonstrate that the use of such powers is a last resort in a terrorism investigation. The period of validity for a wiretap is extended, and the requirement to notify targets that surveillance has taken place can be delayed for up to three years.

Considering this legislation, Senate and House of Commons committees took testimony from witnesses, and as a result the Canadian government proposed several amendments to the original Bill. The preventative arrest and investigative hearings powers expire in 2006, through sunset clauses, and the legislation is due for review by Parliamentary committees in 2004. Both mechanisms are intended to stress the immediate need for the legislation while accepting that circumstances may change to make those powers unnecessary or undesirable. Annual reporting requirements, a three-year review timeframe and sunset clauses also inform the agencies seeking to use the powers. They will be well aware that their use or misuse will attract high-level scrutiny on an on-going basis.

United Kingdom

The two major pieces of legislation in the United Kingdom are the Terrorism Act 2000 and the Anti-Terrorism, Crime and Security Act 2001 (ATCSA). The Terrorism Act was passed by Parliament on 20 July 2000, and came into force on 19 February 2001. This Act replaced previous temporary legislation that was primarily devoted to counter-terrorism in relation to Northern Ireland. ATCSA was passed in the immediate aftermath of September 11, but its title demonstrates that its scope is not restricted to terrorism.

The Terrorism Act came into force almost seven months prior to September 11. In perhaps anticipating the direction of global events it outlaws certain terrorist organisations, makes it illegal for them to operate in the United Kingdom and extends this proscription to include international terrorist groups like al-Qaeda. It provides police with wider powers to investigate terrorism, including stop and search powers, and the power to detain suspects for up to seven days (though any period longer than two days must be approved by a magistrate). It creates new criminal offences including inciting terrorist acts, seeking or providing training at home or overseas and providing training in the use of firearms, explosives or chemical, biological or nuclear weapons. It further provides additional powers applicable to Northern Ireland.[15]

The United Kingdom was already well placed with counter-terrorism legislation, but the government still felt the need to enhance its not insignificant powers. In a 2002 Cabinet Office review of the United Kingdom's terrorism response the government noted that prior to September 11 '... we already had much experience of terrorism and dealing with terrorists. As a result, before last September, we already had legislation in place that made it hard for terrorists to operate ... Many branches of government had robust contingency plans in place. However these measures were designed to counter the threat from terrorism on a very different scale.'[16] With regard to ATCSA the same document notes 'It is tough, but necessarily so and the measures it introduced have had a deterrent and disruptive effect'.[17] ATCSA provides for detention of foreign nationals suspected of involvement in terrorism, strengthens protection and security of aviation and civil nuclear sites, extends hoax laws and increases the penalties for crimes aggravated by racial or religious hatred. It also allows the freezing of suspected terrorist assets at the start of an investigation.[18] As noted, many of the United Kingdom's counter-terrorism provisions are already in the Terrorism Act. The new legislation widens the remit of such powers to crimes that are not related to terrorist offences.

ATCSA is structured in fourteen parts. Parts 1 and 2 address financial issues, including providing law enforcement authorities with the power to freeze cash at the start of an investigation, rather than when a person is about to be charged. This significantly shifts the application of the legislation to the 'suspicion' stage of an investigation, but is intended to prevent funds being used or moved offshore before they can be frozen. It includes an obligation on the financial sector to report when there are reasonable grounds to suspect terrorist financing.

Similar to the US approach, Part 3 removes current barriers to information sharing from customs and revenue to law enforcement agencies. Customs and Excise and Inland Revenue are given a general power to disclose information held by them for law enforcement purposes and to the intelligence services in the defence of national security. Further, public authorities can disclose certain types of otherwise confidential information where this is necessary for the purposes of fighting terrorism and other crimes. There is some concern that the police will not need reasonable suspicion that such a file contains evidence of a crime, merely that it is useful in an investigation.[19]

Part 4 provisions are intended to prevent terrorists from abusing the UK immigration and asylum procedures. Clauses 21 to 32 allow detention of those the Secretary of State has certified as threats to national security and who are suspected of being international terrorists where their removal is not possible at the present time. This derogates from article 5 of the European Council on Human Rights, and is only permitted during time of public emergency, and must be strictly limited to the extent strictly necessary as a result of that emergency. In the current climate, where it appears that the threat of international terrorism is semi-permanent at least in the short term, this provides the Home Secretary with what is effectively the power of indefinite detention where a person faces persecution or torture in the only country to which they could be returned. While it is accepted that the government could not be expected to allow terrorists to go free and continue their planning, it appears that suspected terrorists, who may be legitimate asylum seekers but for their intent, fall through the cracks of the legislation into a Camp X-Ray-style limbo.

Increased penalties for crimes of race or religious hatred are dealt with in Part 5. While seeking to counter in part the backlash against Muslims in the United Kingdom, it could be contended that this also extends the provisions so that a criminal offence could be argued to be religiously aggravated and thus attract a higher sentence.[20]

Part 10 provides police with powers to demand the removal of any item that they believe is being worn wholly or mainly for the purposes of concealing identity, such as a mask or gloves. It also allows for cross-jurisdictional assistance, such as British Transport Police providing assistance to police outside their usual 'railways' jurisdiction. The non-governmental organisation Liberty argues this extends the circumstances under which fingerprints can be taken, and the police can undertake 'examinations to ascertain a suspect's identity'.[21]

Part 12 provides for the retention by communication service providers of certain types of data to assist law enforcement. This includes information about the use made by customers of the communications, such as subscriber details and itemised billing. It does not include the content of such communications and mass trawls and 'fishing expeditions' are not permitted. Effectively this provision, as originally drafted, would have encouraged the storage of millions of lines of data relating to innocent individuals against the possibility that it might be useful in the future. There was an absence of safeguards in the legislation that was corrected, to some degree, when the House of Lords forced the government to restrict this provision to the prevention or detection of crime and matters related to national security.[22]

Part 13 largely introduces miscellaneous measures intended to expedite international counter-terrorism measures. It does, however, make it an offence not to disclose information about terrorism. This failure to disclose information about terrorism was previously restricted to Northern Ireland, passenger and freight information. The measure was included in the previous Prevention of Terrorism Act, but not in the Terrorism Act 2000. While Liberty accepts that it has always been part of British tradition that citizens assist the police it was not a criminal offence not to do so (except in very particular circumstances). Consequently 'the section changes fundamentally the relation between the citizen and the state and imposes a duty to provide further information'.[23]

Australia

Australia's experience of terrorism has been almost accidental. While there have been numerous events in Australia which would fall under any accepted definition of terrorism, they have not been acts perpetrated against the Australian state or its institutions. Many have resulted from overseas inter-ethnic conflicts that simply have had Australia as their location rather than their target. September 11, the Bali bombing and attendant awareness of Islamist and other terror groups operating in our region, and the public naming of Australia as a target by al-Qaeda members have now changed this pattern. The Australian government, along with independent analysts, now considers Australia itself to be a real target of terrorism.

The Australian government introduced its key post-September 11 counter-terrorism legislation into Parliament in February and March 2002. This comparative delay occurred primarily as the House of Representatives was dissolved and the Parliament, including the Senate, was prorogued on 8 October 2001 prior to the general election on 10 November 2001.

The government's main package of legislation was introduced on 12 March 2002. Included were:

- Security Legislation Amendment (Terrorism) Act 2002 [no.2],
- Suppression of the Financing of Terrorism Act 2002,
- Criminal Code Amendment (Suppression of Terrorist Bombings) Act 2002,
- Border Security Legislation Amendment Act 2002, and the
- Telecommunications Interception Legislation Amendment Act 2002.

The Security Legislation Amendment (Terrorism) Act 2002 amended the Criminal Code 1995 to create a new offence of engaging in a terrorist act, modernised Australia's treason offence, and created offences related to membership and other links with a terrorist organisation. An organisation can also be proscribed if the Attorney-General is satisfied that it is a terrorist organisation and the organisation has been identified in a United Nations Security Council decision relating to terrorism. Prior to this Act, Australia had legislation prohibiting types of activities likely to be associated with terrorism, but had no comprehensive legislation targeted at terrorism directly. There was, for example, no legislation dealing with membership of, training with and supporting terrorist organisations.

The Criminal Code Amendment (Suppression of Terrorist Bombings) Act 2002, makes it an offence to place bombs or other lethal devices in prescribed places with the intention of causing death, serious harm or extensive destruction which would cause economic loss. The Suppression of the Financing of Terrorism Act 2002 implements obligations under United Nations Security Council Resolution 1373 and the International Convention for the Suppression of the Financing of Terrorism. The Telecommunications Interception Legislation Amendment Act 2002 amended legislation to recognise terrorism as falling within the most serious class of offences for the purposes of interception warrants. These Acts went through Senate Committee scrutiny and received Royal Assent in July 2002.

On 21 March the government introduced the Australian Security Intelligence Organisation Amendment (Terrorism) Act 2002. This Act sought to provide The Australian Security Intelligence Organisation (ASIO) with the ability to detain and question people under warrant for up to 48 hours in the first instance in order to gather information about terrorist attacks. The bill was referred to the Senate Legal and Constitutional Affairs Committee and the Joint Parliamentary Committee on ASIO, the Australian Secret Intelligence Services (ASIS) and the Defence Signals Directorate (DSD) with a brief to report in June 2002. In August the Attorney General announced that the government intended to accept the majority of recommendations made by the above committees, and the Bill passed the House of Representatives on 24 September. The Senate, however, sought further amendments and the Bill was laid aside in December after the two houses were deadlocked over further changes. The Bill was further revised and reintroduced to the House of Representatives in March 2003. It has passed the House of Representatives and remains before the Senate at the time of writing.

The proposal to allow preventative detention for the purposes of intelligence gathering has been the most contentious element of the Bill. In his second reading to the House of Representatives, the Attorney General noted the need to balance the security of the community with individual rights, but argued the need to provide ASIO with powers to discover offenders 'preferably before they perpetrate their crimes'.[24] In a speech to the New South Wales Bar association in October 2002, he added that 'It is not an understatement to say that this is one of the most controversial pieces of legislation to come before the Federal Parliament'.[25] Provisions in the original Bill denied the right to legal representation to detainees, and removed the right to silence. Safeguards against abuse of these powers have since included notification to the Inspector-General of Intelligence and Security that a person has been detained, limits on the length of interrogation in a 24 hour period, and access to a security-cleared lawyer.

There has been some debate as to the constitutionality of such a detention power. The government's position is that in general the detention powers in the ASIO Bill can be supported through the constitutional power to create offences, together with the Commonwealth's incidental constitutional powers.

In a submission to the Parliamentary Joint Committee on ASIO, ASIS and DSD inquiry, Professor George Williams argued that the detention provisions are constitutionally suspect, as 'the power to detain for punitive purposes exists only as an incident of the judicial function of adjudging and punishing guilt and can not be vested in the Executive'.[26] The government's argument in response has been that detention under the provisions of the ASIO Bill is for the purposes of gathering intelligence regarding serious terrorism offences, not for punitive purposes. Thus, it is constitutionally valid. Perhaps more clearly, what the government has effectively argued here is that it is not constitutionally invalid on the grounds of the non-punitive nature of the detention.

ASIO is not currently empowered to obtain a warrant to question a person. Certainly, the government considers it necessary to provide ASIO with such a power in order to prevent terrorist attacks. However, there remains an awkward balance in providing an organisation that has traditionally operated in secret with coercive information gathering powers. The lengthy parliamentary debate over this provision clearly focuses attention on the challenges that transnational-networked terror combined with the destructive potency of multiple suicide attacks provide to liberal democratic understandings of freedom and security.

THE IMPLICATIONS OF POST-SEPTEMBER 11 LEGISLATION

The legislative responses discussed above collectively challenge traditional notions of the role of law enforcement and intelligence agencies, and in seeking to deal with the 'new' threat of mass casualty terrorism look to apply the skills of both sectors to the problem. In doing so, however, they run the risk of elevating the legitimacy of terror as a tactic.

Definitions of terrorism abound in academia and government. There is general agreement that it has two defining characteristics: the use of or threat of violence; and some form of ideology, whether issue-based, or religious. Two paradigms flow from this: (1) terrorism is a mechanism for revealing the fundamentally fascist nature of the state through its response; and (2) terror is used to terrify for the purpose of making an aspect of state policy untenable. The two methods of choice for achieving these ends in the twentieth century were hostage-taking and bombing.

The conventional response of western liberal democracies has been to treat terrorism as simply criminal, and no more worthy of special treatment than any other criminal act. A successful bomber is just a murderer, regardless of the cause, and will be treated according to the criminal law. Part of the rationale for this approach has thus been to leech out the political meaning of terrorist attacks, thus undermining their potential for success. By doing so, states have not had to resort to emergency legislation, and thus undermine their own liberal foundations. States, then, were aware of the dangers of overreaction. In all four states discussed above, there has been a concerted effort to control reaction to terrorist attacks through legal and constitutional means. While this has certainly posed challenges to traditional notions of civil liberties governments have been acutely aware of those challenges and sought to embed oversight and review mechanisms within the new legislation.

However, since the September 11 attacks governments have considered themselves to be operating under a new paradigm. The advent of suicide bombers places the current focus of counter-terrorism laws and operations on the prevention of attacks, and then on the containment and handling of attacks, rather than the prosecution and punishment of people under criminal law. Ultimately the goal of the new legislation is to detect and punish those lower down the scale of terrorist offences in order to prevent plans from reaching their operational stages. Consequently the focus is not necessarily on the individual suicide bomber but on support mechanisms. Further, law enforcement and intelligence agencies can now focus on the intent of activities that under normal circumstances are not criminal, such as donating to charities. Thus a construction of terrorist criminality is developed which does not focus on a specific event, but rather on the willingness and capacity to carry out a terrorist attack at some (possibly unspecified) point in the future. This is suggestive of 'potential terrorist criminality' as an indicator of an individual's interest to security services, and shifts the burden of proof away from the state.

In the current context, then, states have made a choice fundamentally based upon *raison d'état*. They accept and understand that there are significant civil liberties concerns with counter-terrorism programs. This is evidenced in public debate and in the numerous rights protection amendments to legislative provisions accepted by governments. Ultimately though they consider the state to be under a real and grave threat, and have placed obligation to the community as a whole above the rights of individuals.

There is a paradox here. For if legislative programs are successful in preventing terrorism they may reduce support for the very mechanisms that have achieved that goal. One of the aspects which keeps terrorism in the public eye, and has provided widespread acceptance, if not support for counter-terrorism measures, is the horror of the events of September 11. Reducing the threat will also reduce public support for extraordinary or emergency measures. This apparent paradox has no legitimate resolution, but it is a paradox to which citizens and governments must remain hostage.

NOTES

1. Doyle, Charles (2002), 'The USA PATRIOT ACT: A Legal Analysis', CRS Report for Congress, Congressional Research Service, The Library of Congress, Washington DC, 15 April, p 1.
2. *Ibid.*, pp 2–3.
3. *Ibid.*, p 3. The Fourth Amendment enshrines protection from unreasonable searches and seizures.
4. *Ibid.*, p 5.
5. See Mylroie, Laurie (1995), 'The World Trade Center Bomb:Who is Ramzi Yousef? And Why It Matters', The National Interest, Winter 1995/96.
6. Doyle, Charles (2002), 'The USA PATRIOT ACT', p 20.
7. *Ibid.*, p 50.
8. *Ibid.*, p 52.
9. *Ibid.*, p 54.
10. Department of Justice, Canada (2001), 'Anti-Terrorism Legislation Comes Into Force'. Online. Department of Justice, Canada. Available: canada.justice.gc.ca/en/news/nr/2001/doc_29513.html.27 May 2003.
11. *Ibid.*
12. *Ibid.*
13. *Ibid.*
14. *Ibid.*
15. Home Office, United Kingdom (2003), 'Terrorism: Legislation'. Online. Home Office. Available: www.homeoffice.gov.uk/terrorism/govprotect/legislation/index.html. 27 May 2003.
16. Cabinet Office, United Kingdom (2002), 'The United Kingdom and The Campaign against International Terrorism: Progress Report'. Online. Cabinet Office, United Kingdom. Available: http://www.cabinet-office.gov.uk/reports/sept11/coi-0809.pdf. 27 May 2003, p 11.
17. *Ibid.*, p 15.
18. *Ibid.*, p 15.
19. Wadham, John (2002/3), 'The Anti-Terrorism, Crime and Security Act 2001'. Online. Available: http://www.liberty-human-rights.org.uk/resources/articles/pdfs/the-anti-terrorism-crime-and-security-act-2001.pdf. 27 May 2003.
20. *Ibid.*
21. *Ibid.*

22. *Ibid.*
23. *Ibid.*
24. Commonwealth of Australia (2002), House of Representatives Hansard, 21 March 2002, p 1607.
25. Williams, Daryl (2003), 'The War Against Terrorism, National Security and the Constitution: A Response to Dr Renwick'. (Speech by the Attorney General for Australia to the Constitutional Law section of the New South Wales Bar Association.) Online. Attorney-General's Department.
26. *Ibid.*

16. Australia after September 11: The Intelligence Challenge

Dennis Richardson

This chapter will briefly examine the events of September 11 and the impact they have had upon Australian security. It will reflect upon Australia's security environment and discuss some of the intelligence challenges arising from September 11.

Fundamental to any terror strategy is its capacity to catch us off balance. Two of the prominent elements of September 11 were the location of the attack and the scale of the operation. It was not a surprise that Osama bin Laden and the al-Qaeda network were responsible. In evidence before a Congressional Committee in early 2001, George Tenet, Director of Central Intelligence, had clearly identified al-Qaeda as the number one terrorist threat facing the United States.[1]

Apart from the issue of shared democratic values and the nature of Australia's long-standing alliance with the US, the new networked transnational terror threat posed by al-Qaeda engages Australia's interests, simply by virtue of us being part of the global community. Consequently, the Australian Security Intelligence Organisation (ASIO) has an interest and a responsibility to ensure that those very few Australians with links to international terrorism do not involve themselves in acts of terrorism, either in Australia or elsewhere. The Australian government and its security agencies also have an interest and a responsibility to ensure that foreign interests in Australia are properly protected. This has been rendered more acute by the fact that US interests worldwide are at a significantly heightened level of threat.

THE WIDER REGIONAL CONTEXT

In a broader context, our own citizens can be victims of terrorism abroad – as was the case on September 11 and even more devastatingly was proved by the soft targeting of the Sari Nightclub in Bali. Terrorism has, as we have seen, operated on a global scale for a long time. September 11 and the Bali bombings, therefore, did not mark the globalisation of terror, but it did demonstrate in the most brutal of ways that such a strategy has no boundaries.

Thus, one may ask, what has September 11 meant for Australia's security environment? The difficulty in addressing such an issue is that, all too often, the discussion is forced to either end of the political or law enforcement spectrum. Since the end of the Second World War, Australia, unlike Asia or Europe, has been relatively free of significant terrorist threats. At present, Australia does not face the same intensity of threats as the US and some other countries, although this may change in the wake of the second war with Iraq.

Equally, however, we should be in no doubt that the effects of September 11 and the 'war against terror' announced by George W. Bush after the events in September 2001 have long-term implications.

September 11 and its aftermath, evidently, was not merely a blip on the security landscape, which will simply fade gradually into history. It has profoundly changed the security environment and this transformation will be with us for some years. Consequently, the US and its partners are engaged in a protracted struggle.

There will be further terrorist attacks, as events in Bali and elsewhere have demonstrated. Moreover, as much as it might comfort us to think otherwise, and as much as it might give reassurance to explain the unexplainable, terrorists are generally not insane. Indeed, they are very often highly skilled and intelligent. Above all, they are infinitely patient, striking at times and by means of their own choosing.

Thus, the extraordinary events of September 11 have had profound implications for Australia's perception of its security environment. In particular, Australia's security environment is now characterised by a generally higher level of threat to Australia and to its interests. For many years we have operated in the 'Very Low' to 'Low' zone of the threat spectrum, with threat levels occasionally broaching 'Medium' level.

Our normal operating level is now the 'Low' to 'Medium' zone with threat levels sometimes reaching 'High'. We now have a sustained 'High' level of threat to US, UK and Israeli interests in Australia, and an elevated level of threat to some other diplomatic missions and government visitors.

In terms of the nature of the terror threat or the weaponry deployed, the threat from Chemical, Biological, Radiological and Nuclear (CBRN) terrorist attacks has been raised from 'Low' to 'Medium'. Likewise, the threat to aviation interests has been raised from 'Low' to 'Medium'. Along with these predictable changes, security agencies must now give increased attention to threats to national symbols and infrastructure.

Since September 11 the threat to Australian interests abroad has also increased dramatically. Prior to the Bali bombing, a grenade was thrown into the grounds of the Australian International School in Jakarta in early

November 2001. In December, Singaporean authorities uncovered advanced terrorist planning for an attack against largely western interests. This planning included the Australian High Commission in Singapore. Ultimately, and most violently, the 12 October 2002 bombing of the Sari Club and Paddy's bar on Kuta beach was the first mass casualty attack on Australian citizens.

Some terrorist groups with global reach have a small number of supporters in Australia and it is known that a small number of Australians have trained in al-Qaeda terrorist camps in Afghanistan. Not all of those with such links are in US military custody.

None of this should spark too much apprehension. However, it would be unwise not to recognise that our security environment has changed. The challenge posed by terrorism with global reach does have implications for the conduct of international relations and diplomacy, for our legislative framework, for defence, for law enforcement and for intelligence agencies. We shall focus briefly on the latter. The immediate effect of September 11 for ASIO represented, as it did for many other agencies, a lot of hard work. ASIO went on a twenty-four hour work cycle, problematic for a small organisation and something that was unsustainable over the longer term. Accordingly, we had to reprioritise. That part was not too hard as we simply stopped doing a number of things – indeed, some of what we stopped doing has yet to be resumed. This has caused some angst, but the challenges arising from the new security environment have made such changes unavoidable.

Since September 11, we have had to handle an enormous amount of information, from within Australia, from other agencies and from our liaison partners globally. All the information that is received has to be addressed carefully and deliberately. Inevitably, thresholds of concerns have been lowered. All leads need to be investigated, but these have to be prioritised. Overwhelmingly, investigations have resulted in assessments that have eliminated threats, rather than established them. This process of elimination is an important, often overlooked, part of our role.

A small number of investigations simply highlighted what we already knew, and others revealed what we did not. Undeniably, some of these investigations continue today. In responding to the events of September 11, ASIO – and I suspect many other agencies at both the Federal and State level – were assisted by the planning and exercises which went into preparations for the Sydney Olympics that were staged in 2000.

We were also lucky that, at the time of September 11, our resources had been temporarily supplemented for the Commonwealth Heads Of Government Meeting. Without that fortuitous conjunction, we might have found ourselves in some difficulty. Beyond the additional workload, and more fundamentally, two words can summarise the implications arising for an intelligence agency such as ASIO from the impact of September 11: *mainstream* and *cooperation*

Significantly, September 11 *mainstreamed* terrorism as a major issue in countries such as Australia. We have constantly taken it seriously, and the 2000 Sydney Olympics gave it a relevancy easily understood across the community. Nevertheless, September 11 gave it an unparalleled reality and immediacy. As a result, implications across government needed to be addressed. This has led to the review of counter-terrorism arrangements initiated by the government and has led to the creation of a new Defence and Security division of the Department of Prime Minister and Cabinet to coordinate national security in May 2003.

As with any issue that becomes a major government priority, a lot more actors have a legitimate interest, and the requirement for cross-government cooperation becomes crucial to overall success. This underscores the second word – *cooperation*. Indeed, we have seen cooperation become a by-word globally as some traditional suspicions have been put aside – at least temporarily – in pursuit of a common cause. We witness the same dynamics in Australia, with Commonwealth and State leaders coming together in April 2002 to set national guidelines. At the practical working level, we need to ensure that coordinating machinery and cooperative arrangements are adequate to meet the new challenges, and that the process of review has already commenced and has a good platform on which to build.

For an agency such as ASIO, a central challenge highlighted by the globalisation of terror is the need to ensure that intelligence is properly shared with relevant State and Federal agencies. Moreover – in some cases involving the protection of the national information infrastructure – we will also need to factor in the private sector. As a consequence, we will need to work much harder at being more open, more accessible to our partners, and need to provide information relevant to the practical needs of different clients. Similarly, our partners need to understand that intelligence, like every other profession, has its imperfections. We will not always have the full details, frustrating as that might be.

Beyond government, it is essential that ASIO and other relevant agencies conduct themselves in a manner that instils community confidence and trust. It is important that all community groups feel able to approach us for assistance when subject to harassment or violence. This in particular applies to the harassment and violence directed against Australians of the Islamic faith following September 11. An agency such as ASIO needs to constantly ensure that any activity is directed against only the small number of individuals and groups in Australia with links to terrorism. Consequently, we have a responsibility to ensure that we are not open to any legitimate claim that we target communities. All of us must ensure that the rightness of our task does not blind us to the need to act with integrity, legality and with propriety.

CONCLUSION

Terrorism is an issue that involves Australia, and in respect of which we carry certain responsibilities, whether we like it or not. The threat environment within Australia, and for overseas Australian interests, has changed and will remain changed for the foreseeable future. As an issue, terrorism has been mainstreamed, and this has implications for the way government agencies, and some in the private sector, work together. In this altered context, it is essential that agencies such as ASIO conduct themselves in a manner which enhances community confidence and trust.

NOTE

1.   Woodward, Bob (2002), *Bush at War*, New York: Simon and Schuster.

17. Terrorism Today – Terrorism and International Regimes

Richard Butler

For the ten years following the end of the Cold War, from 1990 until the turn of the century, it became increasingly unclear what the fundamental dynamic of international relations in the early part of the twenty-first century would be. The collapse of the Soviet Union and the resultant end of bipolar competition seemed to remove what had been seen, no matter how reluctantly, as the organising principle of contemporary international relations.

The competition between the United States and the Soviet Union had been desparate and global. It was truly a war, and even though the danger of it turning hot was avoided (in at least one instance – the Cuban missile crisis – this had been a close call), some public figures, scholars, and commentators, seemed to lament the passing of an age where all important values had been clear – the free West versus the 'evil empire' of Soviet communism.

When it was over, we in the West said that we had won the war. The truth was a little more complex, namely, the Soviets had lost. This is not a trivial objection. Much error has flowed from Western triumphalism over the collapse of this Soviet Union. The 'we won' rather than 'they lost' error is one of the best contemporary examples of how incredibly important it is for us to always know the real reason for events.

In 1990, the first President Bush declared that 'a new world order' had emerged and looked forward to: the worldwide spread of democracy; universal adoption of the free market economic system; and global cooperation, including between what had been the major adversaries. For a few months, his vision seemed to have been broadly accurate, in each of the three areas. Certainly this was the case at the Security Council of the United Nations, one of the key centres for the organisation of global political cooperation.

In the previous forty years in the Security Council, the two combatants had each cast some 250 vetos, greatly abusing the original purpose of that unique power in order to defend their empire, in the case of the Soviet Union, and their 'special clients', (such as Israel) in the case of the United States.

Beginning in 1990, the Security Council seemed to enter a vetoless phase. Indeed, there was a comical sanctimony amongst Ambassadors of the five permanent members of the Council, who would place their hand on their heart and exclaim 'Veto? Would I do a thing like that?'

The real answer, actually, was absolutely! As Australian Ambassador to the United Nations, I sat for five years on the committee to reform the Security Council. All proposed reforms were vetoed by the five permanent members. The first test of the new age came in August 1990 when Saddam Hussein sent his army into Kuwait, an action which consituted the first instance, since the foundation of the United Nations, of a member State seeking to absorb a fellow member State.

President Bush said this action would not be allowed to stand and began working, both through the Security Council and in the wider international community, to achieve political legitimacy for the expulsion of Iraq from Kuwait and the military means to achieve that, if that proved necessary. For almost six months the Security Council demanded that Iraq withdraw and backed up this demand by imposing far-reaching sanctions on it. Saddam refused to comply and in January 1991, military action led by the United States with some twenty-nine other countries participating and legitimated by resolutions of the Security Council, began. It succeeded rapidly in forcing Iraq out of Kuwait.

In another unprecented move, the Security Council then established the United Nations Special Commission (UNSCOM). It acted as a sub-organ of the council to bring about the removal of Iraq's weapons of mass destruction capabilities. That commission was led intially by Rolf Ekeus of Sweden, and later by myself. The council had in mind that UNSCOM's job should have taken from between twelve and twenty-four months. In any event, Iraq ejected the commission seven years later, with the job still incomplete.

The United Nations and coalition actions against Iraq did seem, in the first instance, to justify President Bush's assertion that a new world order had been born. The coalition included states from East, West and the Arab world. The far-reaching resolutions of the council on Iraq would not have been possible had there not been an entirely new level of cooperation between Russia and the United States. That cooperation continued for a further few years and was evident in fields other than with respect to the problems in the Persian Gulf and the Middle East. As the years passed, there were increasingly diverse and ever stronger signs of an unease amongst nations about a unipolar world and about some of the policies of the sole super power – the United States.

Two countries in particular were increasingly uneasy – China and France – both also permanent members of the Security Council and therefore in possession of the veto power. Their reasons were different.

China's, as ever, had to do with its abiding obsession – the unity of China. During the period in which I took part in meetings of the Security Council on the Iraq issue, I did not hear of a Chinese intervention which did not begin with the assertion that the fundamental value was the sovereignty of the State and the need for it to be free from any intervention, including multilateral intervention. Its concern was and remains that neither the United States nor the international community would ever be able to intervene on the Taiwan or Tibet issues. China saw the United Nations' actions in Iraq as containing within it the possibility of establishing an example of, if not precedent for, intervention which might, one day, be applied to Tibet in particular.

France's growing hostility to United States' power rested on more self-centred concerns about what it might do to France's role in the world, including the use of the French language. There was also an historic French preference for multi-polarity because of the French belief that such a more complex state of affairs provided a more fertile field for the exercise of fabled French diplomacy.

It was evident that, with the fall of the Berlin Wall, a world had passed away. However, it was not clear what would replace that world. This was the case in spite of: the claims of the then US President; the clarifying actions of a veto-less Security Council; and the virtually universal rejection of the actions of Saddam Hussein.

The coming to power in Washington of the administration of George W. Bush, followed by a series of early policy decisions which signalled that his administration's interpretation of American power was to be selfish and isolationist, did nothing to reduce uncertainty about a unipolar world.

The terrorist attack on the United States on September 11 2001 swept away all such uncertainty. The future use of American power was immediately clarified, in both fact and doctrine. It would be deployed in a war against terrorism, globally.

Bush junior made a series of statements which included the assertions: that those who did not help the United States would be considered to be its enemies; the war on terrorism would be permanent; it gave the United States the right to execute pre-emptive strikes; and, perhaps most extravagantly, what was at issue was a contest between good and evil with respect to which the United States had exclusive right to determine which persons, countries and actions fitted into which of those categories. Among other instances of this was the President's assertion that 'an axis of evil' existed, an assertion which Secretary of State Colin Powell was obliged to spend the subsequent six weeks clarifying or explaining to Congress and around the world.

New relationships were forged by the United States with Russia, China, India, and Pakistan – in each case leading to the setting aside of major issues of concern to the United States in the policies and conduct of those other States. The war on terror fostered more than a few convenient marriages.

Old relationships, such as those with Europe and Japan were at least implicitly downgraded, although within Europe the United Kingdom and its nimble Prime Minister were identified as an exceptional friend of the United States.

The costs of September 11 were massive and still incalculable. What is clear, with respect to financial costs, is that the prosecution of the war on terror has blown away the surplus the administration inherited from President Clinton and Bush's current budgetary proposals involve a level of spending on defense, in the next five years, which is simply astonishing.

There are many other effects of September 11 which could be mentioned and the full implications of which are not yet visible. It is essential to recognise, however, that the reaction of the United States' administration, and to some extent the people of the United States, to the outrages committed has been to place the existence of terrorism in the world and the need for it to be defeated at the centre of all foreign and security policy. What happened on September 11 was an outrage and terrorism must be defeated, but a decision to subjugate all other issues and concerns to the United States policy on terrorism holds the very great danger of obscuring the fact that there are other major issues and conditions in the world which must be dealt with.

Indeed, they may in fact include conditions which have bearing on the very existence of non-state groups prepared to use terrorism as the expression of their hostility to existing conditions, and their determination to change them.

To make this point is not to excuse the massacre of September 11 or, worse, in some implicit way to blame the victim. Nonetheless, we need to know the origin of things, the reason for events, such as the end of the Cold War. If we do not, we will not forge the right policies. This is a practical application of the dictum that if we fail to learn from history's mistakes we will be condemned to repeat them. We need to know accurately how it has come about that there are, now, in existence networks of people and groups prepared to use indiscriminate homicide as an expression of their beliefs or goals.

There are a multiplicity of such sources but I would identify four as being paramount: unreliable and corrupt political systems; economic inequity; the circulation of wrong and often deeply and wilfully misleading information about current events and their origin; and the interpretation of cultural differences in ways which seem to suggest the existence of inherent or implacable hostility amongst various groups of people.

Former Australian Foreign Minister, Gareth Evans, in his recent Cohen lecture at Lehigh University, described cogently this phenomenon:

> With all the understandable post-9/11 preoccupation with terrorism, it is worth reminding ourselves how little the fundamentals of conflict have actually changed. The great dangers come from political problems – some of them with underlying economic and social causes – that are unresolved, unaddressed, incompetently addressed or deliberately left to fester, until they become so acute they explode. Part of the fall-out of such explosions can be terrorism, including international terrorism, but terrorism is not in and of itself a self-driving concept, or in and of itself an 'enemy.' It is not even an ideology, as anarchism was in the nineteenth century. Rather it is a tool or a tactic, resorted to in particular by the weak against the strong – weak individuals, weak groups, weak states.[1]

If a key problem which confronted States, including the United States, in the decade following the Cold War was that of the uses of American power, then it is the case that a consequence of September 11 has been the removal of ambiguity about those uses. American power will be deployed relentlessly against terrorism and its supporters.

This raises two truly serious problems – will the United States alone make all of the relevant assessments and determinations of what constitutes a terrorist and therefore a legitimate target of attack? Furthermore, what will happen to the other international agenda: the alleviation of poverty; the management of the global environment and climate; the management of oil supplies and prices; trade in arms; the non-proliferation of weapons of mass destruction; trade in narcotics; the growth in HIV; and the growing flow of refugees?

These are matters which demand attention and which, if they are not attended to, will increase the impetus of terrorist action against western developed countries, particularly the United States. If September 11 were to become an obsessive concern, and there are signs that this is the case, we will suffer the consequences that typically accompany obsessive behaviour.

Matters of intrinsic importance, which existed before September 11, and continue to exist – such as the growing gap between rich and poor in the world – will be deprived of the attention they demand, because of such an obsession. In addition, at a deeper but dramatically powerful perceptual and psychological level, there are the notions of equity and principle at issue in the response to the acts of September 11.

The notion of equity is one of the most powerful motivators of human action. Simply, if prevailing circumstances, conditions, events, are perceived to be unfair or unequal, then people become at least utterly alienated and very often extremely angry. This is inadequately recognised by the current US administration. It is a dangerous failure.

Equally, the spectacle of western policy makers insisting that certain political principles and principles of human rights must be followed everywhere, or else, but then bending them to the needs of their war on terrorism does not go unnoticed. The history of international relations has always been a dismal one from the standpoint of the consistent observance of principles, even principles solemnly agreed in high councils and then inscribed on parchment – such as in the charter of the United Nations.

This has not escaped the attention of the philosophers from Plato through Machiavelli to E.H. Carr. All call attention to the dangers posed by inequity and failure to attempt to apply agreed principles consistently. The now historic failure, hopefully to be rectified soon, to extend to the Palestinian people the same right which supports Israel – a secure nation-state – has caused untold suffering and cost, both *in situ* and globally. Moreover, it is not unrelated to the problems under discussion throughout this text.

If there are principles which support utter resistance to terrorism and I believe deeply that there are, in both law and morality, then their widespread acceptance will rely, above all, on them being applied to all and applied consistently. In this context, I would call specific attention to an important study, published this year, on the twentieth century's most hideous failure – to resist and prevent genocide.

Samantha Power's book *A Problem From Hell* does many things but certainly makes the case for the absolute necessity for key human principles to be defended, consistently, everywhere.[2] For Australia, there are obvious direct actions that need to be taken to prevent, and hopefully make a contribution to the elimination of, terrorism.

The key such actions are: greatly improved intelligence; strengthened domestic security measures; continued control over the entrance of goods and persons into our national territory; an increase in our level of international cooperation in these areas; and insistence on the continuing development and application of international law designed to deter and punish terrorism.

Action to maintain Australian national security, in the face of what has now emerged as the contemporary terrorist threat, should rest on a basic, logical structure. It begins with our seeking to have the greatest possible advance knowledge of those threats. This means we need to improve our own national intelligence capability. The key limits to that are both financial and the need to preserve the civil and privacy rights of our own people in relation to the actions of the intelligence agencies. We have a reasonable track record in this area, but it can be improved and targeted more sharply on the contemporary threat.

That Australia has suffered little, so far, from the transplantation of ancient disputes from Europe and Asia to Australia, as people from those areas have come here and become Australians, is a major achievement.

The rise of modern terrorism and the increase in its popularity and mystique as the ancient problems have remained unsolved, and the gaps between equity and principle already referred to have grown, means that we may not be so fortunate in the future. We will need a greater quality and quantity of information on what actions terrorist groups may be planning.

Similarly we need a greater degree of international intelligence cooperation in this area. The phenomenon at issue, as with so many activities in the contemporary world, is a global one.

International intelligence cooperation is a take-no-prisoners business. No information is free. Trades of information and careful nurturing of relationships are required and there are inequalities deriving from the differing sizes of power of national intelligence capabilities.

Australia has established specific areas of expertise and capability in this field. It should use those in cooperation with others, to enhance our security. However, it should tread carefully. Above all, it must preserve its independence of judgement. All intelligence materials need the most scrupulous analysis and assessment. They can be erroneous and tainted.

I believe a particular warning is appropriate in the present context. We have a deep and obviously extremely useful relationship with the United States in the field of intelligence cooperation. That should be maintained, but we must take great care to ensure that judgements and objectives driven by US policy and US domestic politics are not uncritically accepted by us as hard, objective intelligence materials when they may not be.

Alliances have their inherent peculiarities, as well as their obvious benefits. They can challenge the independence of the smaller partner. It is not in our national interest for any such challenge to succeed, ever, but perhaps especially when our partner has announced a doctrine of unfettered right to intervene militarily whenever it chooses, associated with the notion that those who are not with them, are against them.

A condition of basic importance to our security is to be able to regulate the entry of goods and people into our national territory. We, like all comparable countries, have done this for a very long time, not least for financial reasons – customs duties, for example. We have particular characteristics which influence our procedures deriving from the fact that we are an island and from the need to keep our plants and animals safe from diseases which have not existed indigenously.

Today's world is increasingly interconnected and complicated. Increased trade has linked nations as never before, sea-borne trade is based on countless numbers of containers. Massive currents of people, increasingly including involuntary flows of refugees, impact upon neighbouring countries. The exercise of surveillance, let alone control of those flows, has become immensely difficult.

A perfect outcome now seems impossible. This is not to say that effectiveness cannot be increased. The logic referred to earlier moves from better information to improved surveillance and control exercised, *inter alia*, on the basis of that information, to strengthen domestic procedures designed to deter and/or prevent terrorist actions.

All of these actions are best conducted within a framework of law, both domestic and international. While terrorists elementally challenge notions of legitimacy, action against them which ignores or bends agreed legal standards would both fulfil the terrorists' worst, demonic, picture of the conventional order, and remove our ability to benefit from a key part of the law – the prosecution and punishment of offenders.

Given the contemporary, post-September 11 challenge, there is a case for the strengthening of existing international law and procedures on terrorism. Australian international lawyers have made outstanding contributions to the development of international law. They should do so again in this field.

The need to engage ordinary Australians and the relevant professions: intelligence and security officials; lawyers; the armed forces; policy advisors – in protecting our security is crucial. This task is not aided, indeed it is dangerously retarded, when those seeking elected office and then to form the government, misrepresent such terrorism, refugee and security issues in order to win elections; and are widely known to have done so, including possibly by recourse to the fabrication of events.

Such action might help with an election in a popular democracy. That this appears to have happened in Australia in 2001 does not necessarily suggest that ordinary Australians are more gullible, more prone to being frightened than their counterparts in comparable countries. Having lived for quite a while in the US, my feeling is that the ability of ordinary Australians to make up their own minds and resist manipulation is very high in comparison with others.

Yet there remains the possibility of politicians exploiting incipient anxiety and xenophobia in circumstances such as faced in August 2001 when the Tampa was approaching Australian territory. Prime Minister Howard and his close colleagues exploited that fear in a manner which harmed the Australian consciousness at home, and damaged our reputation abroad.

What was most disappointing in these events was that rather than seeking to lead the Australian people to a clearer understanding of the inter-connectedness of our world, the Prime Minister shot low to win an election. He and his colleagues have argued that they were merely serving known public opinion. Perhaps, but they certainly did nothing to inform it or lead it to a better place.

Domestic politics aside, these actions do not serve well the need to build the required structures against terrorism. They lead to massive investment in stopping boat people, not real terrorists. The terrorist action which must be feared most is an attack with a nuclear or radiological weapon. This is possible. Such a weapon would not require a missile or aircraft for its delivery, a suitcase would do. The likelihood of this occuring is not minute. Prevention of it will require major international cooperation and continuing defence of the nuclear non-proliferation treaty and other nuclear arms controls. These latter arrangements are currently under great pressure, principally as a result of new US nuclear weapons policies, the development of which has been explained as a response to September 11. There is, at the very least, a lapse in logic here.

For the longer term, the current state of our globalised world indicates that major action is required on three fronts, not because of the problem of terrorism, but because these are the three areas in which profound failure is occurring and great danger can be identified. In each of these areas we need nothing less than a whole new paradigm.

The first of these is in the field of economic equity. Whatever benefits the realignment of global economic relations, commonly called globalisation, have brought in the last twenty years, alleviation of poverty in any comprehensive way has not been one of them. It is the case that while the world is now creating more wealth than ever before there are also more deeply poor people than ever before. This is an unhealthy and dangerous situation, and it has a bearing on the growth of terrorism.

The structures that have both produced this and seek to deal with it are clearly inadequate. They remain rooted in economic, political, administrative and, indeed, ideological constructs which are incapable of bringing about a more equitable distribution of wealth. Some new approaches have been tried, such as that of micro-credit devised by Mohammed Yunnus, but overall, a whole new paradigm for eliminating poverty needs to be constructed.

The post-Cold War cant about free markets fixing it all is manifestly wrong. Some of the world's most successful capitalists, such as George Soros, and successful communists, such as the Chinese, agree that past approaches to this crucial problem don't work.

The second point concerns the field of information. A good deal of the conflict and hostility that takes place between nations and peoples today is abundantly fuelled by information and propaganda that is false. The paradox here, comparable to the poverty paradox, is that this is occurring not in some dark age, but after the information revolution of recent decades.

There are grave perils, in terms of liberty, in any efforts to control information. But there is now abundant evidence that cynical manipulation of information and the media, in the variety of ways that now occurs, is deadly. It sets people to killing other people. What is elementally required is political responsibility. Far too many political leaders, all over the world, manipulate information for the purpose of retaining or extending their own power. Too often they specifically deploy ethnic and religious hatred for those purposes.

People need to know facts not fables and the real causality of events. If they do not, serious error, or worse misfortunes will occur. A new understanding, a new paradigm for responsibility in the creation, dissemination, and use of information is required. It will be very hard to build, especially in the age of the Internet, but failure to build it is not an option.

Thirdly, access to an application of technologies remains critical. In particular, the area of weapons of mass destruction should concern us all. The revolution in applied technologies, especially in the biological and artificial intelligence areas, has not only raised the possibility of solving long-standing problems but also an expansion in the proliferation of means of mass destruction.

The paradigm through which the international community has sought to deal with this problem for almost fifty years is that of the non-proliferation treaties in the nuclear, chemical, biological and missile areas. This paradigm has become flawed because of the failure of major weapon states to carry out their undertakings and problems in enforcement, when breaches occur.

At a deeper level, the perennial problem in the relationship between science and ethics has grown larger, especially in the area of biology. This can be encapsulated in the question: does the fact that something can be done mean that it should be done? Some say yes, in the name of science, but that unqualified affirmation breaks a vital link between science and ethics.

Again, a new paradigm for the application of the products of scientific research which includes consideration of both human benefit and ethical concern is needed. Furthermore, it must be supported by strengthened measures to prevent the proliferation of weapons of mass destruction.

The post-Cold War, post-September 11 landscape has become discernible. The challenges we face are daunting, the stakes at issue are very high. There is much we can do in Australia and by offering Australian cooperation internationally. Nevertheless, the deepest challenge of all is to change this world in some fundamental ways. It will take time. We should start now.

NOTES

1. Evans, Gareth (2002), "Confronting the Challenge of Terrorism: International Relations after 9/11', *The Cohen Lecture in International Relations*, Lehigh University, Pennsylvania, 23 April. Online. Available: http://www.garethevans.dynamite.com.au/speechtexts/LehighLecture23iv02.htm. 13 March 2003.
2. Power, Samantha, (2000), *A Problem From Hell: America and the Age of Genocide*, New York: Basic Books.

Bibliography

Abadinsky, Howard (1994), *Organized Crime*, Chicago: Nelson-Hall Publishers.

Abshire, David (1996), 'US Foreign Policy in the Post-Cold War Era: The Need for an Agile Strategy', *The Washington Quarterly*, 19/2, Spring.

Abuza, Zachary (2002), 'Tentacles of Terror: Al Qaeda's Southeast Asian Linkages', *Contemporary Southeast Asia*, 24/3, December.

Acharaya, Amitav (1993), *A New Regional Order in Southeast Asia: ASEAN in the Post Cold War Era*, Adelphi Papers 279: London: IISS.

Alagappa, Muthiah (1987), *The National Security of Developing States*, Dover: Auburn House.

Alam-al-Din, Riyad (1999), 'Iraq, Bin Ladin Ties Examined', *Al-Watan al-'Arabi*, 1 January.

Alexander, Yonah and Leventhal, Paul (eds), *Preventing Nuclear Terrorism: The Report and Papers of the International Task Force on Prevention of Nuclear Terrorism*, Lexington: Lexington Books.

Alibek, Ken with Handelman, Stephen (1999), *Biohazard*, New York: Random House.

Anthony, Mely and Jawhar, Mohamad (eds), *Confidence Building and Conflict Reduction*, Kuala Lumpur: ISIS-Malaysia.

Arkin, William (1999), 'The Cyberbomb in Yugoslavia', *The Washington Post*, 25 October.

Arquilla, John and Ronfeldt, David (1993), 'Cyberwar Is Coming!', *Comparative Strategy*, 12/2, Summer.

Arquilla, John and Ronfeldt, David (1996), *The Advent of Netwar*, Santa Monica: RAND.

Arquilla, John and Ronfeldt, David (2001), *Networks and Netwars: The Future of Terror, Crime, and Militancy*, Santa Monica: RAND.

Arquilla, John and Ronfeldt, David (eds) (1997), *In Athena's Camp: Preparing for Conflict in the Information Age*, Santa Monica: RAND.

Ayman al-Zawahiri (2001), 'Knights Under the Prophet's Banner – Mediations on the Jihadist Movement', *AL Sharq al-Awsat* (in Arabic), 2 December.

Azzam, Abdullah (1988) 'Al Qaidah al Sulbah', *Al Jihad*, 41, April.

Babcock, Charles (1978), 'Suspects in plot may have thought mafia wanted sub', *Washington Post*, 6 October.

Baldwin, David (ed.) (1993), *Neorealism and Neoliberalism: The Contemporary Debate*, New York: Columbia University Press.

Barber, Benjamin (1996), *Jihad vs McWorld*, New York: Ballantine.

Barber, Richard (ed.) (2000), *Aceh: The Untold Story*, Bangkok: Asian Forum for Human Rights and Development.

Barnaby, Frank (1996), *Instruments of Terror*, London: Satin Books.

Bar-Zohar, Michael (1967), *The Avengers*, New York: Hawthorne Books.

Ben David, Joseph and Clark, Terry (eds), *Culture and its Creators*, Chicago: University of Chicago Press.

Bergen, Peter (2001), *Holy War Inc. Inside the Secret World of Osama bin Laden*, London: Weidenfeld & Nicolson.

Blank, Stephen (2001), 'Narcoterrorism as a Threat to International Security', *World and I Magazine*, 1 December.

Bodansky, Yossef (2001), *Bin Laden: The Man Who Declared War on America*, Roseville: Forum.

Bossard, Andre (1990), *Transnational Crime and Criminal Law*, Chicago: University of Illinois and Office of International Criminal Justice.

Brackett, David (1996), *Holy Terror: Armageddon in Tokyo*, New York: Weatherhill Inc.

Brynjar, Lia and Hansen, Annika (1999), *An Analytical Framework for the Study of Terrorism and Asymmetric Warfare*, Kjeller: Norwegian Defence Research Establishment.

Buccianti, Alexandre (1999), 'Des extremistes musulmans detiendraient des armes chimiques et bacteriologiques, selon un dirigeant islamiste', Agence France Presse, 21 April.

Burns, Tom and Stalker, George (1961), *The Management of Innovation*, London: Tavistock.

Cameron, Gavin (1999), 'Multi-track Micro-proliferation: Lessons from Aum Shinrikyo and al-Qaeda', *Studies in Conflict & Terrorism*, 22/4, October–December.

Cameron, Gavin (1999), *Nuclear Terrorism: A Threat Assessment for the 21st Century*, Basingstoke: Macmillan Press.

Cameron, Gavin (2000), 'WMD Terrorism in the United States: An Assessment of the Threat & Possible Countermeasures', *The Nonproliferation Review*, 7/1, Spring.

Case, William (1996), 'Can the "Halfway House" Stand? Semidemocracy and Elite Theory in Three Southeast Asian Countries', *Comparative Politics*, 28.

Chalk, Peter (1997), *Grey Area Phenomena in Southeast Asia*, Canberra: Strategic and Defence Studies Centre.

Chalk, Peter (1998), 'Heroin and Cocaine: A Global Threat', *Jane's Intelligence Review*, Special Report No. 18, July.

Chalk, Peter (1998), 'Low Intensity Conflict in Southeast Asia: Piracy, Drug Trafficking and Political Terrorism', *Conflict Studies*, January/February.

Chalk, Peter (2000), 'Commercial Insurgency and the Southeast Asian Heroin Trade', *Studies in Conflict and Terrorism*, 23/2.

Chalk, Peter (2000), 'Southeast Asia and the Golden Triangle's Heroin Trade: Threat and Response', *Studies in Conflict and Terrorism*, 23/2.

Chalk, Peter (2000), *Non-Military Security and Global Order. The Impact of Extremism, Violence and Chaos on National and International Security*, London: Macmillan.

Clare, Sian and Morris, Lucie (1998), 'UK Defense Secretary Claims Evidence against Bin-Laden', London Press Association, 23 August.

Conboy, Kenneth and Morrison, James (1999), *Feet to the Fire. CIA Covert Operations in Indonesia, 1957–1958*, Annapolis: Naval Institute Press.

Conrad, Joseph (1907, 1990), *The Secret Agent*, London: Penguin Books.

Cooley, John (2002), *Unholy Wars. Afghanistan, America and International Terrorism*, London: Pluto Press.

Cotton, James (1999), 'ASEAN and the Southeast Asian "haze": challenging the prevailing modes of regional engagement', *Pacific Affairs*, 72/2.

Dalby, Simon (1995), 'Security, Intelligence, the National Interest and the Global Environment', *Intelligence and National Security*, 10/4, October.

Desanctis, Geraldine and Fulk, Janet (eds), *Shaping Organisational Form: Communication, Connection, and Community*, Thousand Oaks: Sage.

Dorman, Andrew, Smith, Mike and Uttley, Matthew (eds) (2003), *The Changing Face of Military Power*, London: Palgrave.

Doyle, Charles (2002), 'The USA PATRIOT ACT: A Legal Analysis', CRS Report for Congress, Congressional Research Service, The Library of Congress, Washington DC, 15 April.

Dudnik, Vladmir (1993), 'Does the Chechen Republic Possess SS-20 Missiles?', *Moscow News*, 17 September.

Dupont, Alan (1999), 'Transnational Crime, Drugs and Security in East Asia', *Asian Survey*, XXXIX/3.

Dupont, Alan (2001), *East Asia Imperilled. Transnational Challenges to Security*, Cambridge: Cambridge University Press.

Edwards, Rob (2001), 'The nightmare scenario', *New Scientist*, 172/2312, 13 October.

Ersanel, Nedret (1994), 'PKK's chemical arms depots', *Nokta* (Istanbul), 30 January.

Esposito, John (1992), *The Islamic Threat Myth or Reality?*, Oxford: Oxford University Press.

Falkenrath, Richard, Newman, Robert and Thayer, Bradley (1998), *America's Achilles Heel: Nuclear' Biological and Chemical Terrorism and Covert Attack*, Cambridge: The MIT Press.

Farrell, Stephen (2001), 'Bin Laden makes nuclear threat', *The Times*, 10 November.

Fealy, Greg (2002), 'Is Indonesia a Terrorist Base', *Inside Indonesia*, 71, July–September.

Fielding, Nick, Laurier, Joe and Walsh, Gareth (2002), 'Bin laden "almost had uranium bomb"', *Sunday Times*, 3 March.

Friedman, Thomas (1999), *The Lexus and the Olive Tree*, London: HarperCollins.

Fukuyama, Francis (1992), *The End of History and the Last Man*, London: Penguin.

Funston, John (1998), 'ASEAN: Out of its Depth?', *Contemporary Southeast Asia*, 20/1.

Funston, John (2002), 'Malaysia: Muslim Militancy – how much of a threat?', *Aus-CSCAP Newsletter*, May.

Gellner, Ernest (1985), *Relativism in the Social Sciences*, Cambridge: Cambridge University Press.

George, Alexander (ed.), *Western State Terrorism*, New York: Routledge.

Gergen, Kenneth (2000), 'The Self in the Age of Information', *Washington Quarterly*, 23/1, Winter.

Gershman, John (2002), 'Is Southeast Asia the Second Front?', *Foreign Affairs*, 18/4.

Gibbon, Edward (1776, 1977), *The Decline and Fall of the Roman Empire*, Harmondsworth: Penguin.

Godson, Roy and Williams, Phil (1998), 'Strengthening Cooperation against Transnational Crime: A New Security Imperative', *Transnational Organized Crime*, 4/3–4, Autumn/Winter.

Goldman, John and Ostrow, Ronald (1998), 'U.S. Indicts Terror Suspect Bin Laden', *Los Angeles Times*, 5 November.

Grunwald, Michael (1998), 'US Says Bin Laden Sought Nuclear Arms; Complaint Cites Alliance with Sudan, Iran', *The Washington Post*, 26 September.

Guelke, Adrian (1995), *The Age of Terrorism and the International Political System*, London: IB Tauris.

Guest, Robert (1995), 'Cult Germ was Claim as Police Find Bacteria', *Daily Telegraph*, 29 March.

Gunaratna, Rohan (2001), 'The Evolution and Tactics of the Abu Sayyaf Group', *Jane's Intelligence Review*, 13/7, July.

Gunaratna, Rohan (2002), *Inside al-Qaeda: Global Network of Terror*, New York: Columbia University Press.

Gutteridge, William (ed.), *Contemporary Terrorism*, New York: Facts on File Publications.

Harding, James (2001), 'Counter-capitalism. Inside the Black Bloc', *Financial Times*, 15 October.

Hawkins, David (1972), *The Defence of Singapore: From the Anglo-Malayan Defence Agreement to ANZUK*, London: United Services Institute for Defence Studies.

Hefner, Robert (2000), *Civil Islam Muslims and Democratization in Indonesia*, Princeton: Princeton University Press.

Henderson, Mark (2001), 'Nuclear reactors vulnerable to attack', *The Times*, 24 September, p 4.

Henderson, Mark (2001), 'Terrorists could make atom bomb by raiding hospitals', *The Times*, 1 November.

Herman, Edward and O'Sullivan, Gerry (1990), *The Terrorism Industry*, New York: Pantheon.

Hernandez, Carolina and Pattugalan, Gina (eds), *Transnational Crime and Regional Security in the Asia Pacific*, Manila: Institute for Strategic and Development Studies and Council for Security Cooperation in the Asia Pacific.

Heydenbrand, I. (1989), 'New Organisational Forms', *Work and Occupations*, 3/16.

Hibbs, Mark (1995), 'Chechen Separatists Take Credit for Moscow Caesium-137 Threat', *Nuclear Fuel*, 20/25, 5 December.

Hiro, Dilip (1989), *Islamic Fundamentalism*, London: Paladin.

Hoffman, Bruce (1986), *Terrorism in the United States and the Potential Threat to Nuclear Facilities*, Santa Monica: RAND.

Hoffman, Bruce (1997), 'The Confluence of International and Domestic Trends in Terrorism', *Terrorism and Political Violence*, 9/2, Summer.

Hoffman, Bruce (1998), *Inside Terrorism*, New York, NY: Columbia University Press.

Hoffman, Bruce (2001), 'A Counterterrorism Policy for Yesterday's Threat', *Los Angeles Times*, 16 September.

Hoffman, Bruce, Roy, Olivier and Benjamin, Daniel (2000), 'America and the New Terrorism: An Exchange', *Survival*, 42/2, Summer.

Holsti, Kalevi (1996), *The State, War, and the State of War*, Cambridge: Cambridge University Press.

Hooper, John (2001) 'Gadafy Told Berlin Diplomat of Libyans' Lockerbie Role', *The Guardian*, 16 May.

Humphreys, Amelia (ed.) (1997), *Terrorism: A Global Survey: a special report for Jane's Intelligence Review and Jane's Sentinel*, Alexandria: Jane's Information Group.

Huntingdon, Samuel (1996), *The Clash of Civilizations and the Remaking of World Order*, New York: Touchstone.

Hussain, Zahid (2001), 'Bin Laden met nuclear scientists from Pakistan', *The Times*, 25 November.

Inglehart, Ronald (2000), 'Globalisation and Postmodern Values', *Washington Quarterly*, 23/1, Winter.

Ingles-le Nobel, Johan J. (1999), 'Cyberterrorism hype', *Jane's Intelligence Review*, 11/12, December.

Isaacson, Jason and Rubenstein, Colin (eds), *Islam in Asia. Changing Political Realities*, New Brunswick: Transaction.

Jackson, Brian (2000), *Technology Acquisition by Terrorist Groups*, Santa Monica: RAND Note.

Jenkins, Brian (1975), 'International Terrorism: A Balance Sheet', *Survival*, No. 17.

Jenkins, Brian (1975), *Will Terrorists Go Nuclear?*, Santa Monica: RAND.

Johnston, Philip (2001), '"Terror Groups" Hiding in the Heart of Britain', *Daily Telegraph*, 28 September.

Joo-Jock, Lim and Vani, S. (eds), *Armed Separatism in Southeast Asia*, Singapore: Institute of Southeast Asian Studies.

Juergensmeyer, Mark (1993), *The New Cold War: Religious Nationalism Confronts the Secular State*, Berkeley: University of California Press.

Juergensmeyer, Mark (2000), *Terror in the Mind of God: The Global Rise of Religious Violence*, Berkeley: University of California Press.

Kahin, Gerorge Mct. and Kahin, Audrey (1997), *Subversion as Foreign Policy. The Secret Eisenhower and Dulles Debacle in Indonesia*, Seattle: University of Washington Press.

Kaldor, Mary (1999), *New and Old Wars: Organized Violence in a Global Era*, Stanford: Stanford University Press.

Kaplan, David and Marshall, Andrew (1996), *The Cult at the End of the World: The Incredible Story of Aum*, London: Arrow Books.

Kedourie, Elie (1980), *Islam in the Modern World and Other Studies*, London: Mansell.

Kedourie, Elie (1994), *Democracy and Arab Political Culture*, London: Frank Cass.

Kegley Jr, Charles and Wittkopf, Eugene (1999), *World Politics: Trend and Transformation*, New York: Worth.

Kell, Tim (1995), *The Roots of Acehnese Rebellion, 1989–1992*, New York: Cornell University.

Kendall, Raymond (1998), 'Responding to Transnational Crime', *Transnational Organized Crime*, 4/3–4, Autumn/Winter.

Keohane, Robert (1984), *After Hegemony*, Princeton: Princeton University Press.

Kissinger, Henry (1994), *Diplomacy*, New York: Touchstone.

Kitfield, James (2000), 'Covert Counterattack', *National Journal*, 16 September.

Klaidman, Daniel and Liu, Melinda (2002), 'Indonesia: Asia's New Weakest Link', *Newsweek*, 4 February.

Klaidman, Daniel and Liu, Melinda (2002), 'Malaysia: A Good Place to Lie Low', *Newsweek*, 4 February.

Koch, Andrew (2001), 'Space Imaging Gets .5m Go Ahead', *Jane's Defence Weekly*, 10 January.

Kurlantzick, Joshua (2000), 'Muslim Separatists in Global Network of Terrorist Groups', *Washington Times*, 2 May.

Kushner, Harvey (1998), *Terrorism in America: A Structured Approach to Understanding the Terrorist Threat*, Springfield: Charles C. Thomas.

Lapidus, Ira (1983), *Contemporary Islamic Movements in Historical Perspective*, Policy Papers in International Affairs, No. 18, Berkeley: University of California Press.

Lapidus, Ira (1988), *A History of Islamic Societies*, Cambridge: Cambridge University Press.

Laqueur, Walter (1999), *The New Terrorism: Fanaticism and the Arms of Mass Destruction*, Oxford: Oxford University Press.

Latter, Richard (1991), *Terrorism in the 1990s*, Wilton Park Papers 44, London: HMSO, November.

Leifer, Michael (1995), *Dictionary of the Modern Politics of Southeast Asia*, London: Routledge.

Leitenberg, Milton (1999), 'Aum Shinrikyo's efforts to produce biological weapons: A Case study in the serial propagation of misinformation', *Terrorism & Political Violence*, Special Edition – The Future of Terrorism, 11/4, Winter.

Lesser, Ian, Hoffman, Bruce, Arquilla, John, Jenkins, Brian, Ronfeldt, David and Zanini, Michele (eds) (1999), *Countering the New Terrorism*, Santa Monica: RAND.

Lintner, Bertil (1998), 'Drug Asian Crisis', *Asia-Pacific Magazine*, 13 December.

Lloyd, Anthony (2001), 'Bin Laden's nuclear secrets found', *The Times*, 15 November.

Lodl, Ann and Longguan, Zhang (eds), *Enterprise Crime: Asian and Global Perspectives*, Chicago: Office of International Criminal Justice.

Lupsha, Peter (1996), 'Transnational Organized Crime versus the Nation State', *Transnational Organized Crime*, 2/1, Spring.

MacFarqhuar, Neil (2001), 'Wahhabis: Adherents to a Strict Form of Islam', *New York Times*, 7 October.

Man, W. K. Che (1990), *Muslim Separatism: The Moros of Southern Philippines and the Malays of Southern Thailand*, Singapore: Oxford University Press.

Marin, Minette (2001), 'It is Decadent to Tolerate the Intolerable', *Daily Telegraph*, 22 September.

Martin, Seamus (1994), 'Mafia threatens to bomb power station', *The Irish Times*, 14 November.

Matthews, Lloyd (ed.), *Challenging the United States Symmetrically and Asymmetrically: Can America Be Defeated?*, Carlisle, PA: United States Strategic Studies Institute.

May, R.J. (1992), 'The Religious Factor in Three Minority Movements', *Contemporary Southeast Asia*, 13/4.

McDonald, Tim (2001), 'CIA to Congress: We're Vulnerable to Cyber-Warfare', *NewsFactor Network*, 22 June.

McGrory, Daniel (2001), 'Al-Qaeda's $1 million hunt for atomic weapons', *The Times*, 15 November.

Mearsheimer, John (1994/95), 'The False Promise of International Institutions', *International Security*, 19/3.

Metz, Steven (1994), 'Insurgency after the Cold War', *Small Wars and Insurgency*, 5/1.

Mir, Hamid (2001), 'Osama claims he has nukes', *Dawn* (Pakistan), 10 November.

Mylroie, Laurie (1995), 'The World Trade Center Bomb: Who is Ramzi Yousef? And Why It Matters', *The National Interest*, Winter 1995/96.

Nacos, Brigitte (1994), *Terrorism and the* Media, New York: Columbia University Press.

Najib, Mohamad and Razak, Abdul (2001), *Defending Malaysia: Facing the Twenty-First Century*, London: ASEAN Academic.

Nathan, Adam and Leppard, David (2001), 'Al-Qaeda's men held secret meetings to build "dirty bomb"', *Sunday Times*, 14 October.

Naylor, R.T. (1995), 'From Cold War to Crime War: The Search for a New "National Security Threat"', *Transnational Organized Crime*, 1/4, Winter.

Nohria, Nitin and Eccles, Robert (eds), *Networks and Organisations*, Boston: Harvard Business School Press.

Nordland, Rod (2001), 'A Dictator's Dilemma', *Newsweek*, 1 October.

O'Brien, Kevin A. and Nusbaum, Joseph (2000), 'Intelligence gathering on asymmetric threats – Part One', *Jane's Intelligence Review*, 12, 10 October.

Orjollet, Stephane (1995), 'Nuke package raises fear of Chechen attacks – but how real are they?', Agence France Presse, 24 November.

Pipes, Daniel (2000), 'Islam and Islamism Faith and Ideology', *The National Interest*, Spring.

Power, Samantha, (2000), *A Problem From Hell: America and the Age of Genocide*, New York: Basic Books.

Pringle, James (1990), 'Tamil rebels face all-out war launched by Colombo', *The Times*, 19 June.

Prins, Gwyn (1990), 'Politics and the Environment', *International Affairs*, 66/4, October.

Pugliese, David (2001), 'Police suspect bin Laden making "dirty" nuclear bombs', *National Post*, 17 October.

Ranstorp, Magnus (1994), 'Hizbollah's Command Leadership: Its Structure, Decision-Making and Relationship with Iranian Clergy and Institutions', *Terrorism and Political Violence*, 6/3, Autumn.

Rashid, Ahmed (2000), *Taliban: Militant Islam, Oil and Fundamentalism in Central Asia*, New Haven: Yale University Press.

Rathmell, Andrew and O'Brien, Kevin (eds) (2000), *Information Operations: A Global Perspective*, Coulsden: Jane's Information Group.

Reader, Ian (1996), *Poisonous Cocktail? Aum Shinrikyo's Path to Violence*, Copenhagen: Nordic Institute of Asian Studies Books.

Reeve, Simon (1999), *The New Jackals: Ramzi Yousef, Osama bin Laden and the Future of Terrorism*, London: Andre Deutsch.

Reeves, Phil (1995), 'Moscow Tries to Play Down Radioactive Chechen Feat', *The Irish Times*, 25 November.

Reeves, Richard, Veash, Nichole and Arlidge, John (1999), 'Virtual Chaos Baffles Police', *The Observer*, 20 June.

Rivera, Temario (1994), 'Armed Challenges to the Philippines Government: Protracted War or Political Settlement?', in *Southeast Asian Affairs 1994*, Singapore: Institute of Southeast Asian Studies.

Roberts, Andrew (2001), 'Bring Back 007', *The Spectator*, 6 October.

Roberts, Brad (ed.) *Hype or Reality: The 'New Terrorism' and Mass Casualty Attacks*, Alexandria, VA: The Chemical and Biological Arms Control Institute.

Rodan, Garry (1998), 'The Internet and political control in Singapore', *Political Science Quarterly*, 113/1.

Rosenau, William, Gay, Kemper and Mussington, David (1997), 'Transnational Threats and US National Security', *Low Intensity Conflict and Law Enforcement*, 6/3, Winter.

Roy, Oliver (2000), 'Islam, Iran and the New Terrorism', *Survival*, 42/2, Summer.

Rufford, Nicholas, Leppard, David, and Eddy, Paul (2001), 'Crashed plane's target may have been reactor', *Sunday Times*, 21 October.

Sager, Ira (2000), 'Cyber Crime: First Yahoo! Then eBay. The Net's vulnerability threatens e-commerce – and you', *Business Week*, 21 February.

Sains, Ariane (1994), 'Ignalina Sabotage Deadline Passes Without Blow-Up', *Nucleonics Week*, 17 November.

Salim, Jilad (1997), 'Secrets of al-Manshiyah', *Al-Watan al-'Arabi*, 31 October.

Schmid, Alex (1996), 'The Links between Transnational Organized Crime and Terrorist Crimes', *Transnational Organized Crime*, 2/4, Winter.

Schwartzstein, Stuart (ed.) (1996), *The Information Revolution and National Security: Dimensions and Directions*, Washington, DC: Center for International and Strategic Studies.

Seow, Francis (1994), *To Catch a Tartar. A Dissident in Lee Kuan Yew's Prison*, New Haven: Yale Southeast Asia Studies, Monograph 42.

Sharaf-al-Din, Khalid (1999), 'Bin-Ladin Men Reportedly Possess Biological Weapons', *Al-Sharaq al-Awsat*, 6 March.

Shargorodsky, Sergei (1995), 'Security Tightened at Nuclear Power Plant after Threat', *Associated Press*, 1 July.

Simon, Sheldon (ed.), *The Many Faces of Security*, Lanham: Rowman and Littlefield.

Simon, Steven and Benjamin, Daniel (2000), 'America and the New Terrorism', *Survival*, 42/1, Spring.

Smith, Steve (2001), 'The United States will emerge from this as a more dominant world power', *The Times*, 19 September.

Soo Hoo, Kevin, Goodman, Seymour and Greenberg, Lawrence (1997), 'Information Technology and the Terrorist Threat', *Survival*, 39/3, Autumn.

Spaeth, Anthony (2002), 'Rumbles in the Jungle', *Time Asia*, 26 February.

Stanton, John (2000), 'A Typical Pentagon Agency Waging War on Terrorism', *National Defense*, May.

Stark, Rodney (1999), 'Rads, Bugs and Gas: The Threat of CBN Terrorism', Department of Defense and Strategic Studies Southwest Missouri State University, 14 May. Master of Science in Defense and Strategic Studies thesis.

Sterling, Clair (1981), *The Terror Network*, New York: Holt, Rinehart & Winston.

Stern, Jessica (1999), *The Ultimate Terrorists*, Cambridge, MA: Harvard University Press.

Stern, Jessica (2000), 'Pakistan's Jihad Culture', *Foreign Affairs*, 79/6, November/December.

Sullivan, Andrew (2001), 'The Damage Clinton Did', *Sunday Times*, 30 September.

Tan, Andrew (2001), 'The Rise of Islam in Malaysia and Indonesia: An Emerging Security Challenge', *Panorama*, 1.

Thely, Benoit (1994), 'Suspect held as threat forces closure of Lithuanian reactor', Agence France Presse, 4 November.

Thompson, James (1967), *Organisations in Action*, New York: McGraw-Hill.

Tiglao, Rigoberto (1995), 'Under the Gun', *Far Eastern Economic Review*, 24 August.

Tucker, Jonathan (ed.), *Toxic Terror: Assessing Terrorist Use of Chemical and Biological Weapons*, Cambridge: MIT Press.

Utley, Garrick (1997), 'The Shrinking of Foreign News; from Broadcast to Narrowcast', *Foreign Affairs*, 76, March/April.

Utley, Tom (2001), 'The Moment I Saw Bush Had Grasped the Point of this War', *Daily Telegraph*, 28 September.

Van Creveld, Martin (1991), *The Transformation of War*, New York: Free Press.

Van Creveld, Martin (1999), *The Rise and Decline of the State*, Cambridge: Cambridge University Press.

Vassylenko, Volodymyr (1998), 'Bin Laden's weapons', *The Times*, 2 November.

Viyug, Marites and Gloria, Glenda (2000), *Under the Crescent Moon: Rebellion in Mindanao*, Quezon City: Ateneo Center for Social Policy and Public Affairs/Institute for Popular Democracy.

Vlassis, Dmitri (1998), 'Drafting the United Nations Convention against Transnational Organized Crime', *Transnational Organized Crime*, 4/3–4, Autumn/Winter.

Wain, Barry (2002), 'Wrong Target', *The Far Eastern Economic Review*, 23 April.

Walker, Tom, Grey, Stephen and Fielding, Nick (2001), 'Al-Qaeda's secrets: Bin Laden's camp reveal chemical weapon ambition', *The Sunday Times*, 25 November.

Waller, Douglas (1998), 'Inside the Hunt for Osama', *Time*, 152/25, 20 December.

Webster, Philip and Watson, Roland (2001), 'Bin Laden's Nuclear Threat', *The Times*, 26 October.

Weiser, Benjamin (1998), 'US Says Bin Laden Aide Tried to Get Nuclear Weapons', *New York Times*, 26 September.

Wesley, Michael (1999), 'The Asian Crisis and the Adequacy of Regional Institutions', *Contemporary Southeast Asia*, 21/1.

Whine, Michael (1999), 'Islamist Organisations on the Internet', *Terrorism and Political Violence*, 11/1, Spring.

Whitworth, Damien (2001), 'America paralysed by 2,300 anthrax scares', *The Times*, 17 October.

Williams, Phil (1995), 'The New Security Threat: Transnational Criminal Organizations and International Security', *Criminal Organizations*, 9/3, Summer.

Woodward, Bob (2002), *Bush at War*, New York: Simon and Schuster.

Woodward, Bob, Kaiser, Robert and Ottaway, David (2001), 'US Fears Bin Laden Made Nuclear Strides: Concern Over "Dirty Bomb" Affects Security', *Washington Post*, 4 December.

Yusufzai, Rahimullah (1999), 'Conversation with Terror', *Time*, 11 January.

Zabriskie, Phil (2002), 'Picking a Fight', *Time Asia*, 26 February.

Zakaria, Fareed (2001), 'The Allies Who Made Our Foes', *Newsweek*, 1 October.

Index